THE INDIVIDUAL, SEX, AND SOCIETY

a SIECUS
Handbook
for
Teachers
and
Counselors

edited by Carlfred B. Broderick and Jessie Bernard

The Individual, Sex, and Society

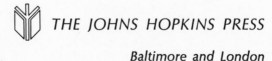

THE JOHNS HOPKINS PRESS

Baltimore and London

The Johns Hopkins Press, Baltimore, Maryland 21218
The Johns Hopkins Press Ltd., London

ISBN-0-8018-1036-1 (clothbound edition)
ISBN-0-8018-1037-X (paperback edition)

Originally published, 1969
Johns Hopkins Paperbacks edition, 1969
Second printing, 1970
Third printing, 1970

Contributors

JESSIE BERNARD, Ph.D., was for many years Professor of Sociology at The Pennsylvania State University and is now retired with the status of Honorary Research Scholar. She is doing independent research, writing, and consulting in Washington, D.C. Among the many books of which she is author or co-author are *American Family Behavior; Remarriage; Dating, Mating, and Marriage; Marriage and the Family among Negroes;* and, most recently, *The Sex Game.* She is a member of the SIECUS board.

CARLFRED B. BRODERICK, Ph.D., is Associate Professor of Family Relationships at the College of Human Development of The Pennsylvania State University. A sociologist, his research has been in the areas of family structure, American courtship, and normal heterosexual social development of children. He is a member of the SIECUS board.

CATHERINE S. CHILMAN, Ph.D., a psychologist, is a specialist in research relating to many aspects of child development and the family. The author of a number of professional and popular articles and books in the field, she is a former teacher of marriage and the family at Syracuse University. She has also had broad experience in speaking and consultation in many parts of the country. She is a member of the SIECUS board.

HAROLD T. CHRISTENSEN, Ph.D., Professor of Sociology at Purdue University, is a past president of the National Council on Family Relations and a former editor of the journal *Marriage and Family Living.* He is the author of *Marriage Analysis* and editor of the *Handbook of Marriage and the Family.* He spent 1957–1958 in Denmark studying the Scandinavian family. In 1967 he was the recipient of the Burgess Award of the National Council on Family Relations, given every second year for the greatest contribution to family research. He is a member of the SIECUS board.

NELSON N. FOOTE, Ph.D., is a sociologist doing research on community development in New York City. He came to New York from the University of Chicago, where he was Director of the Family Study Center. He is co-author of *Identity and Interpersonal Competence, Household Decision-Making,* and *Housing Choices and Constraints,* as well as articles on consumer behavior and family relations. His essay "Sex as Play" has been translated into several languages.

ARTHUR E. GRAVATT, Ph.D., is Professor of Child Development and Family Relationships at the University of Tennessee. His special interests are the role of the family in the community and sex education, and he has organized several workshops for training home economists, medical personnel, health educators, and others in sex education. In 1967 he edited a special issue of the *Journal of the College Health Association* on sex education.

BOONE E. HAMMOND is a research associate in the Metropolitan Affairs and Public Administration Program and Assistant Professor of Sociology at Southern Illinois University, Edwardsville. He was a research associate with the Pruitt-Igoe Housing Study conducted by the Social Science Institute at Washington University, St. Louis. He has presented several papers at professional meetings on the sex life of the lower-class Negro and is also interested in sex deviance, urban studies, and the problems of poverty.

WARREN R. JOHNSON, Ed.D., is Professor of Health Education at the University of Maryland and Visiting Lecturer at the Washington School of Psychiatry. He has directed institutes of sex education for the Washington School of Psychiatry, the National Association of Independent Schools, and the Maryland State Department of Education. He is the author of numerous articles, and his several books include *Human Sexual Behavior and Sex Education* and *Health Concepts for College Students*. He is a fellow of the Society for the Scientific Study of Sex, has been a member of the SIECUS board, and is President of the American Association of Sex Educators and Counselors.

LESTER A. KIRKENDALL, Ph.D., Professor of Family Life at Oregon State University, was one of the founders of SIECUS. He is author or co-author of several books, including *Premarital Intercourse and Interpersonal Relationships, Sex and Our Society,* and *Sex Education as Human Relations.* He served as a consultant in sex education to the U.S. Office of Education and as Director of the Association for Family Living in Chicago.

JOYCE A. LADNER is a research associate in the Social Science Institute and received the Ph.D. in sociology at Washington University, St. Louis. Her areas of interest are the sex behavior of lower-class Negro girls in northern cities and contemporary militancy among American Negroes. Her research on Negro militancy has appeared in *Transaction* and the *Archives of General Psychiatry.*

ROGER W. LIBBY is a graduate assistant in the Department of Child Development and Family Relations at the University of Connecticut. His research interest in parental and professional attitudes toward adolescent sex education in high schools is partly the result of his experience as a teacher in Pasco High School, Pasco, Washington.

CHARLES S. MAHAN, M.D., was Chief Resident in Gynecology and Obstetrics at the Hennepin General Hospital, Minneapolis, working on human reproduction, the impact of antidiuretic hormones on the menstrual cycle, and new types of obstetrical analgesia at the time of writing his chapter. He is at present a Lieutenant in the Medical Corps, stationed at the U.S. Naval Hospital, Quantico, Virginia.

HELEN MANLEY, Executive Director of the Social Health Association of Greater St. Louis, has been publicizing the need for sex education since 1930. As a result of her work in this and related fields, she received the Gulick Award of the American School Health Association. Among the results of her many activities in the field is *A Curriculum Guide in Sex Education.*

ALFRED W. MELTON, JR., Assistant Professor of Family Relationships at the College of Human Development of the Pennsylvania State University, teaches a marriage course and is a marriage counselor. He has lectured and written extensively on the sexual dilemmas of teenagers and their parents.

ESTHER MIDDLEWOOD, now retired as Chief of the Education Section of the Michigan State Department of Mental Health, has been active in the development of community sex education programs for a great part of her career.

JOHN MONEY, Ph.D., is Associate Professor of Medical Psychology and Pediatrics at The Johns Hopkins University School of Medicine and Hospital. The most recent of his many publications is *Sex Errors of the Body.* In 1956 he was the co-recipient of the Hofheimer Prize of the American Psychiatric Association for his research in hermaphroditism, and in 1966 he received the Gold Medal Award for the Children's Hospital of Philadelphia for his contributions to the medical psychology of sex. He is a member of the SIECUS board.

JAMES E. MOORE, Ph.D., is Assistant Professor of Child Development and Family Life at Purdue University, where he is attempting to develop an undergraduate curriculum which integrates the humanities and the social sciences. In 1966–1967 he was a National Institute of Mental Health postdoctoral fellow in marriage counseling at the University of Minnesota. With his wife, who is a public health educator, he conducts sex education seminars.

LEE RAINWATER, Ph.D., is Professor of Sociology and Anthropology at Washington University, St. Louis, and a research associate in its Social Science Institute. Among his many books are *Family Design, And the Poor Get Children,* and *Workingman's Wife.*

IRA L. REISS, Ph.D., is Professor of Sociology at the University of Iowa. His major interests are sociology of the family, deviant behavior, and sociological theory. He is an associate editor of the *American Sociological Review, Journal of Marriage and the Family,* and *Social Problems,* and is on the board of directors of the Midwest Sociological Society and the National Council on Family Relations. He is the author of two books, *Premarital Sexual Standards in America* and *The Social Context of Premarital Sexual Permissiveness.* He is a member of the SIECUS board.

DANIEL N. WIENER, Ph.D., is Associate Professor of Clinical Psychology at the University of Minnesota and Director of Research at the Veterans Administration's Mental Hygiene Clinic, St. Paul. Among the many books of which he is author or co-author are *Discipline, Achievement and Mental Health; Dimensions of Psychotherapy;* and *Short-Term Psychotherapy and Structural Behavior Change.*

Foreword

SIECUS, the Sex Information and Education Council of the United States, was formed as a voluntary health organization in 1964. The headquarters of its modest professional and clerical staff is at 1855 Broadway, New York, New York 10023. Its goal from its inception has been to generate public awareness, understanding, and acceptance of the multiplicity of patterns of human sexuality—to move from a restrictive concept of genital sexuality to the larger dimension in which every individual, at whatever age, boy or girl, man or woman, is seen as a whole, with all his thoughts, feelings, and actions as boy or girl, man or woman. SIECUS has carried forward this purpose through its study guides, its consultant services to communities and schools, and the publications of its board, many of whose members are numbered among the contributors to this volume. *The Individual, Sex, and Society* represents an attempt to move away from the dictionary definition of genital sexuality to identify the new meanings of the term. As such, it well represents the educational effort with which SIECUS has been identified over the years.

Lester L. Doniger
President, SIECUS

Acknowledgments

Earlier versions of Chapters 7, 8, 9, and 11 appeared in the *Journal of Social Issues*, 22 (April, 1966), and appear here by permission of its editors. Chapter 7 was published, in somewhat altered form, as SIECUS Discussion Guide 5; Chapter 16 appeared as SIECUS Discussion Guide 3. Readers should note that Dr. Money's recent book, *Sex Errors of the Body: Dilemmas, Education, Counseling* (Baltimore: Johns Hopkins Press, 1968), represents an expansion of the discussion in Chapter 15 and is especially useful for its illustrations of the conditions described in that chapter.

Dr. Gravatt would like to express his appreciation of the review of the medical aspects of Chapter 14 by Margaret Dowell Gravatt, M.D., of the Ritenour Health Center of the Pennsylvania State University, and Charles W. Rohrbeck, M.D., Fellow of the American College of Obstetrics and Gynecology. The research reported here by Dr. Money was supported by National Institute of Mental Health Grant HD-00325 and Research Career Development Award HD-K3-18,635.

Contents

Contributors   v

Foreword   ix
Lester L. Doniger, President, SIECUS

Acknowledgments   xi

Introduction   xv

PART I: TEACHING ABOUT SEX

Introduction   3

1   Trends in Sex Education   5
   Lester A. Kirkendall and Roger W. Libby
2   Normal Sociosexual Development   23
   Carlfred B. Broderick
3   Socialization into Sexual Behavior in a Negro Slum Ghetto   41
   Boone E. Hammond and Joyce A. Ladner
4   Starting a Program of Sex Education   53
   Helen Manley
5   Some Social and Psychological Aspects of Sex Education   65
   Catherine S. Chilman
6   Sex Education in the Community   83
   Esther Middlewood

Suggested Readings   99

PART II: QUESTIONS OF STANDARDS AND VALUES

Introduction   107

7   Premarital Sexual Standards   109
   Ira L. Reiss
8   Sex and Interpersonal Relationships   119
   Lester A. Kirkendall and Roger W. Libby
9   Sex in the Culture of Poverty   129
   Lee Rainwater
10   Changing Concepts of Masculinity and Femininity   141
   Nelson N. Foote
11   The Impact of Culture and Values   155
   Harold T. Christensen

Suggested Readings   167

PART III: NORMAL SEXUAL FUNCTIONING

Introduction   173

12 Human Reproduction   175
    Charles S. Mahan and Carlfred B. Broderick
13 Human Sexual Response   221
    Alfred W. Melton, Jr.
14 Family Planning   243
    Arthur E. Gravatt

    Suggested Readings   279

PART IV: PROBLEMS

Introduction   283

15 Sex Errors of the Body   285
    John Money
16 Masturbation   319
    Warren R. Johnson
17 Sexual Problems in Clinical Experience   327
    Daniel N. Wiener
18 Problematic Sexual Behavior   343
    James E. Moore

    Suggested Readings   373

    Glossary   379

    Index   393

Introduction

Public demand for sex education programs for young people has been growing throughout the sixties, but the supply of trained personnel has been woefully inadequate. Schools, churches, academic institutions, and even medical and theological schools have been unable to staff programs to examine human sexuality. When summer institutes to train experienced teachers in this new field are set up, there are no guidelines around which training can be organized. This book, the first of its kind, is an attempt to eliminate that bottleneck by making available in one volume an extensive and reliable body of information for sex educators. We hope it will be useful as a textbook in training new teachers and that it will serve as a reference book for those already in the classroom.

The Individual, Sex, and Society distinguishes between the knowledge the teacher seeks to transmit to his students and the knowledge he himself needs in order to do so. What is actually taught will vary from school to school. Some schools will want sex education programs limited to a minimum of factual information. Others will want to explore a much wider range of sexuality, including research into current mores. Between these extremes there is considerable room for choice.

We stress pedagogical knowledge in the chapters that follow, for whatever the personal bias of any teacher with respect to the nature of human sexuality and trends in sexual mores, he must be well versed in current research. But knowledge alone is not enough. Only persons who are at ease with their own sexuality should be asked to deal with it in the classroom, for only they are likely to be successful. No amount of information, no technique, will create a good teacher out of a person whom talking about sexuality makes uncomfortable. There is no disgrace in admitting a feeling of uneasiness about the subject. It is a feeling shared by millions of people—in fact, it is precisely because so many do feel uncomfortable about it that sex education presents special difficulties. No teacher should hesitate to request that he be excused from undertaking this assignment, and no administrator should hesitate to excuse him.

Almost as many views as authors are presented here, but certain themes run throughout these papers: that there is no one sex education curriculum that can be put forth as ideal or complete and that each institution must design a program to meet its own requirements; that the sex education teacher, by being frank, serious, and open in a sense *is* the curriculum and is teaching his way of thinking and feeling about sex (not omitting his own value system) as much as he is the cold facts; that he must have a firm grasp of the current research bearing on his program, though he should never be afraid to say "I don't know"; that he must be prepared pedagogically to deal with the problems, interests, and questions that are peculiar to his students' developmental level; and, last but not least, that sex education is not and cannot be a cure-all for socially undesirable behavior, nor can it guarantee healthy sexuality—what it *can* do is provide a set of constructive alternatives to the values, ideas, and information about sex which young people absorb from television, paperbacks, movies, magazines, newspapers, and their own peers.

The book is divided into four parts. Part I focuses on the practical, pedagogical aspects of sex education. In order to be effective, the teacher must be aware of the developmental level of his students, their knowledge and expectations, and the aspects of sexuality that are relevant for discussion at each developmental stage. He must be able to anticipate the pedagogical peculiarities involved in setting up and participating in a sex education program. It may not be equally obvious why Part II, which places sexuality in its cultural context, is important. However, there is no aspect of an individual's behavior with wider ramifications, no area of his life more completely interwoven with the values of the surrounding culture, than his sexuality. With Part III we move into a more specialized discussion of normal sexual functioning, with a review of the biological process of human reproduction and the physiological process of sexual response, and an examination of their corollary, family planning. Sex educators will find here the tools with which their own knowledge can be broadened and their programs constructed. Sexual anomalies and aberrant or controversial sexual behavior pose special problems for the sex educator and thus are presented separately in Part IV.

It is our hope that these chapters, along with the supplemental readings, the glossary, and the comprehensive index, will constitute a framework within which the sex educator can move toward his goal—the development and expression of the concept of healthy sexuality.

Carlfred B. Broderick
Jessie Bernard

PART I: TEACHING ABOUT SEX

Introduction

Because learning is learning, and because so many readers of this volume already have a thorough grounding in "educational psychology," it may seem anomalous to introduce this volume with a series of chapters which deal, in effect, with the "pedagogy" of sex education. Why, it might be asked, does this area require special consideration? An exciting assignment in English literature, though not very likely to do so, may conceivably arouse a strong emotional response in some students: some may weep at a touching death scene, become indignant at injustice vividly portrayed, and so on. But no subject in the school curriculum has the potential for personal impact that human sexuality has. Both experienced and inexperienced teachers recognize the special and characteristic silence that falls upon a class when discussion turns in this direction. If the teacher is fudging or evading or hiding, the silence and tension continue; the students may even become sullen. But if the teacher is candid and honest, making it clear that he is trying to teach rather than, by implication, rebuke, there will be such a liveliness and release of tension by active participation as may even require the teacher to call for order.

Lester Kirkendall and Roger Libby begin with a historical review of the movement to introduce sex education into the school curriculum and a survey of the current scene in a wide variety of schools and communities. C. B. Broderick, in Chapter 2, then traces the development of the individual as a sexual being over the life cycle. All people do not develop in the same social climate, however, and in Chapter 3 Boone Hammond and Joyce Ladner vividly portray sociosexual development in a Negro ghetto.

The materials in these first three chapters make it abundantly clear that no single approach, no uniform curriculum, would be effective in all schools and groups and that programs should be tailored to the needs of the group and the resources of the community. Nevertheless, it is useful to have at least one example of the development of a successful approach in one community. In Chapter 4 Helen Manley summarizes her work in the schools of one of the suburbs of St. Louis.

Thus far we have been dealing with essentially normal situations. But in almost every class that any teacher will face, at whatever developmental stage, there are sure to be some students who need more than teaching. They need counseling as well. The chapter by Catherine Chilman warns the teacher not to confuse the two functions. He should be able to detect signs that indicate counseling is called for, but he should not attempt to supply it himself unless he

3

has been adequately trained for it as well as for teaching. This is not to say that individual discussion and conversations are out; they may be extremely useful. But serious professional counseling is not a job for the teacher. Like so many of the other contributors, she also warns us not to demand more of sex education than it can honestly offer.

Not all teachers in the field are in schools: many of them work through other agencies. Esther Middlewood describes their contribution to the total picture in Chapter 6. The same general "pedagogic" principles operate in this area of education as in the schools, but special modification is called for when working in the community with an adult audience.

1 Trends in Sex Education

Lester A. Kirkendall and Roger W. Libby

"A trend is a trend is a trend," as Gertrude Stein would say. But is it? We are not so sure. Perhaps *"a trend is an opinion is simply something someone is trying is only something someone has quit trying."* We will attempt in this chapter, nevertheless, to identify trends in sex education and to comment upon them in a way which will be helpful to those working with or expecting to work with sex education programs in the public schools. We will also engage in some interpretations and summarizing observations.

In pursuit of this objective we have reviewed the writings of some of the leaders in sex education since the turn of the century, drawn from the experience of those who have worked with sex education, and garnered ideas from a questionnaire on trends and directions in sex education in the United States which was sent to persons throughout the country who are involved in this area of instruction. Over seventy-five replies were received, and they have been most valuable in helping us to analyze trends and arrive at our conclusions.

ORGANIZATIONAL BACKGROUND

The initial impetus for sex education came from medical organizations and gave it its characteristic stamp for many years. In 1904 Dr. Prince Albert Morrow submitted to the New York County Medical Society plans for an organization "to limit the spread of diseases which have their origin in the Social evil." The movement for sex education began a year later with the organization of the American Society of Sanitary and Moral Prophylaxis, by Dr. Morrow, whose purpose was "to organize a social defense against a class of diseases which are most injurious to the highest interest of human society."[1] The Society published an official journal, *Social Diseases*, later changed to the *Journal of Sanitary and Moral Prophylaxis*. Five years later, in 1910, the American Federation for Sex Hygiene was organized. In 1912, at a meeting of the International Congress of Hygiene in Washington, D.C., a special committee of three doctors made a report on "Matter and Methods of Sex Education," which showed that its authors realized the limitations of the educative effort that had been made. Shortly thereafter, in 1914, the American Society for Social and Moral Prophylaxis and the American Federation for Sex Hygiene merged to form the American Social Hygiene Association.

The term "social hygiene" was broader in conception than "sani-

[1] Quoted in M. A. Bigelow, *Sex Education* (New York: Macmillan, 1916), pp. 229–30.

tary and moral prophylaxis"; in fact, "in its original usage social hygiene inclued a wide range of health and social matters relating to the welfare of society in general."[2] In the United States, however, social hygiene came to mean "those phases of social health which in their essential nature are sexual," and "systematic sex education for both children and adults has from the first occupied an important place in the social hygiene movement."[3] The significance of this organizational sponsorship of sex education lies in the fact that the earlier emphases tended to be on the pathological aspects of sexuality rather than on its normal aspects.

THE LITERATURE

It was not until 1916 that *Sex Education*, the first major work concerned with sex education in the public schools, was published. Its author was Maurice Bigelow, Professor of Biology at Teachers College, Columbia University. This influential and ground-breaking book was followed by a widely distributed and important pamphlet, *High Schools and Sex Education*, published in 1922 and revised in 1939. Written by Benjamin Gruenberg and printed by the U.S. Government Printing Office, it was prepared under the direction of the U.S. Public Health Service in collaboration with the U.S. Bureau of Education. The White House Conference on Child Health and Protection held in 1930 produced a pamphlet entitled *Social Hygiene in Schools* (1932). More recently, several general books, *Sex Guidance in Family Life Education*, by Frances Bruce Strain,[4] *Sex Education as Human Relations*, by Lester A. Kirkendall,[5] and *Human Sex and Sex Education*, by Warren R. Johnson,[6] have appeared. One can see in these books the marked similarity of the basic philosophy of sex education in the public schools over the years as enunciated by the leaders of the field. Throughout, three points have been insisted upon: (1) sex education must go beyond any one or two limited objectives (e.g., prevention of venereal diseases, provision of information on reproduction) to a concern with the effective sexual functioning of happy, socially well-adjusted persons; (2) sex education should reflect a positive, life-enriching approach rather than a negative and repressive view; and (3) sex education is best integrated into the curriculum rather than considered a separate and distinct phase of instruction.

[2] Bigelow, "Sex Education and Sex Ethics," *Encyclopedia of the Social Sciences* (New York: Macmillan, 1934), 1:10.

[3] *Ibid.*

[4] (New York: Macmillan, 1947).

[5] (Sweet Springs, Mo.: Roxbury Press, 1950).

[6] (Philadelphia: Lea and Febiger, 1963).

In spite of the limited objective suggested by Dr. Morrow in 1905, in 1916 Bigelow defined sex education as including "all scientific, ethical, and religious instruction and influences which . . . may help young people prepare to solve for themselves the problem of sex. . . . Young people need instruction that relates not only to health but also to attitudes and morals as these three are influenced by sexual instincts and relationships."[7] Gruenberg in 1922 emphasized an approach which went far beyond the biological: "sex education in the school means not only the presenting of facts, but also the interpretation of meanings and applications, where they happen to fit in with the subject matter of instruction in any or all of the various school courses or subjects that deal with human interests, human relations, human problems."[8]

In 1932 the White House Conference on Child Health and Protection produced a pamphlet, *Social Hygiene in Schools,* suggesting that the "primary aim of social hygiene is the preservation of the family and the improvement and enrichment of family life."[9] Kirkendall sought to reflect a similarly broad, inclusive concern in the title he chose for his book, *Sex Education as Human Relations,* and in 1963 W. R. Johnson said:

educators . . . are furthering the improvement of human relations generally, including the various aspects of sexual adjustment, whenever they predispose young people to feel more involved in mankind than in their feelings against people; to be more respectful of fellow human beings than respectable; to be more loving than lovely; to be capable of friendship and not just of friendliness; to be more accepting of themselves, physically and mentally, than rejecting; to use language with proper awareness of its potency, especially perhaps for evil; and to be free of a feeling of obligation to prescribe how other people, including future mates and children, should live. All this kind of thing is, of course, basic sex education.[10]

The positive, life-enriching point of view is implicit in these quotations. Clearly, efforts to attain this objective will have wide implications for educational practices and instruction. This emphasis was clearly implied from the beginning. Bigelow discussed the aims of sex education as the basis for the organization of instruction and noted the possibility of including sex education in the biological sciences, in literature, and in general health instruction. He opposed special sex education lectures as isolating sex from its proper context. In the first edition of *High Schools and Sex Education* Gruen-

[7] *Sex Education,* pp. 1–2.

[8] B. Gruenberg, *High Schools and Sex Education* (Washington, D.C.: U.S. Government Printing Office, 1922).

[9] (New York: Century, 1932), p. 3.

[10] *Human Sex and Sex Education,* p. 195.

7

berg discussed possible incorporation of information on sex in biology, general science, physiology, physical education, home economics, social studies, and English courses. He considered the special lecture an "emergency device." In the 1939 edition the same recommendation was used but brought up to date and somewhat elaborated. The integrated approach was also espoused by Kirkendall.

One must remember that these were the concepts of the leaders in the field. In general, their views were not followed either by school authorities or by the general public. Bigelow, for example, noted that "personal sex-hygiene" materials are not included in biology textbooks "because educational and public opinion do not stand for such radical lessons in books for schools."[11] What would be his appraisal of today's books?

Unquestionably, there was little sex education in the schools in the 1920's, 1930's, and even in the 1940's. There is also little doubt that when it was included, it was restricted largely to discussion of reproduction. Unquestionably the element of disaster insurance bulked large in what was done—insurance against venereal infection and premarital pregnancy. The emphasis was strongly repressive and the tone, while elevated in terms of hopes and future potentialities, was severely negative so far as youth and the present were concerned.

What changes have occurred? Over the years the element of fear which has permeated the whole question of sex education for children is gradually disappearing. With it the inhibitions against open discussion of the concerns of the young people themselves have also gradually disappeared. This trend is directly related to the expansion of the variety of approaches and techniques used by sex educators. Acceptance and implementation of the broad, integrated approach recommended by the early leaders in the field has been increasing. There has been a movement away from euphemisms and toward using the term "sex" in describing the school program. Sex education has begun at an increasingly earlier age. And finally, and most hopeful of all, systematic programs for the preparation and on-the-job training of teachers in this area have begun to be established. In the following sections, each of these trends is more fully discussed.

DECREASING FEAR, INCREASING OPENNESS

The atmosphere in which sex teaching takes place has gradually become more open, more accepting, less fearful, and less likely to

[11] *Sex Education*, p. 99.

produce opposition. Despite the fears which without doubt still exist, it is nevertheless hard to envision the extent and the depth of those present at the turn of the century. A book published in 1906, *The Renewal of Life*, by Margaret Morley, written for parents, literally bristles and crackles with fear:

since there is very great danger in speaking in public on this subject before children, no matter how well the speaking may be done, it is undoubtedly better not to approach it directly in the schools,—at least in grades below the high school. . . . In dealing with this subject the teacher needs to be as wise as the serpent and as harmless as the dove, not only for her own sake but for the sake of those she wishes to help. . . . Many a life has been lamed and saddened because of the first terrible and ineradicable impressions it received upon this all-important subject. Many a high-minded man and woman have gone through life tormented by images of the first unworthy thoughts. No matter how good the after-knowledge may be, it is almost impossible to erase from the tablets of memory that old first impression.[12]

Another writer, Felix Kirsch, in a book addressed to Catholic parents, at first seems extremely frank and open but suddenly reverses himself. The child must be very persistent if he wants clear answers:

parents and priests have produced no convincing reason why parents should refuse to answer even the youngest child when he asks: "Where do babies come from?" An attempt on the part of the parents to ignore the question may silence the child and drive him elsewhere for information or let him suspect that there is a mystery that the parents do not wish to discuss. . . . What harm could come from frankly answering the question by saying: "Baby comes from God. And God sent with him an angel, who will stay with baby, day and night, and watch over him to keep away danger." If the child persists and wishes further information, further information should be given frankly.[13]

While Bigelow's book on sex education in schools was published just ten years after Morley's, he was clearly less fearful than either Morley or Kirsch. He was insistent on the need to be honest and open about sex: "The policy of maintaining mystery and secrecy concerning sex has failed with adults even more sadly than children. Health and morals have suffered incalculable injury. . . . The wonder is that . . . the world has not developed more sexual vice."[14] But Bigelow was still a product of his time. Fear is clearly evident in his comments about masturbation: "Have children sleep on a hard mattress. The old-time feather bed was dangerous. . . . Do not leave children to their own devices; they may naturally fall into dangerous

---

[12] (Chicago: McClurg, 1932), pp. 24–25.
[13] *Sex Education and Training in Chastity* (New York: Benzinger, 1930), p. 189.
[14] *Sex Education*, p. 15.

play. Privacy is often demanded by the moods of adults, but is dangerous for children."[15] Frances Bruce Strain was still reacting to this atmosphere of fear when she wrote:

Sex teaching is still so uncertain an art, and holds so many possibilities of danger, one hesitates to recommend the addition to it of a flavor of humor. Yet that is what I should like to do. A touch of whimsy here and there along the way does much to keep the whole tenor of the work on an even keel, makes it human. And if now and then something really funny happens or is said and everybody laughs, well—laugh too, why not? . . . It is almost as hazardous to recommend a tinge of good old-fashioned sentiment as it is to recommend a dash of humor.[16]

She also discussed with her teacher readers certain personal qualities about which they needed to be most circumspect—size, dress, manner, voice, speech—all of which, according to Mrs. Strain, bore significantly upon success in this field.

Felix Kirsch reflects both fear and disgust based on religious teachings in his attitude toward nocturnal emissions: "At night, often during an impure dream, this fluid is ejected from the body. There is in this emission nothing to be alarmed about. It is perfectly natural; even the saints had to suffer it." In order to cope with emissions, Kirsch advises boys to "try to think of something else, forget about the emission, say a Hail Mary, and turn over and go to sleep."[17]

Masturbation has always been a subject which brings out fears quickly and clearly (note Bigelow above). Fear and distaste colored Gruenberg's comments on masturbation: "Many boys get into bad habits of handling their external sex organs. Every boy who has done so knows that it is not the right thing to do and is ashamed of himself for doing it."[18] Less fear is present in the 1939 edition. Gruenberg comments that "within a generation we have learned pretty generally that various methods and forms of sensual gratification are practically universal for boys and girls. . . . In considering the subject of masturbation, it is necessary to detach ourselves from earlier moralistic assumptions and vague fears about sex [but] the whole question of masturbation must be handled by the qualified teacher with delicacy, but also with a degree of assurance."[19] We have now arrived at the point where a prominent and respected psychiatrist can write that masturbation has a positive contribution to make to development in "any rational concept of personality

---

[15] Ibid., p. 141.
[16] Sex Guidance in Family Life Education, p. 266.
[17] Sex Education and Training in Chastity, p. 200.
[18] High Schools and Sex Education, p. 51.
[19] Rev. ed. (Washington, D.C.: U.S. Government Printing Office, 1939), p. 67.

structure and social relations. Such a view is by no means mine alone but is shared by many of my professional colleagues who are most knowledgeable and clinically experienced."[20]

None of the respondents to our questionnaire thought that fears of sex and sex education had increased. For each respondent who said there had been no change, eight said fears had decreased. Many reasons were suggested, but most commonly mentioned were the frank and open treatment which sex has been receiving in the mass media and an increasing awareness on the part of parents, teachers, and professional people of the need for sex education, especially for youth. Some of the respondents made points which are valuable in defining the total situation more sharply. One said that he had dealt with situations in which he felt that fears had grown over a period of time, other situations in which there had been no change, and others where fears had decreased. Even this respondent felt that the over-all trend had been toward a decrease in fears.

Some of the changes in methodology and procedure in sex education are probably the result of this freer atmosphere. For example, the respondents to our questionnaire agreed that the sex education lecture (decried by Bigelow), often given by a doctor who was brought in unannounced from the outside, was a thing of the past. Lecturers now are made an integral part of the teaching process, and as such they are likely to be questioned by pupils and involved in discussions of pertinent issues. Our respondents also agreed that discussion with the pupils is commonly invited rather than avoided, as formerly. An illustration of this trend is seen in open-ended films which invite, rather than block, discussion. At the end of the film "Human Growth" the teacher is seen stepping toward the audience, after her class has been raising questions about various aspects of sex, growth, and development, to suggest that the same procedure can be followed in the classroom in which the film is being viewed.

Co-educational classes are no longer unusual and ordinarily are desired by both teachers and pupils, though some questionnaire respondents felt that there were times when segregated classes could provide better instructional situations. In any event, we have moved far beyond Bigelow, who wrote that there "is no reason why the biological studies should not be coeducational through nature-study and biology as far as the development of frogs and birds and, in a general way, of mammals."[21] However, in 1932 the White House Conference report, in discussing instruction of adolescents, suggested that separation "stimulates sex consciousness and

[20] W. R. Stokes, "Modern View of Masturbation," *Sexology*, 27 (1960):588–89.
[21] *Sex Education*, pp. 109–10.

11

urges, whereas free wholesome social intercourse of the sexes tends to minimize tensions and sublimate these urges."[22] Gruenberg was not quite so accepting on this point,[23] but still, in general, he approved of co-educational classes.

Another question which once was the subject of much debate is whether the teacher should be of the same sex as his pupils. Bigelow feared "danger for some boys if they are frankly instructed by attractive young women who are only ten to fifteen years older than their pupils. Hence, I urge great caution if there must be any exceptions to the general rule that teachers and pupils should be of the same sex."[24] Gruenberg felt that the decision on this issue should be determined by the personality of the individual teacher.[25]

Hesitancy still exists, of course, about dealing with certain topics. Any discussion of sexual techniques in intercourse is said to be universally proscribed, as is instruction about contraceptive techniques and devices. These restrictions have, to our knowledge, been breached in individual counseling and small group situations and even, in the case of contraceptive teaching, in high school formal class situations.

It is our impression that there is less tendency now to surround the teaching of sex with an aura of sacredness and sentimentality, which seems to us to have represented a feeling that open discussion was somehow fearful and threatening. We will forego the temptation to illustrate the point with highly sentimental statements from older books. However, some of the respondents foresaw the likelihood of considerable opposition to sex education, stemming from two sources—fundamentalist church groups and parents or persons disillusioned with the failure of sex education to meet their expectations in controlling sexual behavior. The way with which sex educators deal with the moral issue is undoubtedly of great concern. Success or failure here has tremendous implications for the success or failure of the entire program.

Publicity about a "sexual revolution" and "declining moral standards" has without question had considerable influence in bringing some parents to favor sex education. This support has at the same time a certain element of precariousness about it. Several of our questionnaire respondents noted that awareness of the presumed changes in sexual behavior among youths was generating pressure upon the schools to establish sex education programs. But some of these respondents also suggested that these supporters expected

[22] *Social Hygiene in the Schools*, p. 29.
[23] *High Schools and Sex Education*, rev. ed.
[24] *Sex Education*, p. 109.
[25] *High Schools and Sex Education*, rev. ed.

that the schools would in some way be able to reverse the supposed trend toward greater sexual freedom—to put the lid back on, so to speak. What happens if it becomes clear that sex education is not accomplishing this goal?

That the issue of morality is a central one is acknowledged by practically everyone who has worked with sex education programs for adolescents. As an illustration, the National Association of Independent Schools has given priority to the inclusion of sex education in the instructional programs of the schools making up the Association. In the summary report of a two-day institute held in April, 1966,[26] one of the central issues was that of "sex education and morality."

The discussions concerning morality in the schools will undoubtedly parallel the debate going on in the churches. Here the issue is between those who wish to adhere strictly to the legalistic code in which a particular pattern of behavior is regarded as exemplifying morality and those who feel that behavior may vary from one situation to another while still remaining consistent with certain basic principles. Several school systems have already dealt with the moral issue by adopting the latter point of view. They have accepted the concept that the building of relationships which have in them integrity, sincerity, and outreach is a moral position which they can support in good conscience. This approach is acceptable to many religious groups and yet at the same time does not involve the school in "religious instruction" or in supporting any particular creed or dogma.

Premarital intercourse is without doubt the most sensitive of all the issues with which teachers have to deal. Once they were fortified by a well-nigh universally accepted taboo against any kind of premarital sexual expression. Today, however, the teacher is faced with a wide range of opinion, depending upon the writer's particular view on the subject of morals (see, for example, the books listed in the Suggested Readings at the end of Part I). Moreover, rather than being commended, the teacher is now criticized (by some educational leaders at least) when he gives advice or engages in didactic moralism. On this issue and the approach to moral instruction, the teacher is caught in a paralyzing crossfire.

The future development of sex education programs would seem inseparably linked to the success of the schools in resolving the moral issue, bringing us to the question: what shall be the objectives of sex education?

[26] E. Yeomans, *NAIS Institute on Sex Education* (Boston: National Association of Independent Schools, 1966).

BROADENING OBJECTIVES

The objectives of sex education are being broadened. Four objectives which are being emphasized as an integral part of modern sex education can be distinguished. One is a concern with building an understanding of changing sex roles (see Chapter 10, by Nelson Foote). The whole question of male-female interaction in the family, in the business and professional world, at play, and in all of life generally was mentioned by respondents to the questionnaire as almost certain to require greater attention.

A second objective is the spelling out in a concrete and comprehensible way of the place of sex in the individual's personal and family life: the relationship of sex to love, the place and significance of sex in marriage, and the sex education of children.

The development of self-understanding in relation to one's sexual nature and needs is a third objective which a number of respondents recognized as important. It is also an emphasis which is being incorporated in many curricular outlines and units, and, if it can be fully realized, will undoubtedly help greatly in the acceptance of instruction about human sexuality. In the fullest sense, what happens is exactly what has been suggested—"sex education" becomes "education about human sexuality." This is sex in context. We are only beginning to develop this concept, but many leaders and programs are reflecting an awareness of the need and value of linking sexuality with self-understanding. A state-wide program in Kansas has sprung from the combined efforts of the University of Kansas Medical Center, the State Department of Health, and the State Department of Education. Workshops have been developed to help school administrators and teachers to make sex instruction an integral part of all learning about human development. Other programs may relate instruction concerning sexuality to personality and emotional growth; others to the development of an individual identity; others, with a sociological approach, to cultural understanding and adjustment. But regardless of the particular emphasis which may be chosen, the isolation of sex from the rest of life, which has in the past been one of the great deterrents to the effectiveness of sex education, is lessened.

The fourth objective, which was mentioned with much greater frequency than any of the other three by our respondents, is that of helping the pupil arrive at a condition of insight and understanding which will enable him to engage in responsible decision-making. The phrase is much in vogue, but in view of the extent to which youths are expected to, and do, make their own decisions, it seems quite properly so. The realization of this last objective, however, involves much more than simply some procedural variations or methodological innovations. The very foundation of the learning-teaching process is involved. In the past when sex educators have dealt with behavioral issues and moral questions, they have relied mainly on persuasion. Ordinarily, they have presented a view limited to what was generally regarded as acceptable in the community. This, of course, is an attempt to provide guidelines for decision-making, but the intent is to get the pupils to make the decision favored by the community. What happens when teaching is conducted with the full realization that the pupil *will* make his own decision? How does the teacher present the case for or against cigarette smoking, or for or against going into a certain occupational field? A certain teaching procedure designed to facilitate problem-solving and decision-making becomes necessary.

The typical procedure in other decision-making areas is to analyze and interpret the facts established and tested through experience and research in the light of one's own experience and basic philosophy and to arrive at a decision through this process. The question is this: in our teaching about the sensitive areas of human relations—not just sex, but interracial associations, divorce, or cross-sex friendships for married persons—can we look at the various possibilities objectively?

Several writers, i.e., I. L. Reiss,[27] J. W. Hudson,[28] and C. B. Broderick,[29] have been critical of high school and university textbooks and instruction because they seem inadequately grounded in the logical processes of decision-making. Broderick writes: "As a survey of high-school texts will quickly show, what students get in the chapters on boy-girl relations is advice illustrated with case studies, advice illustrated with cartoons, even, occasionally, advice illustrated with data from some study. The problem with advice is that . . . it does not recognize or make use of the students' own experience and insights. These are often extensive. Neither does advice-giving open the way to effective communication between the teacher and the students."[30] The likelihood that the objective of "responsible decision-making" will continue to be undermined by the giving of direct advice is great and is one of the major challenges before family life-sex educators.

Efforts to implement the "decision-making" objective have led to

[27] "The Treatment of Pre-Marital Coitus in Marriage and Family Texts," *Social Problems*, 4 (1957):334–38.

[28] "A Content Analysis of Selected Family Life Education Textbooks Used at the Secondary Level" (Ph.D. diss., Ohio State University, 1956).

[29] "Family Life Education versus Reality," *Journal of Marriage and the Family*, 26 (1964):102–3.

[30] *Ibid.*, p. 102.

a concern with teaching procedures which will provide pupils with some experience in decision-making processes. More and more pupils are being encouraged to ask questions and to contribute suggestions as to what they would like in the program. Discussion among pupils and between pupils and teachers is being emphasized. The dialogue is encouraged by the better and more experienced teachers, particularly those working with adolescents.

A particularly interesting illustration of the emphasis on dialogue was provided by the Elk Grove, California, High School in the spring of 1966. With the help of their teachers the students of this school planned a conference on the theme "Who am I?" All classes were dismissed for the day, speakers were brought in, and discussion leaders were trained to lead forum groups. Six groups were organized, one was on the family, another on personal values. Questions relating to family adjustments, dating, sex education, and preparation for marriage were so predominant that clearly these issues were central concerns of the pupils. A similar conference was held in 1967, centered around family, sex, and dating problems.

Illustrations of the way in which openness in student expression may change the direction or emphasis of programs multiply. In Montana the State Department of Health, working with the State Department of Education, developed a program entitled "Education for Parenthood." In the beginning it was just what the title implied, but the pressure of pupil concern over dating and sexual problems has pushed the program more and more into these areas.

In Orono, Maine, after a series of incidents demonstrating the need for sex education, adult leaders representing parents, school administrators, church and youth agency leaders, and university people decided to plan a series of three meetings for high school youths on the theme "Morality—1964." The need was felt for the opinion of the young people themselves, and a meeting was called with representative youth from the high school. At this meeting "the young people took a dim view of the innocuous and fuzzy language in the proposed title and asked quite frankly what the adults were trying to do (put over on them). They suggested a title for the project that they believed would have more drawing power and was, after all, 'what we are concerned about.' It became known as *The Three P's—Parking, Petting, and Problems.*"[31] Information on reproduction still remains among the objectives of sex education, but it is becoming only one of many, particularly for pupils past the period of early childhood.

[31] M. S. Zink, "A Community Discusses Petting, Parking, and Problems," mimeographed (AAUW Study Groups Report, 1964).

MULTIPLE APPROACHES

In the process of being extended, sex education has produced many and varied instructional and organizational arrangements. Sex education programs are now being developed to span the entire school period, kindergarten through twelfth grade. A number of schools have developed outlines and listings of topics and materials for such programs and are attempting to see that this instruction is implemented throughout the system.

The plans which are followed vary. Most schools in which sex education is a part of the elementary school program utilize incidental instruction. Information on reproduction may be accomplished through keeping animal pets in the classroom; knowledge of nutrition and of male-female parental roles may also be a consequence if the teacher chooses to make it so. Discussion of the arrival of new babies in families, of notions about babies and reproduction held by the children, and of the roles of human fathers and mothers may grow out of the story hours. Joint use of toilet facilities may familiarize kindergarten children with differences in anatomy and physiological processes.

In the middle grades discussions related to the biological and natural sciences may deal with these subjects and other aspects of growth and development more deeply. Boys and girls may be prepared for impending physical maturation in their health classes through the use of films and discussions. In the upper grades definite units designed to fulfill these needs may be included. Ways may be provided for children to ask questions about themselves and the other sex.

At the high school level formal units or informal discussions relating to pertinent aspects of sex may be incorporated in biology, general science, physiology, physical education, home economics, social studies, and English (as suggested by Gruenberg). Counselors may help with the personal sex problems of pupils. Many high schools have instituted family living courses, particularly at the junior and senior level. The Corvallis, Oregon, High School has an elective, co-educational, semester-length family living course in the social studies department which enrolls juniors and seniors. Various topics related to dating, love, mate selection, and marriage are discussed, and sexual questions freely raised and discussed. Particular attention is paid to the function of sex in interpersonal relationships.

The Hayward, California, Unified High School (now joined by the Castro Valley and San Lorenzo high schools) has pioneered in a more elaborate family life program.[32] As he enters the ninth grade

[32] Family Life Education Study Committee, "Progress Report, 1964–65," mimeographed (Castro Valley, Hayward, San Lorenzo Unified High School District, 1966).

each student becomes the advisee of a home room teacher, who serves him as a counselor-adviser for his four full years. In the twelfth grade a course, Sociology I (Family Living Instruction) is taught by this teacher for all of his advisees, enabling him to base his instruction on an intimate knowledge of his students gained from his three years as their adviser. It also provides a combination of group instruction and a personal counseling relationship. In this setting sex questions and discussions are an integral part of both group instruction and individual counseling. The Hayward program has now been expanded to include adult education (for parents in particular) in these areas.

An interesting aspect of the Hayward program is that it is built upon concepts which should, in the opinion of the curriculum builders, be developed grade by grade. Now that this program is being extended from kindergarten through the twelfth grade, a listing is being prepared to describe the full scope of the program. This concept-building approach provides an interesting contrast with programs which are based on a subject-matter sequence (see Chapter 4 by Helen Manley for one example of the former approach).

Anaheim, California, is now working with a program which was initiated, after a one-year pilot study, in the fall of 1964. Following the organization of the school district, it covers grades seven through twelve. In order to allocate time for this instruction, five weeks of the year's health and physical education program have been allocated to "family life and sex education." These time segments are so planned that each pupil is enrolled for five weeks in each grade, in a sequence which proceeds as follows: seventh, self-understanding; eighth, philosophy of life and values; ninth, morals in dating and premarital relations; tenth, human sexuality, engagement, and mate selection; eleventh, communication (dialogue and discussion emphasized); and twelfth, family, marriage roles, and child care. In both the Anaheim and the Hayward programs the teachers have been selected for their interest in the program, and their competence and confidence have been built and supported through continuing in-service preparation.

Other interesting variations include the day conference plan at Elk Grove, California, described above. In Kansas City, Missouri, the health and physical education division has pioneered in televised sex instruction. Team teaching has been used in a number of schools to provide an interdisciplinary emphasis and/or male-female views.

Churches are also moving into the area with great rapidity and, it seems, with less fear of community repercussions than the schools.

Several of our questionnaire respondents noted this development, but they also noted that the liberal churches were unquestionably moving more rapidly in this venture than the more conservative church groups. A number of respondents believed that the churches were outdistancing the schools in their success in building programs, particularly those geared to the needs of adolescents.

EUPHEMISMS FOR SEX EDUCATION

There has been a running debate over the term to be used to designate instruction about sex. The strong taboos surrounding the subject have carried over to the term "sex education," which in the past has excited fears, stirred disapproval, and connoted a narrow, limited approach. The result has been a continuing search for some neutral phrase which would at the same time be clear. As already noted, Dr. Bigelow used the words "social hygiene education," which grew rather naturally out of the prevailing concern for suppressing venereal ("social") diseases. Other names have been suggested and each has had its day and its adherents—"health and human relations education," "education for personal and social living," and "personal and social guidance."

Undoubtedly, "family living" is the most common and acceptable phrase and provides the context for the sex education aspects of the pioneering San Diego program.[33] Instruction concerning sex is naturally set in the framework of family and personal relationships, which is as it should be. It also appears less stark and provides shelter against potential criticism. Unfortunately, however, it is all-inclusive and has permitted those so disposed (and there have been many) to drop the sex education content altogether. Also family living has so many facets that the sex education aspect, which is an area of such importance to adolescents, has often been very inadequately treated even when it is included. Finally, there are many aspects of sexual understanding which are properly taught outside the family life context. There is, furthermore, such a wide range of possible definitions for family life education, as Elizabeth S. Force[34] and others have noted, that precision is extremely difficult.

In spite of these circumstances, many still feel strongly that direct references to sex education imperil the entire instructional program by making it vulnerable to public criticism. The Superintendent of Schools in Anaheim, California, Paul Cook, asked specifically for the term "sex education" to be used, so that the school program would

[33] American Social Health Association, "Family Life Education in San Diego," mimeographed (Washington, D.C.: By the Association, 1961).

[34] "The Role of the School in Family Life Education," *Journal of Marriage and the Family*, 26 (1964):99–102.

be known as "family life and sex education." He believed that sex education is badly needed and that it is time to abandon the subterfuge and evasiveness of the past for a direct statement about what is being taught, yet he wanted sex education put in a broader setting and so included family life. In an outline obtained from another school the program is entitled "health guidance and sex education," a juxtaposition which has come to our attention from other sources.

There is apparently a growing belief that the time has come to use the phrase "sex education" directly as an open and honest effort to get such instruction included in the school curriculum at the proper levels. Such reasoning led to the decision to form the Sex Information and Education Council of the United States as a separate and independent organization. The response to the program of SIECUS has been enthusiastic enough to suggest that both the public and professional educators may now be ready for a much more direct approach than heretofore.

PROGRAMS FOR YOUNG CHILDREN

The emphasis on programs from kindergarten through high school suggests that educators are becoming aware of the need for getting help to pupils early. Youths themselves have always voiced the "too little and too late" criticism. Their views are supported by C. B. Broderick, who has done extensive research on the dating and heterosexual interests and activities of children from the age of ten to the mid-teens (see Chapter 2 below). He has demonstrated that numbers of boys and girls even at age ten have cross-sex interests and experiences that go far beyond the expectations of most adults. He comments:

The findings indicate that for many children a special interest in members of the opposite sex begins in kindergarten or before. Crushes on classmates, teachers, and admired adults of the opposite sex are common throughout grade school. Kissing games are normative at third- to sixth-grade levels, and some kissing "when it means something special" occurs at these ages also. In some communities dating begins for a substantial number of children in the fifth and sixth grades, and going steady is common at the junior high school level. . . . The strong impression emerges that young people increasingly bring more heterosexual experience and sophistication to family-life classes than is assumed by most textbooks and course outlines. . . . By the junior or senior year of high school, when the students are most likely to encounter a family-living course, many have had five or more years of romantic interest in and romantic interaction with members of the opposite sex.[35]

[35] "Family Life Education versus Reality," p. 102.

PROGRAMS FOR TEACHERS

Despite some progress the greatest problem, noted over and over by the respondents to the questionnaire, lies in the preparation of teachers. This weakness is a matter of much concern. Upon its solution depends the future of sex education. Most undergraduate preparatory programs, if they are good, provide prospective teachers with basic information on psychology, human growth, personality development, and sociological awareness, upon which an understanding of human sexuality and sexual behavior can later be built. But few such programs deal directly with sexuality itself or recognize sex education as an aspect of instruction in the public schools.

In-service training of teachers has progressed much further than academic programs—so much so that in every section of the United States summer workshops, weekend conferences, and extension courses dealing with sex education and human sexuality can now be found. Of the two methods in-service training would seem at the moment to be much stronger and far more promising. Even now it reflects the flexibility already noted in some high school instructional programs.

The Kansas workshops for teachers and administrators based upon human growth and development have been mentioned. The State of Minnesota Department of Public Health and Department of Education have on two occasions held weekend conferences in which teachers and others interested in sex education have met with national authorities, viewed and evaluated new materials, and discussed problems. At the University of Oregon and Oregon State University, high school youths and high school teachers have been enrolled as students in the same workshops in an effort to break through communication barriers. Cities like Phoenix, Arizona, Santa Rosa, California, and San Jose, California, have provided special in-service programs for their teachers. The Kansas City Social Health Association, a community agency, has conducted afternoon and evening workshops for teachers in particular districts. Thus we have at present a field of instruction which is alive and moving. The challenge is to provide a firm and sound foundation for it, to arrive at some consensus on its objectives, and to create community support for the programs needed.

2

Normal Sociosexual Development

Carlfred B. Broderick

Nothing can be taught or learned if we disregard the human beings involved. In this chapter, therefore, we focus attention on the student himself, showing the process of his development, so that the teacher will always know approximately where he is when he faces him, what he is ready for, what is going on inside his mind and body. It is as much a part of the teacher's training to know the individuals he is confronting as it is to know the material he is presenting to them.

The sex educator is concerned with at least four questions, no matter what age group he may be dealing with: (1) what is the group's level of information and experience in the area of sex? (2) what are the attitudes of its members toward themselves as sexual beings? (3) what are the attitudes of the members of the group toward the opposite sex as a category of people? (4) what social skills do the members of the group have (or need) to help them relate to the opposite sex in satisfying and appropriate ways? The answers to these questions will vary from individual to individual and from group to group. But it is still of interest to review the meager store of information that is available on the typical pattern of development in these four areas over the life cycle.

THE PRESCHOOL YEARS
Sex Information and Experience

The extent of preschool children's knowledge about sex undoubtedly varies enormously, depending upon the attitudes and circumstances of the adults in charge of the child during these years. Observations in nursery schools and Head Start programs indicate that many children are interested in the differences between the sexes, both physical and behavioral. Some children want to know where babies come from, especially if the birth of a new baby is an important event in their own lives, as it often is at this age. Preschool children rarely appear to be concerned with questions of sexual intercourse or conception unless these matters are brought to their attention by adults or older children.

Attitudes toward Self

Whatever their level of knowledge about sex *per se*, all children learn attitudes about themselves as sexual beings during these years.

Even the parents who never discuss sex as a general topic are forced to deal with it as a characteristic of the child. The two-year-old who leaves his wet pants at the corner and comes home naked is certain to learn something about his parents' attitudes toward public exposure of his genitals. The four-year-old who has his hand in his pants when company comes learns something about the subject from the reaction he gets. The child of any age who comes in upon his parent of the opposite sex dressing or bathing or using the toilet will also learn from the reaction. Obviously, what he learns depends on the reaction, but there is no doubt that he learns something. Multiply these experiences by the number of situations involving sex in one way or another that commonly come up in family living, and it can be seen that the chance of avoiding learning in this area is nil. For better or for worse, the foundations of the child's basic concept of himself as a sexual being are laid in the often unintentional but powerful teaching that goes on during the preschool period.

Attitudes toward the Opposite Sex

It is generally believed that a child's capacity to relate to the opposite sex in a normal way is largely determined by his experiences during these early years. There are at least three factors involved. First, there is basic identification of himself as a member of his own sex. All future relationships with the opposite sex depend on this as a foundation. Most children achieve this identification fairly smoothly. They are constantly reminded of their sex by adults and other children and are rewarded for being appropriately masculine or feminine. In some instances, however, the parents may systematically indicate to the child that they would be more pleased if he were of the opposite sex. Studies show that it is also more difficult to identify with one's own sex if the parent of that sex is viewed as so cruel or so weak that no one would want to be like him.[1]

The second element is early experience with the opposite sex, especially with the parent of the opposite sex. Presumably, if one's early encounters are rewarding, the way is paved for a subsequent trusting, positive attitude toward other persons in this category. Studies of homosexuals seem to show that if the cross-sex parent is

[1] For two good reviews of the literature on the family's influence on sexual identification, see J. Kagan, "Acquisition and Significance of Sex Typing and Sex Role Identity," in *Review of Child Development Research*, ed. L. W. Hoffman and M. Hoffman (New York: Russell Sage Foundation, 1964), 1:137–68; and J. A. Clausen, "Family Structure, Socialization, and Personality," in *ibid.* (1966), 2:1–54.

24

too seductive or too punishing or too emotionally erratic, heterosexual adjustment may be made more difficult.[2]

A third factor that probably grows out of the first two is the young child's feeling about marriage as an eventual way of life for himself. Children play house from the age of about three on, indicating that they have a fair notion of many of the non-sexual aspects of marriage even at this age. One recent study[3] suggests that five-year-olds have a good idea of the group of eligible persons from which they must eventually select a mate (the mate must be outside the immediate family, of the opposite sex, and of the same general age). But more to the point, the majority of them are already committed to the notion of their own eventual marriage. This majority increases each year throughout childhood. The significance of this positive attitude toward marriage is underscored by the further finding that achievement of it seems to be almost a prerequisite to heterosexual progress during the next stage of development.

Social Skills

At this age there is probably not a great deal of difference in the skills needed to get along with one's own or the opposite sex, although this assumption has not been systematically studied. In any case, the more fundamental challenge for the preschool child is to learn the basic skills for dealing with interpersonal relationships in general. At later ages, more differentiated, specifically heterosexual, skills begin to play a bigger role.

MIDDLE CHILDHOOD (SIX THROUGH TWELVE YEARS)

Sex Information and Experience

Although to my knowledge there have been no studies on the information or misinformation which children of elementary school age have about sex, it seems likely that there is perhaps more variation in sophistication at this than at any other age. The effects of widely divergent parental attitudes toward sex are evident in the conversations of children from kindergarten onward. One rural mother told a parent group recently that while she was in the hospital having a new baby she left her kindergartner in the care of a friend who was about seven months pregnant. The little girl, observ-

---

[2] For a review of this literature, see J. Marmor, ed., *Sexual Inversion* (New York: Basic Books, 1965), chap. 1; and I. Bieber, "Clinical Aspects of Male Homosexuality," in *ibid.*, chap. 14, pp. 248–67.

[3] C. B. Farrell, "Awareness and Attitudes of Preschool Children toward Heterosexual Social Relationships" (Master's thesis, The Pennsylvania State University, 1966).

ing her shape, asked whether the babysitter was going to the hospital soon too, and was told, "Not for a couple of months yet." The casual response was "Oh, I guess you were jumped two months later." We may grant that this child's parents might want to spend some time with her discussing the elements of love and tenderness unique to human mating, but one cannot doubt that this young lady had a firm grasp on what are often called "the facts of life."

Contrast this with the experience of another girl of the same age who was staying with her grandmother while her mother had a baby, and said to her, "Grandma, I know that babies grow inside of their mothers, but how do they get out?" To which her grandmother replied, "I think it's terrible to fill children's heads with filth like that." The little girl persevered: "But Grandmother, you must know how they get out; you had Mommy." The answer (and this was in the 1960's, not the 1890's) was this: "I found your mother in a cabbage patch and that's where she found you, too. Now let's hear no more about it."

Probably most children are less well informed than the first little girl and more honestly dealt with than the second little girl. Although there are no statistics on it, it is probably true that the majority of children form some notion of pregnancy and childbirth and of their relation to sexual intercourse before they leave elementary school. They learn from parents, from older brothers and sisters, from other children and even, in a growing number of cases, from professional educators in a school or church setting.

On several occasions I have had questions from groups of fifth- and sixth-graders after viewing a film such as "Boy to Man" or "Girl to Woman."[4] One doesn't know what the questions might have been if the films had not been shown first, but in these circumstances the girls ask questions about menstruation and pregnancy, and often about whether one can get pregnant through any other means than sexual intercourse. Boys' questions may also touch on pregnancy and intercourse, but in addition they frequently ask for definitions of terms (including slang terms) which they have heard but not understood. In communities where preadolescent dating occurs, either sex may ask questions on sexual conduct, questions that are more typically encountered at later ages. Not infrequently, there are questions about "the pill," about birth out of wedlock, and about differences in size and shape of genitals (boys) and of bodies (girls).

Occasionally a question reminds one that even at these ages some

[4] These films are both produced by Churchill Films, 662 North Robertson Boulevard, Los Angeles, California 90069, priced at $90 for black and white prints and $180 for color.

children have experienced sexual exploitation by adults or by older children and that others have experimented with sex with children of their own age. Kinsey's data on children's sexual experience are now woefully out of date, since they were collected mostly from adults during the decade of the 1940's and describe behavior experienced in the 1930's and earlier. Nevertheless, it is instructive to realize that his sample of males reported that by age twelve about 20 per cent had masturbated, 30 per cent had been involved in homosexual play (mostly handling another boy's genitals), 40 per cent had experienced heterosexual play (including exhibition and looking, as well as touching), and an estimated 15 per cent had attempted intercourse with a girl.[5] Among the females, about 15 per cent reported that they had masturbated, about 20 per cent reported homosexual experience (excluding looking), and about 30 per cent reported heterosexual experience (including looking and exhibition).[6] No current data are available, but it does seem safe to assume that the current generation is no less experienced than its parents.

Attitudes toward Self

Little is known about how children of elementary school age feel about themselves as sexual beings. Lacking direct data, inferences must be based on their behavior. The very fact that boys and girls tend to grow apart more and more during these years (reaching a maximum segregation at about age twelve) suggests the possibility of role discomfort, as though they need to practice their roles separately before they can interact with the opposite sex.[7] Another evidence of growing awareness of sex role expectations is revealed in Kinsey's data. Among girls the active incidence of heterosexual play *decreased* as puberty approached. The same was true for those boys who eventually went on to college, although not for others. Where the decrease occurs, it seems likely that it is caused by older children's increased awareness of the social significance of sexual behavior.[8]

[5] These data and a great deal of additional information are, of course, available in the chapters on preadolescent sexual development in each of the Kinsey volumes (A. C. Kinsey et al., *Sexual Behavior in the Human Male* [Philadelphia: Saunders, 1948]; Kinsey et al., *Sexual Behavior in the Human Female* [Philadelphia: Saunders, 1953]).

[6] See n. 5 above.

[7] See C. B. Broderick, "Socio-Sexual Development in a Suburban Community," *Journal of Sex Research*, 2 (1966):1–24; and Broderick and S. E. Fowler, "New Patterns of Relationships between the Sexes among Preadolescents," *Journal of Marriage and Family Living*, 23 (1961):27–30.

[8] Kinsey et al., *Sexual Behavior in the Human Male*, p. 174; *Sexual Behavior in the Human Female*, p. 111.

Attitudes toward the Opposite Sex

In a recent series of studies in Georgia,[9] Pennsylvania,[10] and Missouri,[11] considerable information has been gathered on the process by which attitudes and social involvement with the opposite sex progress, at least from age ten onward. It has already been noted that the foundation for further sociosexual development seems to be a positive attitude toward marriage. The exact proportion varies from one part of the country to another, and from one type of community to another, but typically about 55 to 60 per cent of the ten-year-old boys, about 65 to 70 per cent of the twelve-year-old boys, about 80 per cent of the ten-year-old girls, and 90 per cent or more of the twelve-year-old girls are sure that they want to get married some day. Those that have not yet come to this conclusion tend not to become involved with the opposite sex at all, either in fantasy or in reality, during preadolescence. For these children, and only for them, the concept of preadolescence as a period of "sexual latency"[12] has real validity.

Those who do accept marriage as something they want to become involved in themselves sooner or later take the next step and single out a particular member of the opposite sex as their girl friend or boy friend. As often as not, at the younger ages this chosen sweetheart may never be aware of his selection. The child keeps his choice largely to himself, perhaps sharing his fantasies with one or two close friends. In only about one-fifth of the cases was the attachment found to be reciprocated by the sweetheart. Nevertheless, these attachments, as well as crushes on adults, entertainers, and others, can be seen to have a real function. They provide an opportunity to rehearse intense emotional involvement in the complete safety of one's own imagination. The eleven-year-old girl who is smitten by some recording artist or televison star or, for that matter, by the boy who sits in the row next to hers in school, can play out

[9] Broderick and Fowler, "New Patterns of Relationships between the Sexes among Preadolescents."

[10] C. B. Broderick, "Social Heterosexual Development among Urban Negroes and Whites," *Journal of Marriage and Family Living*, 27 (1965):200–4; Broderick, "Socio-Sexual Development in a Suburban Community"; Broderick and G. P. Rowe, "A Scale of Preadolescent Heterosexual Development," *Journal of Marriage and the Family*, 30 (1968):97–101.

[11] Broderick and Rowe, "A Scale of Preadolescent Heterosexual Development"; Rowe, "Patterns of Interpersonal Relationships among Youth Nine to Thirteen Years of Age" (Ph.D. diss., Florida State University, 1966).

[12] For many years Freud's suggestion that in the years just prior to puberty there is a turning away from all interest in the opposite sex was widely accepted. In recent years it has become increasingly obvious that nothing quite that clear-cut happens in most children.

scenes of great tenderness or ecstasy in her own mind without fear of rejection, exploitation, or, in fact, any consequences at all. The same is true for boys. Girls are more likely than boys to have these fantasies, probably because they are more heterosexually oriented than boys at these ages. Typically, about half of the boys and three-fourths of the girls report having a sweetheart of their own age, and somewhat smaller percentages report crushes on familiar adults or public figures of various kinds.

From crushes, the next step is love. Adults, of course, smile at the notion of preadolescents claiming to be in love, and indeed at every age studied, from ten to seventeen, young people themselves tend to discount any "loves" prior to the current one. Previous experiences are reclassified as having been only "puppy love" or a "crush." Despite these disclaimers, when it is experienced, "love" seems to have some impact on those involved. Between 40 and 50 per cent of the boys and between 50 and 60 per cent of the girls between ten and twelve years of age claim at some time that they are in love.

Once this point is reached, there is some evidence that the imagination turns not only to idle romantic fantasies but to more concrete wishes. This is illustrated by the fact that, of the boys who claim they are not in love, only 20 per cent think it would be more fun to go to the movies with a girl than with another boy, but for those who claim to be in love, over 40 per cent would prefer a female companion at the movies.

The ultimate step would be actually to take a girl out on a date. In some parts of the country it is still very rare for preadolescents to date; in some communities studied the percentage was as low as 5 per cent. In other communities, however, well over half of the twelve-year-olds reported having had one or more dates. As in the case of "love," some of these early "dates" may be designated by older children as "not *really* dates." Even allowing for some re-definition of a date at later ages and for the fact that it is generally several months between dates at these early ages, it remains true that in some communities the more precocious boys and girls may begin to date while in grade school. It is my observation that this pattern is more likely to be found in the South and the Pacific Coast states than in the East and Midwest. It is also most likely to be found among the middle classes in urban or suburban areas, and least likely in the rural areas.

Social Skills

At the time when boys and girls are rehearsing emotional commitment in the safety of their own imaginations, they are also likely to be rehearsing some of the social skills which they feel are useful in boy-girl relations. One example is playing kissing games at parties. In a kissing game one has the opportunity to practice an activity important in later boy-girl relations without taking responsibility for choosing one's partner (who is determined by some chance factor), and without risking being rejected, since everyone in the game is committed to abide by the rules. Also, the probabilities of kissing leading to more serious physical or emotional involvement is minimized by the structure of the situation. The incidence of kissing games varied tremendously among the communities studied. In one small town in Missouri no child had ever played kissing games, while in one urban setting in Pennsylvania the large majority of children over ten had had some experience with them.

Almost the same range is evident in the case of social dancing. In many communities from coast to coast fifth- and sixth-graders in the middle- and upper-class areas are given formal instruction in social dancing and the etiquette that goes with it. In fact, on the West Coast there are chains of dance studios that cater particularly to this age group. I have newspaper clippings of elementary school proms and fancy balls from many parts of the country. Of course, this sort of activity requires parental sponsorship, and therefore in many communities social dancing does not begin until junior high school or even later.

In view of the extraordinary range of experience and inexperience, involvement and non-involvement, at this age, it is clear that no single curriculum could be expected to meet the needs of every group. Each teacher must have some means of determining the information, experience, and emotional involvement of the children in his own class; if not, his material may be completely inappropriate for his students.

ADOLESCENCE
Sex Information and Experience

In the period from seventh through twelfth grade there is a steady shift from an emphasis on questions about menstruation, conception, and sexual intercourse to questions about the social relationships between boys and girls and about sexual mores. Girls want to understand boys' motivations better. Why are they so interested in sex? What will they do and think if a girl rejects their advances? If a girl doesn't? What are good ways to cope with boys? As an increasing number have had experience with petting and with sexual intercourse,[13] either first-hand or vicarious, more questions

---

[13] Recent data on the sexual experience of adolescent boys and girls are lacking. The best we have are those of Kinsey, which are now a generation old, and the

are asked on how far they should go under various circumstances ("Should a Christian girl ever pet?" "Is sex all right if you really love a boy? If not, why not?" "What's wrong if he only does it with his finger?"). Boys are likely to ask similar questions, in some cases challenging the adult world to defend traditional values and in other cases asking for guidance because of a real lack of self-direction.

Some educators have observed, however, that the question of standards and values is most urgent at about the tenth-grade level and that beyond that age young people apparently have made their basic decisions and by twelfth grade the questions mostly focus upon the psychology of boy-girl relationships rather than upon sex specifically. Questions about sex range from how to achieve sexual adjustment in marriage, to whether a boy ought to marry a girl if he gets her pregnant, to whether frigidity is physical or psychological.

It would seem that the information needed by adolescents is primarily in the realm of human interaction and decision-making, with some attention also to dynamics of personality. Information gradually becomes less important than meaning. The over-riding question of adolescents is, "What part ought sex to play in my life now?"

Attitudes toward Self

It can be observed that in adolescence there is a close tie between feelings of self-esteem and feelings of sexual adequacy. Clinicians frequently find that the boy who is insatiable in his need for sexual conquest is more likely to be motivated by a need for reassurance that he is masculine than by an unmanageable biological sex drive. Similarly, a girl's seducibility may be more a function of her feelings of worth and lovability than of her need for physical stimulation and release.

One recent study[14] attempted to get at young people's feelings about themselves by having them write stories about a cartoon showing a boy and a girl sitting or standing together. These stories showed that the boy and girl were most often viewed as being uneasy and at a loss for words. Moreover, contrary to expectations, the

---

study of Michael Schofield (The Sexual Behavior of Young People [Boston: Little, Brown, 1965]), which is more recent but which was done in England, not the United States. Based on these sources, it may be said that well over 90 per cent of the boys of high school age may have masturbated but that only about 25 per cent of the girls of similar age have done so. About 80 per cent of both boys and girls have petted by age eighteen. About half of the boys and about 15 per cent of the girls have had actual sexual intercourse by eighteen years of age. Each of these activities varies with social class, religious devoutness, race, region, and so forth.

[14] C. B. Broderick and Jean Weaver, "The Perceptual Context of Boy-Girl Communication," Journal of Marriage and the Family, 30 (November, 1968), in press.

older the respondents were, the more prone they were to see the couple as feeling inadequate in the situation. In other words, experience with the opposite sex did not lead to a more comfortable feeling but rather to a sharper awareness of one's own vulnerability. It is probably in this context that going steady should be evaluated, that is, as a strategy for reducing social anxiety and uncertainty. This interpretation is supported by the findings in the same study that the older the respondents were (the age range was ten to seventeen), the less likely they were to think that one had to be in love to go steady.

Attitudes toward the Opposite Sex

Like every other society, ours has the problem of maneuvering its young people into marriage. It is interesting to note that we are very successful in doing so. About 94 per cent of our population is married by the age of forty. This is all the more remarkable because, with its emphasis on freedom of choice, our society depends upon the voluntary efforts of individuals to achieve this goal. As has been noted, beginning in infancy, a series of pressures are applied calculated to motivate children to get married some day. In addition, there is a systematic program for involving adolescent boys and girls in each other's social world. Boys are under considerable pressure to find female companions for various social events and girls are under similar pressure to accept and even to encourage such invitations. Initially, the contract between the boy and girl for these events is limited to enjoyment of the date itself, but there are powerful forces at work to keep the relationship from stopping there if the first date is a success. For one thing, lining up a different girl for each occasion takes energy, and there is a strong motivation for regularizing successful relationships through steady dating or some other similar arrangement. But even beyond these considerations, the boy has been taught to press for whatever degree of physical intimacy the girl will allow, and the girl has been taught to press for whatever emotional and social commitment she can obtain from the boy. As the relationship develops with these two forces at work, what began as casual and limited tends almost inevitably either to become more "serious" (that is, involve more intimacy and more commitment) or else to be broken off altogether.[15]

If this analysis is correct, then adolescents see the opposite sex from two viewpoints. On the one hand, it is evaluated as a pool of

[15] For a somewhat more detailed discussion of the intimacy-commitment spiral, see my "Steady Dating, the Beginning of the End," in *Teenage Marriage and Divorce*, ed. S. M. Farber and R. H. L. Wilson (Berkeley, Calif.: Diablo Press, 1967), pp. 21–24.

eligible partners for recreational events. On the other hand, it is also a pool of candidates for a relationship of increasing intimacy and commitment. There is evidence that the predominance of one viewpoint over the other depends upon several factors. First is the duration of the relationship itself. The longer a boy and girl go out together, the more difficult it is to keep out of the intimacy-commitment spiral. A second factor is the social acceptability of the partners. One study has shown that if the partners' social background or personal values are far apart, the relationship is unlikely to progress very far.[16]

Third, there are circumstantial or feasibility factors. Those who plan to go on to college or who have other firm plans for their lives after high school is over tend to avoid the spiral, while those who have no such plans tend to move from one level of commitment to another until they are married.[17] At present about 50 per cent of all girls do get married while they are still in their teens, so that the process described here runs its full course within the experience of many adolescents.

Social Skills

At this and at subsequent ages, most of the social skills needed to cope with the demands of heterosexual relationships are not very different from those needed to cope with social relationships in general. Probably the key assets that can be acquired at this stage are self-understanding and sensitivity to others. It is not accidental that nearly all "functional" courses on dating and courtship include material on these important qualities. Various approaches have been used to try to develop these insights—autobiographies, personality inventories, interaction in small groups, personal therapy, etc. Some of these techniques and others have also been used to increase understanding of the opposite sex. Although the effectiveness of various approaches has not been adequately evaluated, the widespread recognition of the need for social skills is noteworthy.

Another entirely different type of skill, which many family life educators see as important at these ages, is birth control. The question of whether young people should be instructed in the effective use of contraceptives will doubtless be debated for a long time to come, both on moral and practical grounds. If the trend toward general liberalization in our society continues, however, it does

---

[16] A. C. Kerckhoff and K. E. Davis, "Value Concessions and Need Complementarity in Mate Selection," *American Sociological Review*, 27 (1962):298–303.

[17] See *ibid.* and A. J. Schneider, "Measurement of Courtship Progress of High School Upperclassmen Currently Going Steady" (Ph.D. diss., The Pennsylvania State University, 1966).

seem likely that a majority of adolescents will receive instruction, mostly informal, but also formal, in the various aspects of birth control.

It is probably also true that this generation of teenagers will have available to them more reliable information on effective techniques of sexual stimulation than any previous generation has had. It is not clear, of course, whether this information will be directly translatable into action, but one presumes that if there is any change from one generation to the other, it is likely to be in the direction of greater competence in this area.

AFTER HIGH SCHOOL, BEFORE MARRIAGE
Sex Information and Experience

Up through the age of about seventeen the majority of young people have at least one important thing in common: school. Beyond that age their life circumstances begin to diverge more and more. A considerable number marry shortly after high school. Of those who do not, some go on to college, some go into the armed services, some go to work. Some continue to live at home with their parents, and some live away from home, more or less on their own. In describing the level of sexual experience in these various groups, we are handicapped again by the fact that most of the data are badly out of date. We have no way of knowing whether the behavior patterns of twenty or more years ago, when some of the key studies were done, are present today.

Petting, which of course covers a very wide range of finely graded sexual interactions, is the commonest form of sexual behavior during the late teens and early twenties. There is some evidence that there is more petting among middle- and upper-class young people than among lower-class groups, more among steady and engaged couples than among casual couples, and so forth. But the central fact is that this is the most frequent sexual practice for all groups of this age. As at the younger ages, the question of how far to go in petting becomes a matter not only of moral values but of bargaining between boys and girls. Indeed, there is very little evidence of any widely accepted strictures governing the matter in our society, except those relating to the intimacy-commitment bargaining cycle. This perhaps explains why the major focus of this age group tends to be less upon morals and standards and more upon matters of strategy in boy-girl relations. There is particular concern for the impact of present behavior upon eventual marriage, and both boys and girls are concerned with finding that balance of sexual expression and sexual restraint which will lead to the best marital union. Unfortunately, there is no very convincing scientific evidence which the educator can offer as a guide. There is some evidence that a more conservative approach tends toward a more stable marriage,[18] but in the final analysis such choices cannot be determined on the basis of the results of research but must grow out of the individual's own long-range system of values.

The proportion of unmarried youths who have experienced sexual intercourse also varies from group to group. Kinsey found that by age twenty about 25 per cent of girls with a high school education or less and about 20 per cent of girls with a college education reported having had coitus. By the same age almost 70 per cent of college boys and an even larger number of lower-class men had reported the experience.[19] Of course, both Kinsey's studies and others indicate that with each successive year of age the proportion of unmarried girls who are virgins decreases and also that the closer a girl is to marriage, the greater is the likelihood that she has had coitus. The best data we have from various studies is that something close to 50 per cent of American women have had sexual intercourse before marriage, although most commonly this occurs with their future husbands.[20]

In addition to petting and intercourse, it is also true that nearly half of all unmarried women in this age group masturbate from time to time. There is a wide range of individual variations, but there can be no doubt that for a significant number of women, this practice is a major sexual outlet during this period of their lives. Again, there are social class differences, in that the better educated groups are somewhat more likely to masturbate than others.

For a more detailed discussion of the level of sexual experience at this stage of life, the reader is directed to the excellent review in Robert Bell's *Premarital Sex in a Changing Society.*[21]

Attitudes toward Self

The range of attitudes toward oneself at this age becomes so complex, even more so than in the case of sexual behavior, that it is difficult to summarize. One factor that probably plays an important part in the single girl's sexual self-image is the fact that by the age of twenty she is already a member of a minority. If she is in college,

[18] W. R. Reevey, "Premarital Petting Behavior and Marital Happiness Prediction," *Journal of Marriage and Family Living*, 21 (1959):349–55; D. G. Shope and C. B. Broderick, "Level of Sexual Experience and Predicted Adjustment in Marriage," *Journal of Marriage and Family Living*, 29 (1967):424–27.

[19] Kinsey's data on lower-class men are considered quite unreliable because so many of his cases were prisoners.

[20] Kinsey et al., *Sexual Behavior in the Human Female*, pp. 330–31.

[21] (Englewood Cliffs, N.J.: Prentice-Hall, 1966).

of course, most of the other girls around her are also unmarried, but by the age of twenty-four most girls, whatever their education, are aware that the large majority (actually about 85 per cent) of women in the same age group are married. For the girl who is fairly confident that she will eventually marry the boy she is going with, of course, this causes little worry. Similarly, for the girl who does not want to be married, this is no problem. But the girl who wants to become married but sees no immediate prospects may question her own desirability.

Contrary to the popular image of gay bachelorhood, there is also a smaller but significant group of males who feel that they are single not by choice but because of inability to attract a desirable mate. It must be presumed that this is a period of crisis for both of these groups in their attitudes toward themselves as sexual beings. The situation is likely to be made worse if, in their loneliness, they turn to masturbation or other forms of sexual activity which in their own eyes, are demeaning.

Persons not in these groups who are unhappy about their experiences in the windings of the intimacy-commitment spiral may also find reasons to doubt their own worth. But it is probably true that, in general, this period of life is more supportive to one's sexual self-image than any other, if only because the process of courtship is, by definition, flattering.

Attitudes toward the Opposite Sex

From society's point of view, the most important final goal of male-female relationships is responsible parenthood. In pursuit of that goal, society has an investment in every potential parent's achieving the capacity to relate to the opposite sex with trust and concern for the other's welfare. Nevertheless, man's needs for sexual fulfillment and emotional response can be exploited like any other needs. It would appear that one of the key elements in sociosexual development, then, would be learning to reject relationships based on exploitation in favor of relationships based on mutual concern. Some of this process of learning undoubtedly occurs in the process of growing up, so that whereas some people avoid exploitation under any circumstances, others take this as a usual approach to situations. In his book, *Premarital Intercourse and Interpersonal Relationships*, Lester Kirkendall has traced the process by which many individuals progress from exploitative to supportive relationships with the opposite sex.[22] The process is courtship. Thus it may be that the almost universal goal of marriage is itself one of the chief factors in the development of positive relationships between the sexes.

[22] (New York: Julian Press, 1961). See also Chapter 8 below.

Social Skills

The social skills required of this group do not differ materially from those required of adolescents. The substantially greater stability and success of marriage contracted by those twenty years old and older, as compared with those contracted by teenagers,[23] does lead to the conclusion that there is a real difference in the level of competence in interpersonal relations between the two groups. Thus, although the demands may be the same, the more mature group appears to have the advantage in achievement.

EARLY IN MARRIAGE

Although it is naïvely believed by young people that sexual experience automatically assures rather complete understanding in sexual matters, this is patently untrue. According to one study of middle-class couples, done in 1946,[24] only a little over half found sex mutually satisfying from the beginning. After several years only 10 per cent more had achieved satisfactory relationships. Lee Rainwater, in a study reported more fully in Chapter 9, got essentially similar results except that the lowest income group was found to be even more likely to find difficulty in achieving satisfactory sexual adjustment than the middle class. These studies would seem to indicate that there is learning to take place in the sexual area even after marriage, at least for a considerable proportion of the population. Further evidence of this is Kinsey's finding that on the average women's sexual responsiveness increases throughout the first decade of marriage.

Judging from the content of marriage handbooks designed to smooth the way to more successful sexual relations, the information needed by young married couples is of three types. First, the erotic potential of men and women and ways of taking advantage of them must be understood. Second, some grasp of human relationships and the principle of give and take as they apply to all areas of life, including the sexual, must be present. And last, but by no means least, there must be a positive attitude toward one's own and one's partner's sexuality.

A number of communities are aiming educational programs at this group (see Chapter 6 below), although in many cases sexual adjustment is secondary to education for parenthood. Of course, it is the

---

[23] According to one study (J. T. Landis and M. G. Landis, *Building a Successful Marriage*, 4th ed. [Englewood Cliffs, N.J.: Prentice-Hall, 1963]) the percentage of divorces if both partners are under twenty years of age is 20.2, compared with 10 per cent if both are in the twenty- to twenty-five-year group.

[24] J. T. Landis, "Length of Time Required to Achieve Adjustment in Marriage," *American Sociological Review*, 11 (1946):668.

philosophy of most sex educators that education for sexual adjustment in marriage starts in infancy, but there are at least some promising indications that efforts at the time of marriage can bear fruit.

MIDDLE AGE

It is widely observed that middle age is a difficult period sexually. It is a period of decreasing sexual powers, of increasing dissatisfaction with all aspects of marriage including the sexual, of generally unflattering physical change. It is the period when women are most likely to have an extra-marital affair. It is the time of the menopause, with all of the physical and psychological stresses which accompany that important event.

All of these things serve to indicate that the sexual difficulties of middle age are closely related to self-image and self-confidence. As A. W. Melton has pointed out,[25] a positive attitude toward oneself as a sexual person is not enhanced by the obvious interest and involvement of one's own adolescent children in sexual interaction. Children's activities and concerns tend to focus their parents' attention on their own sex lives. Often the results of this re-examination are not reassuring. H. Feldman has shown that marital integration, including sexual closeness, tends to lessen with the birth of each child.[26] In a longitudinal study, P. C. Pineo has shown that after twenty years of marriage most couples reported being less satisfied with every aspect of it, including the sexual.[27] Cuber and Harroff found that only about one-sixth of their sample of stable upper middle-class marriages could be rated as "vital," and that about half were dominated by a feeling of mutual antagonism, either passively or actively expressed.[28]

Despite these gloomy data, I know of few programs aimed at helping this age group achieve a more positive self-image and a more satisfactory heterosexual relationship. Various counseling facilities may be utilized by a few. Some may be influenced by the attempt of medical and mental health groups to alter the public concept of menopause as an end of sexuality. But the majority are left without help in their difficulties. Whatever the reason for this

[25] "Sexual Communication and the New Morality" (Address to the Annual Meeting of the National Council of Family Relations, San Francisco, Calif., August, 1967).

[26] "Sexual Adjustment in Early Marriage" (Address to the Annual Groves Conference on Marriage and the Family, Kansas City, Mo., April, 1966).

[27] "Disenchantment in the Later Years of Marriage," *Journal of Marriage and Family Living*, 23 (1961):3–11.

[28] J. F. Cuber and P. B. Harroff, *The Significant Americans: A Study of Sexual Behavior among the Affluent* (New York: Appleton-Century, 1965).

neglect, it seems safe to predict that new programs will be developed to meet the needs of this group.

LATER YEARS

In aging, waning sexual prowess is often confronted by ridicule. Unhappily, when asked to consider the sexual life of this group, even medical doctors and persons in the mental health professions may share this attitude. I recently led a discussion of Isadore Rubin's excellent book, *Sexual Life after Sixty*,[29] in the staff meeting of a mental health clinic. An onslaught of raucous, good-humored comments about how the meeting was certain to be short (presumably due to lack of content) had to be weathered before the subject could be seriously broached.

It is true that the proportion of men who can achieve intercourse diminishes steadly, from about 75 per cent at age sixty to 30 per cent at seventy to about 14 to 20 per cent at eighty, but a substantial group of older men remains, and their sexual needs and capacities are real and legitimate. In addition, those men who are impotent may have feelings about their own incapacity which should be worked with. The situation with women is somewhat different because there is no exact equivalent to male impotence. The woman's organs may show some deterioration and lack of lubrication, but her sexual activity is more likely to be governed by her husband's desires than by her own.

A related question is that of widows and widowers, who are without legitimate sex partners and who, for that matter, are in a poor position to compete for any sex partners, legitimate or not. Unlike any other age group, their unmet sexual needs are seen as ludicrous at best and lascivious at worst; their attempts to meet their affectional needs through remarriage, for example, are met with winks and leers and, often, disapproval.

The problems of aging are many-faceted. Our society is just now beginning to respond to their need for adequate sustenance and for medical care, and some time may elapse before proper attention is paid to the serious question of the sexual needs of the elderly.

[29] (New York: Signet Books, 1965).

3 Socialization into Sexual Behavior in a Negro Slum Ghetto

Boone E. Hammond and Joyce A. Ladner

Broderick's chapter indicated in a general way the course of normal hetero-sexual development in the larger society. The experience of groups in this heterogeneous society varies tremendously, however. In this chapter Hammond and Ladner provide a vivid insight into the sexual socialization process in one important subculture, the Negro ghetto.

In recent years social scientists have attempted to understand the problems of the lower-class Negro. In spite of the volumes of data collected in the past few years, many important areas remain totally unexplored. Individuals born in Negro ghettos live their entire lives there, in conditions that have been virtually unchanged for decades. Too often we are unable to understand the ever-present problems of marital disruption, illegitimacy, and promiscuity. An examination of the early socialization patterns of the lower-class Negro child may be a step toward understanding these problems.

This paper deals with sexual socialization patterns of lower-class Negro preadolescents and adolescents, i.e., the attitudes and behavior patterns relating to sexuality and the ways in which they are formed as the child moves toward adulthood. Much of the literature on childhood socialization shows that much of what is passed from one generation to the next is through the parent-child relationship,[1] so that, in part at least, the parent's perception of his environment will be passed on to the child. Further, through social interaction with his family, peers, and others, he becomes conscious of and understands his world. As he becomes aware of the sexual behavior patterns and attitudes around him, the child begins to learn the role of sex in his subculture. The goal of our study was to identify the influences, pressures, and circumstances involved in this process.

The data come from a study currently under way at the Pruitt-

---

[1] See A. Bandura and R. H. Walters, *Social Learning and Personality Development* (New York: Holt, Rinehart and Winston, 1963); E. H. Erikson, *Childhood and Society* (New York: Norton, 1950); S. W. Bijou and D. M. Baer, *Child Development: A Systematic and Empirical Theory* (New York: Appleton, 1961).

Igoe Housing Project in St. Louis.[2] The sample size numbers roughly 150 males and females, but we worked intensively with only about half of the sample. The age range of our respondents is five through eighteen. Although the project has an all-Negro population, we feel that much of the data are applicable to lower-class behavior in general. In the main, we present the data as descriptive because our findings are only preliminary.[3]

The area of sex has traditionally been clouded with mystery. Discussion of sex was, and to a great extent still is, held in great secrecy even among close friends. Slowly these ideas are disappearing, but the general air of secrecy and mystery remains. The trend of scientific research in sexual matters has followed this same pattern somewhat, although there have recently been changes. Indeed, the pioneering work of Kinsey, Ramsey, Masters, and others[4] has been received with a mixed reaction based in great part on mythical ideology.

For many years, one myth which has been considerably popular has been that of "Negro sexuality." The Negro lower class has been characterized as having stronger interests in sex than other groups and, in fact, an insatiable desire for sexual relations. The entire characterization is, of course, absurd in all of its aspects. The idea of continuous sexual enjoyment in the lower class has been disproved by Lee Rainwater and others.[5] Unfortunately, many people still believe it to be a reality, and it is especially unfortunate that a

[2] This paper is based in part on research aided by a grant from the National Institute of Mental Health, No. MH-09189: "Social and Community Problems in Public Housing Areas."

[3] We have presented these findings in detail elsewhere. See Boone Hammond, "The Contest System: A Survival Technique," mimeographed (Masters Honors Essay Series, Social Science Institute, Washington University, St. Louis, 1966); Joyce Ladner, "Deviance in the Lower Class Adolescent Sub-Culture" (Masters Honors Essay Series, Social Science Institute, Washington University, St. Louis, 1966); Boone Hammond, "The Contest System: Some Notes on Lower Class Negro Sexual Relations" (paper presented at the Midwest Sociological Society meetings, Madison, Wis., April, 1966).

[4] A. C. Kinsey et al., Sexual Behavior in the Human Male (Philadelphia: Saunders, 1949); Kinsey et al., Sexual Behavior in the Human Female (Philadelphia: Saunders, 1953); G. V. Ramsey, "The Sexual Development of Boys," American Journal of Psychology, 56 (1943):217–33; W. H. Masters and V. E. Johnson, Human Sexual Response (Boston: Little, Brown, 1966). For a cross-cultural view, see C. S. Ford and F. A. Beach, Patterns of Sexual Behavior (New York: Harper, 1951).

[5] Rainwater deals with the myth of lower-class sexuality and the "natural man" in several papers, e.g., "Some Aspects of Lower Class Sexual Behavior," Journal of Social Issues, 22 (April, 1966):96–108; "Marital Sexuality in Four Cultures of Poverty," Journal of Marriage and the Family, 26 (1964):457–66; "Crucible of Identity," in The Negro American, ed. K. Clark and T. Parsons (Boston: Houghton Mifflin, 1966).

substantial number of lower-class Negroes have themselves absorbed much of this myth, making it a kind of "self-fulfilling prophecy." It has become an in-group cultural ideology, widely disseminated through folklore, the press, and popular music. As a "group member" (i.e., a member of the Negro lower class), one is alleged to manifest much of the behavior embodied in the myth. Despite the myths and stereotypes relative to sexuality among lower-class Negroes, however, sex does play a major role in their lives. We shall focus on the importance of sex and its impact on the socialization of the child.

It is a commonplace in America to think of children as asexual. C. B. Broderick expresses this middle-class conception thus: "By cultural definition pre-adolescents are held to be without sexual interest or capacity, and the investigator is liable at least to ridicule for attempting to find what is not there and at worst to persecution for imperiling the morals of children by putting unnatural ideas into their heads."[6] We found in our investigation that the "unnatural" ideas were already there. We will now attempt to describe how they develop.

The destructive social and economic forces of the Negro ghetto often create a situation in which the young child is exposed to sex-socializing influences almost constantly. Beginning at about age five (and sometimes earlier), he begins to become aware of the area of sex to which he has often been blatantly exposed, and he absorbs as much of it as he is able to comprehend. The basis of the child's comprehension is partly a function of the amount and degree of exposure and partly of his maturational level.

The belief that preadolescents are asexual in their interests and capacities does not apply to a large segment of Negro lower-class culture. In fact, in many cases we found the very opposite view accepted. Some parents believed that even preadolescents were sexually sophisticated. A number of mothers boasted of the sexual conquests of their young sons, while other parents expressed strong concern for the potential trouble that could develop for their sexually precocious sons and daughters. One mother who apparently had experience with preadolescent sexuality had this to say: "These kids grow up fast in this project. The five and six year old heifers [girls] know as much about screwing as I do. My six year old boy has already punched [had intercourse with] two or three of these fast chicks and I'm teaching my four year old boy how to be a lady killer too. I can't hide the facts of life from them because they

[6] C. B. Broderick, "Sexual Behavior among Pre-Adolescents," *Journal of Social Issues*, 22, no. 2 (April, 1966):6–22.

can see them every day on any stairway, hall, or elevator in the project."

Similar examples could be given, but they all illustrate the basic point that the idea of asexual childhood is almost inconceivable to this group. Instead, the child is held to be highly sexual in his interests and capacities, and it is expected that he will become aware of sex as soon as he is able. Moreover, the parents' concern is how to protect the child and prevent him from becoming involved in sexual activities based on this knowledge. On the other hand, some parents use the number of these early sexual encounters as criteria for predicting the sexual capacities of the child in later life. Thus the mother quoted above expected her son to become a "lady killer," meaning highly promiscuous when he reached young adulthood. There is far more reservation about girls because of the graver consequences that may result. However, strong sexual involvement does not carry the same stigma in the ghetto as it does in middle-class society, and this attitude often leads to their early awareness, interest, and involvement in sexual activities.

One is able to determine to some extent the important role sex plays by noting its prevalence in everyday conversation. In place of mystery and secrecy we find open discussion among all age groups of both sexes. The theory and practice of sex are discussed in great detail and debated heatedly. If there is any mystery surrounding an issue, it is there only because the scientific facts have not yet sifted down to the discussants. Whether the issues are backed by scientific evidence or not, the point is that sex is talked about openly and freely.

Given the open discussions of sex as a lower-class pattern, we make the following proposition: one of the major ways in which the child receives sexual socialization is by a process of learning from and through the conversation of others. Through exposure to everyday conversations involving sex, the child begins to learn the details of the sexual role that he must later assume. It is true that this information would not be absorbed by most middle-class children, for the reason that they lack general exposure to the sexual area. It is a fact of middle-class life that parents have great control over the areas of life to which the child is exposed. In order for the middle-class child to experience the "normal" stages of development, the parent feels obligated to keep him from most "controversial" areas, topics, and discussions. Johnny is told to run along when adults are discussing a "controversial" topic because they are talking "grown-up" talk. Thus, the middle-class child is frequently in his teens before any great interest in sex beyond the exploratory stage is generated. In contrast, the lower-class child is frequently exposed to all areas of life, both physical and existential, long before the middle-class child is even aware of their existence. The early age at which the lower-class child receives constant and "uncontrolled" exposure forces him to become precocious about matters from which middle-class children are shielded.

Among the negative aspects of living in slum (and particularly public) housing is the lack of privacy both in and out of the apartments.[7] This gross lack of privacy forces into public and semipublic areas behavior which would normally be conducted in private. In the absence of more convenient facilities, stairways, halls, corridors, elevators, washrooms, parking lots, and lobbies, which are used to gain access to apartments, work areas, and recreational spaces, are also the main locations in which sexual activities of all kinds take place. The child can frequently see various forms of sexual behavior, including sexual intercourse, in these areas. Because of crowding within the apartments privacy here too becomes a commodity virtually impossible to obtain. The overcrowded conditions in the home sometimes allow the child to observe sexual intercourse taking place. The visibility of these acts, then, becomes an important factor in the acquisition of sexual patterns. In view of this, we make a further proposition: a second major way in which the child learns about sex is through actual observation of sexual activity in its many and varied forms.

The essence of the situation is given by a sixteen-year-old girl: "It's too much sex down here . . . and it's happening everywhere, all over the building, in the hallways, and it's just too much, you know. They don't care where they have it, in the washroom . . . they don't care." There is an abundance of evidence to bear her out. A fourteen-year-old girl tells how her mother had resolved a disagreement with her (the mother's) boy friend: "They done got good now, 'cause I heard them bed springs rocking all last night. Ain't that right, mother?" Dirk, an eleven-year-old, and his ten-year-old buddy followed Dirk's older brother up to the family apartment. Dirk's buddy relates the incident: "They went up to Dirk's house. They were in the bedroom, in the bed. He got on her and started rolling. They were in there for a long time. They took off their clothes . . . and cuddled up in bed. Me and Dirk was peeking in there." Two eight-year-old boys tell us about thirteen-year-old Dan, who had forced fourteen-year-old Candy into a middle hallway: "he had a man size penis and he was down there hurting her cause she say let me up. He told her to shut up and slapped her. . . . She

[7] See on this point U.S., Department of Health, Education, and Welfare, *Slums and Social Insecurity*, Division of Research and Statistics Research Report no. 1, prepared for the Social Security Administration by A. C. Schorr, esp. chap. 1.

was crying. . . . He put his hand over her mouth. Then we slammed the door and he stopped because of the noise. . . . Then Candy came out . . . she could barely walk. Then Dan came out all smiling." From these examples the role that observation plays in the learning process is obvious.

Our third proposition results from the first two. Once the child has heard enough and seen enough, he will attempt the act himself. We propose that the third major way in which the child becomes socialized is by actually participating in some form of sex play himself. In the lower class, experience is indeed the best teacher. Seven-year-old Barbara tells of her experience: "I don't mind boys 'doing it'[8] to me. But I ain't too crazy about it because it gives me heartburn." Although she is referring to the general attitude of males, eight-year-old Kathy does show that she has had enough sexual experience to comment on the situation: "I don't like any of the boys around here cause they 'do it' with you and then they 'do it' with somebody else and they act like yourself ain't yourself." As an indication of how early sexual experience can begin, we have the story of Bernard. A group of teenage boys was with a nineteen-year-old girl who was "letting everybody feel all over her. Everybody that came into the hall. There was a little boy named Bernard. Bernard was all up under her dress playing with her [genital area]. She liked it too. [How old is Bernard?] Bernard is four or five."

From the data collected it appears that among adolescents the most important socializing influences are conversations of peers, and adults; observation of these groups; and actual participation in or imitation of the acts themselves. There is no systematic pattern or sequential ordering of these influences. The child may observe a sexual act, engage in it, and later hear a conversation about it. What may at first have been imitative play then comes to have a new conceptual meaning for him. The point should be stressed, however, that most of these children are exposed to sex at such an early age that they have not had the opportunity to formulate convictions which would sustain them against sexual involvement. It was uncommon for most children studied to reach the age of five or six without having acquired some knowledge of sexual intercourse, either from seeing the act or from hearing peers or older persons talk about it. By the time they reach the age of seven, many have themselves often tried to have intercourse. The formation of early opinions on sex derives from early exposure, but acceptance of

[8] Various terms are used to describe the act of sexual intercourse. Some of the more popular ones are "do it," "screw," "trim," "get some drawers," and "work out."

such behavior is developed long before the child is able to evaluate it critically.

The meanings attached to the sexual act are probably unclear at first. In the initial stages, sexual gratification and orgasm are not the objectives and results, although they may sometimes occur.[9] Most of the early behavior is imitative and can be viewed as a form of play and entertainment or recreation.[10] Soon, however, usually during adolescence, it becomes a matter of serious concern. For most lower-class children there is no "sexual rite of passage," or relatively sex-free period lasting until the mid-teens, at which point the youngster starts to become sexually aware. Instead, sex play can be thought of as a continuum beginning in preadolescence and increasing as adolescence approaches. The adolescents in this study ranked both the discussion of and participation in sex high in relation to their other interests and concerns. Teenage girls, when asked to list the most serious problems of girls they knew, most often listed problems that were directly and indirectly related to teenage sexual involvement. This included problems of dating, lack of parental understanding, etc.

Sex as a form of play now gives way to more pressing concerns and a correlation develops between the stresses of ghetto life and the role of sex. What was once sex-as-fun-and-games is now broken down into two categories, sex as fun and sex as a strategic game of survival. The poverty, emotional deprivation, crime and violence, etc. of the ghetto force the adolescent to be concerned with problems which are vital to his livelihood and subsistence. He is faced with conflicts, choices, and decisions related to sex which are linked, in many cases, with ultimate survival.

What the adolescent girl decides with regard to sexual relations with a boy can result in pregnancy, illegitimacy, and a situation unfavorable to both her welfare and that of her child. Her decision to drop out of school because of pregnancy can mean that she will work at unskilled or low-skilled jobs for the rest of her life. Most of these decisions are based on examples set by mothers and older females, who serve as role models. The sexual indulgences of adolescents are often rationalized with the expression, "everybody does it." Girls see their mothers and older female relatives engaging in these activities, and mothers are in a difficult position to chastise their daughters when they can often be reminded of their own deviant activities. The same is true of males. In essence, then, children are socialized into an environment where the controls

[9] Broderick, "Sexual Behavior among Pre-Adolescents," p. 15.

[10] See Kinsey et al., *Sexual Behavior in the Human Male* and *Sexual Behavior in the Human Female.*

which would prevent or at least delay early sex activities are either very weak or non-existent. Their precocity is, in a very real sense, superimposed on them by the environment.[11]

In the remainder of this paper we will focus briefly on the role of sexual activity among lower-class adolescents. It is interesting to note that despite the high rate of promiscuity there is seldom any planning as to when and where sexual acts are to take place. The theory is that if the feeling is there, a time and place can always be found. Thirteen-year-old Kathy states it this way: "I just get in the mood and if he in the mood with me we just go on and get with it." Usually the place is in a hall, washroom, elevator, stairwell, or one's apartment if adults are away. When plans are made to have intercourse in a hotel, motel, or rented room, the girl's partner is usually an adult. Teenage boys seldom have the necessary money (transportation, room rent) and a sixteen-year-old female will prefer an older man because he can provide these facilities. The following quote illustrates the girl's preference for the bed:

Q. Do you have it in the bed in your mother's apartment?
A. No. In a hotel or motel. Somewhere like that.
Q. How old are the boys who take you to a hotel room?
A. Mostly nineteen or twenty or around that age.

Although planning seldom takes place, there is always the expectation that, if the social situation permits, intercourse will take place. The norm is to "take care of business" ("T.C.B.") whenever and wherever one can.

In this housing project, as in other lower-class areas, age-appropriate behavior norms are in general similar to those for higher status groups. One must keep in mind, however, that relative to the middle class, adherence to and enforcement of these norms are much less stringent. That is, there is more permissiveness, although, theoretically, children are expected to respect adults and "stay in their place." Unlike middle-class culture, however, we have noted a distinct difference in the observance of this norm on many occasions. In numerous instances when the child oversteps his role and behaves like an adult, he will be treated as such. This reaction extends to the sexual area as well. For example, a ten-year-old boy who approaches an adult female for sexual intercourse probably will not be reprimanded for his lack of respect for an adult female. Rather, he will be denied intercourse on the grounds that he is incapable of performing the act because of his youth. On the other hand, a ten- or eleven-year-old girl who makes sexual advances will, more often than not, be accommodated by some older male (teen-

[11] See the studies by Kinsey, Hammond, and Ladner, cited above.

age boys and men). The normal age barriers between the sexes, i.e., the laws governing statutory rape, are virtually inoperative here. One project functionary (reflecting both the problem and his viewpoint) told me that "you can do it to any of these whores [girls] at any age and don't have to worry about a thing. These forty-year-old dudes are doing it to these thirteen- and fourteen-year-old girls like pussy is going out of style." When I asked him whether he would do it to one of the young girls, he answered, "Before they can get their drawers down."

Adolescent participation in sexual activities also serves more specific and meaningful purposes. It should be viewed as an integrative function which provides the participants with a sense of togetherness: they share common experiences which they can discuss with each other, and the boy and girl share a feeling of "belonging" to each other, a sense of togetherness, identity, utility, and enjoyment. In the later adolescent years, however, sex for girls takes on the important function of being a form of exchange, primarily for material goods and services (gifts, money, etc.). Some economically and emotionally deprived girls are able to gain access to certain necessities from boy friends through their participation in sexual activities.[12]

Teenagers in this environment as elsewhere, want to engage in "teenage activities" (to own clothes, records, phonographs, money, to go places, etc.), but there is a gross lack of resources with which to do so. Their desires are no different from those of their middle-class counterparts. In their day-to-day struggle for survival, males and females may have learned that delayed gratification and strong interpersonal relationships are to be viewed positively, but the insurmountable pressures of emotional and physical deprivation cause them to reject such goals. It is necessary, then, that the young child be taught to "go for himself" and to get what he can in any way necessary. Thus, girls have been known to engage in sexual intercourse in exchange for a movie date, a ride in a car, food, and other things that will take them out of the housing project and away from the depressing and deprived family life. The male in turn offers these things because he knows the girl is desirous of them and can offer what he wants in exchange.

Sex is also exchanged for other things. In many acts of intercourse there is an exchange of emotions or a reciprocal obligation to please the partner. Sex is also used as a flight into fantasy or an escape from overwhelming ghetto problems. A fifteen-year-old girl says: "When I have intercourse, I get a thrill. I just forget about all my

[12] See Ladner, "Deviance in the Lower Class Adolescent Sub-Culture," p. 47.

trouble. It makes you forget that you don't have the kinds of things you need for school, the money to buy your lunch and clothes to wear and stuff like that. I play hooky sometimes because I don't have those things but then I 'do it' and have a good time and I don't have to worry about those things." In many cases sex is used as a means of keeping the peace and avoiding trouble. Girls sometimes submit to the advances of males out of fear that they will be harmed, or that the boy will break off the boy friend-girl friend liaison. Finally, when one is bored and there is nothing else to do, one can always turn to sexual intercourse. As a thirteen-year-old girl says, "When we are hanging around the building and don't have anything else to do and boys come around, we might start playing with them and before you know it all of us are mellow [having sex]." In a similar statement another girl explains: "We sometimes do it for kicks, and you don't have to like the boy to do it with him. You do it 'cause you can be mellow when you don't want to play cards or watch TV."

As can be expected, the result of so much sex play is pregnancy. In spite of this there seems to be little concern for the consequences of sex. Only a few boys and still fewer girls ever consider protection.[13] At least half of the adolescent females in our sample had adequate knowledge of the various types of contraceptives and ways in which they could be obtained. Indeed, one-fourth of the girls could describe in sophisticated language how each of the contraceptives we listed was to be used. Despite this knowledge, the majority of girls do not use them. The three major reasons given for non-usage are belief in the old wives' tale about their ill effects, unavailability of a contraceptive at the time of intercourse, and embarrassment—i.e., reluctance to purchase materials such as EMKO foam on the open market, to secure a prescription for pills, a diaphragm, or an intrauterine device from a doctor, or to ask the partner to use a condom. Moreover, a small number of girls express the desire to have a child to give them a sense of responsibility and a feeling of security. One girl stated: "I would be grown if I had a baby. I'd have something that I could call my own and someone to depend on me." Some express strong moral opposition to controlling fertility, which is another reason for not taking advantage of contraceptives.

In addition to pregnancy there is the growing problem of venereal disease. Large numbers of teenage boys and fewer girls are treated for venereal disease at public health clinics. Some of them have contracted the disease from the same girl. These are only two of the

---

[13] See K. Clark, *Dark Ghetto* (New York: Harper and Row, 1965), p. 71.

negative consequences of sexual indulgence that are attributable not only to permissiveness but also to ignorance of hygiene and birth control. When such knowledge exists, most often it is not put into practice.

We have attempted here to explain some of the factors involved in lower-class sexual socialization patterns. In doing so, we wanted to show that learning about sex at an early age indicates an increased probability that sexual activities will be engaged in early and that this pattern will continue throughout adolescence into adulthood. Not every child becomes involved in the situations that we have described. Indeed, many never do. Others may experiment but have strong enough parental controls to give them the proper perspective on sex. Unfortunately, however, these controls are too often lacking, and the influences of peers, deviant role models, and deprivation have a stronger impact. In view of the availability of both a sexual partner and a place to carry out the act, control over such activities becomes problematic. Moreover, because of the importance assigned to sex in this environment, one finds a more permissive sexual attitude than in the middle class. When we realize that lower-class children have a desire for material objects as well as for the emotional and recreational outlets enjoyed by middle-class children and lack the resources necessary to obtain them, we can understand why sex is used as a substitute, as a medium of exchange, and for prestige, identity, and entertainment.

Only by delving deeper into these dynamics and processes can we solve these problems. The behavior patterns described here permeate the ghetto community. They are multi-generational and will persist until the social, political, and economic forces which produce them are removed. The success of programs for change will depend entirely upon the level of commitment of those with resources adequate to effect it. There must be total, long-term involvement by the urban political structure, schools, social service organizations (voluntary and governmental), business community, and any other group that possesses the resources needed.

4   Starting a Program of Sex Education

Helen Manley

*In this chapter, Helen Manley, a teacher with years of experience in the
public schools, explains what the term "sex education" has and has not
meant and gives us the benefit of her observation of and participation in
the inauguration of sex education programs. She provides a set of guidelines to follow, and re-emphasizes the importance of prepared teachers.
She then summarizes the topics (which include reproduction but by no
means exclude other topics) which she has found pertinent in her own
experience. Although neither SIECUS nor the editors of this volume are
willing to lay down a prescribed curriculum for courses dealing with
human sexuality, the experience of those who have worked in this area
can be useful as a starting point. Every teacher will have to decide which
topics his own students want or need discussed and the content may well
vary even from class to class within a school and will certainly vary among
schools. The material included under the heading "dating behavior," for
example, will not be identical in, let us say, an extremely progressive
school and a parochial school. But students in both are entitled to have
such subjects discussed.*

The curriculum related to sex education in each school district
will be planned to meet the needs of the children in that area at
their various developmental stages and to allow variations among
neighborhoods in the district. Children come to school from different homes, socioeconomic classes, racial and cultural backgrounds, religions and ideologies. The objectives of sex education
are the same for all of these children, but the means of achieving
them may vary widely. Care and discrimination must therefore be
used in the selection of materials and in the choice of staff.

Educators, including curriculum consultants, principals, and teachers, are equipped to plan, but a large and representative advisory
council of citizens of the community is an essential adjunct. A few
guidelines for development of a program are provided here.

1. Approval of the school authorities should be obtained. The members or
   directors of the Board of Education and the administrative officers must
   understand the curriculum and give it their strong support. All the
   teaching personnel should be informed of the plans and their support
   should be sought.
2. There should be understanding on the part of the community. Citizens
   should be informed of any new plans for the education of their children, in the area of sex no less than in, let us say, the so-called new

mathematics. Awareness of the need for sex education has been evident for decades, despite its deplorable lack of availability in the schools. The abundant evidence of the need for sex education can be emphasized in talking to PTA's, service organizations, church groups, or others interested.

3. Sex education should fit smoothly into the curriculum. There should be nothing special or different or unusual about it; there should be nothing about it that suggests that it is daring. If special equipment is needed, or if small discussion groups are used, these should not be made to seem extraordinary. All children should be involved; no special permission should be required.

4. The program should be constantly and thoughtfully evaluated. Suggestions should be welcomed. Communities change rapidly, and citizens need to be kept aware of the sex education program. Scientific information expands, and the program must keep pace.

5. Teachers must be well prepared. Because of the fundamental importance of the teacher, as noted throughout this volume, special emphasis should be placed on his preparation.

THE TEACHER

The teacher is the most vital factor in the success of any sex education program, but teacher training has been least adequate here. In the traditional curriculum for teacher preparation, the area of "sex education" has found little place. Even today few, if any, colleges have specific courses to prepare such teachers (let alone the ordinary college student). Naturally, the subject of sex cannot be completely excluded from the training of teachers, for it is a major variable in all psychological studies of individual differences and is a major component of many courses in psychology. It is also a major variable in all studies of social structure, including those of the division of labor on the basis of sex present in all societies. In more concrete form sex appears in courses in child development, home economics, guidance, health, and personal and family living.

But all too often sex has been dealt with either incidentally or from a purely biological or institutional point of view. Nowhere has it been dealt with as a teaching area in which a future teacher would have to be proficient, which presents unique pedagogical problems. One purpose of this book is to make available a text for persons preparing to teach at any level, from children in the primary school grades to mature participants in professional workshops or school internes.

In the elementary school all teachers should be free of inhibitions about the subject and should be able to answer children's questions without embarrassment. Those who participate in the program in the secondary schools should have some knowledge of the basic sciences of biology, anatomy, and physiology. The success of the teacher is not based on his sex, marital status, or parenthood, but rather on his understanding of human interrelationships, his life experience, and his sensitivity.[1] Some of the characteristics of the successful sex education teacher are:

1. A thorough liking and sympathetic understanding of children and youths and a trust and belief in his pupils.
2. A positive attitude toward sex. This would come more easily from one who had himself experienced a satisfactory family life.
3. Good common sense and judgment, which would include sensitivity to the morals, customs, and ideals of the community.
4. A spontaneous, dignified sense of humor. Laughter, however, is never acceptable when it is at the expense of or embarrasses a student.
5. Knowledge of the scientific background materials: this is part of the body of knowledge of doctors, nurses, and students of health education. However, it is perhaps the area of proficiency most easily acquired. Books, charts, and many other visual aids are readily available, and the student will respect an occasional "I don't know, let's look it up."

Certified teachers have already studied psychology, child growth, and methods of teaching. Elementary school teachers may lack background in the biological sciences, but the information needed to teach children of this age can be easily acquired. In the secondary school sex education would probably be placed in the areas of the sciences or health, where teachers have some knowledge that would be transferable. In general, however, teachers have had little or no preparation for sex education and may feel inadequate or averse to adding this subject to their heavy schedule. Some lack a broad view of sexuality and have associated sex solely with the genitals and vulgarity. Others think they need much more information in the areas of physiology and anatomy to do the job. It is true that most college graduates emerging as teachers do lack background in the area called health, which has been neglected or omitted from the curriculum of the public schools for several decades. High school graduates enter college having little or no health instruction, and teachers' colleges find that their students come with a poor background in health and a very short time in which to develop it. The curriculum for prospective teachers of health has also been generally inadequate.

A vicious circle develops: with little demand for health teachers, strong majors in health education have been lacking. Administrators, however, more and more of whom are realizing the child's

[1] See Helen Manley, *A Curriculum Guide in Sex Education* (St. Louis, Mo.: State Publishing Co., 1967), p. 12.

need for sex education, are not waiting for improvement in the undergraduate curriculum but are setting up extensive in-service programs. All teachers in the school system must understand the need for sex education, how it is being planned for the school system, and their specific part in it. They may also need some experience in what is called sensitivity training in order to examine their own attitudes toward human sexuality and free themselves from any prejudice or inability to speak comfortably about this area of the curriculum.

AN ILLUSTRATIVE PROGRAM

I noted above that there seems to be a developing consensus about the general contents of a program or course in sex education, but I repeat that there is no perfect, correct curriculum suitable for all schools in all communities. The material that follows is only one example and is presented not as a model but as a suggestion as to what may be included. It is specific enough to assure that each child get the necessary information and flexible enough to allow for the teacher's judgment and creativity in using it. It is based on the assumption that sex education in the schools starts at kindergarten and continues through twelfth grade, as it fits smoothly into the total educational program. This does not mean that fragments of information are imparted at each grade level, but that each teaching opportunity is used, that children's questions are answered, and that at certain maturity levels specific areas of sex education are stressed.

Primary Grades

Many learning experiences in the primary grades are based on human and family development. The child's family may contain mother, father, brothers, and sisters. New babies are arriving in the homes of these children; they are eager, interested, and curious. The child may have received excellent sex information or may have had negative experiences. The teacher may merely be strengthening what the child has learned, or he may be establishing new attitudes and values in the area of sexuality.

The objectives for each child in these early years can be stated as follows:

1. Acquisition of a wholesome attitude toward his body.
2. Use of correct terminology and vocabulary in reference to all parts of his body.
3. Understanding of the value of having a family and being a good family member.
4. Understanding of the elementary facts of reproduction.

5. Knowledge that boys and girls are different, and that each sex is very important.
6. Lessening or preventing unnecessary handling of the body.
7. Ability to talk about the body openly and without embarrassment.

The daily routine presents many opportunities to attain these objectives. Routine toilet procedures can be used to emphasize correct terminology. New babies at home stimulate questions about their origin; care of growing things in the classroom provides opportunities for study of the growth and development of living things and arouse queries such as "How do plants grow?" "How do animals grow?" "How do I grow?" At the end of the primary grades a child should know:

1. Where babies come from.
2. How the baby gets into the mother.
3. How the baby gets out.
4. The sex differences between boys and girls, and the reasons for these differences.
5. That living things begin from a seed.
6. That human beings are mammals.
7. How the mammal feeds its young from its own body.
8. How the baby lies in the mother's body.
9. The part the hospital and doctor play in the birth of a baby.
10. The importance of the family.

His vocabulary should include:

abdomen	reproduction
bowel movement or defecation	sperm
breast	stomach
egg	urination
nipple	urine
penis	vagina
pregnant	wean

Children will have questions, and appropriate moments for discussion will present themselves frequently. Teachers should seize upon these moments to discuss facts, standards, and values.

Intermediate Grades

In the intermediate grades, however, some formal teaching must also occur. The age level for teaching various facts depends upon the children and the administrative setup. Before human reproduction is specifically highlighted, background information on cell structure and other systems will make for better understanding. All this can be embodied in the health and science curriculum. Objectives for these grades might be stated as follows:

1. Stress on and continual development of a healthy attitude toward sex.
2. Emphasis on the wonder, as well as the science, of reproduction.

3. Provision of a scientific vocabulary for a dignified discussion of bodily processes.
4. Establishment in students of ease and freedom in talking frankly about sex, and asking any puzzling questions.
5. Helping preadolescents understand the changes taking place in their bodies, and the variance in individual growth patterns.
6. Appreciation of the role each member of the family plays.
7. Assistance to each child in assuming his own sex role.
8. Development of an understanding of social customs and conventions.

Vocabulary

abdomen	genitals	placenta
adolescent	glands	pollen
anus	hatch	preadolescent
bladder	heredity	pregnant
born	hormones	puberty
breast	identical	rectum
breeding	male	reproduction
Caesarean	mammal	scrotum
chromosomes	mating	Siamese
egg	menstruation	sperm
embryo	multiple births	testes or testicles
endocrine	navel	twins
Fallopian tube	nipple	umbilical
feces	ovary	urinate
females	ovulation	urine
fertilize	ovum	uterus
fetus	pelvis	vagina
foreskin	penis	vulva
fraternal	pituitary	womb
genes		

In the intermediate grades these specific areas of the sex education curriculum would be covered:

I. Your growth and development
   A. Living things make new life
   B. You started from two cells:
      1. Egg or ovum from mother
      2. Sperm from father
      3. Sperm enters egg—fertilization
   C. You, the fertile cell, need nourishment and air
   D. The creation of you, a baby
II. The birth of the baby
III. Changes in your body as you grow
   A. Similarities in boys and girls
   B. Differences in boys and girls
   C. Variances in individuals
IV. Reproductive organs and functions

A. Boys
B. Girls
V. Variations in childbirth—position, Caesarean, multiple
VI. Heredity

Junior High School

The early adolescent faces many critical moments. He needs scientific knowledge along with much sympathetic understanding. The development of primary and secondary sex characteristics gives him a decided awareness of sex, and the irregularity of this development and its variance among individuals require some basic knowledge of physiology. While his interest may change almost in minutes from childish pursuits to adult desires, he is anxious to be grown up and to assume his sex role. In planning sex education consideration must be given to the subject area in which it is taught and to the vast discrepancy in the sex experiences that may occur between the ages of twelve and fifteen. Some children will have done some sex experimenting, while others should be referred to the intermediate program. The unit can be placed at the seventh-, eighth-, or ninth-grade level or can be taught in graded amounts each year. At this very difficult age a teacher or counselor should be readily accessible to boys and girls to talk with, and to answer questions. The objectives of the unit in junior high school are these:

1. Provision of scientific information on growth and sexual maturity.
2. Development of respect for human relationships and understanding of social mores.
3. Encouragement of discussion of sex between boys and girls in scientific language, and with dignity and lack of embarrassment.
4. Provision of honest, frank answers to the sex questions and problems of youth.
5. Development or improvement of family relations of students now and of ideals for their future families.

The following topics might be covered:
I. Body changes in adolescence
  A. General
    1. Spurt of growth
    2. Change in proportions
    3. Unevenness in growth
    4. Variations that may be puzzling—one breast larger than the other, one testicle lower, etc.
  B. Boys
    1. Primary
      a. Development of reproductive organs: testes, scrotum, penis, prostate
      b. Erection of penis
      c. Emissions

      2. Secondary
      Growth of beard, hair on body, increased musculature, change of voice, newly activated sweat glands
  C. Girls
    1. Primary
    Fuller development of reproductive organs: ovary, uterus, vagina, Fallopian tubes
    2. Secondary
    Widening of pelvic bone, growth of hair, rounding of body contour, breast development, newly activated sweat glands

II. Physiology of sex
  A. Function of male reproductive organs, including seminal emissions and erections
  B. Function of female reproductive organs
  C. Masturbation
  D. Homosexuality

III. Reproduction
  A. Conception, mating
  B. Pregnancy
  C. Birth, with variations
  D. Inheritance

IV. Boy-girl relations, dating
  A. Kinds of dates
  B. Behavior and responsibility in dating
    1. How to ask, accept, or refuse
    2. What to do
    3. What not to do
    4. Signals of going too far
    5. Possible results of going too far: loss of respect for self and each other, pregnancy, venereal disease

V. Being a parent
  A. Responsibility of being a parent
  B. Responsibility of being a son or daughter

VI. A family
  A. What makes a family
  B. Your responsibility in your family
  C. Your future family

Vocabulary

abdomen	congenital	Fallopian tube
abortion	contraceptives	fertilization
adolescent	contraction	fetus
birth canal	egg	fraternal
cervix	ejaculation	genes
chancre	embryo	genitals
chromosomes	emission	gland
clitoris	epididymis	gonorrhea
conception	erection	heredity

homosexual	ovum	sperm
hymen	pelvic	sterile
infatuation	penicillin	syphilis
insemination	penis	tampon
intercourse	petting	testes
labor	physiology	testicle
masturbation	pituitary	twins, Siamese
mating	placenta	urethra
menopause	prostate gland	uterus
menstruation	puberty	vagina
nuclei	scrotum	venereal
ovary	seminal vesicle	vulva
ovulation	sexual intercourse	womb

Senior High School

Senior high school students today have high intellectual potential and need to be challenged by the sciences, which supply information, and by the social sciences, which study behavior. In the sex-oriented world in which they live, scientific answers and sympathetic help are required to establish a basic philosophy for living a satisfying life as an adult. The administrative setup of the school will determine how this phase of education is structured. In some schools it may be taught progressively, at the tenth-, eleventh-, and twelfth-grade levels; in others it is made part of a required health or science course in one of these grades.

The objectives of a senior high school program are:

1. To develop understanding and appreciation of the family in our culture and of the student's responsibility as a member of his family now and in a family of his own in later years.
2. To develop appreciation of the importance of meaningful human relationships.
3. To build a mature knowledge of the physiology of sex.
4. To help in choosing a mate and preparing for marriage.
5. To assist in developing values as a basis for decision-making.

The teaching unit might cover the following:

  I. The family as a basic unit of society
    A. History: types
    B. Parent-child conflict
    C. Improving family relations
  II. Maturing
    A. Physical change in males and females (review)
    B. Emotional development
    C. Dating behavior
  III. Marriage
    A. Considerations in choosing a mate
    B. Readiness for marriage

IV. Reproduction
   A. Pregnancy
   B. Birth processes, prenatal care
   C. Unwed parents
   D. Birth control
   E. Scientific research
V. Heredity
   A. Principles and facts
   B. Superstitions
VI. Sex involvement
   A. Normality of sexuality
   B. Fallacies and truths
   C. Homosexuality
   D. Masturbation
VII. Sex in the world today
   A. Abuse: promiscuity, illegitimacy, venereal diseases
   B. Control
   C. Ideals and standards of behavior

SOME SUGGESTIONS FOR ADMINISTRATORS AND TEACHERS

Whatever ideals may be held up for sex education, they will not be feasible in every school, and there will be details of administrative procedure that will have to be worked out. One such detail is segregation of the sexes. If, as is ideal, sex education is planned as an integral part of the curriculum, it will be taught as part of all areas. If, however, it is segregated as part of, let us say, the physical education program, in which boys and girls are separated, then, of course, this would be impossible. Even if the sexes are not segregated, junior high school boys and girls should have some segregated periods to permit typical girls' or boys' questions; conversely, even if the sexes are segregated, there should be some classes held together for discussion of such topics as dating and boy-girl questions.

Teaching about sex follows the pattern of all good education. There is no single way to teach, but the good teacher is sensitive to the class and develops the program accordingly. Many opportunities for weaving sex education into the total curriculum will be afforded, and the good teacher seizes and uses them. They occur especially frequently in the elementary school, with the advent of a new baby or new puppies or the discovery of four-letter words. For older children, the occurrence of words in the newspapers and magazines such as "rape" or "abortion," facts mentioned in history, such as "illegitimate sons" of rulers or descriptions of the succession of kings; great classics of literature, such as *The Scarlet Letter* or *David Copperfield*; new scientific discoveries in, for example, genetics, offer opportunities for the teacher in more advanced grades if he is willing to use them.

In addition, good audiovisual materials are now available. (They should not, however, be over-used.) Other methods might include, according to age, lectures, small buzz sessions, role-playing, dialogue, visits to laboratories, museums, enlistment of resource people, and even research projects. It goes without saying that encouragement of questions and undismayed replies are important and often lead to further learning, especially because for so long these questions may have been evaded by parents and teachers.

5

Some Social and Psychological Aspects of Sex Education

Catherine S. Chilman

Catherine Chilman here emphasizes some of the dynamics involved in the interplay between teacher and pupil in sex education.

This paper presents some suggestions based on observation, experience, social, psychological, and educational theory, and some collateral research. It is impossible to buttress these suggestions with evidence because no research has been done on how information about sex is best imparted, what its content should be, or what the effects of sex education are. The research-minded reader may take many of the suggestions made as areas for study. One such area would seem to be the determination of the impact that various forms of sex teaching have on the information, attitudes, and behavior of those who participate in sex education courses.

Sex education, as defined here, is primarily intended as general education, in contrast with programs planned for students who are preparing for a career in scientific sex research. It focuses on information that will be of use to the student in his own life as an individual, as a family member, as a participant in the community, and as a member of the work force. Although many of the principles presented might well apply to education in any setting—a church, a clinic, or a community—the school is the main focus of this discussion. The framework established, let us now consider some of the issues raised by the ambitious, broad goals of sex education.

GOAL LIMITATIONS

Resistance, fear, anxiety, and confusion about sex education are obvious and often-noted stumbling blocks to the achievement of its goals, but there are other blocks that are not so readily recognized. For instance, education alone is unlikely to bring about changes in attitudes and behavior toward sex. This is probably true of most subjects taught in the schools but is apt to be particularly true of subjects which are heavily laden with emotional content and are intimately concerned with basic human drives. Although the schools cannot handle such a task alone, it is sometimes assigned to educators and sometimes assumed by them.

Although education is a strong acculturating force, human behavior is determined by many factors—cultural, experiential, biological-constitutional, and situational—and sex education, no matter how well planned and how expertly carried on, probably cannot deeply affect an individual's functioning in this area. Moreover, much behavior and feelings which seem to be directly related to confusion, ignorance, or anxiety about sex may have quite different roots. Sex anxiety of deviant behavior can be a displacement of an individual's problem in an area other than the sexual. For instance, someone who feels that he has been basically deprived as an infant or small child may compulsively seek to meet his dependency needs through sexual activity. Anxiety, hostility, and rebellious feelings can take the form of sex problems, just as sex-related problems can masquerade as other difficulties, such as a compulsive drive to achieve. Thus, educators who seek to deal singlehandedly with such complex problems are going far beyond their proper boundaries.

Education about sex is only one of a number of ways of helping people to understand their sex needs and drives better and to handle these needs and drives in ways that provide satisfaction to themselves and to the society in which they live. In working toward the achievement of such goals as helping people of all ages to live comfortably and responsibly as sexual beings in today's world, sex educators will most profitably coordinate their efforts with those of other professionals and non-professionals in the formal and informal organizational networks of the community.

Some schools, recognizing that student problems, attitudes, and behavior are based on a multiplicity of factors, seek to create a multi-service school system complete with physicians, social workers, psychologists, and recreational leaders. While such an approach seems laudable, an argument can be advanced that the school, in developing its own network of services, is creating a separate world of its own rather than interacting with the community. Other separate service worlds are created around health facilities and places of employment. It seems as if a more open educational and service system is needed to put the school in closer touch with the larger world rather than submerging it in a world of its own. After all, students and their parents live in the larger world.[1]

But beyond this, it is important simply to bear in mind that al-

[1] It is recognized, however, that in some instances the larger community does not have the needed services available and that there are practical problems in securing funding and proper administration of a coordinated approach involving the total community.

though sex education has the potential to help many people, it cannot be expected to solve the basic human problem of how to be happy, though civilized.

INDIVIDUAL AND GROUP DIFFERENCES

It has become a truism among educators to note that each student and each class is different from every other. If the subject matter is sex, however, certain differences take on added significance, which must not be ignored.

Individual Life Experiences

Every person learns a great deal about sex, whether or not he is given specific instruction. He has gathered up a good deal of information from his family, friends, and other sources, and he learns, as he lives, a great deal about what it means to be a male or a female. Learning is far more than an accumulation of specific facts that can be repeated and theories that can be formulated. Human beings learn how to feel and how to behave from the time they are born, both through a conscious, rational process and through an unconscious or pre-conscious process of being and reacting.

In a sex education course the student's life experience in his own family is apt to be especially crucial. His attitudes, feelings, experience, and information regarding sex are deeply ingrained. Much of his learning occurred within the family when he was very young and has probably been repressed or suppressed, because the primitive sexuality of infancy and early childhood is usually redirected by parents into socially acceptable channels. Moreover, the emotional ties, both positive and negative, with parents, siblings, and others significant to him affect the way in which he will relate to sex education.

As already suggested, the individual's sex behavior and feelings are affected by his total personality and functioning. His life experience as a person in interaction with his environment and with people outside his immediate family—in the neighborhood, at school, at play, and at church—is important.

Some individuals are more likely to act on the basis of factual information than are others. One view of personality typology classifies individuals in three major behavioral groupings: rational, impulsive, and autonomous or anti-authoritarian. The rational individual tends to seek for facts and reasons and, in general, to guide his behavior accordingly. The impulsive person is more likely to be unimpressed by facts and to rely more on feelings and intuition. The autonomous person values what he can find out for himself and tends to reject other sources of knowledge. It is obvious that sex education, as presented through lectures, books, films, and discussions, would tend to make a stronger impact on those persons who are oriented toward rationality than on those who are oriented toward impulsivity or autonomy.[2]

The Current Life Situation

Each student brings to a class in sex education the life situation he is in at the moment. Although it seems inadvisable for the educator to address himself to individual life situations in a personal way, it is important for him to be aware of the range of possibilities. For example, students' parents or siblings may be involved in sex-related deviant behavior. The student himself may be in such a situation. When one is teaching adolescents or young people, it is highly possible that at least one of the students in a class may be pregnant with an illegitimate child. Persons living in socially disorganized neighborhoods are often exposed to a wide range of sexual activities. In teaching, the educator may refer to such situational problems and experiences and refrain from value-laden statements about the "rightness or wrongness" of such behavior. The realistic problems can be discussed and the community services that are available for assistance presented. For instance, it is relevant to discuss various kinds of community services that may be used by unmarried mothers. This is but another example of the interaction of the educational system with that of other informal and formal systems in a larger society. The sex educator probably needs to know a good deal about his students as individuals and also about the neighborhoods from which they come, the kinds of families in which they live, and the resources within the community.

Variations in Cultural Patterns

The content of sex education, although its focus is objective and impersonal, will, of course, vary, depending on the makeup of the group that is to be educated. One of the factors that affect what will be taught and how it will be taught is the cultural pattern that group members bring with them. Some of the variations in these patterns

[2] The discussion here of the role of individual life experiences in the formation of personality, particularly in relation to sex behavior and attitudes, is highly condensed. Persons preparing to teach in the field of sex education will need to take at least several basic courses in psychology, particularly developmental psychology and the dynamics of individual behavior. While a full reference bibliography to the dynamics of individual personality development and sex behavior would be far too extensive to present here, a few selected readings are listed at the end of Part I.

are described in the papers in this book by Rainwater, Reiss, and Christensen.[3]

In general, it is important for educators to be sensitive to cultural differences among students. These differences are particularly important in certain subjects, especially those that are closely related to the student's family. Children and young people usually have been more deeply influenced in their cultural patterns by their family than by anyone else. These patterns include values, goals, attitudes, beliefs, and customs. They are generally deeply ingrained in the person's life and affect his total style of living. They are not lightly tossed aside, partly because to change one's culture involves changing one's concept of self and of belonging to one's family. To imply that the cultural values that a student brings to school are inferior or inappropriate would seem to imply deficiencies in him and in his parents. Such an implication is likely to bring about a conflict of affection and loyalties within the student. Values about sex which are different from those to which the student has been exposed at home or in his neighborhood can be presented as another way of looking at the subject, not as *the* way or a *better* way.

It cannot be assumed that an individual has a certain set of values, customs, and attitudes simply because he belongs to a certain group, since the tapestry of cultures is infinite in its variations, and individuals gaze upon it in an infinite number of ways. Still, there is a general similarity in values and attitudes among members of national, religious, ethnic, and regional groups. In the United States we have a great diversity of cultures, and these vary not only in the terms mentioned above, but in terms of the socioeconomic level of the student's family—the occupation, education, and income of his parents. Moreover, there are variations between the sexes in their cultural attitudes in many areas, including sex values, behavior, and attitudes. These intersex variations are partly based upon social class and national, ethnic, and religious background. Further understanding about the various cultures that students bring with them to the classroom may be gained by the teacher through reading and study; such understanding can be greatly enriched by listening with empathy and sensitivity to what students say, watching what they do, and studying what they write.

[3] The subject of cultural differences and their impact on human behavior (including sex behavior) is vast. The sex educator is advised to take relevant courses in sociology and anthropology. The papers presented in this volume by Rainwater and Christensen should be useful, and further references are given at the end of this part.

Physical and Developmental Factors

Each student brings his physical as well as his cultural and experiential self to the educational setting. His stage of physical development and growth will greatly affect his interest and motivation to learn about sex. Differences in development can be particularly "touchy" for the educator who is working with young people between the ages of eleven and sixteen, partly because the individuals in the class will be at such varying stages of growth.[4]

There are also differences of a physical and psychological nature between boys and girls, apart from the obvious anatomical ones. To what extent these differences are culturally induced and to what extent they are biologically innate is not known. At any rate, boys in our culture are more clearly aware of their specific sex drives and more genital in orientation than girls. Girls tend to perceive their sex needs in a diffuse way and to put emphasis on "romantic love" rather than direct sexuality. Generally speaking, girls engage in less direct sex discussion and sex exploration with their peers than do boys, and they tend to become directly aware of their sexuality through a sex relationship. It appears that they have to be awakened to the physical aspects of sex through personal experience.

The differences in male and female anatomy are held to be largely responsible for the differences in sexual awareness, in that the male sex organ is readily stimulated from infancy onward, whereas this is not so likely to happen with females in the normal course of events. It is also quite possible that the relative lack of sexual awareness of girls and some young women may be strongly related to the cultural proscriptions against female sexuality. Whether or not these male-female differences in sex awareness are culturally or biologically induced, however, the fact remains that, in our culture,[5] these differences are usually present. As female sexuality is more overtly accepted in our society, the two sexes may become more similar in their sex attitudes and behavior.

For those who are engaged in sex education of children and adolescents, it is useful to bear in mind that, with the exception of sexual awareness, girls, on the average, develop more rapidly than boys and are apt to be ready for dating, courtship, and marriage several years earlier than boys. Although the male sex drive tends to be more overt and direct, the female, on the average, reaches

[4] There are a number of excellent basic textbooks on child and adolescent development, including a discussion of differences between the sexes, some of which are listed in the suggested readings.

[5] When the phrase "our culture" is used here, it refers to the predominantly white, middle-class culture of this country. Minor variations for subcultures in the United States occur (see the Suggested Readings and Chapters 3, 7, 9, and 11).

puberty several years earlier than the male. In terms of social and emotional development, cultural factors and earlier maturation tend to create a higher level of sophistication in interpersonal relationships among girls than among boys of the same age.

Such over-all differences in rate of development create a complex teaching situation for the sex educator dealing with preadolescents and adolescents. Male-female differences have been one reason why some educators have planned separate educational sessions for the two sexes. Such an approach, though it is likely to be simpler and less controversial, hardly seems to be sound. A basic purpose of sex education is to promote greater understanding and healthier relationships between the sexes and to aid in more effective communication between males and females, and sex education offered to separate groups would seem likely to widen the unfortunate communication and relationship gap which already exists.

Other aspects of the physical characteristics of individual students are important to keep in mind. Among them is the possibility that biological-constitutional differences in people may affect the nature of their sexuality and their perception of it. This is an area in which research evidence is meager, although some studies have been made along these lines. For instance, it has been found that there are great differences in babies at birth in their response to stimuli and their readiness to form relationships with those who care for them. Some infants are passive and slow in tempo and readily take to a dependent, "cuddling" relationship with their parents. Other infants are observed to be aggressive, highly active, and comparatively independent. Of course, it should be recalled that the original endowment of infants is shaped by the learning experiences that occur throughout life.

Further elaboration of the intricate kaleidoscope of human sexuality may clarify the discussion. The psychosomatic functioning of human beings is now becoming understood: physical, emotional, and intellectual functioning is, indeed, a dynamic interaction system. It is recognized, for instance, that emotional upsets and learned response patterns are very likely to be reflected, in one way or another, in food intake, digestion, and elimination. It is also recognized that emotional disturbances have effects on the functioning of the heart (including the entire respiratory and cardiovascular system). The role that individual differences and learned behavior play in the functioning of these systems is less obvious, but further research is likely to reveal intricate associations.

Just as these physiological systems are basic to the life process and therefore engender basic human drives for food and air, so the reproductive system is basic to the life process—perhaps *most* basic because it is fundamental to the survival of the race. Sex drives are psychologically as well as physically central and, just as emotional factors and learned responses affect the intake and use of food and air, so sex and reproductive functioning is psychosomatic in nature. Moreover, it is important to think of the psychosomatic concept as a two-way principle; i.e., somatic (physical) factors affect emotional and intellectual (learning) behavior, and vice versa. For example, a digestive upset of physiological origin clearly affects one's emotional state and motivation and capacity to learn. It also affects one's sex drive and response. Conversely, feelings, attitudes, and information can affect many aspects of physical functioning, including capacity for sex arousal and response. The old cliché, which came first, the chicken or the egg?, is most appropriate here and, as often happens in folklore and proverbs, reflects the intuitive wisdom born of deeply felt experience.

Individuals may have specific physical problems about which they are fearful and anxious. On the other hand, they may be unaware of existing physical difficulties. A course in sex education can be of great use in leading students to seek medical help for such difficulties. The function of the teacher in such instances would be to refer students for appropriate medical help. (See Chapter 15 by John Money for a full discussion of the needs of persons with physical handicaps affecting their sexual functioning.)

SUGGESTED PRINCIPLES FOR EDUCATIONAL METHODS

The foregoing section has briefly sketched some of the major ways in which students vary in their needs and capacities. Now it is appropriate to turn to a consideration of how these factors may provide guidelines for teachers in the area of sex.

Sex Education vs. Counseling and Therapy

In courses such as family life or sex education, which deal with emotion-laden material, the teacher is often tempted to take on the role of counselor or therapist. The temptation becomes particularly strong when students show the need for individual help. There has been a great deal of confusion about this point, and I shall attempt here to clarify the distinction between education and therapy. Education is addressed to what might be termed the rational, objective, conscious component of the individual's personality. Personal counseling and, more intensively, therapy are addressed to the individual's subjective emotional concerns and unique life experiences and situation. Education seeks to help students plan and behave more effectively because of objective information they have gained; counseling and therapy seek, among other things, to help the emotionally upset person feel better so that he can act more in the light of objective facts than in terms of the twisted perceptions induced by confused emotions.

It is highly doubtful that sex education would be useful to persons who have deep-seated neurotic problems and who suffer from strong anxiety, fear, guilt, and conflict. For such people, personal counseling or psychotherapy is generally indicated. Sex education may be useful in opening up an area that has caused them great concern but which they have not clearly identified. Teachers who are alert to individual students can provide a highly useful function in helping them recognize the need for personal help and in sending them for such help, and the educator must therefore know what resources in the school and community are available. Sex education is also unlikely to be effective in reaching the person who has poor control over his own behavior. Persons who "act out" their impulsive drives in a repetitive and antisocial way usually need help from a trained therapist.

It seems essential to differentiate clearly between the roles of the educator, the counselor, and the therapist. There are several reasons why the distinction should be maintained. First, the educator is not trained to handle deep emotional problems. He should be able to recognize them and keep them in mind while he is teaching, but should avoid discussion of them on a personal basis. If the concerns of individuals are discussed in a subjective and particularistic way, it is likely that a great deal of conflict will be activated. The feelings that the teacher arouses are apt to be too complex for him to handle. Of course, such disturbances can also have repercussions among other students in the group. Second, the situation tends to rule out therapy, especially if the setting in question is a public school with the intention of educating children. Students, their families, and the taxpayer are usually committed to education, not treatment of emotional problems, in the schools. This is the condition under which most schools are founded and supported. A private school is freer to set its own goals and may more readily move from the educational to the treatment process. However, if the school does move into the area of treatment, this fact should be made clear to the students and to their families. Another problem that faces the teacher who may get involved in therapy is that if sex education is part of a course, it is usually necessary for the teacher to give grades, to keep attendance, to be concerned about course credits, and to be accountable to all his students. One of the essential aspects of counseling and therapy is acceptance of the patient as he is and what concerns him as an individual, with the main focus on his feelings and his freedom to make plans for himself.

The main focus of the educator is on ideas and facts, and his primary responsibility is to the students whom he teaches. The roles of teacher and of counselor thus are different in focus, although the counselor sometimes gives information and the teacher, if he is a good one, is sensitive to the feelings and the life situation of individual students.

The Search for Values

Some sex educators, particularly those who are strongly oriented toward research and scientific impeccability, favor a "value-free" approach to teaching. According to them nothing should be taught that is not backed by research evidence or academically respectable theory, an approach that seems itself a value. A subject which is as deeply emotional as that of sex and family life would not seem to lend itself to a completely intellectual approach. The importance of feelings, motivations, and values, as well as of facts, needs to be recognized.

Young people, especially adolescents and youths, are usually hungry for guidelines. They frequently want to know "what is the right thing to do." Therefore, the educator may, if he wishes, discuss his own values but should make clear that they are his own and that the student may freely agree or disagree with them. In some publications on sex education, the personal values of the writers are presented as if they were facts. Research evidence is sometimes either misinterpreted by the writer or carefully chosen so as to back up his point of view. It is important that the teacher recognize biases such as these in publications and also in his own thinking. It would seem most appropriate to present values for what they are: culturally and personally induced life styles, not absolute truths based on a careful sifting of research evidence. In this sense, the research-oriented sex educator has a good point when he deplores value-laden teaching. However, as discussed earlier, students bring deeply ingrained values to the classroom with them. They may be unable or unwilling, partly because of their own cultural background, to accept new knowledge and attitudes.

Values taught as facts may be seriously misleading and may set up conflicts in individuals and produce guilt and needless fears. For example, it is sometimes said and taught that premarital sexual experimentation will eventually create problems in married life. This is far from clear. Whether such experimentation would or would not affect later marital harmony is probably closely associated with the attitudes, beliefs, and situations of the individuals concerned.

In a discussion of values and ethics, the educator may feel under pressure to put forth a value system which he himself does not wholly accept. While it may be natural for him to feel pressure to do so, it would seem inadvisable for him to present any views as his own unless he truly accepts them. Students, especially as they grow out of childhood, are quick to note a lack of complete honesty and integrity in their teachers and other adults. Part of the current youth revolt is based on the perceived "phoniness" and hypocrisy of adults. Commonly held social values can be presented as such, without claiming them as one's own. Part of the educational process would seem to be a recognition, understanding, and examination of social values, which is not synonymous with their espousal or personal adoption.

Free discussion among students about values can be very useful. This often works most effectively when small groups of not more than seven or eight are used: a direct learning experience is provided as people discover that there are many different ways of looking at the same question. One of the potential uses of the small group is to promote communication among people; another may be the development of new cultural patterns through their exploration and acceptance by peer groups. The teacher, who has leadership skills and can establish freedom within limits, is likely to find the small group method one of several helpful approaches in sex and family life education.

In order to learn more about the attitudes, interests, and informational levels of a group of students, the teacher may find it helpful to begin with some form of questionnaire. Of course, a questionnaire is not possible for very young children, and difficulties present themselves in the teaching of functional illiterates. Ingenuity is needed to adapt to such situations, but for the more usual groups, questionnaires, rather than a verbal discussion, are suggested. One is more likely to get only socially acceptable questions and attitudes and to hear from the more aggressive, verbose students when reliance is placed on oral questioning alone. In order to get a relatively uninhibited set of expressed interests and attitudes, it is a good idea to ask for anonymous answers and to make it clear that this is not a test that will be graded. Repeated use of questionnaires and written responses from students can be useful because new questions may arise as the course goes along.

The Teacher as Pseudo-Kin

A class in sex education is apt to take on many of the aspects of the student's own family in terms of the student's perception. The teacher may be perceived as pseudo-parent and the classmates as brothers and sisters. This perception is likely to occur in many educational (and other interpersonal) settings, but the subject matter in sex and family life education is likely to intensify family-related feelings. It is important that the teacher be aware of this tendency and realize that emotional reactions, even though repressed, may be especially intense. The educator is not usually trained to deal directly with these emotions, as already noted, but he must recognize their validity and strength. For instance, some students with particularly warm feelings for their own parents may transfer a sense of admiration and devotion to the teacher—very gratifying to him, but not a situation for which he can take full credit. The aware and psychologically mature teacher is able to avoid using such student devotion to satisfy his own need to feel loved and significant. Personal intimacy between teacher and student carries many dangers for both: such deep, subjective ties belong primarily to the student's family, friends, and—in the event that he needs help with emotional problems—to a professional counselor. If the student and teacher are not of the same sex, interpersonal relationships may require particularly sensitive handling, especially for teachers who are working with preadolescent or adolescent youths.

The family life and sex educator needs insight into his own psychological makeup and emotional needs so that he can handle the subject matter in this field with objectivity, empathy, calmness, and honesty. He needs to be secure in his own feelings about himself, or herself, as an adult male or female. If he feels overly anxious about his desirability or competence as a sex partner, guilty about his own sexuality, or hostile toward his own or the opposite sex, these feelings are likely to adversely affect his behavior with his students as well as what he teaches. Since students learn from what teachers do as well as from what they say, particularly in terms of the courses under discussion, sex and family life educators must either be remarkably mature, psychologically strong people, or must secure personal help for their own feelings and attitudes from a trained counselor or therapist.

Not only are affectionate or sexually tinged feelings transferred from family members to teachers, but hostile and guilty feelings as well. It may be useful to bear in mind that, just as the educator cannot take full credit for all the devotion that may come his way, he does not have to assume the total burden of dislike, resentment, boredom, and resistance that some students offer. These student attitudes are more readily accepted if the teacher is aware that he is likely to be, in part, a stand-in for a rejecting, nagging, or over-possessive parent. Unlike the parent, the teacher need not be and should not be subjectively involved. If the teacher can help a student keep his hostile feelings under control by giving him firm, mild, consistent discipline along with respect and understanding, not only will the student's disturbing behavior be more easily handled but an important lesson may be learned: that interpersonal relationships in a pseudo-family setting can be rewarding and that hostile feelings can be understood and controlled.

The pseudo-familial nature of the class in sex and family life education has much to offer apart from the subject matter itself. Within the limits imposed by the fact that the class is an educational, not a clinical, setting, boys and girls, men and women, may learn to relate to each other as valued and valuable human beings—human beings first, male and female human beings second. They may learn to work together through class projects. They can learn together about such subjects as male and female anatomy, reproduction, childbirth, the psychosocial relations between the sexes, and so on. As boys and girls, men and women, learn together through books, lectures, audiovisual aids, discussions, and work projects, many fears and anxieties about sex and masculinity and femininity are likely to diminish.

While such discussions are apt to be more meaningful in an atmosphere of freedom, such freedom can readily exceed its bounds. A few clearly understood ground rules, spelled out in advance and repeated if necessary, are likely to help. Such rules might include the principle that discussions are not to include personal, subjective revelations about the students' or teachers' own specific family life, sex behavior, functioning, fears, fantasies and so on. Learning experiences can be structured so as to keep material of this sort in a more objective framework. For example, a student may ask what he should do about his own desire to have premarital sex relations. This can easily be put into a more general focus by commenting that this is a concern of many young people and that answers cannot be given in reference to particular individuals because each individual has his own set of circumstances and experiences. The discussion can then go on to a general presentation of pros and cons around this question.

In the use of small group discussions or buzz sessions the subject matter can be structured by the teacher so that a topic is discussed, rather than personal experiences. The same kind of general framework is suggested for role playing—a device often used—and apparently with excellent results, if the teacher is aware of sensitive areas and of the subjective material that may be exposed. Interest in group therapy, group dynamics, and sensitivity training has prompted some experimentation, and the educator who is well acquainted with the students he is teaching and who is well trained in the complexities of human personality and the structure and functioning of small groups can use devices such as role playing, psychodramas, and buzz sessions effectively.[6]

The School Environment

The impact of the total environment on human behavior, interests, and attitudes has already been stressed. In translating this concept into methods of sex education, it is helpful to consider the total school environment as a living laboratory. One major goal of sex education is that of helping people of opposite sexes to feel at ease in their everyday relationships with one another. Open communications, shared interests and activities, attitudes of trust and respect— these qualities are associated with wise mate selection, marital satisfaction and stability, and sexual gratification within marriage. Boys and girls are more likely to learn some of these skills in an educational setting if the total environment—classroom, playground, lunchroom, "outside activities"—is structured in such a way as to provide opportunities for the two sexes to talk, work, and play together in an atmosphere of positive acceptance of individual likeness and differences. This basic principle applies to administrators, faculty members, and students equally. In some schools, competitions between boys and girls are encouraged. It would seem wise to avoid such practices because one educational goal is to help the sexes interact harmoniously rather than conflict with each other.

Student Evaluations

I have found it useful to arrange for frequent anonymous written student evaluations of course content and methods while it is in process in order to learn more about its strengths and weaknesses. An evaluation at the end of a sex education program is not particularly helpful in serving the group at hand, and it may not have meaning for teaching another group because the next one may be quite different. Groups contain a variety of individuals, and it is hardly possible that all students would be satisfied or dissatisfied. As mentioned earlier, each person brings with him his own particular style of functioning and learning and an educational program will be perceived differently by different people. In working with groups the educator can hope to be "successful" only with a portion of the group. If the educator appears to be meeting the needs of the majority, this is probably the best that he can ask.

[6] The use of a variety of teaching techniques with small groups is based on a large body of research and theory in the social and behavioral sciences. The sex educator will probably find it useful to take related courses in such fields as social psychology. See the readings for references.

Tests

The topic of sex is so laden with emotion and confusion that students may perceive what has been presented in a course in very different ways. Some may even become more confused than they were in the first place because of the particular blocks they bring to learning in this area. Therefore, well-constructed tests to identify points of student confusion would seem to be important. Problems arise for the teacher in a formal educational setting, who therefore probably has to give each student a grade. Graded tests may introduce an extra note of anxiety that may cloud the picture. Therefore it is probably wise to give both graded and ungraded tests in an attempt to eliminate or reduce this factor.

Teaching Methods

Sex educators, like other educators, tend to favor a particular teaching style. Some lean toward the lecture, some toward free discussion, some toward visual aids, some toward student projects, and some toward other devices such as the use of role-playing and problem-solving. Because of variation in individual personalities, levels of intelligence, and learning styles, it is likely that different methods have different values to different students. An experimental approach seems to be called for, which may be aided by the student evaluations and tests that have been mentioned. However, it is found that a teacher needs to be true to his own style and to feel at ease with himself in relation to the educational method he is using, and thus student evaluations may be but one guide in course content and teaching method.

Involvement of Parents and the Community

This topic is handled in considerable detail elsewhere in this volume (see particularly Chapters 4 and 6), and therefore only a passing reference will be made here to the importance of involving the parents, school administrators, faculty members, and opinion-makers in the community in sex education programs. This may be particularly appropriate just before a new program is launched. Because sex education is often new to a community; values and beliefs about sex are rapidly changing; parents and other adults, like students, bring the complexities of their total life experiences and cultural patterns to the topic; and the proposed program is almost sure to create some anxieties and misconceptions—an orientation program for the adults involved would seem to be in order. Such a program might include an overview of the proposed course content and teaching methods (fantasies about what is involved in sex education are apt to be far more lurid than the actual fact of the matter). A fringe benefit may be the provision of information and attitudes to adults, which are important to them in their own lives as individuals as well as parents. Many adults did not receive such education when they were young, new information is constantly made available, and new issues arise for men and women as they reach different stages in their growth and development.

Sex Education in the Curriculum

There is a great deal of confusion as to "where sex education belongs in the curriculum." While the arguments go on, it is likely to end up nowhere. In an ideal situation, it would occur naturally in the many courses in which the subject comes up, such as English, history, biology, social studies, and art, and would be discussed by both men and women teachers. Since sex is a pervasive and natural part of life, it probably should be treated as such. However, we are a very long way from a general acceptance by schools and citizens of the naturalness of sex and its relationship to most subject matter. As it is now, it is likely that special courses in sex education are needed at the various educational levels in the schools and that they may be taught by specially trained persons. Because this is a new subject for most schools and very few people have training for teaching it, it is probable that at the present time sex education will be placed wherever a teacher is available who is prepared and wishes to teach this material.

There are also suggestions that sex and family life education courses should be lifted from the regular curriculum and offered in a series of meetings as non-credit courses. One of the reasons for this suggestion is that in a course that seeks to help students with their everyday problems there can be considerable confusion as to whether the teacher is primarily an enabling leader or a functioning part of an educational system. This issue can be particularly acute when the teacher is called upon to grade students, check attendance, set standards for classroom behavior, and discipline refractory individuals.

There are sound arguments for and against offering sex and family life education as a non-credit course. One of the arguments against such a move is that the students who are most in need of it might be the ones who would be the least likely to involve themselves in it if it did not offer credit. If a teacher can make clear to himself and his students that he is concerned for them as individuals, that his liking and respect for them is basic and is not altered by how well they behave in class or do on tests, then the more formal and structured side of a course need not interfere with its more human aspect. In a sense, it can be constructive for students in a sex education program to learn that they are free to feel as they wish and to inquire as they wish but that at the same time their behavior must be kept within limits and must conform to certain standards. In society, there will aways be standards and limits on sex behavior.

SUMMARY

Some suggested basic principles for sex education to help students with their own lives have been presented here. They derive largely from educational, social, and psychological research and theory and from the author's experience as a teacher and counselor in the field. Determination of whether or not they are sound must await evaluative studies of operating programs.

Since sex education seeks to affect a fundamental and complex aspect of human behavior, it should be based on an understanding of the multiple causes of human behavior and of the society in which such behavior occurs. Education constitutes only one way of affecting human behavior, and sex educators would be well advised to coordinate their efforts with medical, social service, and religious personnel in the community. Because sex education deals with deep-seated, highly personal feelings and needs of individuals, teachers and counselors in this field should be particularly sensitive to individual differences of students in cultural background, life experience and current situation, and physical development. A class in sex education may carry with it social and psychological undertones of the family group, and the sex educator will probably benefit from understanding the individual and group dynamics with which he is dealing. He is also likely to need considerable psychological maturity in order to handle his own role in the situation as a leader aware of, but controlling, his own subjective feelings.

It would seem desirable that the sex educator make a clear differentiation in his mind between the separate but related functions of education and of therapy. He should be aware of particular problems and be ready and able to refer those with serious difficulties to appropriate medical and counseling personnel. It is likely that sex education will be particularly effective if carried out in a democratic atmosphere in which open communication between the sexes is encouraged and in which each individual is given an equal sense of identity and worth, first as a person and second as a male or a female. This is a relatively new, experimental field. Educators are likely to find it a challenge to their ingenuity and their own capacity to learn and to grow.

6 Sex Education in the Community

Esther Middlewood

Much of the present volume is aimed at teachers in a school setting and offers the kind of knowledge they will need in facing youngsters in a classroom. But no one imagines that this channel of communication is the only one. A large audience has to be reached outside the school, and this chapter shows how sex education can be implemented in a community setting.

The word "education" automatically suggests "school" to most persons, but it is probably true that the schools provide the smallest and least significant proportion of one's lifetime educational experiences. Family, friends, work and leisure, church, the mass media, and the surrounding community begin a child's education before he goes to school and continue it long after he graduates. In no area is this observation more true than that of human sexuality.

From the many types of learning and teaching experiences outside the school which have an influence on sexual attitudes and understanding, I have selected for discussion more or less formal programs systematically presented through the mass media and community organizations. Unfortunately, even this goal must be further restricted by the lack of research on the number and effectiveness of such programs throughout the country. This chapter, then, is based upon my personal observation and experience, augmented by scattered reports of other programs which were available to me.

THE NEED FOR COMMUNITY EFFORTS

Most community efforts, of whatever kind, grow out of a felt need of the people—a recognition of inadequate information in a vital area. This has been the case with adult sex education programs throughout the country. Although there have been various national movements to interest people in the subject, it seems that they succeed only in cases in which the community itself has already sensed the need. However, awareness of a problem does not inevitably produce a remedy, and the history of local sex education efforts is a mixture of moving successes, dismal failures, and the whole range of intermediate experiences.

One significant factor in success or failure is the source of information that is drawn upon. Many sex educators are self-appointed, poorly trained, and attitudinally biased to a serious degree. A doctor is not necessarily a qualified teacher of sex, nor is a pastor. The former may have a knowledge of the physiology of sex but no understanding of sex roles, value systems, or total personal involvement. The latter may have some understanding of the morality of sex and of personal involvement in it while he is utterly lacking in awareness of current social attitudes and pressures. Neither may have the ability to teach. Both may acquire further knowledge as they move into this new experience, but this does not happen by chance. Training is essential if a community plans to utilize its lay leadership for sex education programs.

In addition to the question of source of information, there is also the question of organization and follow-through. All too often sex education for adults is a matter of a single lecture by a local doctor sponsored by a church or parent-teacher organization or child study group. Although one cannot discount the possibility that such programs may have good effects, it seems doubtful that the consequences of any one-shot approach can be far-reaching. The purpose of this chapter will be to explore and evaluate the array of approaches and resources that have been used in various communities.

THE RANGE OF APPROACHES AND PROGRAMS

Uses of the Mass Media

In any educational program, when one wishes to reach a large number of people, one thinks of the mass media: newspapers, national magazines, radio, and television. The limitation of these agencies as educational tools is that typically they do not provide for give and take or personal involvement on the part of the person at whom the information is aimed. Experience has shown that, especially in areas with emotional content, some type of personal involvement is a vital factor in a change of attitude. Nevertheless, the power of the mass media should not be underestimated. An article in color in *Life Magazine* on the development of the human fetus has impact: the significance of that impact is not clear. Many readers may be engrossed and learn much. Some may be repulsed and may have their negative feelings toward sex reinforced. However, some who cannot accept this material as presented through mass media alone would have profited greatly had they been given an opportunity to discuss the same material in a small group in a comfortable setting.

It is sometimes possible to combine this mass approach with more intimate experiences. In one community a local radio station sponsored a program during which listeners could telephone in questions, for subsequent reply. The questions were to deal with the problems of youth. Most of the calls received concerned problems relating to sex information and sexual behavior. The need for greater public understanding of sex was apparent, and, as a result, the county health department was asked to cooperate in designing a program which would help as many people as possible.

The public health nurse of the county contacted forty women, and they agreed to assist in carrying out a community experiment. They met at the health department for six training sessions, in which they studied patterns of psychosexual maturation, the concept of self in sex expression, appropriate ages for giving biological information to children, and the social-sexual expectations society imposes upon youth, with the resultant confusion. They also reviewed early sex patterns and incest temptations and taboos. They read literature on the subject so that they could lead discussions with confidence. They also studied group involvement and group dynamics to aid them in the task of leadership. Each leader was then asked to invite ten to fifteen people in her own neighborhood to join her for morning coffee in her home each week. The group listened to a broadcast presented by the local radio station, and after each program discussed the material presented with a trained leader. Following each morning presentation, the leaders convened in the afternoon to discuss problems which emerged in the home groups or "listening posts," as they were called.

A very successful program was carried on in St. Louis, Missouri, utilizing the mass media. A medical doctor, B. G. Glassberg, conducted a series of radio programs dealing with sex during which anyone could call in to ask questions, to be answered by him later in the program. A set topic was discussed during the first ten to fifteen minutes, and questions were answered for the rest of the hour. The program is reported to have been unusually frank and honest and was helpful to people who inquired. It was also apparent that many of the questions telephoned to Dr. Glassberg were of great general interest, although one always wonders whether questions asked really reflect concerns of large numbers of people or whether individuals who are prone to ask startling and rather difficult questions, simply to provoke a difficult situation, tend to dominate the callers. It is the feeling of those involved, however, that such a program does afford an excellent opportunity to help people obtain information which would be difficult for them to get in any other way.

Another use of the mass media is to advertise resources which are available. In keeping with the usual study guide format, the

1967 Michigan Child Study Program, which focused upon sex education in the family, provided a leadership guide for each topic.
Topics include "What Sex Information Do Children Need?" "Marriage Is More Than a Contract," and "Sex Problems of Youth." In
addition to outlining the topics these guides suggest reference
materials and the use of resource people from the local community.

The use of local consultants is not without its hazards, of course.
In one instance that came to my attention, it was readily apparent
that the consultant was directing the discussion in a moralistic, in-
hibitive, and over-restrictive manner. Many of his comments con-
sisted of platitudes and clichés which have been applied to marriage
relations for far too many years and have little significance today.

One might ask whether it is worth while for large groups to attempt to discuss such difficult topics with little or, as in the example
above, uncertain help from experts. There is no reliable information
on the success or failure of the many such groups. Some measure of
success is reflected in the continued demand for these study guides
and for similar series developed for use in certain church groups,
parent-teacher groups, and so forth.

In all these cases it is clear that the impact of the mass media was
vastly increased by the use of organized small-group discussions as
a follow-up.

Institutionally Centered Programs

There are other community programs supported by public and
private funds, which have permanent facilities and staffs. In addition to such specialized organizations as Planned Parenthood and
programs of the various religious denominations, there are a few
institutions with sex education as a major goal. Three outstanding
examples are the Merrill-Palmer Institute in Detroit, the Cleveland
Health Museum, and the Flint, Michigan, program (sponsored by
the Claire Elizabeth Fund). The last will serve as an example of
institutional programs.

The Flint program[1] was sponsored through a local trust fund and
developed out of a program for maternal health, which was the
initial purpose of the Claire Elizabeth organization. The program in
sex education was developed by Dr. David Treat and involves both
children and parents. The pattern has been emulated by many communities throughout the United States. In brief, parents and children
were brought together to hear a lecture on sex, in which the Dickin-

---

[1] Information regarding this program is available from Dr. George Chamis,
Director of Family Life Education, Flint Public Schools, Flint, Michigan.

son models were used to explain biological processes. Later, films were included in the sessions. The program has been described in detail many times, and it is doubtless familiar to those who are interested in sex education.

The Flint program has many strengths, but also raises some questions. Insofar as parent education is concerned, it seems excellent. However, it appears to me to be unreasonable that children should be taken out of school to a central location in a community for sex education, traveling by bus for long distances to a rather unnatural setting, when they learn about all other forms of life and receive all other scientific information in the schoolroom. On the positive side, it has the real advantage that parents know exactly what has been presented to their children. The feeling seems to be that the communication between child and parent is best if both receive the same information. Whether this advantage is outweighed by the awkwardness and remoteness of the centralized meeting, the size of the groups, and the inhibiting effects on learning of an attempt to involve children and adults at the same level are questions raised by many educators. It is my view that the facts that adults need to know may be beyond the interest and understanding of children of most ages. Adults also need to delve into their own feelings apart from children. Children, too, have needs peculiar to themselves which need not be shared with parents initially. Parents need their own opportunity for learning, but not with their children. They need to keep avenues of communication open between them and their children so that when the occasion is presented they can make use of it.

In all fairness to the Flint program, it must be said that the community has responded to the stimulus provided by the program and has developed a complete program for children within the public schools. In addition, the portion of the program aimed at young people, both married and unmarried, has continued and is of excellent quality. There probably are few communities where as much intensive work is being done, largely as a result of a concentrated effort by a single, well-endowed institution. Whatever the strengths and weaknesses of the Flint program, it and the other efforts being made prove the feasibility of a systematic institutional approach and provide the opportunity to learn from the mistakes, as well as from the unquestioned achievements, of these pioneers.

A Community-Wide Approach

Although it is desirable to have substantial private or public funds behind any ambitious adult education program, it is not necessary.

What is necessary is dynamic local leadership combined with competent professional help. The success of the Kelso, Washington, program[2] illustrates the point. A member of the county medical auxiliary asked for assistance from SIECUS in initiating a program of sex education. Dr. Mary Calderone, Executive Secretary of SIECUS, agreed to visit and recommended as one particularly useful device in enlisting the support of community leaders the Sex Morality Teaching Record Kit.[3] The first meeting at the local level was held in the home of a community leader. Included were the superintendents of the public schools of Longview and Kelso, the president of Lower Columbia College, and representatives of parent-teacher groups, the county ministerial association, the community guidance center, the county medical association, and the medical auxiliary, the organizing agency.

Although the group recognized that the schools were providing reliable information about reproduction, it was agreed that the program should be expanded to include discussions about attitudes and values relating to sex. It was further agreed that the only way to implement such an expansion would be to educate adults as well as children. Other immediate steps advocated were an opportunity for teachers to participate, establishment of discussion groups for parents, and organization of a community council to coordinate sex education activities. Dr. Calderone added to those recommendations the suggestion that more men be involved, that orientation meetings be held for high school and college students, and that an outside speaker be brought in to talk to the public school students.

Much of this has been accomplished, and the community looks ahead to even greater growth of the program. The citizens are concerned—but what is more important, they are designing and implementing a sound, locally supported program.

Some communities have had success even without publicity and effective outside help. In one suburban community[4] the schools for many years had offered a course in reproduction and sex hygiene at the fifth- and sixth-, ninth-, and twelfth-grade levels, as well as education for parents. Parents had supported the program but felt it left much to be desired, and suggested that the school re-examine it. The task was assigned to a committee under the auspices of the

[2] See the National Education Association Journal for January, 1967. For further information, contact the National Education Association, 1201 16th Street, N.W., Washington, D.C. 20036.

[3] $10.00. Prepared by H. F. Southard of the National Board of the Y.W.C.A., 600 Lexington Avenue, New York, N.Y. 10022.

[4] Oak Park, Michigan. For further information write to the Oak Park Public Schools, Attention of the School Nursing Section.

school nursing office. A few classroom teachers and junior high school principals were involved after it was determined that the junior high schools should be the target for the expanded program. They worked throughout a summer reviewing materials, designing the curriculum, and planning a four-day training workshop for the teachers involved. The program was instituted in the fall of 1967, and a new working committee was established to assess the elementary school and secondary school involvement. All of this was accomplished without city-wide meetings or publicity of any sort.

It might be helpful to look at the progression of events that led to action on sex education in two communities with contrasting approaches.[5] In one town a physical education instructor and a health educator with a special interest in venereal disease control, both teaching at the college level, took the initiative. They conferred with a member of the adult education staff of the university, a committee of interested college personnel was called together, and it was decided to include some delegates from schools and social agencies in the area. The name given to the group was "council" because it was felt that the word defined its function most precisely.

The council met monthly for a time and finally decided to hold a two-day conference for school principals, health educators, and physical education instructors. At this meeting an outside speaker was brought in to broaden the discussion. Instead of focusing on sex education, the group began to look at the larger topic of family life education. Its scope grew, and the local council of churches, the county medical society, and other social agencies were involved in a two-day, county-wide meeting on "sex," with outside specialists used. There were mass student meetings, a PTA-sponsored meeting for the public, a general teachers' meeting, and a meeting of the local council of churches. Because many school systems within the county were involved, each representative was to report to his own community any part or all of the experience. In at least four instances some positive action occurred, while in two there has been a negative reaction, as a result of this approach. An assessment of its effectiveness remains to be made. It should be noted that (1) the initiative and motivating energy came from sources extraneous to the schools themselves; (2) there may not have been enough awareness of similar experiments in the past; (3) consultants' services were available; and (4) although one might expect changes in course offerings in adult education curricula, development of educational opportunities for parents, increased involvement of social agencies

[5] Kalamazoo, Michigan. For information write Miss Margaret Large, Women's Health Education, Western Michigan University, Kalamazoo.

in their own programs of adult sex education, etc., there is no mention of adult involvement other than mass meetings.

In contrast to this design is one that provides less opportunity for general social awareness, but which may afford a sturdier basis for growth. The question of better sex education arose in another urban community of comparable size but with one school system rather than within a county unit. For many years the school had arranged to have local physicians give three lectures on sex to eleventh-grade boys and girls, and both the school superintendent and the doctors knew that this was too little and too late. Classroom teachers met with the physicians and in lieu of a better plan decided to continue to use them but to hold classes for eighth- and tenth-graders as well. On the understanding that this was done for expediency, they also hired a family life specialist to assess the over-all program and set up a pattern for the future.

The family life specialist set up a committee that included faculty members and some persons in the community as consultants—doctors, the school nurse, a few parents, a minister, etc. Elementary school teachers, junior high school teachers, senior high school teachers, and those concerned about community education were included. They saw their area of concern as ranging from kindergartners through adults. Adults were not there simply to support an in-school program but because a bona-fide need for greater knowledge about sex and sexuality among adults was felt. The committee then began to design the school program based upon the responses to questionnaires given to seventh-, eighth-, and ninth-graders and one given to fifth- and sixth-graders in twenty of the elementary schools.

The results have been varied and interesting. Growth has been slower initially, but progress is more stable. The school system has added an assistant director of family life education and has developed a good program of in-service sex education training for teachers. There have been several two-day workshops for ancillary personnel, so that all individuals involved in any way in the school and community program are cognizant of goals, teaching materials, precautions, etc. Teachers receive in-service training as part of their regular twelve-session self-improvement training program, in which all of them are involved.

We should note the following features of the program: (1) it was initiated within the school; (2) the community was involved but was not allowed to impose its views; (3) the goal has consistently been that of educating all ages, from kindergartners to adults, with the school assuming responsibility for preschool and adult education; (4) the energy was generated within the group itself, rather than from outside authorities; and (5) there were no unnecessary public meetings.

The Church

In talking of the community and sex education programs, one must be aware of the work which is being done by church organizations. The Methodist Conference on the Family, held in Chicago in 1967, is a good illustration of the energy expended in such programs by the church. The Cana Conference of the Roman Catholic Church, of Father Umbiorsky's design, is another attempt to deal with sexual needs in a religious framework. Whatever our feelings are in regard to religion and sex information, it is apparent that no matter what kind of factual information is presented about sex, the individual must assess it in terms of the philosophical framework within which he functions. If the church presents a program which is sufficiently well founded on facts about current practices, current moral concepts, and sociological and psychological knowledge, it can be most useful. Both the Methodist and the Catholic programs represent serious attempts to solve the problem of disseminating information on sex and instruction designed to help individuals who find themselves in difficulties in the sexual area of their lives. Other larger churches, such as the Unitarians and the Episcopalians, have included sex education in their programs.

There are some who argue that sex information is best obtained from the church itself, especially in the case of parents and young people, who are trying to establish their value systems, and certainly of couples who plan to be married in the church and to conform to the general philosophy of the church to which they belong. Established churches have a certain homogeneity which enables them to assess sexual practices and concerns in the light of their philosophy. Many churches have done an excellent job of sex education within the framework of their youth programs. As a matter of fact, in the United Church of Christ study guides for youth programs much attention is paid not only to family life education but to sex information specifically. In one community[6] junior high school students spent six weeks reading and discussing the sex information contained in these materials. First their parents were called together for two meetings in which the materials and the general information which was to be presented were reviewed. Such topics as the meaning and significance of adolescence, body changes in adolescence, sex information, reproduction, and, finally, the students' personal assessments of sex were discussed. Questions were answered

[6] Lansing, Michigan. For information write Mrs. Dale Granger, Director, Family Life Education, Lansing Public Schools.

honestly. Boys and girls met together, and at the last meetings they had an opportunity to ask questions of a panel of qualified persons. Those persons included a psychologist, a physician, and some young college students who could answer some of the questions asked about current sex activities and practices. Such programs are not unusual, but the kind of material presented varies greatly. One senior high school group completely rejected the course because the minister involved was platitudinous, exhortative, and beside the point. It is imperative that we reply with complete honesty to the questions which are asked if we hope for adherence to the ethical values which church groups advance.

An exciting new approach is being planned for the subteens of the Methodist youth group of the Methodist Michigan Conference. They are planning the sessions themselves, with guidance, and are utilizing role-playing, using adults to play the roles and themselves as discussion panels. Such programs have been used successfully with older children but the current program is a new venture.

Other Community Institutions

Closely related to church youth groups are the sex education programs conducted by such organizations as the Y.W.C.A. and the Y.M.C.A. There are many such programs. Some deal with the problems of young people, some with the unwed mother, some with pre-courtship, and a few deal with sex adjustment of the young married. These programs vary as much as those presented by the church, and their success is almost totally dependent upon their leadership.

One of the most extensive programs in the United States which can be used effectually to impart sex information is the Agricultural Extension Service. The Service is designed to reach large numbers of people in a rather intimate way. It enables leaders to talk with people in comparatively small groups, so that discussion can become a part of whatever information is presented. Unfortunately, the Extension Service is most effective in teaching skills. However, I suppose that if we are concerned only with the transmitting of information, information about sex can be passed on as readily as glovemaking or some of the other topics which are presently presented. The philosophy of this paper, however, is to assume that more than biological information is necessary. Thus the method of training discussion leaders for local groups is not ideal for developing leadership. Attempts are being made to modify existing leadership training programs and afford greater in-depth training. One suggestion is that one individual in a local unit might become the family life leader for any topic which is presented in that general area. That leader can attend a series of meetings and become well versed in a variety of topics, including sex information, so that if the group should show interest in family life education he could attend a session for training in the specific area requested and then return to his group as a leader in this area of learning.

CHALLENGES

Re-Creating and Developing Leaders

In recent years there have been many more professionally led adult discussion groups on sex than ever before. Planned Parenthood provides leadership in this area. Sometimes physicians help local groups at Y.W.C.A.'s. Certainly the family service agencies are rendering a real service, especially in meeting with groups from deprived areas. Despite these real achievements, however, one of the most pressing needs is for more and for better-trained leaders. Professional groups are trying to do their part by introducing courses in family life education into the curriculum of medical schools and theological seminaries. Social workers, nurses, physical education, health, and home economics teachers, and many others are being trained in this area. But lay leaders must be trained also to provide leadership at the community level.

In Michigan, as has been mentioned, there is a Parent Education Associates group, now numbering some seven thousand persons, who have been trained for three years or more to lead parent education groups. Some of these women have been involved in the program for fourteen or fifteen years. There are approximately fifteen hundred in training now. The Parent Education Associates are drawn from many walks of life. They have varied educational backgrounds and are drawn from all economic levels. The one essential requirement is that the individual be a family member who has found a certain enjoyment in the rearing of children, and that she in turn be willing to devote time to meeting with other parents in discussion groups. They do not become pseudo-experts, nor do they try to set up groups in which they dictate or admonish parents about current practices of child-rearing. The experience which they hope to provide is an informal discussion in which parents can freely express their ideas about their own problems and those of their children and their husbands, as well as those that arise from the interaction of the members of the family.

The leader is trained in basic child growth and development concepts—not child-rearing practices, but the way people function, some of the problems they experience in adjustment, the significance of aggression, and the importance of understanding individual differences in terms of growth patterns and needs. They learn about psychosexual maturation patterns, although not in an academic framework; and they try to appraise social situations as they exist, and not as they might ideally be conceived in a nostalgic recapturing of the past, so that they tend to be much more effective than the usual parent education leader in more highly stylized programs.

During their period of study, the associates learn something about group dynamics, the elements of good discussion, and the use of sociodrama and role-playing, and various films and materials. Thus the interest of the programs as they are carried out in the community is heightened. After a three-year training program, they meet once a month for approximately three hours, they assume leadership in their own churches or in established ongoing programs of parent education, such as child study. They assist in small group discussions at grade levels within their own schools, such as those of preschool mothers, or in any one of a variety of ways. They do not establish new organizations within the existing structure. It would seem that some such program is needed on a much broader basis if local leaders in adult sex education are to be provided in adequate numbers.

Adult Sex Education in the Culture of Poverty

In the work done with deprived families it is becoming apparent that we do not as yet know these people well enough to be of great help to them. Workers have too often either imposed middle-class views or have depended upon sociological descriptions which too often miss the deep, emotional undertones. Many ascribe great casualness regarding sexual activity to the poor. They judge, on the basis of survey findings, that the activity reflects inner feelings accurately. This assumption can be questioned.

In long-term contact with small groups of women, some of whom had as many as nineteen children by various males, one begins to be aware of many other feelings, and deep anger about being sexually used, which emerge in many ways. It is often assumed that child-bearing would decrease if adequate information could be given about contraceptive practices, yet in one meeting mothers discussed the problem which confronts them when men with whom they have intercourse secretly puncture condoms while professing that they are protected. These women understood the masculine need of impregnation for men who have little other in life to prove their manliness.

To help these women and their men or their middle-class counter-parts it is clearly not enough to see that contraceptive information is available to them. They understood the use of condoms but did not use this knowledge as a guide to their behavior because they also understood the male need. The problem, then, was to help them find more appropriate ways to support their men while pro-tecting themselves, as women, from repeated unwanted pregnan-cies. It is my conviction that such a change in behavior cannot be achieved by mass lectures, pamphlets, etc. It requires establishment of small groups operating over a long period of time and developing competent local level leadership. Society must allow for this type of learning if it hopes for change.

But even now changes do occur—if not massive social changes, then at least very real individual changes. In one group of women with more children than they wanted, the discussions led not only to changed feelings about contraception but to changed feelings about themselves. One had recently purchased a mirror " 'cause now I can look at myself; 'cause I likes me better," and she saw her life with eight children in a different perspective. One left the house where she had lived to move into a house which had a key because as she said, she had a "good enough job for what I've got now without more children" and intended to lock out the men in her life.

Mothers of the poor, for all of their apparent casualness about sex, have an amazing capacity for shyness, prudery, and hunger for knowledge about their own bodies and the sexual design of the male. Hovering over and through it all are such questions as "How can we help our children to make the most of sex in their lives?" "How can our boys become men when they don't see 'men'?" "How soon should our girls know about 'the pill'?" We are far from having the answers, and we too must learn from them.

If we admit to not knowing the answers, at least we are trying to develop some. In my own state, Michigan, the Merrill-Palmer Insti-tute, the State Department of Social Welfare, and the State Depart-ment of Mental Health are all attempting programs in sex education as a part of work with groups of A.D.C. mothers; the Family Service Association works with "ENABLE"; the State Department of Health works through local units in educational programs about prenatal care and venereal disease. Unfortunately, such efforts are sporadic and are only a beginning.[7]

[7] Further information on Michigan programs is available from the author, Box 8, Haslett, Michigan 48840.

Financial and Operational Support

It has already been noted that solid financial support is one element that helps to assure the success of a community program. Most often the programs that succeed and endure have a firm base in some solvent organization, whether it be a philanthropic foundation or a public agency such as the school district. Government at all levels is increasingly responsive to the needs in this area. Through mental health, social welfare, special grants, and many other channels support is becoming available for well-conceived local programs. Not least important is the leadership at the state level. To use my own state again as an example, Michigan, under the auspices of the State Council on Family Relations, is attempting to coordinate the efforts of all persons with responsibility for statewide sex education programs—government agencies such as health (prenatal care, maternal health, venereal disease, and illegitimacy), mental health (parent education, growth and development, sex adjustment and aberrations), social welfare (strengthening family design, illegitimacy), education (the whole problem of learning for growth from kindergarten through adult life), and others less involved. In addition to government agencies, the state council of churches, state child study organizations (such as the cooperative nursery organization), and the broader adult education structures all can and must provide leadership. State councils, in turn, can look to the National Council on Family Relations and SIECUS for guidance in this effort.

CONCLUSIONS

If community involvement in sex education is to be carried on by a variety of people, and with as many patterns of presentation of both method and content as there are people involved, we may draw the following conclusions:

1. We need research which is not only sociological and descriptive. We need to know a great deal more about people themselves and the significance of human relationships in all phases of life. Our sexual practices may be so rigidly controlled by a moralistic view, or so casually imposed by poverty and expedience, that they do not fulfill human needs. Hypererotic or sexually deviant behavior may be so blatantly paraded that normal persons doubt their own normalcy.
2. We need much better training for those who are called upon for leadership in education, and we would hope that distortions of viewpoint, whether they are inhibiting or verge on an exhibitionistic freedom, are not imposed as codes of behavior.
3. We must utilize all structures for teaching in our communities, such as extension programs, the churches, adult education in the public schools,

to help human beings to an understanding of self. This makes sex education a necessity.

4. Sex education should be free of personal bias, unless the responsible group has the obligation to its own membership to assimilate the member, as in homogeneous groups with a given philosophical framework.

5. Innovations must be founded upon historical considerations. No community needs to "start from scratch." We can learn from the success and failures of other communities. Sex in an erotic society is enticing, and sex education will interest a segment of the population at any given time. The real test comes when a given community combines to assess its strengths and weaknesses. Then, and only then, can we look at the existing patterns and problems and design a program to meet the needs of the individual community.

Suggested Readings: Part I

COURSE CONTENT

Bigelow, M. A. *Sex Education*. New York: Macmillan, 1916.
A pioneering effort to define needs, objectives, methods, and content in sex education. No longer in print, but available in many libraries.

Duvall, E. M. *Why Wait Till Marriage?* New York: Association Press, 1965.
Represents the extreme of the conservative approach to sexual morality. Chastity is put forward as the ideal for both sexes. Written for high school and early college ages.

Ellis, A. *Sex without Guilt*. New York: Lyle Stuart, 1966.
(Also available in a Dell paperback.)
Represents the extreme of the liberal approach to sexual morality. Suggestions are given so that the reader may enjoy premarital intercourse, masturbation, etc., without guilt or fear. Very easy to read.

Gruenberg, B. *High Schools and Sex Education*. Washington, D.C.: Government Printing Office, 1939.
A revision of the 1922 publication, this pamphlet continued the emphasis on the integration of sex education in the school curriculum. No longer in print, but available in some libraries.

Grunwald, H. A., ed. *Sex in America*. New York: Bantam Books, 1964.
Chapters on puritanical and liberal sex codes provide a range of views of sexual morality. Lester Kirkendall, Walter Stokes, and Mary Calderone are some of the contributors.

Hudson, J. W. "A Content Analysis of Selected Family Life Education Textbooks Used at the Secondary Level." Ph.D. dissertation, Ohio State University, 1956.
Ten high school textbooks published from 1945 to 1954 were analyzed. Sex was treated in only three of the texts examined. The results of the study illustrate the need for more comprehensive high school family life and sex education textbooks.

Johnson, W. R. *Human Sex and Sex Education*. Philadelphia: Lea and Febiger, 1963.
A chapter on theories of sex education presents seven differing approaches. The concluding chapter comments on the place of sex education in a changing world.

Kirkendall, L. A. *Premarital Intercourse and Interpersonal Relationships*. New York: Julian Press, 1961. (Also available in Matrix House paperback.)
A research study of interpersonal relationships based on case histories of 668 experiences of premarital intercourse reported

by 200 male college students, the emphasis is on the differing motivations and consequences of premarital intercourse. Suggestions relating to decision-making within an interpersonal relationship provide a basis for an approach to sex education.

Kirkendall, L. A. *Sex Education as Human Relations.* Sweet Springs, Missouri: Roxbury Press, 1950.

A general book on the objectives and methods of sex education in the schools. Copies are still available.

Reiss, I. L. *Premarital Sexual Standards in America.* New York: Free Press of Glencoe, 1960.

A classic sociological study of premarital sexual standards, the results indicate a trend away from abstinence toward permissiveness with affection.

Reiss, I. L. *The Social Context of Premarital Sexual Permissiveness.* New York: Holt, Rinehart and Winston, 1967.

An extension of Reiss's earlier research into premarital sexual standards, this is the first sociological study of a national probability sample of premarital sexual attitudes. An integrated theory of sexual permissiveness is formulated.

Reiss, I. L. "The Treatment of Pre-Marital Coitus in Marriage and Family Texts." *Social Problems* 4 (1957):334–38.

Demonstrates the great difficulty which exists in developing an objective, balanced treatment of this subject. The treatment of the psychological effects of premarital intercourse and the relationship between it and marital success or failure should be especially noted.

Strain, F. B. *Sex Guidance in Family Life Education.* New York: Macmillan, 1947.

Discusses the incorporation of sex education in school family life programs.

"Teacher Exchange for High Schools and Colleges." *Journal of Marriage and the Family* 20 (1967):374–89.

Several articles deal with the content and nomenclature of sex education courses.

TEACHING TECHNIQUES

California School Health 3, No. 1 (1967). (Entire issue devoted to sex education.)

Child Study Association of America. *Sex Education and the New Morality.* New York: By the Association, 1967.

Duane, M. "Sex Education—a Small Experiment." *Family Planning,* 1962. (Reprints available from SIECUS, 1855 Broadway, New York, N.Y. 10023.)

Gendel, E. S., M.D. "Sex Education Patterns and Professional Responsibility." *Southern Medical Journal*, 1966. (Reprints available from SIECUS.)

Harper, R. H., and Harper, F. R. "Education in Sex." In *The Encyclopedia of Sexual Behavior*, edited by A. Ellis and A. Abarbanel. New York: Hawthorn Books, 1961.

Johnson, W. R. *Human Sex and Sex Education—Perspectives and Problems*. Philadelphia: Lea and Febiger, 1963.

Kirkendall, L. *Sex Education*. SIECUS Discussion Guide 1. New York: SIECUS, 1956. (Available from SIECUS.)

Levine, M. I., and Seligman, J. H. *Helping Boys and Girls Understand Their Sex Roles*. Chicago: Science Research Associates, 1953. (Available from Science Research Associates, 295 East Erie Street, Chicago, Ill. 60611.)

Manley, H. "Sex Education: Where, When, and How Should It Be Taught?" *Journal of Health and Physical Education*, 1964.

Rubin, I. "Transition in Sex Values—Implications for the Education of Adolescents." *Journal of Marriage and the Family*, 1965. (Reprints available from SIECUS.)

Shaffer, T. E., M.D. "The Role of the Schools and Community in Sex Education." *Journal of the American Medical Association*, 1966. (Reprints available from SIECUS.)

Southard, H. "The Revolution in Sex Education—What Schools Can Do." *Teaching and Learning*, 1967. (Reprints available from SIECUS.)

PSYCHOLOGY, SOCIOLOGY, AND CULTURE
Developmental Levels

Douvan, E., and Adelson, J. *The Adolescent Experience*. New York: Wiley, 1966.

Grinder, R. E., ed. *Studies in Adolescence*. New York: Macmillan, 1963.

Kuhlen, R. G., and Thompson, G. C. *Psychological Studies of Human Development*. New York: Appleton-Century-Crofts, 1963.

McCandless, B. R. *Children and Adolescents: Behavior and Development*. New York: Holt, 1961.

Maccoby, E. E. *The Development of Sex Differences*. Stanford, Calif.: Stanford University Press, 1966.

Mussen, P., and Conger, J. *Child Development and Personality*. New York: Harper, 1956.

Thompson, G. *Child Psychology*. New York: Houghton Mifflin, 1962.

Personality

Bell, N. W., and Vogel, E. F. "Family and Personality." In *Modern Introduction to the Family*, edited by Bell and Vogel. Glencoe, Illinois: Free Press, 1960.

Ehrmann, W. W. "Marital and Non-Marital Sexual Behavior." In *Handbook of Marriage and the Family*, edited by H. T. Christensen, New York: Rand McNally, 1964.

Erikson, E. H. *Childhood and Society.* New York: Norton, 1950.

Handel, G. *The Psychosocial Interior of the Family.* Chicago: Aldine, 1967.

Kagan, J. "Acquisition and Significance of Sex Typing and Sex Role Identity." In *Review of Child Development Research*, edited by M. M. Hoffman and L. W. Hoffman, Vol. 1. New York: Russell Sage Foundation, 1964.

Lindgren, H. C. *The Psychology of Personal Adjustment.* New York: Wiley, 1961.

Mussen, P., and Conger, J. *Child Development and Personality.* New York: Harper, 1956.

Witmer, H., and Kotinsky, R., eds. *Personality in the Making.* New York: Harper, 1952.

Social Psychology and Group Behavior

Bonner, H. *Group Dynamics, Principles, and Applications.* New York: Ronald Press, 1959.

Cartwright, D., and Zander, A. *Group Dynamics: Research and Theory.* 2d ed. New York: Harper, 1960.

Coyle, G., and Hartford, M. E. *Social Process in the Community and Group.* New York: Council on Social Work Education, 1958.

Foote, N. N., and Cottrell, L. S., Jr. *Identity and Interpersonal Competence.* Chicago: University of Chicago Press, 1955.

Hare, H. P., Borgotta, E. F., and Bales, R. F. *Small Groups, Studies in Social Interaction.* New York: Knopf, 1955.

Lindzey, G., ed. *Handbook of Social Psychology.* Vol. 1, *Theory and Method.* Reading, Mass.: Addison-Wesley, 1954.

Stock, D., and Thelen, H. A. *Emotional Dynamics and Group Culture.* New York: New York University Press and National Training Laboratories, 1958.

Swanson, N., and Hartley, H., eds. *Readings in Social Psychology.* New York: Holt, 1952.

Marriage and the Family

Burgess, E. W., and Cottrell, L. S., Jr. *Predicting Success or Failure in Marriage.* New York. Prentice-Hall, 1939.

Komorovsky, M. *Blue Collar Marriage.* New York: Random House, 1964.

Rainwater, L. *Family Design.* Chicago: Aldine, 1965.

Terman, L. M. *Psychological Factors in Marital Happiness.* New York: McGraw-Hill, 1938.

Cultural Differences

Bronfenbrenner, U. "Socialization and Social Class thru Time and Space." In *Readings in Social Psychology*, edited by E. E. Maccoby, T. M. Newcomb, and E. H. Hartley. New York: Holt, 1958.

Cavan, R. S. "Subcultural Variations and Mobility." In *Handbook of Marriage and the Family*, edited by H. T. Christensen. New York: Rand McNally, 1964.

Chilman, C. S. *Growing Up Poor*. Welfare Administration Publication, no. 13. Washington, D.C.: Government Printing Office, 1956.

Dager, E. Z. "Socialization and Personality Development in the Child." In *Handbook of Marriage and the Family*, edited by H. T. Christensen. New York: Rand McNally, 1964.

Erikson, E. H. *Childhood and Society*. New York: Norton, 1950.

Kinsey, A. C., et al. *Sexual Behavior in the Human Male*. Philadelphia: Saunders, 1948.

Kinsey, A. C., et al. *Sexual Behavior in the Human Female*. Philadelphia, Saunders, 1953.

Sussman, M. B. *Sourcebook in Marriage and the Family*. New York: Houghton Mifflin, 1963. See esp. chaps. 4 and 5, pp. 194–284.

PART II: QUESTIONS OF STANDARDS AND VALUES

Introduction

In the last chapter of this unit (Chapter 11) Harold T. Christensen defines a value as "a standard of reference, a criterion for judging the relative worth and importance of things." In the field of sex education there are at least two areas of value conflict that color every other area. First, there is the question of whether premarital intercourse is ever morally justified, or, more broadly, what values ought to guide young people in their decisions in the sexual area. Several of the authors in this unit address themselves to the question, but one's position seems to boil down to one's basic moral assumptions. In general, traditionalists assume the intrinsic validity of religious and cultural prohibitions, while liberals reject them. Of course, the liberals in turn must find a new set of assumptions, such as Reiss's affection (Chapter 7) or Kirkendall and Libby's interpersonal relationships (Chapter 8), from which to develop a new set of criteria.

Although several of the contributors to this volume make their own (generally liberal) values very plain, it is not the intention of the editors to argue for one position or another. Rather, in the spirit of Christensen's chapter, it is our goal to illuminate the range of values, the consequences of various value orientations or value-behavior discrepancies, and the premises upon which values are based.

There is a second equally hotly contested and emotion-laden area of decision-making upon which we do take a stand, however. Many accept the view that ignorance protects innocence and preserves virtue while knowledge and questioning corrupt. We reject this assumption on both empirical and philosophical grounds. It is our assumption that children (and adults) can make wise choices, whatever their value position, only if they are informed about the issues involved. Whatever one's final decision on the correct level of sexual intimacy permissible before marriage, the problem of how to make the sexual side of life meaningful and fulfilling continues. It is to this latter point that this book is primarily directed.

7   Premarital Sexual Standards

Ira L. Reiss

Whatever values the teacher himself holds, he cannot ignore the variety of values which obtain in a pluralistic society. Ira Reiss makes it very clear that several standards with respect to premarital sexual relations are, so to speak, "fighting it out" on the current scene and that the one that seems to be dominant demands affection as a criterion for judging any relationship. As we have noted, different schools will use this information in different ways, but no teacher can afford to ignore it.

The best way to gain insight into premarital sexual standards today is to start with the realization that among young people abstinence is not the only nor necessarily always the dominant standard. This is a fact that all of us must face, whether or not we approve of such a state of affairs. The researches of Kinsey,[1] Ehrmann,[2] and, most recently, myself[3] make this apparent. On the other hand, one key characteristic of the new permissiveness is, as seen in the researches mentioned, its relatively heavy reliance on affection and its low evaluation of promiscuity. There is a good deal of premarital sexual permissiveness, but for the most part it is regulated, particularly for females, by the affection of the participants. It is the objective of this paper to spell out in greater detail what this regulation involves and to examine some of the research. It should be understood that the present analysis reflects middle-class American standards and deals only with heterosexual kissing, petting, and coital relationships and not with homosexuality or masturbation.

[1] A. C. Kinsey et al., *Sexual Behavior in the Human Male* (Philadelphia: Saunders, 1948). This is the famous study of males in America that broke ground for future research. The Kinsey study on females, like the volume on males, remains a classic and important reference for all interested in the area. See A. C. Kinsey et al., *Sexual Behavior in the Human Female* (Philadelphia: Saunders, 1953).

[2] W. W. Ehrmann, *Premarital Dating Behavior* (New York: Henry Holt, 1959). The book is excellent for its analysis of male-female sexual differences. It is the classic statement of how going steady and love relate to sexuality and contains an interesting analysis of social class differences and sexual behavior, based on a study of Florida college students.

[3] See *The Social Context of Premarital Sexual Permissiveness* (New York: Holt, Rinehart and Winston, 1967), the first empirical sociological study to use a national sample of adults and samples of students to test and develop an integrated theory of premarital sexual permissiveness.

TRENDS IN PREMARITAL SEXUAL PERMISSIVENESS

Recent Changes

The common belief that the proportion of non-virginity has risen markedly during the past twenty years is not supported by the research. The best source for data on trends comes from the Kinsey studies, which show that the big change in female non-viriginity occurred in the group born after 1900. There was comparatively little difference in non-virginity among females born during the first, second, and third decades of this century. Differences were found, however, among these three birth groups regarding petting to orgasm. There was a sharp increase in this activity in each group, but there was no comparable rise in non-virginity. When one examines the more recent studies by Ehrmann, Freedman, Kirkendall, Schofield, and myself,[4] made in the 1950's and 1960's, the same results appear. Thus, although the evidence is not perfect, it does suggest that there has not been any change in the proportion of non-virginity for the past four or five decades equal to that which occurred during the 1920's.

Why has this widespread belief in a sharp increase in female non-virginity developed? Visibility is the first reason. There are almost 200 million Americans today, whereas fifty years ago there were only approximately half that many. When there are more people doing the same thing, one is prone to believe that something new is happening. When twice as many people do something, it becomes more noticeable even though the percentage remains the same. There is also a greater willingness to talk about what is going on. This talk increases public awareness. Then too there appears to have been a change in *attitudes* about sexuality. (I have presented recent evidence on this.[5]) Although the same percentage of females

---

[4] See Ehrmann, *Premarital Dating Behavior;* M. B. Freedman, "The Sexual Behavior of American College Women: An Empirical Study and an Historical Survey," *Merrill-Palmer Quarterly of Behavior and Development,* 11 (1965):33–48, a detailed study of eastern college girls with more recent data than the Kinsey studies; L. A. Kirkendall, *Premarital Intercourse and Interpersonal Relationships* (New York: Julian Press, 1961), which stresses the importance of the interpersonal relationship in the sex lives of two hundred college students; M. Schofield, *The Sexual Behavior of Young People* (Boston: Little, Brown, 1965), a recent, carefully executed study of English teenagers with much fascinating information that can be compared with American findings; my *The Social Context of Premarital Sexual Permissiveness,* cited above, and "The Sexual Renaissance in America," *Journal of Social Issues,* 22 (April, 1966):1–137, a special issue with contributions by such authorities as Robert Bell, Jessie Bernard, C. B. Broderick, Harold Christensen, Paul Gebhard, Lester Kirkendall, Roger Libby, Lee Rainwater, Robert Sherwin, and Clark Vincent.

[5] See *Premarital Sexual Standards in America* (New York: Free Press of Glencoe, 1960) for an analysis of the major social science studies on premarital sex and an

have coitus, more of them accept this behavior as proper. Such a change in attitudes is a bold and direct attack on the established standard of abstinence and may raise the level of public awareness and anxiety. It takes time for the public to become aware of widespread changes, and the factors mentioned have slowly brought about this awareness.

It may be interesting to note that there is a similar misconception about divorce. The divorce *rate* (the number of divorces per thousand married females) has not changed radically in the past twenty-five years. The rate was slightly higher in the 1940's than in the 1950's; it has been rising slightly in the 1960's.[6] Despite this fact, there is widespread belief that the divorce rate has been sharply increasing. In reality, the sharpest sustained increase occurred at about the time of World War I. It was generally maintained during the 1920's and fell somewhat during the 1930's, then rose somewhat during the 1940's. There are more people today who have been divorced, and there is more public discussion of divorce, thus visibility is greater. Here too one can see the myopia which afflicts the public vision. One of the key values of social science research is that it can help serve as a corrective lens for the "common sense" view of society.

As noted above, there have been changes in attitudes since the great breakthrough in sexual behavior during the 1920's. The non-virginal unmarried female in the 1920's may well have been a rebel; the non-virginal unmarried female during the 1960's may well be a conformist. The unmarried male is today probably a tamer sexual creature than his father or grandfather was in the 1920's. He is less likely to visit a prostitute and more likely to value affection as an element in sexual relations. This is not to deny that in perhaps the majority of instances of male premarital coitus affection is still lacking, but rather to assert that coitus with affection may well be at an all-time high.

Four Major Premarital Sexual Standards

The major premarital sexual standards that exist today are four: *abstinence*, which forbids intercourse to both sexes; the *double standard*, the Western world's oldest, which allows males to have coitus but not females; *permissiveness with affection*, growing in popularity, which accepts coitus for both sexes when a stable,

---

attempt to develop from them a coherent view of American sexual standards, and *The Social Context of Premarital Sexual Permissiveness*.

[6] U.S., Department of Health, Education, and Welfare, "Divorce Statistics Analysis: U.S. 1962," Series 21, no. 7. This is a regular publication of the National Center for Health Statistics and contains good national data and analysis.

affectionate relationship is present; and *permissiveness without affection*, which accepts coitus for both sexes on a voluntary basis regardless of affection. This last standard has a quite small number of followers, but it is most newsworthy and thereby the public is misled as to the number of its adherents.

The question of love and how to recognize it is important to many of these value systems.[7] Most people seem to mean by love a subjective feeling of deep affection based upon a close relationship with another person. One might think that males could exploit females by pretending love, but it is believed that the female of today is quite sophisticated and is not often fooled by "a line." However, she may deceive herself in order to justify her own sexual behavior.

During the nineteenth century abstinence and the double standard were dominant. Lest we mythologize our past, we must remember that this was one of the "golden" periods of prostitution and that, television notwithstanding, in the real Old West the dance hall girls did more than dance. Cities in the east spawned their own brand of houses of prostitution. It would seem that abstinence was then, as it is now, predominantly practiced by females. It is hard to estimate how many females also adhered to the double standard, but one can say that a sizable number believed they must accept the fact that "this is a man's world." Many males were affected by abstinence more as a source of guilt feelings than as a restriction on their behavior.

The real shift in the twentieth century was not from an era of purity and abstinence believed in and practiced by both sexes, but from a strong double standard, powerful repression on the part of many females and some males, and vast networks of underground sexuality, both professional and non-professional, involving some of the world's most extensive "hard core" pornography, and established prostitution. It should be noted that in the past two thousand years the Western world has not succeeded in bringing to adulthood as virgins the majority of males in even one generation.

The open type of courtship system and marital choice that was evident in America even in the nineteenth century came into full acceptance in the twentieth. Without chaperons, in a large city, with privacy available in cars, apartments, and hotels, the young person came to exercise his or her judgment as to permissible sexual activity. Under the stress of their own sexual drives and the

---

[7] See A. Ellis and A. Abarbanel, eds., *The Encyclopedia of Sexual Behavior* (New York: Hawthorn Books, 1961). This is the most complete and authoritative source available in this area and contains articles by approximately a hundred experts in the field.

permissive dating system of urban society, young people adopted sexual codes that were considerably more liberal than those of their parents. I have documented the high association between a participant-run courtship system and the acceptance of premarital coitus.

In the 1920's the new system burst upon the public consciousness of Americans. The growth of an industrialized and urbanized society and the autonomy implicit for generations in our marital and family system had bred a new type of courtship. The highly permissive behavior of the 1920's was probably accompanied by a great deal more guilt and self-recrimination than is now the case. Young people today have the benefit of the therapeutic effects of open discussion, and they have two generations of permissive behavior behind them. The psychological aspects of this situation are discussed in a recent report by the Group for the Advancement of Psychiatry.[8]

Recent evidence indicates that even females who accept abstinence are likely to accept intimate forms of petting, sometimes to the point of orgasm, when they are involved in an affectionate relationship, while males who accept the double standard are likely to permit themselves intercourse with a female whom they love. Thus all our premarital sexual codes have been "liberalized." Abstinence is still the dominant code for most females and for a sizable minority of males, particularly those under twenty. The double standard is still the dominant code for many males and females, but permissiveness with affection has today achieved respectability and a sizable following among both sexes. The choice of a premarital sexual code has become, among young people, a legitimate choice among valid alternatives, and even many of those who accept abstinence defend the right of others to choose permissiveness. The legitimation of choice goes along with the trend toward more permissive sexual attitudes.

CONFLICTING VALUES

Some Causes of Permissiveness

Parents are under pressures from their courting children, and they are also responsible for them. Consequently, they are generally less permissive than their children or, for that matter, than they were themselves as adolescents. They exert their strongest influence in the values they pass on to their children during their early years, and in many cases these values are unintentionally permissive. This re-

---

[8] *Sex and the College Student* (New York: Atheneum, 1966), a widely read publication with psychoanalytic leanings but with much practical advice for the college administrator.

sult is to be expected because parents themselves were quite permissive when in the courtship role and thus they tend to stress such things as pleasure, autonomy, and psychic satisfaction—all congruent with permissiveness. It is estimated that a few hundred thousand girls each year are pregnant when they marry; a similar number of single women undergo illegal abortions each year, and an equal number become unwed mothers. Venereal diseases also involve hundreds of thousands of young people. (Anderson, Gebhard, and Vincent[9] offer specific and relevant data and discussion of these problems.) Parents are naturally concerned lest their offspring become part of these statistics. However, it should be noted that despite reports in the popular press the venereal disease rate of teenagers is relatively low compared with that of older persons.

The difficulties of doing anything about the consequences of greater permissiveness are apparent. The same parents who decry the consequences favor a free courtship system—a system that encourages permissiveness. Even more paradoxical is the stress parents place on love as the basis for marriage and happiness. Ehrmann's research findings indicate that love is a key factor in promoting sexual intercourse. The more parents stress love, the more likely it is that children will engage in coitus. In short, the causes of our high permissiveness are often activities of which parents approve and are therefore unlikely to alter.

Control of Its Consequences: Contraception

Disseminating contraceptive information would probably reduce the premarital pregnancy rate, yet many people fear that it would encourage permissiveness. One may question this assumption because the available evidence indicates that it is one's basic values and the pressures of a given situation that actually determine whether or not intercourse takes place. Knowledge of effective contraceptive measures may be a minor factor in such a decision, but it would rarely be the determining one. It has been pointed out above that most of the increase in premarital sexual activity occurred before technical advances in contraception became wide-

[9] O. W. Anderson, *Syphilis and Society: Problems of Control in the United States, 1912–1964*, Research Series 22 (Chicago: Center for Health Administration Studies, 1965), gives a good historical account of our effort to control syphilis. The analysis of trends is elementary, but good references are provided. P. H. Gebhard et al., *Pregnancy, Birth, and Abortion* (New York: Harper, 1958), analyzes the Kinsey data and gives some important findings on premarital pregnancies. Gebhard became Director of the Institute of Sex Research at Indiana University when Kinsey died in 1956. C. E. Vincent, in *Unmarried Mothers* (New York: Free Press of Glencoe, 1961), demonstrates the presence of unwed mothers within the middle classes and compares them with other unwed mothers.

spread. Moreover, groups best informed about contraception are not necessarily the most permissive. Boys are not necessarily better informed than girls, Negroes than whites, the lower classes than the upper classes, and yet permissiveness varies considerably among these groups.

Although one may still object for religious or moral reasons to dissemination of such information, rightly or wrongly, there is a rapid increase in the willingness of the federal and state governments and of private groups to provide contraceptive information and, in many cases, contraceptive devices as well. This development does not mean that parents fully accept the new permissiveness. Rather, for some it is a concession made for the sake of prevention of premarital pregnancy and venereal disease.

It should also be clear that premarital pregnancy cannot be controlled by "devices" alone. Attitudes have to change also. Many females will not use a diaphragm or "the pill" because of the implication that they are prepared for coitus all the time. Such women must be emotionally carried away for coitus to occur. Such a negative self-image often blocks the effective use of contraceptive devices. Contraceptive information can lessen the number of unwanted pregnancies, but deeper attitudinal changes regarding the acceptability or non-acceptability of premarital coitus are required to solve the problem.

FUTURE DIRECTIONS
The Societal Setting

The choice of a premarital sexual standard is a personal one, and no amount of facts or trends can "prove" the superiority of one standard to another. Thus the individual is theoretically "free." In reality, broad societal and cultural pressures are difficult to overcome. The courtship system characteristic of twentieth-century America has been developing here since the appearance of the first white man. It utilizes a stress on autonomy of choice that echoes our frontier days and suits the high mobility of today's small families and the equalitarianism of our male-female marital relations. Our religious institutions stress autonomy of choice, as does our political system. The governmental dissemination of contraceptive information and the generally liberal censorship decisions by the Supreme Court show a permissive trend within our political institutions. The churches also seem to be in part more accepting to the views of such men as Bishop James Pike, Harvey Cox, and John Robinson.[10]

[10] See J. A. T. Robinson, *Christian Morals Today* (Philadelphia: Westminster Press, 1964), for a statement of a permissive position by an English bishop.

115

(See also the famous Quaker Committee statement.[11]) The mass media are beginning to present information on unwed mothers and venereal disease. All these institutional structures are responding to the society around them in displaying increased permissiveness.

Sex and Affection

The permissive sexual standards of today are linked with young people's notions about love. Females in particular associate sexuality with stable, affectionate relationships, and males seem increasingly to value the association of sexuality with affection. Our going steady, pinning, and engagement customs all evidence this fact. The trend is toward the acceptance of sexual permissiveness in an affectionate context, i.e., person-centered rather than body-centered.[12] This change can be seen in abstinence with the acceptance of petting when affection is present, in the double standard with acceptance of coitus for females when in love, in the popularity of permissiveness with affection, and in the lack of a widespread following for permissiveness without affection.

The Scandinavian countries have developed even further than we a type of affection-centered premarital sexual permissiveness[13] (see Chapter 11). We seem to be heading toward a Scandinavian type of sexuality, although this statement should be qualified, in that a country of 200 million people can never accept a single sexual standard. Change will be slow, and the old standards will surely not vanish. The four competing sexual codes described above will exist into the foreseeable future. The respectability of abstinence, however, has now been extended, in some degree, to other sexual codes, and it seems that permissiveness with affection will have a larger role to play in courtship in America in generations to come. It is interesting to note in this context that many Scandinavians view American women as more promiscuous than they. They feel that the American female defines "sex" in terms of coitus alone and therefore pets intimately with many boys while remaining a virgin. The Scandinavian female is less casual about petting, but when her affections are involved, she is more likely to have coitus.

Although this paper discusses the middle class in America, the reader should be aware that this class is diverse and that there are

---

[11] See A. Heron, ed., *Towards a Quaker View of Sex* (London: Friends Home Service Committee, 1963), the report of a committee of English Quakers that created quite a stir when first issued. It takes a permissive religious position.

[12] See R. R. Bell, *Premarital Sex in a Changing Society* (Englewood Cliffs, N.J.: Prentice-Hall, 1966), for an analysis of our sexual standards with emphasis on the role of society.

[13] See Ellis and Abarbanel, eds., *The Encyclopedia of Sexual Behavior.*

groups of young middle-class Americans in which most girls and perhaps a large proportion of boys will continue to accept abstinence. There are smaller groups in which the vast majority of both sexes will accept permissiveness without affection. Abstinent people will stress the importance of saving coitus for marriage, and permissive people will emphasize its physical and psychic rewards. The point being made here is that the new middle class in our country has, on the average, gone in a more permissive direction. This is not a sudden change—it is not a revolution. It is, rather, a gradual evolution of a courtship system that reflects our society. It is a broadening of our image of masculinity and femininity. The topic of the development of masculinity and femininity requires detailed treatment and cannot be discussed here.

Young people stress the "rational" examination of the consequences of permissiveness. If one wishes to examine the consequences of adherence to a sexual standard, one is confronted by the fact that they depend upon the person involved and his situation. Christensen and Carpenter[14] have shown that the consequences of coitus in Denmark, Indiana, and Utah differ considerably (see also Chapter 11). Such findings encourage young people to tolerate standards other than their own. One may object to this tolerance because of the belief that one sexual standard is correct for all, regardless of its consequences, but such a position encounters opposition among many young people today. Those in authority who accept one sexual standard as correct for all must proceed softly if they wish to gain adherents among them.

SUMMARY

Sexual attitudes and behavior today are more open than ever before. (For more specific information on how various social groups differ from each other, see my most recent national study.) Realistically speaking, one can expect the gradual growth in permissiveness to continue. Now that our sexual attitudes and behavior have moved closer together, we may well witness a more rapid increase in permissive sexual behavior and/or attitudes. Organizations like the Sex Information and Education Council of the United States are aware of this extensive cultural change and know that our current knowledge about sex, though increasing, is still limited and that it is important to comprehend our sexual customs more thoroughly. Our sexuality is not an isolated aspect of ourselves but is a reflection of

[14] H. T. Christensen and G. R. Carpenter, "Value-Behavior Discrepancies regarding Premarital Coitus," *American Sociological Review*, 27 (1962):66–74. This is an important comparison of college students in Denmark, Indiana, and Utah.

the kind of people we are and the kind of society in which we live. Whether or not one approves of the direction in which we are moving, one may well want to gain a clearer picture of the nature of our system.

8   Sex and Interpersonal Relationships

Lester A. Kirkendall and Roger W. Libby

Kirkendall and Libby discuss in greater detail the standard which Reiss has shown to be emerging and show the significance of the quality of the interpersonal relationship in sexual matters.

Many influential people are moving toward the belief that sexual morality must be regarded in terms of relationships rather than in terms of a fixed code of sexual behavior. This view is held even by liberal religious leaders, who argue that the first consideration in sexual morality must be genuinely responsible sexual conduct guided by a sincere regard for the rights of others. In other words, the shift is from emphasis upon an act to emphasis upon the quality of the relationship surrounding it.

If an increasing concern for sex as an interpersonal relationship is important to the sexual renaissance, and we think it is, then clearly we must know how sexual functioning interacts with human relationships. An extensive psychological literature has been developed to explain individual functioning; individual differences, individual growth patterns, individual cognitive development have all been explored. But relatively little is known about "relationships" as such—their components and what causes them to flourish or to wither and die, and there is a need to develop a field of psychological research devoted to them. As a psychology and sociology of relationships is developed and research findings provide a tested body of content for teaching, parents and educators may take a new stance: they may become less concerned with interdicting sexual expression of any kind and more concerned with developing an understanding of those factors which facilitate or impede the development of interpersonal relationships.

It is only within the last few years that research has been done on the interpersonal aspects of sexual adjustment. That this is a fruitful area for study is already evident from some of the recent results. One generalization can be made from the findings at this point: a sexual relationship is an interpersonal relationship, and, like other interpersonal relationships, is affected by social, psychological, physiological, and cultural forces. The effort to remove sex from the context of ordinary living, so characteristic of our culture, obscures this simple but important generalization.

THE EFFECT OF AFFECTION ON SEXUAL BEHAVIOR

W. W. Ehrmann[1] examined the association of premarital sexual behavior and interpersonal relationships. He studied the progression of individuals through increasingly intense stages of intimacy as they moved toward or rejected premarital intercourse, the attitudes with which acquaintances, friends, and lovers regard sexual intimacy, the controls exercised, and other factors which help develop certain feelings and attitudes in interpersonal relationships.

In discussing the differences in male-female attitudes which are found as affectional ties deepen, Ehrmann writes:

males are more conservative and . . . females are more liberal in expressed personal codes of sex conduct and in actual behavior with lovers than with non-lovers. In other words, the degree of physical intimacy actually experienced or considered permissible is among males *inversely* related and among females *directly* related to the intensity of familiarity and affection in the male-female relation. . . . Female sexual expression is primarily and profoundly related to being in love and going steady. . . . Male sexuality is more indirectly and less exclusively associated with romanticism and intimacy relationships.[2]

Similarly, Michael Schofield, in a study of 1,873 London boys and girls between the ages of fifteen and nineteen, found that "girls prefer a more permanent type of relationship in their sexual behaviour. Boys seem to want the opposite; they prefer diversity and so have more casual partners. . . . there is a direct association between the type of relationship a girl has achieved and the degree of intimacy she will permit."[3]

One of the present authors conducted a study[4] which centered upon an examination of the association which was believed to exist between interpersonal relationships and premarital intercourse. Three components of an interpersonal relationship were posited—motivation, communication, and attitudes toward responsibility—and the impact of premarital intercourse on them was analyzed. A group of 200 college-level males reported sexual liaisons with 668 females. These liaisons were arranged along a continuum of affectional involvement. The continuum was divided into six segments or levels which ranged from prostitutes, where affection was rejected as a part of the relationship, to fiancées, a level involving deep affection.

[1] W. W. Ehrmann, *Premarital Dating Behavior* (New York: Henry Holt, 1959).

[2] *Ibid.,* p. 269.

[3] M. Schofield, *The Sexual Behavior of Young People* (London: Longmans, Green, 1965), p. 92.

[4] L. A. Kirkendall, "Characteristics of Sexual Decision-Making," *Journal of Sex Research,* 3 (1967):201–12; Kirkendall, *Premarital Intercourse and Interpersonal Relationships* (New York: Julian Press, 1961).

The changing character of the components was then studied as one moved along the continuum. It was found that communication at the prostitute level had a distinct barter characteristic. At the second (pickup) level there was a testing and teasing type of communication. At the deep affectional and the fiancée level there was much concern for the development of the kind of communication which would result in understanding and insight. Similarly, the apparent character of the motivation central to the sexual relationship changed from one end of the continuum to the other. As depth of emotional involvement increased, the focus changed from a self-centered to a relationship-centered one, and increasing emotional involvement resulted in an increasing readiness to assume the responsibilities involved in the sexual relationship.

The study thus provides clear evidence that the consideration of premarital intercourse in crude terms—equating intercourse with a prostitute with intercourse with a fiancée—submerged many nuances and shades of meaning. Until these interpersonal differentiations are taken into account, there is little chance of any realistic or meaningful understanding of the character of premarital intercourse.

THE EFFECT OF SEXUAL INTERCOURSE UPON AFFECTION

E. W. Burgess and P. Wallin have explored the possibility that premarital intercourse may strengthen the relationship of engaged couples who engaged in it. They asked eighty-one men and seventy-four women who reported having had premarital intercourse whether they felt the experience had strengthened or weakened their relationship. Some 92.6 per cent of the men and 90.6 per cent of the women attributed a strengthening effect to intercourse, and only 1.2 per cent of the men and 5.4 per cent of the women considered intercourse to have a weakening effect. The remainder noted no change either way. Burgess and Wallin comment:

This finding could be construed as testimony for the beneficial consequences of premarital relations, but with some reservations. First, couples who refrained from having premarital intercourse were not asked whether not doing so strengthened or weakened their relationship. They might have reported unanimously that their relationship had been strengthened by their restraint.

Such a finding could be interpreted as signifying one of two things: (a) that both groups are rationalizing or (b) that given the characteristics, expectations, and standards of those who have intercourse, the experience strengthens their relationships, and, similarly, that given the standards of the continent couples the cooperative effort of couple members to refrain from sex relations strengthens their union.[5]

[5] *Engagement and Marriage* (Philadelphia: Lippincott, 1953), pp. 371–72.

Premarital Intercourse and Interpersonal Relationships analyzes the data and presents a reinterpretation of the findings of Burgess and Wallin, and a more complex interplay than simply a reciprocating association between sexual experience and the strengthening or weakening of a relationship is suggested:

Some deeply affectionate couples have, through the investment of time and mutual devotion, built a relationship which is significant to them, and in which they have developed a mutual respect. Some of these couples are relatively free from the customary inhibitions about sexual participation. Some couples with this kind of relationship and background can, and do, experience intercourse without damage to their total relationship. The expression "without damage" is used in preference to "strengthening" for it seems that in practically all instances "non-damaging" intercourse occurred in relationships which were already so strong in their own right that intercourse did not have much to offer toward strengthening them.[6]

THE INFLUENCE OF INTERPERSONAL RELATIONS IN SEXUAL BEHAVIOR

Several studies have linked sexual behavior at the adolescent or young adult level with presumed causes in childhood, particularly some sort of deprivation, usually of affection. This view, of course, will be nothing new to those familiar with psychiatric literature. An interesting study which demonstrates this linkage is reported by Harold Greenwald. Greenwald studied twenty call girls, prostitutes ministering to a well-to-do clientele. He found that "many of the tendencies which lead to the choice of the call girl profession appear early in youth." The childhoods of these girls appeared to be lacking in genuine love or tenderness. "The fundamental preventive task, then, becomes strengthening the family as a source of love and growth."[7] A. Ellis and E. Sagarin, in their study of nymphomania,[8] also suggest that it has its roots in inadequate childhood relationships.

In studies made at the San Francisco Psychiatric Clinic, E. G. Lion[9] and B. Safir[10] found that promiscuity was related to personality deficiencies, and that these in turn were related to homes characterized by disorganization, weak or broken emotional ties, and lack of loyalties or identification with any person or group. If a tie of this

[6] *Premarital Intercourse and Interpersonal Relationships*, pp. 199–200.

[7] *The Call Girl* (New York: Ballantine Books, 1958), p. 182.

[8] *Nymphomania* (New York: Julian Messner, 1964).

[9] E. G. Lion et al., *An Experiment in the Psychiatric Treatment of Promiscuous Girls* (San Francisco: City and County of San Francisco Department of Public Health, 1945).

[10] *A Psychiatric Approach to the Treatment of Promiscuity* (New York: American Sociological Hygiene Association, 1949).

kind does exist, it would seem logical that increased ability to develop personal relationships (arising, for example, through therapy) should result in some change in the sexual pattern. Support for this view comes from B. Berelson and G. A. Steiner. In their inventory of scientific findings concerning human behavior, they say that "changes toward a more positive attitude regarding sexual activity and toward freer, more enjoyable sexual activity than the patient was previously capable of having, are reported as correlates of psychotherapy from several camps."[11]

S. R. Graham obtained information on the frequency and degree of satisfaction in coitus from 65 married men and women before they began psychotherapy and compared the data from these couples with similar information from 142 married men and women who had been in treatment for varying periods of time. The results indicated, with certain reservations, that psychotherapy did free individuals for "more frequent and more satisfactory coitus experience."[12]

Let us look at the logic of this conclusion from another angle. If disorganized and aberrant sexual patterns are most frequent among adolescents or young adults who have experienced some form of emotional deprivation in childhood, it seems reasonable to hypothesize that those who experienced normal emotional satisfactions should be more conventional in their sexual practices. Since most studies deal with persons who are recognized as problems, this possibility is not well documented, but there is some evidence to support this view.

M. B. Loeb, in a study of junior and senior high school students, attempted to differentiate between those who do and those who do not participate in premarital intercourse. He advanced these conclusions:

First, teenagers who trust themselves and their ability to contribute to others and have learned to rely on others socially and emotionally are least likely to be involved in irresponsible sexual activity. Second, teenagers who have learned to be comfortable in their appropriate sex roles (boys who like being boys and wish to be men, and girls who like being girls and wish to be women) are least likely to be involved in activities leading to indiscriminate sexuality.[13]

[11] B. Berelson and G. A. Steiner, *Human Behavior* (New York: Harcourt, Brace and World, 1964), p. 290.

[12] "The Effects of Psychoanalytically Oriented Psychotherapy on Levels of Frequency and Satisfaction in Sexual Activity," *Journal of Clinical Psychology*, 16 (1960):95.

[13] "Social Role and Sexual Identity in Adolescent Males," *Casework Papers* (New York: National Association of Social Workers, 1959).

In his analysis of British teenagers Schofield found that "girls who got on very well with their fathers were far less likely to be sexually experienced," that "boys who did not get on well with their mothers were more likely to be sexually experienced," and that "girls who got on well with their mothers were less likely to be sexually experienced."[14] Both these studies point to a greater degree of sexual restraint, and probably of sexual responsibility, in children whose early affectional relationships have been satisfying.

SEXUAL BEHAVIOR PATTERNS AND DEVELOPMENTAL LEVELS

Maturity and developmental levels represent still other factors. C. B. Broderick has made some interesting studies on the appearance and progressive development of various sexual manifestations.[15] In a study of children in a suburban community he found that for many of them interest in the opposite sex begins in kindergarten or before. Kissing "which means something special" is found among boys and girls as early as the third and fourth grades. In some communities dating begins for a substantial number of children in the fifth and sixth grades, while "going steady" is common at the junior high school level.

The level of maturity at which such experiences are encountered apparently has some importance. Schofield found, for example, that "Those who start dating, kissing, and inceptive behavior at an early age are also more likely to have early sexual intercourse."[16] Level of maturity has consequences even for the sexual experience of adults, according to A. Maslow. In his study of self-actualized people he makes several comments about the character of sexual functioning and sexual satisfaction in people who are considerably above the average so far as emotional health is concerned. He says: "sex and love can be and most often are very perfectly fused with each other in (emotionally) healthy people"; "self-actualizing men and women tend on the whole not to seek sex for its own sake, or to be satisfied with it alone when it comes"; "sexual pleasures are found in their most intense and ecstatic perfection in self-actualizing people." Maslow goes on to say: "These people do not need sensuality; they simple enjoy it when it occurs."[17]

Maturity in this context is closely allied to interpersonal compe-

---

[14] *The Sexual Behavior of Young People*, p. 144.

[15] "Socio-Sexual Development in a Suburban Community," *Journal of Sex Research*, 2 (1966):1–24; Broderick and S. E. Fowler, "New Patterns of Relationships between the Sexes among Preadolescents," *Marriage and Family Living*, 23 (1961): 27–30.

[16] *Ibid.*, p. 73.

[17] *Motivation and Personality* (New York: Harper, 1954), pp. 241–43.

tence and the capacity for closeness, and these studies further underscore the significance of the quality of the interpersonal relationship in determining the quality of the sexual relationship.

FUTURE RESEARCH

The theme of this chapter has been that a concern for interpersonal relationships as the central issue in the management of sexuality is displacing the traditional emphasis on the avoidance or renunciation of all non-marital sexual experience. Social scientists who wish to understand this shift should be aware of four key requirements.

1. *It will be necessary to commit ourselves fully to the study of relationships rather than simply reflecting on them occasionally.* In the area of sex, there has been overconcern with the physical act. The senior author of this chapter, while doing the research for his book *Premarital Intercourse and Interpersonal Relationships,* became aware that he was giving undue attention to the act of premarital intercourse, even while he was trying to set it in the context of the interpersonal relationship. As a consequence, crucial data were ignored. For example, in selecting subjects, if one person had engaged in much caressing and petting but had renounced the opportunity for intercourse many times, while another person had merely gone through the physical act a single time, the latter was defined as a subject for the research and the first was bypassed.

With this realization came the determination to examine the decisions made by individuals concerning sexual behavior regardless of whether they had had intercourse. The result is a recently completed preliminary study in which 131 non-randomly-selected males were interviewed.[18] Of this group 72 (55 per cent) had not had intercourse, but apparently only 17 (13 per cent) had never been in a situation which required a decision about it. Of these last, 11 had made a firm theoretical decision against intercourse, leaving only 6 who had never faced the issue in fact or in theory. In other words, when one considers sexual decision-making as an aspect of interpersonal relationships rather than focusing on whether or not the act of intercourse has occurred, one greatly increases the number of potential subjects and the range of interpersonal behavior available for study.

We offer one further illustration of the reorientation in thinking necessary as we come to accept a concern for relationships as the central issue. The view which emphasizes the quality of interper-

[18] L. A. Kirkendall, "Characteristics of Sexual Decision-Making," *Journal of Sex Research,* 3 (1967):201–12.

sonal relationships as of foremost concern is often labeled "very permissive" when sex standards and behavior are under discussion. This conclusion is possible when the sole concern is whether the commission of a sexual act is or is not acceptable. Certainly the emphasis on interpersonal relationships diverts attention from the act to its consequences, but once in this position, one finds oneself in a situation which is anything but permissive. The outcome of relationships seems to be governed by principles which are unvarying and which cannot be repealed. The fiats of parents or the edicts of deans can be tempered, but there is no averting the consequences to a relationship of dishonesty, lack of self-discipline, and lack of respect for the rights of others. If one wishes warm, accepting interpersonal relationships with others, these practices are self-defeating, and no one, regardless of his position of authority, can alter this fact. Proclamations and injunctions will be of no avail. There is no permissiveness here!

2. *Conceptual definitions will have to be developed.* Several social scientists have begun work on this. N. N. Foote and L. S. Cottrell,[19] for example, have identified six components of interpersonal competence: health, intelligence, sympathy, judgment, creativity, and autonomy. W. C. Schultz[20] has developed the FIRO test to measure interpersonal behavior in terms of three interpersonal needs: the need for inclusion, for control, and for affection. Another study that was cited[21] centered around three factors: motivation, communication, and readiness to assume responsibility. Communication and motivation have both been frequently recognized aspects of interpersonal relationships.

However, the conceptualization of relationships in a manner which will permit effective research is still at an embryonic level. Many factors in relationships (for there are undoubtedly many) have still to be determined, and instruments for their measurement must be developed and perfected. Interpersonal relationships as a field of psychological study should be developing concurrently, for only in this way can we broaden our horizons.

3. *Methods and procedures will have to be devised.* The perceptive reader will have noted that while studies have been cited which, in our estimation, bore on interpersonal relationships, all of them except that of Burgess and Wallin[22] obtained their information on

---

[19] *Identity and Interpersonal Competence* (Chicago: University of Chicago Press, 1955).

[20] W. C. Schultz, *FIRO: A Three-Dimensional Theory of Interpersonal Behavior* (New York: Rinehart, 1958).

[21] Kirkendall, *Premarital Intercourse and Interpersonal Relationships.*

[22] *Engagement and Marriage.*

interpersonal relationships by using individuals rather than pairs or groups as subjects. Would we not get a different view of premarital intercourse if we could interview both partners to the experience rather than one? Methods of dealing with couples and groups and procedures which can zero in on that subtle, intangible, yet real tie which binds two or more people are needed. Some such work has already been done, but it has not been applied to sex and interpersonal relationships.

4. *The most important problems will have to be isolated.* Opinions will naturally differ as to what these problems are. We would suggest, however, that since sex relationships *are* interpersonal relationships, the whole field of interpersonal relationships, with sex as an integral part, is appropriate for study.

One of us (Kirkendall) has scattered suggestions for further research throughout his book, mentioned above. Such problems as the importance of time spent and emotional involvement in a relationship as a factor in determining whether a relationship can sustain intercourse, the factors which produce "loss of respect" when sexual involvement occurs, the meaning to a relationship of sexual non-involvement, factors which impede or facilitate sexual communication, and knowledge of various kinds of success or failure in sexual relationships should be examined. How do the emotional involvements of males and females engaged in a sexual relationship differ, and how do they change as the relationship becomes more (or less) intense? How nearly alike, or how diverse, are the perceptions which males and females hold of the total relationship and of its sexual component at various stages in its development? How does the rejection of a proffered sexual relationship by either partner affect the one who extended the offer? What is the reaction of the person receiving it, and what produced it? If there are no sexual overtures to the relationship, how does this affect it?

Which value systems make it most (and least) possible for a couple to communicate about sex? To adjust to the tensions which may accompany intercourse or its cessation? Which enable a couple to cope most effectively with the possible trauma of having their relationship become public knowledge, or of pregnancy?

In what diverse ways do premarital sexual experiences affect marital adjustments? What enables some couples who have been premarital sexual partners to separate as friends, while others are bitter and hostile? What relation has maturity in other aspects of life to maturity in assessing the meaning of and coping with sexual overtures of various kinds in the premarital period? The questions could go on endlessly, yet the selection of important areas for research remains one of the important tasks before us.

9

Sex in the Culture of Poverty

Lee Rainwater

Quantitative data from the Kinsey report and other studies have shown that it is a mistake to assume that sexual values and practices are alike in all social groups. Rainwater reports an attempt to pinpoint qualitative as well as quantitative differences between groups. We do not yet know how universal these patterns are, but awareness of them is clearly a necessity.

An article dealing with lower-class sexual behavior might be expected to picture a group of happy, godforsaken sinners whose sexual gratification is far greater than that of middle-class respectables.[1] However, what little empirical research there is on lower-class sexual behavior—and, more important, on subjective responses to sex in the lower class—tends to present quite a different view.[2] Because we have most comparative information on sexual relations

---

[1] John Dollard has analyzed some of the attitudes that white Southerners have toward Negroes, attitudes which compound both the positive and negative views of lower-class naturalness (*Caste and Class in a Southern Town* [New Haven, Conn.: Yale University Press, 1937]). In his analysis he perhaps took somewhat too seriously the notion that lower-class Negroes gain from the greater sexual freedom allowed them by the caste system. Allison Davis, an insufficiently appreciated pioneer in the study of lower-class cultures, seems to have also been taken in by the myth: "In the slum, one certainly does not have a sexual partner for as many days each month as do middle class married people, but one gets and gives more satisfaction over longer periods, when he does have a sexual partner" (*Social Class Influence on Learning* [Cambridge, Mass.: Harvard University Press, 1952], p. 33).

[2] The shift from the happy impulse-free version of lower-class sexual life to a more jaundiced view is paralleled by a similar shift in the understanding of lower-class delinquency. David J. Bordua, in comparing the work of Frederick Thrasher in the 1920's with that of Walter Miller, Albert Cohen, Richard Cloward, and Lloyd Ohlin, comments:
All in all, though, it does not seem like much fun any more to be a gang delinquent. Thrasher's boys enjoyed themselves being chased by the police, shooting dice, skipping school, rolling drunks. It was fun. Miller's boys do have a little fun, with their excitement focal concern, but it seems so desperate somehow. Cohen's boys and Cloward and Ohlin's boys are driven by grim economic and psychic necessity into rebellion. It seems peculiar that modern analysts have stopped assuming that "evil" can be fun and see gang delinquency as arising only when boys are driven away from "good" ("Delinquent Subcultures: Sociological Interpretations of Gang Delinquency," *The Annals of the American Academy of Political and Social Sciences*, 338 [1961]:136).

within marriage for lower-, working-, and middle-class couples, we will begin by discussing sex within the context of marriage.

LOWER-, WORKING-, AND MIDDLE-CLASS SEXUALITY
Marital Sexuality

Within all classes marital sexual relations provide the major sexual outlet for most men and women during their sexual careers and are considered most preferable and desirable. Other outlets are usually seen by participants as compensations or substitutes rather than as preferable alternatives. I shall start, then, with a comparison of the way in which husbands and wives in the lower, working, and middle classes evaluate marital sexuality.

The material which follows is drawn from my larger study[3] of marital sexuality as part of the context for decisions on family size. The study was based on interviews with 409 individuals—152 couples and 50 men and 55 women not married to each other. Thus 257 families were represented. The respondents were drawn from Chicago, Cincinnati, and Oklahoma City and were chosen from upper-middle- to lower-lower-class whites and upper-lower- and lower-lower-class Negroes. They were asked to discuss their feelings about their sexual relations in marriage, the gratifications and the dissatisfactions they had, the meaning of sex in their marriage, and the importance it had to them and to their spouses.

Emerging from the answers to these questions is a continuum of enjoyment of sexual relations that ranges from very great to strong rejection. The complete range is most marked among women, of course. Men only rarely say that they are indifferent to or uninterested in sexual relations, but women present the whole gamut of responses from "if God made anything better, He kept it to Himself" to "I would be happy if I never had to do that again; it's disgusting." On the basis of each individual's response to the questions, he was classified as having either great or mild interest and enjoyment in sex, having slightly negative feelings about sex, or as rejecting sexual relations. Table 1 presents the results of this classification. (Because there were no differences between the upper and lower portions of the middle class, they were combined in the tables.)

It is apparent that as one moves from higher to lower social status the proportion of men and women who show strong interest and enjoyment declines. The proportion of men showing only mild

[3] See *And the Poor Get Children* (Chicago: Quadrangle Books, 1960), and *Family Design: Marital Sexuality, Family Planning and Family Limitation* (Chicago: Aldine Publishing Co., 1965).

TABLE 1: Attitudes toward Marital Sexual Relations, by Social Class

Attitude	Social Class		
	Middle	Upper-Lower	Lower-Lower
Husbands			
Highly positive	78%	75%	44%
Mildly positive	22%	25%	56%
No. of cases	56	56	59
Wives			
Highly positive	50%	53%	20%
Mildly positive	36%	16%	26%
Slightly negative	11%	27%	34%
Totally negative	3%	4%	20%
No. of cases	58	68	69

interest and enjoyment increases as one moves to the lower-lower-class level, while the proportion of women who are slightly negative or rejecting in their attitude increases steadily as one moves from the middle class to the upper-lower to the lower-lower. (There is a small but consistent tendency for Negroes in the lower-lower class to show somewhat more interest in sex than similarly situated whites[4]).

It would seem, then, that social class is closely related to one's marital view of sexual relations as a valued and meaningful activity. This result is consistent with the Kinsey studies,[5] which found that for women erotic arousal from any source is less common at lower educational levels, that fewer such women ever reach orgasm, and that its frequency among those who do is lower. The pattern is less clear-cut for men, as far as frequency goes, but it is apparent that foreplay is less elaborate at lower educational levels, most strikingly with respect to oral techniques. At lower educational levels there is

[4] It should be noted that the careful and detailed study of blue-collar marriages by Mirra Komarovsky (*Blue Collar Marriage* [New York: Random House, 1964]) reports that there were no differences in sexual enjoyment between high- and low-status wives within the working class (status was determined by high school education or lack of it). I have an explanation for this difference in findings between two studies which parallel each other in most other respects, but the reader should be aware of Komarovsky's contrary findings (see especially her pp. 93–94). However, the less educated wives did view sex as more of a duty, and refused less often.

[5] See P. H. Gebhard et al., *Pregnancy, Birth and Abortion* (New York: Harper, 1958); A. C. Kinsey et al., *Sexual Behavior in the Human Male* (Philadelphia: Saunders, 1948), and *Sexual Behavior in the Human Female* (Philadelphia: Saunders, 1953).

somewhat less versatility in positional variations in intercourse, but more interesting is the fact that the difference between lower and higher educational levels increases with age because positional variations among lower-class men are rapidly abandoned, while the decline among more educated men is much slower. This same pattern characterizes nudity in marital coitus.

The higher elaboration of the sexual relationship among middle-class couples which Kinsey's findings suggest is apparent in the qualitative data presented here. The longer the lower-class man is married, the more likely he is to express a reduced interest in and enjoyment of sexual relations with his wife, as well as reduced frequency of intercourse. In the middle class, while reduced frequency is universally recognized, there is much more of a tendency to put this in the context of "the quantity has gone down, but the quality gets better and better." An examination of the very small body of literature dealing with attitudes toward sexual relations in lower-class populations in other countries suggests that this pattern is not confined to the United States.[6]

Having observed that lower-class husbands and wives are less likely than middle-class couples to find sexual relations gratifying, we wonder why. The major variable that controls this class difference seems to be the quality of the conjugal role relationship in the two classes. Middle-class couples were found much more likely to have patterns of jointly organized activities outside the home and joint interests than working- and lower-class couples. Following Bott,[7] couples who showed a fair degree of separateness in their conjugal role relationships were classified as *highly segregated*, those who showed a very strong degree of joint participation and joint involvement in each other's activities as *jointly organized*, and couples who fell between these two extremes as having conjugal role relationships of *intermediate segregation*. Very few working- or lower-class couples showed the jointly organized pattern, but there was variation in the intermediate-to-highly-segregated range. When the influence of this variable on sexual enjoyment and interest was examined, a very strong relationship was found.

Table 2 indicates that it is primarily among couples in highly

---

[6] See O. Lewis, *Life in a Mexican Village: Tepoztlan Restudied* (Urbana, Ill.: University of Illinois Press, 1951); my "Marital Sexuality in Four Cultures of Poverty," *Journal of Marriage and the Family*, 26 (1964):457–66; E. Slater and M. Woodside, *Patterns of Marriage* (London: Cassell, 1951); B. M. Spinley, *The Deprived and the Privileged* (London: Routledge and Kegan Paul, 1953); and J. M. Stycos, *Family and Fertility in Puerto Rico* (New York: Columbia University Press, 1955).

[7] E. Bott, *Family and Social Network* (London: Tavistock, 1957).

TABLE 2: Attitudes toward Marital Sexual Relations among Lower-Class Couples, by Degree of Role Segregation and Race

Attitude	Degree of Role Segregation			
	Intermediate*		High	
	Whites	Negroes	Whites	Negroes
Husbands				
Highly positive	72%	90%	55%	56%
Mildly positive	28%	10%	45%	44%
No. of cases	21	21	20	25
Wives				
Highly positive	64%	64%	18%	8%
Mildly positive	4%	14%	14%	40%
Slightly negative	32%	18%	36%	32%
Totally negative	—	4%	32%	20%
No. of cases	25	22	22	25

* Includes the few jointly organized couples.

segregated conjugal role relationships that wives reject or are somewhat negative toward sexual relations. Similarly, it is primarily among couples in less segregated conjugal role relationships that husbands and wives express great interest and enjoyment in sexual relations. These results suggest that the lower value placed on sexual relations by lower-class wives, and to a lesser extent by lower-class husbands, can be seen as an extension of the high degree of segregation in their general conjugal role relationship. Such couples emphasize separateness in their other activities, therefore separateness comes to be the order of the day in their sexual relationship. Since the wife's interest in sex tends to be heavily dependent upon a sense of interpersonal closeness and gratification in her total relationship with her husband, it is very difficult for her to find gratification in sex in the context of a highly segregated role relationship. A close and gratifying sexual relationship is difficult to achieve because husband and wife are not accustomed to relating intimately to each other.

It may well be that a close sexual relationship serves no particular social function in such a system, since the role performances of husband and wife are organized on a separate basis, and no great contribution is made by a relationship in which they might develop their ability for cooperation and mutual sensitivity. Examination of the six negative cases in our sample—those in which, despite a highly segregated role relationship, the wife enjoyed sex a great deal—indicates that such women were able to bring to the relationship their own highly autonomous interest in sex. To the extent that such wives were dependent upon their husbands for stimulation, encouragement, and understanding, they seemed to be dissatisfied.

Husbands whose wives do not enjoy sexual relations are not particularly comfortable about this fact and either express some guilt or try in various ways to conceal the state of affairs from both themselves and the interviewers. However, they seem to make few attempts to correct the situation; in fact, half the men in highly segregated relationships overestimated their wives' enjoyment of sex, as compared with only 21 per cent of men in less segregated relationships. Lower-class men in highly segregated relationships seemed to make few efforts to assist their wives in achieving sexual gratification and placed little emphasis on the importance of mutual gratification in coitus. While 74 per cent of the lower- and working-class husbands with intermediate relationships gave some spontaneous indication that they valued mutual gratification in the sexual relationship, only 35 per cent of husbands in segregated relationships spoke of mutual gratification. It is not surprising, then, that 40 per cent of wives in segregated relationships spontaneously indicated that their husbands were inconsiderate of them in sexual relations, compared with 7 per cent of wives in intermediate relationships. Similarly, 38 per cent of wives in highly segregated relationships spontaneously indicated that they considered sex primarily as a duty, compared with 14 per cent of wives in intermediate relationships.

These differences among classes, and within the lower class between couples in intermediate and highly segregated role relationships, continue to appear when the focus of inquiry is shifted from degree of enjoyment of sexual relations to the question of the psychosocial functions which people think sex serves for them. Two common themes stand out when couples talk about what sex "does" for men and women. One is that sex provides "psychophysiological" relief—it gets rid of tensions, relaxes, and provides sensual pleasure in the form of orgasm. The other emphasis is on the emotional gratification that comes from closeness with one's partner, a growth of love, a sense of oneness, of sharing, of giving and receiving. Almost all of the respondents who mentioned the second function also mentioned the physical aspect, but varied quite widely in mentioning it alone or in combination with emotional closeness. Table 3 provides distributions of the emphasis on these two themes by class and role relationship.

TABLE 3: Attitudes toward the Function of Marital Sexual Relations, by Social Class

Function	Middle Class	Lower Class	
		Intermediate Role Segregation	High Role Segregation
Husbands			
Emotional closeness and exchange	75%	52%	16%
Psychophysiological pleasure and relief only	25%	48%	84%
No. of cases	56	40	21
Wives			
Emotional closeness and exchange	89%	73%	32%
Psychophysiological pleasure and relief only	11%	27%	68%
No. of cases	46	33	22

Premarital Sexuality

Although we know less about lower-class non-marital sexual relations than about marital sexual relations, a fair amount of data on the relationship of non-marital sexual relations to social status (educational level) was gathered by Kinsey. The considerable literature dealing with lower-class adolescent peer groups also provides some insight into the place of premarital sexual relations in the activities of young lower-class boys and girls.

The Kinsey studies of white males and females show that before the age of twenty both lower-class boys and lower-class girls are much more likely to have premarital coitus than are middle-class boys and girls. However, even lower-class girls are not as likely to have premarital sexual relations as are middle-class boys: the cultural double standard seems to operate at all class levels. Further, above the age of twenty, status seems to influence premarital coitus in opposite ways for men and women: middle-class girls are more likely than lower-class girls to have premarital relations, perhaps because lower-class girls are so quickly drawn off into marriage, while lower-class boys continue to have premarital relations.

From the Kinsey studies, we know that there are very great differences in the extent to which white and Negro females engage in premarital coitus. While the social class influence is the same in both groups, in the teens the number who have had premarital coitus is on the order of three to four times higher for Negro girls than for white girls. Thus, while at age twenty only 26 per cent of white grammar-school-educated girls have had premarital sexual relationships, over 80 per cent of Negro girls of comparable age and education have.

These findings are consistent with the literature which deals with the peer group systems of white and Negro lower-class adolescents and young adults.[8] In the white lower class there is a great deal of emphasis on the double standard. White lower-class boys are expected to engage in sexual relations whenever they have an opportunity and pride themselves on their ability to have intercourse with many different girls. A reputation for "making out" is valuable currency within the boys' peer groups; there is much bragging and competition (leading to not a little exaggeration) about their sexual conquests.

The girls' position in this group is a much more complex one. White lower-class groups tend to grade girls rather precisely according to their promiscuity, with virgins highly valued and often protected, "one-man girls" retaining some respect from those around them (particularly if in the end they marry the boy with whom they have had intercourse), and more promiscuous girls quickly put into the category of the "easy lay." In groups, then, although boys are constantly encouraged to engage in sexual relations, efforts are made to protect girls from sexual stimulation and even to conceal from them elementary facts about sex and about their future sexual roles. Mothers do not discuss sex with their daughters, usually not even menstruation. The daughter is left very much on her own with only emergency attention from the mother—for example, if she is unable to cope with the trauma of the onset of menses or seems to be getting too involved with boys. When women at this level assess their own premarital knowledge of sex, they generally say that they were completely unprepared for sexual relations, either marital or premarital, that no one had ever told them much about sex, and

[8] H. R. Cayton and St. C. Drake, *Black Metropolis* (New York: Harper and Row, 1962); K. Clark, *Dark Ghetto* (New York: Harper and Row, 1965); E. F. Frazier, *The Negro Family in the United States* (Chicago: University of Chicago Press, 1939); A. W. Green, "The Cult of Personality and Sexual Relations," *Psychiatry*, 4 (1941):343–44; B. Hammond, "The Contest System: A Survival Technique," mimeographed (Master's Honors Essay Series, Social Science Institute, Washington University, St. Louis, 1966); my "Marital Sexuality in Four Cultures of Poverty," and "The Crucible of Identity: The Negro Lower Class Family," *Daedalus*, 95 (1966): 172–216; J. F. Short and F. L. Strodbeck, *Group Process and Gang Delinquency* (Chicago: University of Chicago Press, 1965); and W. F. Whyte, "A Slum Sex Code," *American Journal of Sociology*, 49 (1943):24–31.

that they had only a vague idea of what was involved. There is little evidence that in this kind of white lower class subculture girls find the idea of sexual relations attractive. Although they may have fantasies of romantic love, they seem to show little interest in sexual intercourse specifically.

In the Negro lower class these clear-cut differences between the amount of sexual activity permitted girls and boys (and men and women) are absent. Indeed, at age fifteen, according to the Kinsey results, more grammar-school-educated Negro girls have experienced coitus than have white boys of the same age; this relationship continues at the high school level. With over 60 per cent of grammar-school-educated Negro girls having had intercourse by the age of fifteen and over 80 per cent by the age of twenty, it seems clear that within the Negro slum community, whatever the attitudes involved, lower-class Negro girls are introduced to sexual relations early and engage in them much more frequently than white girls once they have started. There are well-established patterns of seduction within Negro slum communities which Negro boys employ. They are sharply judged by other boys and girls on their ability to employ these techniques, and boys show considerable anxiety lest they be rated low on these skills. As is well known, this high degree of sexual activity leads to a high rate of illegitimate births.

These bald statistics might lead one to believe that among lower-class Negroes there is a happy acceptance of pre-marital sexual relations, somewhat along the line of the natural man myth mentioned at the beginning of this chapter. However, close observation of peer group activities of late adolescent and early adult Negro males and females indicates that such is not the case.[9] In the first place, attitudes toward sexual relations are highly competitive (among sex peers) and heavily exploitative (of opposite sex). Slum Negro boys typically refer to girls, including their own girl friends, as "that bitch" or "that whore" when they talk among themselves. Often Negro girls who do engage in sexual relations in response to the strong "lines" of the boys who "rap it to" them do not seem to find any particular gratification in sexual relations, but rather engage in sex as a test and as a symbol of their maturity and their ability to be "with it." Over time, a certain proportion of these girls do engage in sexual relations out of desire as well as for extrinsic reasons. However, it seems clear that the competitive and exploitative attitudes on both sides make sexual gratification an uncertain matter.

In discussing marital sexuality, it was noted that a high degree of conjugal role segregation seems to interfere with achieving maximum gratification. A parallel factor seems to operate in connection

[9] See Clark, *Dark Ghetto*, and Hammond, "The Contest System."

with premarital relations. Because of the culturally defined and interpersonally sustained hostilities that exist between the sexes, it seems difficult for both boys and girls to develop a self-assured and open acceptance of sex for pleasure, much less for the heightened sense of closeness it can provide. When one seeks to study the meaning and function of sexual relations in such a complex situation as the Negro lower-class community, one becomes aware of how much more subtle and ramified the issues are than the traditional categories of sex research would indicate.

THE SEXUAL RENAISSANCE IN THE LOWER CLASS

As the working class has attained greater prosperity and a sense of greater economic stability since World War II, there seems to have been a shift from the traditional working-class pattern of a high degree of conjugal role segregation and reliance by husbands and wives on peer groups of their own sex for emotional support and counsel. Elsewhere Handel and Rainwater and Komarovsky[10] have discussed the appearance of a modern working-class life style among those families who are in a position to partake of the "standard package" of material and social amenities which represent the "good life" for the ordinary American. We have seen that among couples with the least conjugal role segregation there is the greatest probability of a strong interest in sexual relations and an emphasis on sex as an extension of the emotional closeness that is valued in the husband-wife relationship. We can predict, then, that a movement in the direction of greater cooperation and solidarity based on an interpenetration of conjugal roles will carry with it greater sexual cooperation. This increased closeness is both an expression of and functional for the new, self-sufficient nuclear family, in which working-class husband and wife now rely less on outsiders and primary groups for support and more on each other. In this sense a "good" sexual relation between husband and wife can be seen as one of the major strengths of this adaptable nuclear family, which Clark Vincent has argued is necessary in our industrial society.[11]

But what of those members of the lower class who are not participating in the prosperity and security which the great majority of the working class has known for the past twenty years? In recent years there has been mounting evidence that sex-related pathologies of

[10] G. Handel and L. Rainwater, "Persistence and Change in Working Class Life Style," in *Blue Collar Worlds*, ed. A. B. Shostak and W. Gomberg (Englewood Cliffs, N.J.: Prentice-Hall, 1964), pp. 36–42; Komarovsky, *Blue Collar Marriage*.

[11] "Familia Spongia: The Adaptive Function," *Journal of Marriage and the Family*, 28 (1966):29–36.

the Negro ghetto—for example, illegitimate births, venereal disease, and drug-encouraged prostitution—are increasing rather than decreasing.[12] It seems clear that so long as the socioeconomic circumstances of slum Negroes do not improve, we can expect only a worsening of a situation in which sex is used for exploitative and competitive purposes. There is much less evidence concerning white slum groups; it may well be that the rates for sex-related pathologies increase less because the white poor are not confined to ghettos which serve to concentrate the destructive effects of poverty, but instead tend to be more widely dispersed in the interstices of more stable working-class neighborhoods.[13] In short, though there is some evidence to support the notion of a "sexual renaissance" in marital sexuality in the modern working class, we see no such evidence in the less prosperous lower class.

PARADIGMS FOR FUTURE
RESEARCH ON LOWER-CLASS SEXUAL BEHAVIOR

It is probably fair to say that the scientific study of sexual behavior has been plagued by an obsessive preoccupation with the larger public dialogue on the subject and the value conflicts and contradictions evident in that dialogue. Researchers have often focused on the determination of whether sex under particular circumstances is good or bad, or whether particular customs interfere with pleasure or are conducive to it. While these are legitimate concerns, they have tended to distract social scientists from an effort simply to understand sexual practices in their full human context. It has been suggested here that a close examination of lower-class sexual behavior tends to disprove certain stereotypes that are widely held and are not unknown among social scientists themselves. But more important, lower-class sexual behavior must be understood both in the immediate context of relevant interpersonal relations (marital, peer group, etc.) and in terms of the position of the actors within a marital and social structure and the stresses and strains of that position. Such an understanding can only come about through careful empirical research which does not take for granted supposed "facts" but examines these interrelations empirically.

Once we have an adequate picture of the sexual behavior of individuals in a particular situation, we can begin to ask questions about the role of this behavior in other aspects of the individual's interpersonal relations. We can ask what is the function of particu-

[12] Clark, *Dark Ghetto*, and D. P. Moynihan, "Employment, Income and the Ordeal of the Negro Family," *Daedalus*, 94 (1965):745–70.
[13] See Short and Strodbeck, *Group Process and Gang Delinquency*.

lar forms of sexual behavior for the individual and for the groups to which he belongs. We can ask, rather than assume in advance that we know, what goals the individual is striving for through particular kinds of sexual behavior. It seems to me that Freud's real legacy in the study of sexual behavior was to show that sex is not simply sex but a complex behavior built out of elements which go back genetically into dim childhood history and cross-sectionally into other vital interests which the individual seeks to maximize and protect. Just as any other applied field of social science profits from contending theoretical paradigms, so the study of sexual behavior will profit from a widespread application of the diverse conceptual tools at our disposal.

10 Changing Concepts of Masculinity and Femininity

Nelson N. Foote

It is becoming increasingly clear that sexuality is far more than a mere biological phenomenon. Sex roles are as important as bodies, and the achievement of healthy sexuality depends as much on coming to terms with roles as with body functioning. A human being with a female body can mate and give birth to an infant, but she has to learn how to be a wife and mother. What is more, sex roles are drastically changing. Masculinity is not the same today as it was in the nineteenth century, when, for all intents and purposes, it was identical with aggressiveness, nor is femininity the same. Nelson Foote analyzes some of these changes.

A perceptive young woman of college age tells me that the fate of masculinity is a burning issue among women as well as among men because the fate of femininity is inextricably intertwined with it. The perils of "Momism" have been decried for years by our domestic critics, while Europeans and other foreigners have pointed out the weakness of American males of both the younger and the older generations—the disoriented adolescent and the henpecked middle-aged husband, both of whom seem to be pushed around by women. My purpose here is to bring the story up to date.

As my informant quite baldly puts it, unmarried girls of her age no longer face the dangers of pregnancy and economic helplessness. In these respects they are far freer than their grandmothers and have at last almost achieved the role in society toward which the social ideals of freedom and equality have led them and which contemporary America makes possible. Many of them feel more capable of achieving real intimacy with the opposite sex than were their mothers. However, like their mothers, they want to marry and have a family, and here is where they run into difficulty.

The redefinition of the masculine sexual role has not kept pace with the redefinition of the feminine sexual role. As a rule, there is no one among a college faculty or staff to tell boys how to become men, or even where to go to find out. By maintaining the practices of using grades as the principal measure of worth, of housing and feeding students in sex-segregated groups in dormitories, and of requiring full-time attendance (which forestalls the experience of earning a living), the colleges stand in the way of a contemporary redefinition of masculinity instead of aiding in the process. Much of the current unrest and discontent of young people in college arises in part, I believe, from this frustration of adult masculinity.

The young men and young women facing adulthood today also have a common problem, which they share with all previous generations: the familiar dilemma of dependence versus independence. Becoming an adult entails great gains and great losses, so nicely and powerfully opposed as to justify the use of the word "dilemma." Let us recognize, however, that the dilemma is two-fold. Parents are also ambivalent about the development of independence by their children, during their years together and even afterward. There are gains and losses for the parent as well as the child when the child becomes an adult. The more the parent cares about his child, the more concern he feels about whether, left alone, the child will act wisely. He is tempted to intervene by making decisions for the child—perhaps not overtly, because he knows that adulthood consists of being able to decide for oneself, but by bribery, cajolery, concealment or disparagement of alternatives, or by indicating disapproval or dismay in subtler ways.

One of the important differences between today's young people and their parents, however, is the much greater factual knowledge about sexual physiology and the pleasures of sexual experience. Perhaps in earlier, more sequestered, communities, parents could prevent children from engaging in sexual experience before marriage simply by keeping them in ignorance. At this date, efforts to suppress such information seem merely irrational squeamishness or hypocrisy to the young. Even the efforts of educators to break down remaining barriers to the dissemination of reliable information about sexual physiology—a kind of mopping-up operation following a battle already won—has an old-fashioned, dated quality in the eyes of modern young people. "Sex information" may be what their parents needed and did not get when they were young, but they are moving into a different terrain. An indication of the parental prejudices and anxieties which may prevent inclusion of the new issues in formal curricula, just as "sex information" was blocked in the past, is the controversy over the age at which the "facts of life" should be presented in the elementary schools—a controversy which seems tame in comparison with the confrontation of the burning issue of what is happening to masculinity.

For many centuries masculinity was identified with physical strength, military bravery and aggressiveness, even brutality. Nowadays, however, except for a dwindling minority, male occupations in the developed nations are white-collar pursuits which place no premium on physical strength. Warfare is, for the most part, carried on by technicians, who are not required to engage in the traditional military tasks demanding raw courage and endurance of pain and hardship. Despite the wars in Korea and Vietnam, the chances that a man will be killed in an auto crash are today much greater than the chances that he will be killed in combat. As William H. Whyte pointed out several years ago in *The Organization Man*, a man can live his whole life in this country and never have a chance to find out whether he is a coward or not, in the traditional sense. Whyte makes the point that aggressiveness tends to be more and more out of place in contemporary America: the ability to get along congenially with other people is what is necessary for economic survival.

Once more, let me repeat that I am referring to a marginal change, a shift in emphasis, not a total replacement of one set of virtues with another. The traditional expressions of masculinity represent a conservative set of standards to which the panicky male may revert when under pressure of challenge and self-doubt. The boy who joins the Marines in order to bolster his confidence in his masculinity is a familiar example. The more violent forms of sport may also perform this function. Symbolically, the firing of guns at animals or people seems to boost the morale of some men who find themselves humiliated by their everyday experience at work, at home, or in their community.

It is likely that there will always be a few remaining occasions in social life when physical strength, bravery, and aggressiveness will be demanded of men, but the day when the ordinary citizen has constant need of this kind of prowess is well behind us. Persons who desire to live dangerously must join the armed forces or the police, or take to crime, and some, of course, do so. (From time to time a writer of fiction or drama will make plain the meaning of such gestures, but the humanities teacher who applies such observations to real life is rare.) The occupations of the majority require virtues of other kinds—the philologically inclined will note the derivation of the word "virtue."

In the past men concealed their tender feelings, which had no part in masculinity as then defined. In practice, this meant that men were awkward, shy, and uncomfortable in situations where demonstrativeness was in order. They were embarrassed to show affection, grief, disappointment, appreciation of beauty, or even ordinary pleasure, except in a very inhibited way, lest they seem unmanly. As with the names of the colors, most men of the older generation have a dearth of words for describing either their feelings or their relations with other people. The image of the taciturn male hero is traditional in our culture. Affection has been expressed in overt actions, which is not a bad practice except that the meaning of actions is often harder to interpret than the meaning of words, and many sons have grown up wondering whether their fathers really care for them. Strength (not necessarily physical) and courage, coupled with tenderness, will probably remain masculine characteristics prized by women for many centuries to come. Fortified by a more secure masculinity, men may be able to be more openly tender as well.

To turn from the general image of masculinity to sexuality specifically, there are many traditions of the male role, in our culture as well as others. In some male subcultures the physical satisfaction of sexual intercourse is itself the goal; in others, the ideal is prowess in seduction; in still others, women's admiration for its own sake. The past two decades have been distinguished by the appearance of a new ideal—a man's masculinity is gauged primarily by his ability to provide sexual satisfaction for his partner. As this ideal becomes widespread, a higher valuation is being placed on companionship between sexual partners, both before and after marriage, in the home and out of it. The social segregation of the sexes has been dissolving quite rapidly in all but the more conservative social groups. Not only do couples join in more and more daily activities but, with the upgrading of income and education, there has been a general increase in joint socializing outside the home. More couples spend their time with other couples, usually friends of similar age and interests, rather than with relatives, and the current popularity of sports like skiing and boating reflects this pattern.

Co-education has become almost universal at all levels of schooling. Architects no longer design separate school entrances for girls and boys. Out of co-education, especially at the college level, an even more advanced form of companionship is emerging, termed "colleague marriage" by certain sociologists, in which husband and wife work together as well as play together and share the tasks of home and family.

The familiar division of labor between men and women was largely based on the physical strength required for the task. As this requirement becomes less important, men and women are increasingly found in the same occupations. Whether it was necessary or not—and it probably was necessary when most male work was performed out of doors—when women can and do hold the same jobs as men, there is far less reason for the division inside the home to be retained. It survives simply because almost all husbands are employed outside the home and most married women are not. The proportion of employed married women has been rising so rapidly since World War II, however, that in a few more years we can expect the Bureau of Labor Statistics to announce that non-working wives are in the minority—in fact, the B.L.S. did announce in late 1966 that 50 per cent of a sample of college women graduating in 1957 were working.

As women go to work, some of the older definitions of masculinity and femininity are being subjected to intensive challenge, and one may expect extensive changes as the new patterns become stabilized and are communicated, taught, and learned. In the household where both husband and wife work, children observe and criticize their parents' solutions to the problems presented and form their own notions of how they will live. Such situations present, by the way, an easy opening to discussions with students of future models of masculinity and femininity.

We can be sure that the future manifestations of masculinity will, as always, represent various kinds of complementarity with femininity; each set of characteristics and virtues will continue to differ, and the differences will continue to be prized. But what will these newer distinctions be, as the older ones fade away? To what extent do male and female sexuality as we have known them depend upon retention of complementary masculine and feminine social roles?

Some of the changes visible among the younger generation—pants on women, long hair on men—are conspicuous symbols of rejection of received customs. But let us note the difference between these particular symbols and those of, let us say, the 1920's and 1930's, when feminists began to invade a few of the occupations hitherto reserved for men. Those were the days of the "battle-axes"—women who cut their hair short, wore tweed suits of masculine cut, began to smoke, and even lowered their voices by an octave in order to resemble more closely the men whose privileges they wished to acquire. The colorful pants women wear today are exceedingly varied, but any observer would have to concede the femininity common to nearly all of them, partly their color, partly their cut, partly the choice of fabric, partly their diversity of style, partly their relation to the other items of clothing and coiffure which make up the ensemble. All in all, the fact that women can now enjoy the comfort and convenience of wearing pants when it is comfortable and convenient to wear them indicates that they enjoy rights formerly denied. But they no longer have to give up their femininity to enjoy these rights: instead, the ingenuity of millions of them, and of the manufacturers who serve them, has been unleashed to invent infinite variations on the theme of femininity in pants. If human imagination can produce such a cornucopia of expressions of femininity utilizing such an unpromising medium as this simple garment, we have as yet only a glimpse of how far the theme of femininity can be elaborated when women begin to take over the design of the offices in which they work, the cars they drive, the houses they live in, and the other goods they buy.

But when women are no longer segregated, dependent, and inferior, what is masculinity going to look like? If we think of those younger males who demonstrate in various ways that they have departed from traditional definitions—by their longer hair, their interest in the arts and social action, their disinterest in business and economic competition, their companionship with the other sex, their antagonism to war, their delight in conversation in a group—and wonder about their sexuality, the question almost answers itself. Their free and open interest in sexual experience, their matter-of-fact discussion of it, and the separation they make between sexual experience and procreation are breathtaking to many members of the older generation. On the other hand, what happens privately remains private, between the man and the woman, rather than being the topic of boasts in male gatherings, as was more characteristic of a generation ago. Where men of the past generation oscillated in their attitude between squeamishness and prurience, one never far from the other, the younger generation of men seems closer to a unified, positive attitude of appreciation toward the joys and values of sex. Men want masculinity, just as women want it for them. They want to maintain it in their occupational role, just as working women maintain their femininity. Most of them see the question not as what is the direction in which to go, but how to get there.

Let us return to my informant. Looking at the boys of her age, she notes several specific problems that have to be dealt with. First of all, in the co-educational college, her friends among boys tend to be much nearer her own age than in earlier decades, while girls of, say, twenty-one, seem to themselves further developed toward adulthood than boys. Second, while the girl is still being supported by her parents, just as the boy is, it is a bigger burden to his self-esteem to remain dependent because one of the foremost tests of masculinity traditionally has been the man's ability first to support himself, then to provide a home for his wife and family. Another informant of mine—a boy who is a classmate of the girl quoted—tells me that some boys get married to prove they are adults but then are disconcerted to find that having to remain dependent upon parents after getting married is even harder to bear. A situation in which their wives work to support them, which means that they must quit school to do so, although common among graduate students, is especially troublesome for undergraduate men to accept.

The boy who goes from high school into college, even if he

moves away from home, does not experience a qualitative change in economic self-sufficiency which tells him he is an adult and no longer an adolescent. Self-support may not be an absolute requirement, but in its absence there must be an adequate substitute. Boys who have dropped out of school for a year, for example, and have either been successful in a full-time job or somehow discovered their true vocation, often come back to school feeling that their manhood has been established in this respect. Those who plan to remain in the university in graduate or professional school, not out of indecision or to evade the draft but because advanced study represents a definite vocational plan, less often suffer from the onus of financial dependency. Among the dwindling segment of young people who do not go to college and at nineteen or twenty years of age are already supporting themselves, this problem is not so visible, but among dropouts or graduates from high school who do not get established in an occupation, it is much more acute than among college students. The threat to masculine identity is most serious of all when the traditional masculine roles have decayed, and not even a hint exists of where and how to look for new ones. Such unemployed young males would be ideal recruits as storm troopers abroad or at home, whatever the cause.

The gravest aspect of the matter for most male college students, however, is not their economic dependence upon their father but their emotional dependence upon their mother. It is this dependence which most disturbingly impinges upon their relations with a girl. What their girl friends often discover is that, just as these young men moved without a qualitative change from high school to college, they have often moved from being mothered at home to being mothered by a girl friend or a wife. Every woman a young man has known may have sheltered him, with the result that he has not learned how to play the role of stronger protector himself.

There are many aspects to masculinity, but for the purpose of this analysis it may be helpful and not distort reality too much to confine it here to strength. The virtue of strength is pre-eminent in the thinking of my informant, and she says that it is pre-eminent in the thinking of other college girls. They want strength in their men, usually not mere physical strength in the traditional sense. The man who uses his muscles and fists when strength of other kinds is required is at best a comical figure. At worst, his ways of dealing with his wife and children may have tragic consequences, as in the murders of wives and children by husbands in certain immigrant groups when their manhood is threatened by American conditions. What is masculine strength in non-physical terms? Groping for a solution, some boys try to manifest masculinity by acts of daring, such as motorcyle riding or breaking the law. Some girls do in fact respond to these manifestations with excitement, but the counterfeit, suicidal nature of such gestures sooner or later is apparent and they are abandoned.

Strength in the non-physical sense—moral strength—is manifested in many ways. It would be foolhardy and presumptuous to attempt here to devise for an entire generation the varied patterns of expression by which they will exhibit moral strength. That occasions for its employment are ample, however, is readily demonstrable. The ordinary white-collar employee has daily need of moral strength in order not to succumb to fear of the boss. Seeking a new job takes great courage. It takes self-respect and self-confidence to face up to mistakes, to abandon failing enterprises, to seek out opportunities, and make drastic changes in one's way of life. It takes moral strength to exercise responsibility for one's group and community, to assert one's ability to influence one's environment instead of surrendering to it, to make one's voice heard when one has something important to say.

Many fathers do not tell their sons about their work because they are ashamed of the humiliation it imposes upon them. Too many of them are not willing to challenge the system that forces them to live as only half-men. It is not surprising that when the fathers are loath to present themselves as models many boys do not identify with their fathers. The fact that fathers work away from home is not a sufficient explanation of their estrangement from their sons. A girl can identify with her mother, but a boy wants another model. There is a myth that the man who is pushed around at work compensates by coming home and lording it over his wife and children. If there were some way of obtaining accurate data, I believe that the facts would prove the opposite: the subservient employee is subservient at home, although he may be tyrannical in his dependency.

Powerlessness and impotence are not synonyms, but neither is emasculation entirely a figure of speech. It may give European critics some quiver of superiority to disparage American men for their weakness, but they do this from the standpoint of a conservative tradition which is still relatively strong, except in England, even among those who have shed some of its external trappings. When European men encounter the crisis of masculinity which is common here, however, American men may be well up the mountain on the other side of the valley. We see signs of progress already in the rejection by many young men of the empty way of life in which personal worth is evaluated only by status in a hierarchy, rather than by the value of one's product. The widespread search for meaning in their vocation is a sign that young men, especially in the colleges, see a connection between society and family, work and worth, social role and sexuality. They want to be men, and the more perceptive among them recognize that they seek adulthood in ways different from those of their fathers.

The great dynamic of family life is this criticism of one generation by the next, the decision to raise one's own children differently from the way one was raised oneself. Playing the role of father poses tests of masculinity more rigorous than playing the role of husband. Despite the separation between sexual experience and procreation through contemporary acceptance of contraception, and perhaps even because of it, the decision of a man and a woman to produce a child together is far more conscious, purposeful, and serious than ever before. It is becoming more of a commitment—in another time one would have said sacrament. Marriage can be regarded as to some extent experimental, with no great harm done if the experiment fails, and nowadays having children is regarded more and more as the real commitment which marriage itself used to represent.

The Scandinavian pattern of deferring marriage until after pregnancy, while traditional, assumes a peculiarly contemporary significance in this perspective and may come to constitute a model to young people in other countries. Many young people whose parents separated while they were growing up and suffered from that situation have vowed not to subject other human beings to it, preferring not to have children until they can feel fully confident of providing them a harmonious and joyous family environment. Hence we can surmise that the paramount expression of masculinity, which is to be a good father, especially towards one's son, is a goal toward which the new generation is groping. We may come to the conclusion, therefore, that just as sex education comprises far more than sex information, family life education comprises far more than sex education. These conclusions have implications for educators themselves.

Within the past several years, the proportion of male teachers in public high schools in the United States began to surpass that of female teachers. Thus far these numbers remain comparable, and from the standpoint of sex education among high school students, it seems ideal that the ratio remain about half and half in every high school, so that pupils during adolescence may be exposed to models of both sexes, because teachers, next to parents, are probably the most influential adults in the social development of students. In the co-educational colleges, of course, women faculty members are extremely scarce—a deficiency needing rapid correction and which may be corrected if male college teachers become much harder to hire.

The task of education is to move from the transmission of mere words to ways of life. Long ago school teachers were usually male, but a generation ago the typical high school teacher was a spinster. If male teachers became scarce, female teachers who were married and had children of their own were scarcer. During the Depression married women were often driven out of teaching to open their jobs to others who, as the saying went, did not have husbands to support them, while nowadays, by contrast, bachelors and spinsters are regarded almost with suspicion; people wonder why they remain unmarried. While this expectation that the normal adult will marry may put unfair pressure upon the few who do not, from the standpoint of presenting students with models of adults to emulate, the trend toward employment of married teachers can only be welcomed.

Students take intense interest in courtships and marriages among their teachers. They seem to recognize that teachers who have children of their own show more understanding of students in certain respects than do teachers lacking parental experience. It seems very likely that the combined weight of the examples set by all their married teachers has more impact upon students than whatever may be taught in a formal way about sex and the sexes in a separate course in the curriculum. Hence in terms of ultimate effect it may be far more important to introduce sex education into the training of teachers than into the curricula of students. If ways can be found to imbue teachers with a high degree of enlightened self-awareness about the impact of their example upon the behavior of students, it seems likely that the accomplishment of some specialist concentrating upon the transfer of information about sex will be paltry by contrast.

Let us put aside the old image of the coach or physician who calls the boys together at the principal's request to tell them the facts of life or the newer image of the social scientist reciting statistics from surveys, and imagine a male English teacher in a high school who has explicitly accepted as a part of his responsibility helping both his male and his female students to clarify their standards for judging masculinity and femininity. How can he face his students unless he is honest and objective toward his own attitudes and behavior? Faced with the portrayal in both fact and fiction of the problem of maintaining masculinity in the modern world, the teacher of literature who confines his attention to the physical facts of life is guilty of evasion. For example, how can one express any attitude whatsoever toward the non-hero of *Rabbit, Run* by John Updike without revealing as much about himself as about the principal character? Yet of the books I have read in recent years, few reveal so well the relationship between occupation and sex role. The perils of failure in manhood and womanhood are bared here as few parents could ever present them, and the book cries out for discussion by high school students. The repetitious mischief of the characters in John O'Hara's novels appears dated and unimportant by contrast, yet if there were time it would be instructive for a teacher to have a class compare these two authors, because O'Hara has as sure an ear for the 1920's as Updike has for the 1960's.

Imagine a discussion of how the role of the father could be played heroically in contemporary circumstances, as it was in Ole Rölvaag's *Giants in the Earth*. The study of novels like these is so superior in terms of application to real life and to criticism of real life that any other approach to sex education except the role-playing of life situations seems inferior and evasive. The use of fiction, like the use of role-playing, permits each individual to face the kinds of problematic situations that his education should be preparing him to handle. While a retreat from anxiety is always left open, through the ostensibly fictional nature of these situations, an opportunity for objectivity, autonomy, and control is also made available through presenting hypothetical alternatives to reality.

Young people today, especially in the colleges, are demanding that what they study be relevant to their lives. This does not mean that they simply want vocational training. It means that education must relate to the many tasks of living they face, in the present as well as the future. It means that they want education which will enable them to judge truly and confidently the relative worth of the various kinds of employment open to them, and not just their income potential. They want in fact what liberal education is supposed to provide in theory, the ability to understand and criticize and shape the world they are entering. The moment is therefore propitious for bringing more squarely into the curriculum the consideration of what masculinity and femininity should mean in practice today. Delegation of this matter to narrow specialists will be not only an evasion of a very large responsibility but will exacerbate the frustration of this generation with the irrelevance of much that they are taught. In this sense, the plea that is being made for sex education in the schools is representative of a wider need for relevance in education. A well-articulated and skillfully led movement for sex education, supported by sympathetic members of the older generation, could well serve as the spearhead of the general demand for educational change. Its proponents, therefore, have everything to gain from making common cause with other champions of change and from demanding major reforms rather than small concessions from the upholders of past practices.

I have used the example of the English teacher, but I could equally well refer to the teacher of mathematics and science, languages and social studies. One of the scandals of American education is the degree to which young women are discouraged from entering the technical fields based on science and mathematics and are persuaded early in life that they are incapable of doing so. Every teacher of such subjects should struggle against this superstition every day of his teaching career, should contest it openly and explicitly as part of his obligation as a teacher. But, to repeat an earlier point, he will not be successful in doing so unless he himself in his training has confronted the question of whence these attitudes emanate. The same task devolves upon every teacher of foreign languages whose male students suffer from the opposite assumption that only girls are good at languages. Social studies seem to escape somewhat the prejudice that they are the peculiar prerogative of one sex or the other, but this fact itself seems highly appropriate to include in discussion of learning problems among students of both sexes.

The education of teachers, I have said, is not complete without sex education, and, I might add, their sex education is not complete without some awareness of the peculiar variations that occur between the sexes among the various fields of learning. None of these relationships is fully understood at present. Who can say why women have become great musicians while none have so far become great composers? Why have they done better as novelists and poets than as dramatists? It is remarked again and again that women in general seem quantitatively higher in empathy than men, yet in the arts, where empathy is so highly demanded, women seem to have lagged behind. Are these merely further examples of the discrimination so long practiced against women in occupations outside their homes?

This chapter began with the observation made by my informant that women have been the first to move toward a new definition of their sex role. As she put it, their new capability for intimacy with men is the result of their increasing ability to assimilate their active femininity, to coordinate career and marriage. She indicated that many young women wonder whether to blame themselves, whether they have become too strong, whether they should try to help their boys become men by returning to passivity, sweetness, and dependence. But such retrogression is unworkable and unrealistic. Instead, boys must develop the strength to command the respect and love of modern young women. It is only as men find new sources of strength to master their social environment that they will succeed in establishing their new definition of masculinity, and only if they do succeed can women become secure in their new definition of femininity.

The mighty themes of masculinity and femininity have exerted a far more powerful influence on human history than the conventional historians who specialize on wars and empires seem to realize. Beneath the noise of conquest and defeat the spectacle of human creativity has been evolving. When manhood and womanhood come to be defined more fully in terms of what they create, when each man and woman becomes the perfect audience for the distinctive performance of the other, then we may be justified in speaking, as some recent writers have, of a sexual renaissance.

11

The Impact
of Culture and Values

Harold T. Christensen

This section on values ends with Christensen's sociological analysis of the place of values in society and in science. He illustrates his point with data from three diverse groups of college students: a group from the conservative, largely Mormon, intermountain culture, a group from the midwestern secular American culture, and a group from the liberal Danish culture.

No individual lives entirely alone. He spends most of his time in groups and is a member of the larger society. What he thinks and does, and how he feels, is to a considerable extent determined by the social environment around him. His interactional experiences, and the culture in which they take place, mold his personality and direct his behavior. Furthermore, he, in turn, exerts some influence over society. Man is a part of the group and the group is a part of man; he both influences others and is influenced by them. As Charles Horton Cooley pointed out about half a century ago,[1] the individual and society are but two different aspects of the same thing. In view of this, the claims of certain people that "what we do is our own business" and their occasional attempts to "go it alone" just do not make sense.

A basic element of every culture consists of its mores—the prescriptions and proscriptions that the society considers important to its welfare. They are surrounded with positive and negative sanctions, rewards and penalties. They may also be called the society's norms. When norms become internalized an individual is said to have values and a conscience. Values are thus the counterparts within an individual of group norms. They are the criteria one uses in choosing among alternatives. Though closely related to beliefs and attitudes, they are not identical with either: a belief is the conviction that something is real or true; an attitude is an internal state of the personality that pressures toward action, a "tendency to act"; a value is a standard of preference, a criterion for judging the relative worth or importance of things, ideas, or events. Although values tend to be checked against beliefs and, in turn, form the basis for attitudinal states, alone they are simply the standards or criteria used in decision-making.

[1] *Human Nature and the Social Order* (New York, Scribner, 1902).

The discussion that follows focuses on the issue of premarital sex, with a view to testing the value variable as it relates to behavior and its consequences. To test the general model, I will draw heavily upon my own cross-cultural research. But it is toward a general theory of value relevance that I hope to build, in the belief that such a theory, applied to the sex problem, may offer clarification and make moral decision less difficult.

CHANGING SEXUAL VALUES

It is clear that in the contemporary world two opposing value systems are battling it out. On the one hand, the traditional Judaeo-Christian position is that sex outside of marriage is wrong, period. God has said so; the justification for the edict transcends the reason of man; there is no need for proof and no room for argument. On the other hand, the relativistic or situational position is that the rightness or wrongness of non-marital sex depends upon particular conditions. Morality is not something intrinsic to the act or something supernaturally imposed: it rests upon the over-all effects of a given behavior within a specific setting. Because effects can be expected to vary with situations, the moral implications of an act will be different at different times and places.

To the traditionalist, the "new morality" is nothing more than immorality. To the modernist it is the rigid insistence upon chastity that is immoral because, he believes, self-denial under certain circumstances may work against emotional health and because the arbitrary traditionalist position stultifies free inquiry. In this age of science it is the modernist-relativist who frequently has the best of the argument, simply because his approach is more in keeping with the dominant themes of the day. (This is offered as an observation, not a value judgment.)

But does one need to choose between the absolutist and relativist positions? Isn't it possible that some values are absolute and others relative? Or that a given act may have elements of both? Support for this view is to be found in a recent article by F. Ivan Nye.[2] Nye distinguishes between what he calls intrinsic values, valuation of things for their own sake, and instrumental values, valuation of things for their power to produce desirable outcomes. This dichotomy is, of course, essentially the same as that of the absolutist and relativist positions described above. While recognizing the difficulty of identifying intrinsic values, Nye did specify several: life itself, freedom from chronic pain or discomfort, freedom from severe fear or

[2] "Values, Family, and a Changing Society," *Journal of Marriage and the Family,* 29 (1967):241–48.

anxiety, freedom to make choices, and the condition of loving and being loved. Any given property, he says, can possess both instrumental and intrinsic value. He notes a movement over time toward instrumental valuation of family behavior and hopes that this trend will continue so that changes in family structure can be objectively evaluated and carried out.

SCIENCE AND VALUES

Having recognized the arguments for a relative, as opposed to an absolute, morality, we may ask what science can add to the field of morals, if anything. Can there be a sociological basis for decisions on proper behavior? If by "proper" is meant something that is intrinsically or eternally right, the answer is no. If we mean simply that it coincides with group norms and hence escapes negative group sanctions, the answer is yes. Though the sociologist cannot decide what is *best* in an absolute sense, he can determine what is most *functional* to the systems involved, and thus help decide what is best in a relative sense.[3] His task is to determine cause-and-effect relationships which can aid the non-scientist (including the scientist himself, in his role as a citizen) to set up criteria for moral decisions. The scientist cannot, in his professional role, make choices among the alternatives of relativistic (normative) morality, but he can clarify them, and this is his contribution.

Normative morality is defined as any code of right and wrong that is founded upon the operations of normative systems. Only by knowing how these systems interrelate, how personal behaviors deviate from social prescriptions, and what the consequences of such deviations are can there be any rational basis for moral decisions. Thus normative morality is relative rather than absolute. It attempts to put science in the place of polemics and to see questions of right and wrong in terms of the measurable and variable consequences of the behavior involved.

THE PRINCIPLE OF VALUE RELEVANCE

As will be demonstrated below, values affect both behavior and the consequences of behavior. People tend to act in general accordance with their values, and the consequences of their actions will

[3] According to the structural-functional school, human activities tend to become organized into intra- and interdependent systems, which perpetuate themselves only by maintaining necessary degrees of balance or equilibrium. There are personality systems and social systems—and subsystems of each—all interrelated. When an activity is in harmony with, and helps to maintain, a system, it is said to be functional; when the reverse is true, dysfunctional. It is thus possible to use system maintenance as the criterion against which the propriety of behavior is decided. This essentially is what I mean by a normative morality.

depend upon how closely they conform or fail to conform to those values. The effects of behavior are thus modified by the values held, and so values must properly be regarded as intervening variables. The theory put forth here is that negative effects of behavior are in direct proportion to the amount of value-behavior discrepancy present. I have called the observation that the values that people hold represent important and relevant data for understanding and evaluating their behavior the "principle of value relevance," which may be described as follows:

In simplest terms, *the principle of value relevance means that the values people hold are relevant to their behavior and to the outcome or effects of this behavior:* in other words, it means that the family sociologist not only may but must deal with values as part of his data. What people believe, or perceive, or desire, or expect determines how they act and react in reference to the situations they face—even more so, very often, than the reality factors outside their mental-emotional systems.

Values may be dealt with as *dependent variables*, shaped by forces outside the individual, such as family interaction; as *independent variables* which influence one's behavior and relationships, including that which takes place within the family; and as *intervening variables*, which are so because they intrude themselves into a process to affect both its direction and its outcome. Since the meanings attached to things and events depend upon the values people hold, it is this last named—values as intervening variables—which carries the most promise for the family researchers of the future.[4]

AMERICAN SEX NORMS IN CROSS-CULTURAL PERSPECTIVE

My research into permarital intimacy patterns covers three cultures: sexually permissive Denmark, the moderately restrictive midwestern United States, and the highly restrictive Mormon country (Utah and surrounding states) in the western United States. Selection of these particular cultures was in part based on the need for a wide range of norms and practices in order to test more reliably the effects of specific practices in relation to their norm (or value) settings. The data were gathered approximately ten years ago by means of questionnaires administered to university students and the record linkage technique, applied to samples of the general population.[5]

[4] "The Intrusion of Values," in *Handbook of Marriage and the Family,* ed. H. T. Christensen (Chicago: Rand McNally, 1964), pp. 997–98.

[5] George R. Carpenter collaborated on the questionnaire. Ten journal articles reporting various aspects of this study have been published. Much of the present chapter is drawn from the most recent of these ("Scandinavian and American Sex Norms: Some Comparison with Sociological Implications," *Journal of Social Issues,* 22 [1966]:60–75). Since the article listed and summarized all previous ones, it alone will be cited here.

The Norms

The sex norms of Denmark are known to be highly permissive; those of the midwestern United States moderately restrictive, and those of the Mormon country highly restrictive. In Denmark—which is broadly typical of all Scandinavia—sexual intercourse during engagement is a tradition at least three or four centuries old, and in recent years the practice has spread to include the "going steady" relationship; now, as earlier, many Danes tend to wait for pregnancy before going ahead with the wedding. In the United States, including the Midwest—which may be taken as a fair cross-section of the country—chastity, though frequently violated and considerably liberalized in recent decades, is still the dominant norm, supported strongly by the Judaeo-Christian tradition. Mormon country, of course, is part of the United States, but because of the particular religious culture which pervades it, it is unique in many respects. There chastity is a highly institutionalized norm supported by strong positive and negative sanctions. With orthodox Mormons, "breaking the law of chastity" is among the most serious of sins.

Because those who make up the society tend to internalize its norms, one would expect to see cross-cultural differences similar to those just reported in expressions of personal attitude. This was found. Questionnaire returns revealed that Danish students, in comparison with others, (1) gave greater approval to both premarital coitus and postmarital infidelity; (2) approved earlier starting times, in relation to the marriage date, of each level of intimacy—necking, petting, and coitus; (3) approved a more rapid progression in intimacy from necking to coitus; and (4) scored significantly higher on a Guttman-type scale, which combined ten separate additional items into a measure of "intimacy permissiveness."[6]

Because a person's behavior tends to correspond with his values (including internalized norms), it follows that behavior can be used as an indicator of norms. Using this approach it was found that Danish subjects, more than others, (1) had participated in premarital coitus; (2) had gone on to coitus from petting, that is, fewer of them had engaged in terminal petting; (3) confined premarital coitus to one partner, had first intercourse with a "steady" or fiancée, and hence were less promiscuous (this generalization holds for males only); (4) had given birth to an illegitimate child; (5) had conceived a first legitimate child premaritally; and (6) had postponed further conception following the wedding, hence the low proportion of early postmarital conceptions in this group.[7]

[6] *Ibid.*, p. 62.
[7] *Ibid.*, p. 63.

In virtually all of these attitudinal and behavioral measures, as well as in most of those cited below, the Mormon area fell at the opposite or restrictive end of the continuum, with the Midwest in between, though closer to the Mormon than to the Danish standard, which is why it is labeled "moderately restrictive." Generally speaking, the norm in this country is one of early, frequent, and random dating, with a gradual narrowing of the field, development of intersex intimacy, delaying of coitus until after the wedding, and the strong expectation of marital fidelity. These patterns differ, of course, from one subgroup to another, and, as mentioned above, the Mormons are known to be among the strongest adherents to convention and chastity. Elsewhere, individual variability is great, and the trend over time has been toward liberalization. Especially noticeable is the increased incidence of coitus during the engagement period, which is a move in the direction of Scandinavian practice.

The Danish system provides a sharp contrast. There dating (which is a relatively recent innovation) starts later, is less widely practiced, and is more likely to begin with a "going steady" arrangement with an expectation of eventual marriage. Furthermore, all levels of sexual intimacy are accepted once the relationship is firmly established, and the progression toward coitus is relatively rapid. As a matter of fact, the Danes do not draw a sharp line between technical chastity and coitus (as do Americans). They regard petting and coitus as belonging together and see them both as appropriate in a relationship based on love and oriented toward marriage. Actually, in Denmark both "going steady" and engagement mean more in terms of commitment and privileges than they do in America, and the wedding probably means less, relatively speaking. It is to be noted, therefore, that the greater sexual permissiveness of Denmark (and all of Scandinavia, for that matter) does not necessarily imply looseness or promiscuity; intimacy is simply made a part of the courtship-marriage process.

Nevertheless, it must be observed that there seems to have been a spreading or generalizing of this marriage-oriented permissiveness to non-marital situations, for the Danes questioned gave greater approval than Americans to all of the propositions regarding intimacy, and also reported higher rates of illegitimate births. Though the recent trend in Denmark is toward the adoption of American dating patterns, and though the cultures on both sides of the Atlantic are moving together, differences in sex norms are still striking.

Consequences of Violations

Our cross-cultural data made it possible to test the hypothesis

160

that negative effects of behavior will be greatest when the behavior is out of line with the values (or norms). It was noted above that sexual behavior tends to coincide with sexual norms in each of the three cultures: Denmark was most permissive and the Mormon area most restrictive with regard to both norms and behavior. We still know nothing of the relative proportion of individuals in each of the three cultures who violate their own values (internalized norms). For each culture, therefore, the percentage who approved premarital coitus was compared with the percentage who actually had experienced it. The results showed that in Denmark substantially more approved than had had experience, while for the two American samples the reverse was true: substantially more had had experience than approved, and this discrepancy between experience and approval was greatest for the Mormon area.[8]

The explanation for the Danish pattern probably lies in the permissive norms of that culture, coupled with the youth and hence lack of marriage orientation of many of the respondents. The explanation for the American pattern, especially that of the Mormon area, probably lies in the restrictiveness of the culture, coupled with biological and peer pressures upon individuals to violate the norms.

Because restrictiveness in a culture seems to cause a large proportion of individuals to violate their own standards, one might expect such a culture to produce a higher proportion of individuals suffering from guilt, frustration, and maladjustment. To test this assumption, males and females who had had premarital coitus were given an opportunity, by responding to a check list, to say whether or not it was voluntary and to indicate their predominant feelings the day following the experience. The proportion of those whose first coital experience was *not* "voluntary because of desire"—and, hence was the result of either a felt obligation or actual coercion— was found to be highest in the Mormon area and lowest in Denmark. The proportion experiencing subsequent guilt, remorse, fear, or other negative feelings was also highest in the Mormon area and lowest in Denmark.[9] Thus, both involuntary participation and negative reactions following the event were greatest in the most restrictive culture and least in the most permissive culture.

Estimated dates of conception for first children in marriage were calculated by subtracting 266 days (normal period of uterogestation) from the date of the child's birth. When these were plotted, distinct cultural patterns were evident.

In the Mormon group the line climbed somewhat smoothly to its

[8] *Ibid.*, p. 64.
[9] *Ibid.*, p. 65.

one peak, one month after marriage, and then tapered off. In the midwestern group the line became bimodal, with one peak two months before marriage and a second and higher peak one month after marriage. In the Danish group the line showed a single peak five months before the wedding: more first children were conceived then than at any other time, even in the months immediately following marriage.[10] The interpretation seems clear: in Mormon areas the negative feelings accompanying premarital coitus are apparently strong enough to force marriage; in the Midwest there is a tendency to marry immediately after pregnancy becomes established (about two months from conception) in an attempt to hide the fact and so escape public scorn; in Denmark there is little or no pressure to hurry the wedding, even when pregnancy occurs.

By matching marriage, birth, and divorce records it was possible to arrive at divorce rates for various birth-interval categories. Comparisons of divorce rate differentials between the rather clearly distinguished premarital and postmarital conceivers revealed that premarital conceivers showed up with higher divorce rates than postmarital conceivers in all three cultures, though in Denmark the difference was small. Percentage differences by which divorce rates in the premarital exceeded those in the postmarital pregnancy group were highest in the Mormon area and lowest in Denmark.[11] Thus, though divorces are frequently associated with premarital pregnancy, this relationship is strongest in restrictive societies: permissiveness regarding premarital pregnancy apparently tends to cancel out some of its otherwise negative effects.

Admittedly, these data do not exhaust the possible consequences of premarital pregnancy, yet they include crucial points and suggest what a more comprehensive analysis might find.[12]

It would seem that the negative consequences of norm deviation tend to vary directly with norm restrictiveness, probably because

[10] *Ibid.*

[11] *Ibid.*, pp. 65–66.

[12] Though I use the terms "effects" and "consequences," it is recognized that association is not the same thing as causation and that the latter has not actually been established. It is possible, for example, that a selective process is operating with reference to divorce rate differentials. In the restrictive Mormon culture disproportionately more divorce-prone individuals might be in the premarital pregnancy category if it should be established that persons who become pregnant before marriage are also prone to divorce. The presumption is that cultural restrictions would tend to prevent premarital pregnancies among those whose personalities are most conformist. The matter needs further study, but I would hypothesize that selectivity, if it exists, is only part of the explanation and that an important remainder would be causal.

deviation in the more restrictive societies represents a larger gap between norms and behavior and hence constitutes a greater offense.

Male-Female Differences and Similarities

One may now ask whether the permissiveness or restrictiveness of sex norms in any way affects the convergence or divergence of male and female subcultures. The two extremes on our permissiveness-restrictiveness continuum, Denmark and the Mormon area, showed the greatest convergence of male and female attitudes. Furthermore, proportionately more respondents from these cultures, especially the Danes, believed in a single standard of sexual morality. As for behavior, however, only Denmark showed a strong convergence of male and female patterns. As a matter of fact, the most restrictive culture—the Mormons—showed the most divergence in this respect, a fact which, when we recall its homogeneity of male and female attitudes, indicates that disproportionately large numbers of Mormons fail to practice what they profess.[13]

These data suggest some plausible hypotheses. The single standard of sexual behavior in Denmark probably indicates a freeing or liberalizing of the female, whereas among the Mormons it probably indicates a taming or conventionalizing of the male. The stress on authority, conformity, and participation in the church is reinforced by the presence of a lay priesthood involving most males twelve years of age and older. As for behavior, in Denmark, where there is little stigma attached to premarital sex activity, behavior tends to follow norms, and male-female similarity in attitude becomes male-female similarity in behavior as well. Among Mormons, where the norms set by the church are somewhat utopian, the stronger sex urge among males,[14] plus the general double standard, makes it likely that more males than females will violate the norms and that the gap between the sexes will increase.

Scientists look for uniformities in nature; out of analysis comes synthesis and general theory. In the spirit of science, sociologists and those in kindred disciplines search for principles of human behavior that can be generalized over time and across cultures, but the social scientist also sees the peculiarities of each culture and takes a position of cultural relativism. Nevertheless, not everything is relative. Certain relationships that hold to some degree in all

[13] "Scandinavian and American Sex Norms," pp. 66–67.

[14] Though male-female differences in biological sex drive are open to some question, there can be little doubt but that in our culture most males have stronger *learned* sexual drives than females.

three cultures have been suggested above—higher divorce rates among those pregnant before marriage, for example. I will give three further illustrations: (1) females are more conservative in sexual matters than males, almost without exception and regardless of the measure used and whether attitudes or behavior are considered; (2) approval of premarital coitus increases with each increase in a couple's involvement and/or commitment, but the reverse is true of extra-marital coitus; and (3) premarital pregnancy is most common among young brides and grooms, among couples who have civil rather than religious weddings, and among blue-collar workers.[15]

SUMMARY AND CONCLUSIONS

We have seen that in the three cultures studied sex patterns show both similarities and differences. If everything were generalizable across cultures, one could look to these universals as bases for a uniform morality;[16] if everything were culture-bound, one could conclude that nothing is fixed and morality is entirely relative. As it is, no such pat conclusion is possible. By this I do not mean to imply that the notion of absolute or ultimate values has been refuted. Such a question is beyond the reach of the scientist. It is clear, however, that the scientist can provide generalizations about relationships of variables that concern moral issues, that he can study values as data, without making value judgments, and that thus he can contribute to the resolution of ethical problems.

The Mormon culture was used in this analysis in order to accentuate contrasts. However, the more typical American culture has these same differences compared with Scandinavia, though to a lesser degree, and the explanations might be expected to be similar: in the United States there is more terminal petting, younger marriage ages, more guilt associated with premarital petting, a greater tendency to hurry the wedding when pregnancy occurs, a disproportionately high divorce rate associated with premarital pregnancy, and so on. Some of my Danish acquaintances, in defense of their system, have even suggested that the restrictiveness of American culture—including its emphasis upon technical chastity while at the

---

[15] "Scandinavian and American Sex Norms," pp. 68–69.

[16] Even if it could be demonstrated that the consequences of given sexual acts are the same in all places and at all times (which it cannot), the scientist still could not conclude that these effects are fixed, for he is committed to the study of empirical data. He is within his proper sphere in studying questions of universality, but he must not permit himself to reach questions of absolute or ultimate morality.

same time permitting petting—has resulted in an increase in cheese-cake publications, hard-core pornography, prostitution, and homo-sexuality.

What, then, can be said about the relative merits of the Scandi-navian and American sexual systems? Nothing by way of ultimate judgment. In terms of behavioral consequences, which is the view of normative morality, there are both functional and dysfunctional practices within both cultures, but when a behavior is recognized as dysfunctional, it is only with reference to the normative system in which it exists. Whether, in order to obtain equilibrium, one should change the behavior to fit the system or the system to fit the be-havior or a little of both is a problem for religion or philosophy, not science.

In recent years American sexual practices have been moving in the direction of the more liberal Scandinavian norms. Reiss, for example, characterizes the Swedish norm as "permissiveness with affection" and points out that this standard has grown in popularity in our own country over the last century.[17] It must be remembered, however, that the function or dysfunction of American sex practices must be seen in terms of American sex norms, and unless the latter are liberalized as rapidly as the former, there will be an increase in strain (dysfunction). There is some evidence that this is happening. But whether or not the gap separating prescription from practice is increasing, it exists, and its existence calls for objective investigation and analysis.

Within the framework of normative morality, an act is "good" if it succeeds and "bad" if it fails in terms of a set of understood criteria. There has been little attempt to relate non-marital sexual behavior to its measurable consequences, which may be presumed to exist. The existing objective studies (as well as causal specula-tions) of this problem have been concerned with possible effects upon the individual, his mental health and adjustment; upon the pair relationship, whether it is made mutually reinforcing or endur-ing; and upon the community or society, whether there are inter-connections between sexual controls and societal stability. It is our contention that a theory of normative morality must draw upon culturally relevant research relating to all of these effects.

A final question is whether normative morality will actually work; that is, will a rational understanding of the consequences cause a person to alter his behavior? A suggestion that it will not is pro-

[17] I. L. Reiss, *Premarital Sexual Standards in America* (Glencoe, Ill.: Free Press of Glencoe, 1960), pp. 126–45.

vided by the continuing increase in cigarette smoking, in the face of the report of the Surgeon General of the United States: convincing evidence of smoking's harmful effects made scarcely a dent in the practice. A suggestion that it will work, however, comes from Muuss. He found that the causal nature of human behavior can be taught in the schools, even at very young ages, and that where this method supersedes the traditional judgmental approach the child is "less punitive, less anxious, more tolerant, more democratic, more responsible, more secure, has fewer conflicts, and shows better school adjustment."[18] It appears that information alone is not the answer, and neither is motivation alone. Perhaps information and motivation both work best when they are complementary and hence mutually reinforcing. Perhaps man over time will become more rational and will increasingly look to the consequences of alternative courses of action to guide him in his decisions.

[18] R. E. Muuss, "Mental Health Implications of a Preventive Psychiatry Program in the Light of Research Findings," *Marriage and Family Living*, 22 (1960):155.

Suggested Readings: Part II

INTERPERSONAL RELATIONSHIPS

Berelson, B., and Steiner, G. A. *Human Behavior.* New York: Harcourt, Brace, 1964.
Propositions and findings from social scientific research cover almost every aspect of human activity. Research associated with the family, sexual behavior, and psychotherapy will be of special interest to sex educators.

Burgess, E. W., and Wallin, P. *Engagement and Marriage.* Philadelphia: Lippincott, 1953.
A classic study of dating, engagement, sexual relationships, and prediction of marital success. Reactions of spouses to premarital intercourse are explained. The marital relationship is discussed in terms of sex and interpersonal relationships.

Ehrmann, W. W. *Premarital Dating Behavior.* New York: Bantam Books, 1959.
A thorough study of dating, sex roles, and sexual behavior and attitudes of modern youth. Relationships between ideas of love, sex codes, and heterosexual behavior are explored. The sex educator will find the chapter on intimacy relationships and sex codes of special interest.

Foote, N. N., and Cottrell, L. S., Jr. *Identity and Interpersonal Competence.* Chicago: University of Chicago Press, 1955.
Basic principles of interpersonal competence are related to self-identification and competence in relationships, sexual and otherwise.

Grunwald, H. A., ed. *Sex in America.* New York: Bantam Books, 1964.
Chapters by such authorities as Walter Stokes, Lester Kirkendall, and Rollo May discuss the sexual revolution, interpersonal relationships, and sexual morality in a changing world. This is a paperback of much worth to the sex educator.

Hettlinger, R. E. *Living with Sex: The Student's Dilemma.* New York: Seabury Press, 1966.
Problems of youth are discussed objectively and creatively by a professor of religion. The emphasis on responsible decision-making instead of traditional dogma makes this an effective and stimulating volume for students, teachers, and parents.

Kirkendall, L. A. *Premarital Intercourse and Interpersonal Relationships.* New York: Julian Press, 1961. Also available in Matrix House paperback.
A research study based on 668 premarital intercourse experiences reported by 200 college-level males. The emphasis is on

the differing motivations and consequences of premarital intercourse in relationships of varying importance. The effect of premarital intercourse on marriage is discussed and suggestions are made for the successful integration of sex and interpersonal relationships.

Maslow, A. H. *Toward a Psychology of Being.* New York: Van Nostrand, 1962.

A basis for satisfying interpersonal relations is presented. The sex educator may find this approach useful.

Wilson, J. *Logic and Sexual Morality.* Baltimore: Penguin, 1965.

A most unusual approach to the study of interpersonal relationships and sexual morality. The author, an English philosopher and former professor of religion, does not pretend to be able to resolve the sexual dilemma. Instead, he explores the irrationality of absolutist positions and suggests a rational approach to sexual morality. One section deals with a rational approach to sex education. This book is a must for sex educators.

CULTURE AND VALUES

Bell, R. R. *Premarital Sex in a Changing Society.* Englewood Cliffs, N.J.: Prentice-Hall, 1966.

Uses sociological analysis to view premarital sex in its many ramifications. Reports most of the available research; a liberal slant.

Christensen, H. T. "The Intrusion of Values." In *Handbook of Marriage and the Family,* edited by Christensen. Chicago: Rand McNally, 1964.

Analyses of various aspects of the problem of value intrusion into the domain of family sociology, including discussions of opposing positions and of reasons for considering some of these intrusions as legitimate and others illegitimate.

Croog, S. H. "Aspects of the Cultural Background of Premarital Pregnancy in Denmark." *Social Forces* 30 (1951):215–19.

Provides the historical and cultural setting for the widespread acceptance of premarital pregnancy in Denmark, which is typical of all of Scandinavia.

Duvall, E. M. *Why Wait Till Marriage?* New York: Association Press, 1965.

Builds a case for premarital chastity. Addressed to teenagers.

Ehrmann, W. W. "Marital and Nonmarital Sexual Behavior." In *Handbook of Marriage and the Family.* Chicago: Rand McNally, 1964.

Focuses upon the social significance of virtually all aspects of heterosexual behavior. Draws heavily upon research and is objective.

Linner, B. *Sex and Society in Sweden.* New York: Pantheon Books, 1967.

The most recent and complete discussion of Swedish sex culture, including sex education programs and other involvements of society in this area. Written for the American reader by an outstanding Swedish educator and counselor.

Nye, F. I. "Values, Family, and a Changing Society." *Journal of Marriage and the Family* 29 (1967):241–48.

Treats the conflicts and changes in family values, including sexual morality. Builds a typology of "intrinsic" and "instrumental" values.

Reiss, I. L. *Premarital Sex Standards.* SIECUS Discussion Guide 5. New York: SIECUS, 1967. (Available from SIECUS.)

A succinct statement of the major premarital sexual standards that exist in America, together with discussion of conflicting values and actual and anticipated trends.

Reiss, I. L., ed. "The Sexual Renaissance in America." *Journal of Social Issues* 22 (1966):1–140.

A special issue focusing upon recent changes, and forces affecting change, in American sex attitudes and practices. The eleven contributors are noted for their work in this field.

Svalastoga, K. "The Family in Scandinavia." *Marriage and Family Living* 16 (1954):374–80.

Summarizes major features of the Scandinavian family system, including its liberal sex norms.

PART III: NORMAL SEXUAL FUNCTIONING

Introduction

In Part I we discussed the pedagogical aspects of sex education; in Part II the societal aspects. It seemed appropriate also to include non-technical but authoritative and current reviews of the fields of reproduction (Chapter 12), sexual response (Chapter 13), and family planning (Chapter 14). Together with the Glossary of Technical Terms at the end of the book, these materials should prove a valuable resource to teachers who have to answer questions in areas in which their own academic training may be slight. These materials will also serve to help those whose training in these areas was obtained before some of the striking new breakthroughs in sexual and reproductive research were achieved to bring their knowledge up to date.

12 Human Reproduction

Charles S. Mahan and Carlfred B. Broderick

Illustrations by Paul Stevenson

Some of us have been heard to complain that too much of what passes for sex education is little more than instruction in human plumbing. On the other hand, no one denies the central importance of biology. In this chapter the authors attempt to go beyond a simple description of the plumbing and draw upon recent research to present a picture of how and why the reproductive system works the way it does.

Human reproduction is a complicated and fascinating process. Like every other area of our biological functioning, it has been surrounded by an aura of mystery and superstition. Gradually many superstitions have been successfully undermined by medical research. It is only fair to admit, however, that many mysteries remain even today to challenge the next generation of scientific investigators.

The present chapter is an attempt to present a comprehensive review of this subject in terms that are easily understood by an intelligent layman, while reflecting the latest scientific knowledge.[1] It is organized in six sections. The first section traces the development of maleness and femaleness from conception through pubescence. Section II explains the process of sperm production and ejaculation in the male. The following section describes the four phases of the female reproductive cycle and the part each plays in the monthly process of ovulation and menstruation. Conception and Implantation then traces the sperm through its odyssey to the egg, and follows the fertilized egg from the moment of conception to implantation in the uterine wall one week later. Section V focuses first upon the development of the newly formed life through the embryonic and fetal stages to birth, then describes the mother as she experiences her pregnancy over this same period. The sixth and last section briefly outlines the events between the beginning of labor and the six-week checkup after the baby is born.

Illustrations have been provided where they may aid in visualizing various aspects of the subject. It is hoped that they may be useful

[1] For a general review of the subject see J. Botella-Llusia, *Obstetrical Endocrinology* (Springfield, Ill.: Thomas, 1961); C. S. Keefer, *Human Ovulation* (Boston: Little, Brown, 1963); C. B. Lull and R. A. Kimbrough, *Clinical Obstetrics* (Philadelphia: Lippincott, 1953); and E. R. Novak and J. D. Woodruff, *Gynecologic and Obstetric Pathology*, 5th ed. (Philadelphia: Saunders, 1962).

in teaching as well as learning these concepts. An attempt has been made to explain each technical term when it is first used, but a glossary is appended to the book for easy reference.

I. DEVELOPMENT OF MALE AND FEMALE REPRODUCTIVE SYSTEMS

Male or Female?

An individual's sex is determined from the moment of his conception. It depends upon whether the egg in his mother's body was fertilized by a male-determining or a female-determining sperm cell from his father. All that a child inherits biologically from his father is contained in the twenty-three *chromosomes*[2] crammed into that sperm. All of his mother's contribution is contained in the twenty-three chromosomes found in the nucleus of the egg she produced. Only one of these forty-six chromosomes really determines the child's sex. In all eggs there is a chromosome called "X" which bears the genes for the female reproductive system and for many other vital things besides. No one can live without an X chromosome from his mother. Sperm are of two different types, however. Some carry an X chromosome just as the egg does, while others carry instead a tiny runt called the Y chromosome. Tiny though it is, it carries the genes for maleness. A Y-bearing sperm unites with the egg to form a boy; an X-bearing sperm unites with the egg to form a girl (see Fig. 12–1). Thus, at the moment of conception, while he is still a single cell, a most vital factor in the life of the individual is already determined.

Experiments and observations with animal and, to a more limited extent, with human sperm reveal that Y-bearing (male) sperm tend to have small round heads, while X-bearing (female) sperm tend to be somewhat larger and more nearly oval in shape.[3] Y-bearing sperm travel faster, but X-bearing sperm live longer (the female advantage over the male in longevity begins there and continues thereafter). Despite their general hardiness, apparently something happens in the process of sperm production that cuts down the initial number of X-bearing sperm. Microscopic studies of human sperm show many more round- than oval-headed ones, and it has been estimated that 120 to 160 male conceptions occur for every 100 female conceptions.[4] By birth, the greater hardihood of the

---

[2] A chromosome is a bar composed of a long string of genes, or units of inheritance. Each gene controls some specific characteristic of the individual.

[3] L. B. Shettles, "Conception and Birth Ratio," *Obstetrics and Gynecology*, No. 18 (1961), pp. 122–30.

[4] L. B. Shettles, "Human Spermatozoan Populations," *International Journal of Fertility*, 7, No. 2 (1962).

Figure 12–1. Determination of sex.

female has already begun to show, however, as the ratio of live male births to live female births is only 106:100. This figure is the result of the larger number of male deaths between conception and birth. By the time they have reached their early twenties the number of boys and girls is the same, and in every later age group there are more females than males in the world.

For some reason, not fully explained as yet, young parents are more likely to have boys than are older parents, although the difference is a small one and of little practical importance. For equally obscure reasons, children conceived by artificial insemination tend to be predominantly male. This finding has been demonstrated dramatically among cattle, but at least one study of humans[5] also supports it.

It is possible to discover the sex of an unborn fetus by taking a sample of cells from the amniotic sac in which the fetus floats and examining it, although few doctors would be willing to do this just to satisfy the curiosity of the parent. Soon after conception takes place, one of the two X chromosomes in the female curls up tightly near the edge of the nucleus of the cell. As the cell divides, this characteristic is passed on from cell to cell. When specially dyed, this coiled X chromosome appears as a spot at the surface of the nucleus of most cells in the female organism, making it readily

[5] S. Kleegman, "Therapeutic Donor Insemination," *Fertility and Sterility*, No. 5 (1964), pp. 7–31.

detectable, as the male lacks this spot in his cells. This same test can be used to determine the genetic sex of individuals who may have developed, for various reasons, some of the physical characteristics of both sexes.

Fetal Development of the Sex Organs

0–6 Weeks. For the first six weeks of life the fact that some embryos are developing under the control of forty-four regular chromosomes, one X chromosome, and one Y chromosome, while others are under the control of forty-four regular, one fully functioning X, and one coiled X chromosome, seems to make little difference. The tiny organism is busy growing and developing its basic structure. Although it does not yet look human, it has developed a clearly discernible head whose primitive eye sockets and ear membranes are already evident. Arm and leg buds are developing into real limbs, and along the back a long double row of buds is beginning to grow around the body to become the ribs and muscles of the back and chest. Inside, the forerunner of the spinal cord and the brain are already clearly differentiated, a primitive heart has begun to function, and a primitive gut is beginning to develop into a more complex set of structures.

Just in front of the gut, which at this point is a single tube running from the head to the base of the tail, is a ridge of tissue out of which the main internal organs of urination and of reproduction will develop. In this ridge one can already find the beginnings of the gonads or sex glands, but at this point they are neither male nor female in their structure. There is an outer rim of cells which look very much like the cells of the ovary, and in the center are tubules which are suggestive of the testes. On the outside of the body in the region where the external genitals are to develop there is a hump with a cleft running down its underside. The hump is suggestive of the male, the cleft of the female (see Fig. 15–2).

7–12 Weeks. During the second six weeks of life many of the structures of the fetus (as we may now call it) have become differentiated. The face begins to take on a human appearance: lips, chin, and nose take on a recognizable shape. The hands and feet have developed separate fingers and toes. The main muscles of the body are in place, and the fetus has a finished appearance even though it is still so small that its feeble movements cannot be felt by its mother. It would fit nicely into the palm of one's hand.

It is during this period that the genes of the Y chromosome begin to assert themselves. In some way the production of the male hormone, testosterone, is triggered, and this hormone in turn stimulates the development of the complex system of tubes in the until now undifferentiated gonads. These tubes become the sperm factories of the male in later life, as will be seen in greater detail in Section II below. The genital hump begins to grow and to assume the general shape of the penis, also in response to testosterone. The slit running down its underside gradually closes, forming a hollow tube within—the urethra. Every boy has the evidence of this original cleft, however, in the pink seam that runs down the full length of his penis on its underside.

At first, the female lags behind the male, and for a time the female fetus is distinguished chiefly in that it does not develop tubules and does not show a similar degree of growth of the penis. Despite the slowness of its growth, of course, it does retain a penis-like organ, the clitoris, which is, in effect, the head of the penis, somewhat undersized for lack of testosterone to stimulate its growth. The walls of the cleft, which in the male come together to form the shaft of the penis, in the female remain open and deepen under the influence of estrogen, the female hormone. These walls eventually become the inner lips (labia minora) and vestibule (area into which urethra and vagina open).

Two patches of discolored skin which first appear during this period below and on each side of the genitals also begin to develop differently. In the male these patches eventually become the scrotum, the bag which houses the testes. In the female they develop into the fleshy outer lips (labia majora) which protect her genital area. In addition, the female begins to respond to her own hormones by developing structures that have no close parallels in the male, namely, the vagina and the womb or uterus.

13 Weeks–Birth. All of the developments which began in the earlier periods continue throughout the prenatal period under the influence of a good deal of hormone stimulation. The male's capacity to produce testosterone is particularly vital to his development because he has no other source of it, while the female fetus, if lacking a supply of its own hormones, can develop adequately by drawing on the mother's supply. For this reason, when there are hormonal difficulties it is more common to find a feminized male than a masculinized female.

Perhaps the most dramatic event of this period is the dropping of the testes through the abdominal wall into the scrotum. Throughout most of prenatal life the testes remain in the abdomen in essentially the same position as the ovaries. During the last months of pregnancy, however, the growth of the tissue around them gradually maneuvers them down to the wall of the lower abdomen, and finally, at some time between the seventh month and birth, they descend through two openings in the abdominal wall into the scrotum. The reason for this move is that sperm cannot be manufactured at body temperature. Hanging outside the body, the testes are at a temperature two degrees cooler than the rest of the body. Boys whose testes, for some reason, do not descend are invariably infertile unless they have the testes brought outside by means of a surgical operation.

It is also interesting to note that the most common type of rupture or hernia in men is the result of a weakness in the abdominal wall where the testes went through. If this opening does not close as it should, it may rupture under pressure and permit part of the intestine to intrude into the scrotum. This gap must then be repaired surgically.

In the same period the vagina in the female, which has till now been a solid area of cells, becomes an actual (or at least a potential) space or pocket. Thus, both males and females are born into the world with a full set of the organs they will need in reproduction. Moreover, the female is born with all of the egg cells she will ever have—about 500,000 of them.

Puberty

From birth until about eight or nine years of age nothing very impressive happens in a child's sexual development. His hormone supply, which was relatively high during the crucial months of fetal development, is very low during early childhood. At about eight years a gradual buildup of testosterone and the estrogens begins in both boys and girls, although testosterone predominates in the male and the estrogens in the female. By about ten or eleven the level begins to increase dramatically, especially in the female. By twelve or thirteen years her estrogen level is over eight times as high as it was at ten to eleven. At the same time the pituitary, or master gland, located in the center of the skull at the base of the brain, sends out substantial quantities of F.S.H. (follicle-stimulating hormones) to stimulate the further development of eggs in the female and the manufacture of sperm in the male. In addition, at this time another pituitary hormone in the male, I.C.S.H. (interstitial cell-stimulating hormone), triggers still higher levels of testosterone production.

The results of this bombardment of hormones are first apparent in the female. Some time between the ages of ten and fourteen, usually, the girl first begins to notice pubic hair developing in the thick, inverted triangular pattern common to adult women. Within a month or so her breasts begin to bud, and within the year she will probably have her first menstrual period. Meanwhile, she is growing perhaps three inches per year in height, her hips are broadening in proportion to her height, and she is developing that layer

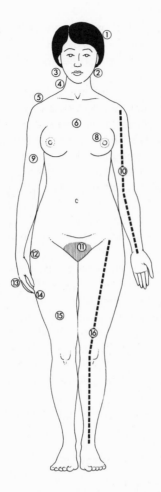

Figure 12–2. Primary and secondary sex characteristics of mature female, about age twenty.

1, head hair: female's is longer, more lasting. 2, facial hair: very faint in female; usually perceptible only in later years.
3, features: more delicate in female; face rounder, broader; head relatively smaller, rounder (from top); eyes set farther apart. 4, neck: shorter, more rounded. 5, shoulders: more rounded, softer, sloping. 6, chest: narrower, smaller. 7, body hair: very light and faint. 8, breasts: well-developed nipples; surrounding rings (areolae) large. 9, muscles: formations largely concealed by fat layers. 10, arms: "carrying angle" bent.
11, pubic hair: straight across; point grows down. 12, hips: wider, more rounded. 13, hands and feet: smaller, narrower, more delicately shaped. 14, thighs: more conical (wider at top but shorter in length). 15, legs: shorter; contours more even and rounded. 16, angle of thigh and leg: as with "carrying angle" of arm, angle is formed at knee, giving "knock-kneed" effect.

of fatty tissue under her skin which gives mature females their "rounded" appearance (Fig. 12–2). There is some evidence that she may not produce fertile eggs very regularly for a year or two after her first menstruation.

Trailing her by about a year, the boy is likely to notice pubic hair when he is somewhere between eleven and fifteen. A few months later he will probably experience his first ejaculation, either through masturbation or a wet dream, although his sperm count may not yet be very high. During the same period his voice will begin to change and hair will appear under the arms and perhaps on the chest. His body will broaden in relation to his hips. His muscles will develop more markedly than the girls'. Eventually he will surpass her in height and develop a beard (Fig. 12–3).

The exact onset of these changes varies from individual to individual and also from culture to culture. In addition to sex and genetic factors, age at puberty seems to depend on good nutrition. As the level of nutrition has improved in the Western world over the last century, the average age of first menstruation in girls has dropped correspondingly at a rate of approximately three months every ten years.[6] At the present time the average age of onset appears to be about 12.5 years. The age of first ejaculation for boys seems to be about 13.5, although different studies tend to come up with somewhat different averages. At whenever age it occurs, puberty completes the process of maturation by which men and women become physically able to play their respective parts in the process of procreation.

II. THE MALE REPRODUCTIVE SYSTEM

Genesis: Production of Sperm

In contrast to the sexually mature female, who typically produces one egg per month, the male produces millions of sperm per day from pubescence onward. Within his testes are well over a mile of tubing, each tubule being scarcely thicker than a human hair. Sperm are continuously being manufactured along this entire length. These tubes coil back and forth in the testes, and Figure 12–4 shows a cross section of one of them.

The process of forming sperm involves three steps and begins with the rather ordinary-looking cells that lie closest to the outer edge of the tubules. Each of these cells has the same number of chromosomes as any other body cell: forty-six, including an X and a Y chromosome. The first step is not at all spectacular. This original cell divides just as any other cell might divide, forming two cells,

[6] D. Hubble, "Earlier Puberty," *Clinical Pediatrics*, No. 5 (1966), pp. 410–14.

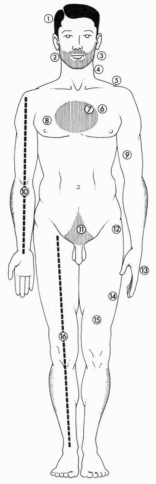

Figure 12–3. Primary and secondary sex characteristics of mature male, about age twenty-four.

Height: taller than female by about 6 per cent. Weight: heavier by about 20 to 25 per cent. 1, head hair: shorter; may fall out with age. 2, facial hair: grows throughout adult life. 3, features: more pronounced; heavier brow; squarer jaw; bigger nose, ears, teeth; face longer; head (front to back) longer. 4, neck: thicker, longer; larynx one-third larger and longer. 5, shoulders: broader, squarer. 6, chest: larger in every dimension. 7, body hair: much more evident, particularly on chest and arms. 8, breasts: rudimentary in size. 9, muscles: bigger, better developed, more obvious. 10, arms: longer, thicker; "carrying angle" straight. 11, pubic hair: grows up to point, forming triangle. 12, hips: narrower. 13, hands and feet: larger; fingers and toes heavier, stronger, blunter. 14, thighs: more cylindrical with bulge of muscles. 15, legs: longer, bulging calves. 16, angle of thigh and leg: as with "carrying angle of arm," forms straight line, thigh to ankle.

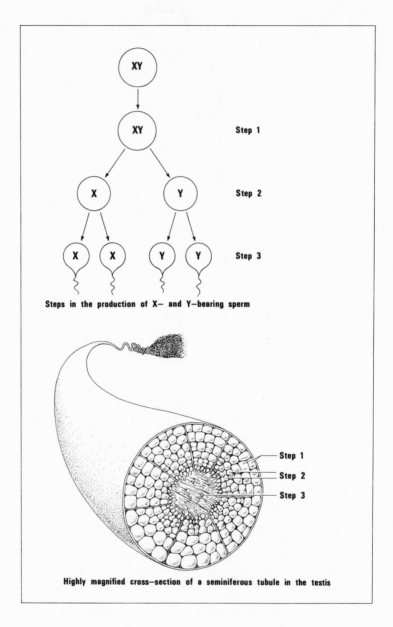

Figure 12–4. Production of sperm.
Step 1: the original cell divides, forming two identical cells each with forty-six chromosomes, including an X and a Y.
Step 2: the new cell splits in two; one chromosome from each pair is allotted to each cell; each of these cells has only twenty-three chromosomes, including an X or a Y. Step 3: the two new cells divide again into sperm cells; two are X-bearing and two are Y-bearing; all twenty-three chromosomes each.

each like the mother cell (Fig. 12–4, *Step 1*). One of these stays put and in effect replaces the mother cell at the edge of the tube. Its destiny is to serve as the original cell for future divisions of the type just described. The other cell is forced inward toward the middle of the tubule. This is the cell that responds to the pituitary hormones by dividing in a way unlike any other cell in the body. Instead of duplicating itself as all other cells do, this special cell lines up all of its chromosomes into twenty-three matched pairs, with X and Y paired with each other. Then it splits into two cells, one chromosome from each pair being allotted to each cell (*Step 2*). The result is two cells that have only half the number of chromosomes of all other body cells. These two new cells are forced further toward the center of the tubule and each divides again in the usual way, duplicating itself exactly (*Step 3*). This final division forces these four cells, which we may now properly call sperm cells, into the innermost ring of the tubule. Two of them are Y-bearing sperm cells and two are X-bearing sperm cells.

Once they are forced into the center of the tubule they join the other sperm being formed all around them and are moved along until at last they are emptied into the collection tubes, or *epididymis* (plural, *epididymides*) which lie against the testes in the scrotum. When the sperm enter these collection tubes, they appear inert and lifeless under the microscope. But in the two to four weeks that it takes them to traverse these collection tubes, something happens. Perhaps in response to the fluid produced by the tubes themselves, the sperm seem to come alive. Although still lethargic in comparison with their later level of energy, they can be observed to move their tails and propel themselves about in a limited way.

They are now prepared to move up into the body for storage. The *vas deferens* (plural, *vasa deferentia*) is a fourteen- to eighteen-inch tube connected at one end to the collection tubes in the scrotum. At the other end it flares out into a sort of sperm reservoir called the *ampulla*, deep in the abdomen. This is where sperm are stored to await ejaculation. The sperm travel from the scrotum to this reservoir without much effort of their own. They are helped along by the movements of tiny hair-like structures and by a series of muscular contractions of the walls of the vas deferens, which work like the swallowing muscles of the throat.

Once in the reservoir they stay until they are released into the *urethra*, the tube which takes them out of the body through the penis. They are expelled by the hundreds of millions into the urethra in the process of ejaculation. Failing that, they continuously dribble out into the urethra and are passed off, without notice, in the urine.

Exodus: The Mechanism of Ejaculation

The focal point of the entire male reproductive process is the moment of ejaculation. At this moment the responses of several very important organs must be coordinated by the body. The penis must be erect so as to form an efficient nozzle, the valve at the opening to the bladder must be tightly closed so that the ejaculation does not back up into the bladder instead of being forced out through the narrow nozzle of the erected penis, and the sperm reservoir (ampulla) itself must contract, along with two other important organs, the *seminal vesicles* and the *prostate*, at the right moment.

Penis. The penis is the external male sex organ and serves several purposes. In its non-erect state it is an efficient viaduct and nozzle for emptying the urinary bladder. In its erect state it serves as an equally efficient viaduct and nozzle for the much smaller volume of fluids that are involved in ejaculation, and also serves as an efficient instrument for penertating the vagina so that the sperm may be deposited inside the female where they will find their way to the egg.

The penis consists of two parts, the *body* or *shaft* and the *head* or *glans*. The penis is especially designed to become erect. It is almost completely filled by three strips of spongy material that run its length (Fig. 12–5). These strips are covered by two long muscles. When the penis is stimulated either by touch or imagination, blood rushes to these spongy tissues and cannot get out because of a valve system that closes the exits. Thus the penis becomes hard and erect and is able to perform its part in the reproductive process.

The head or glans of the penis is made up of the same materials as the shaft, but in addition is richly supplied with nerve endings which make it highly susceptible to stimulation. The sleeve of loose skin which covers the head of the unerected penis is called the *foreskin*. In erection it pulls back out of the way to expose the head of the penis to the fullest stimulation. For thousands of years the Jews and some other Near Eastern peoples have cut off the foreskin of baby boys as a part of a religious ceremony. This simple operation is called *circumcision*. Today most parents choose to have this done by a doctor soon after birth for health reasons; it is intended to prevent secretions from accumulating under the foreskin and causing irritation.

Seminal Vesicles. Inside the abdomen, just above the point at which the vas deferens from the testes enters into the urethra, lie the two seminal vesicles (Fig. 12–5). "Vesicle" means "little bladder" or sac. "Seminal" refers to the fact that until recently it was believed that the semen or sperm were stored here. Although research has dis-

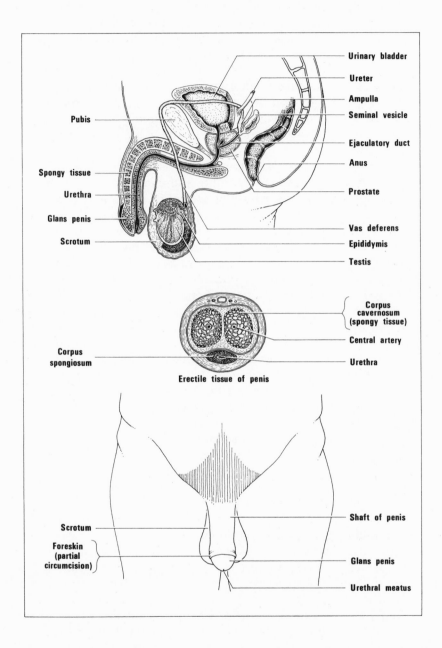

Figure 12–5. Male reproductive system.

proved this idea,[7] the name sticks. But even though they do not serve as the sperm reservoirs, the seminal vesicles play a very important role. In response to stimulation by the hormone testosterone they supply the largest part of the fluid which is involved in ejaculation. This fluid is rich in sugar content, and when the sperm join with the seminal fluid at the point of ejaculation, they react to this high-energy nourishment by becoming much more active. Where before they were sluggish, conserving their energies, now they come to life in preparation for their long journey inside the female.

It is believed that when the sugar level of the seminal fluid is too low, it may contribute to infertility in the male because without this vital nourishment even healthy sperm do not seem to be able to function adequately. Another interesting function of the seminal vesicles may be to contribute to the male sex drive. It is believed by many, although it is difficult to prove, that part of the explanation for the apparently greater urgency of the male's sex drive than the female's may be caused by pressure on the vesicle walls when they are too full. They partly empty when ejaculation occurs, and two, or at most three, ejaculations within a span of a few hours may deplete them almost entirely. It takes about two days for them to fill up again. As has been mentioned, if they are not emptied through ejaculation they dribble into the urethra in unnoticed amounts and are passed off in the urine. The theory tying these vesicles to male sex drive is based on the fact that any irritation of the organs connected with ejaculation can cause erection and what might be intepreted by the individual as pressure for sexual release.[8] Thus the male sex drive may indeed be "more pressing" than the female's, at least to the extent that a full seminal vesicle (and for that matter, a full ampulla) may irritate the surrounding sensitive tissue. It should be added, however, that the body is fully equipped to drain off these excess fluids without ejaculation, so that the view that ejaculation is a necessary function in the male, comparable to menstruation in the female, is without foundation.

Prostate Gland. Surrounding the juncture of the ampulla, the seminal vesicles, and the urethra is a ring-shaped gland about the size of a walnut called the *prostate*. It performs several important functions. First, it adds its own contribution to the fluid of ejaculation. Prostatic fluid includes citric acid, which acts on the sperm to make them even more mobile. It also includes chemicals which, it is believed, may help to make the female tract more hospitable to the

---

[7] R. S. Hotchkiss, *Fertility in Men* (Philadelphia: Lippincott, 1944).

[8] A. C. Guyton, *Textbook of Medical Physiology*, 3d ed. (Philadelphia: Saunders, 1966).

sperm. Finally, at the point of orgasm it contracts around the various tubes that join together in its center and acts as an auxiliary pump to help the seminal fluid along its way.

In older men the prostate can cause a great deal of difficulty. Because not only the sexual fluids but also urine must pass through it on the way out of the body, it is extremely important to the well-being of adult men, and sometimes becomes the site of cancer or other diseases. Doctors regularly check on its condition by inserting a gloved and lubricated finger into the rectum and determining its size and shape through the rectal wall.

The Moment of Ejaculation. A more complete treatment of the male climax or orgasm will be found in the following chapter, but at this point it should be noted that at the peak of sexual excitement, in response to a complex set of messages sent along the nerve paths from the body and the brain, almost all the muscles in the pelvic region contract. The bladder does not empty because the round valve muscle at the entrance is tightly closed in a spasm. The rectum is tightly closed also. But the contents of the sperm reservoir (ampulla) and seminal vesicle are forced into the urethra, where they are pushed along under considerable pressure by the contracting of the prostate and the muscles of the penis itself. The fluid finally passes through the constricted nozzle muscle at the end of the penis and, in the case of sexual intercourse, into the female vagina.

In all, the total volume of ejaculated fluid averages less than a teaspoon, but it may contain up to half a billion sperm, newly energized by the nourishment provided by the seminal and prostatic fluids which make up the largest part of its volume. What happens to this horde of sperm in the female tract will be discussed after the female reproductive system has been described.

III. THE OVULATION-MENSTRUATION CYCLE

As we have seen, the production of sperm is a day-in, day-out continuing process, punctuated only by voluntary ejaculation from time to time. The production of eggs, by contrast, involves an involuntary recurring cycle of events that gives a rhythm to the reproductive life of women which is absent in men. The ovulation-menstruation cycle, as it may be called, has four phases. Only the first phase is involved in the production of the egg, but the other three phases are equally vital in the whole reproductive process. This process is governed by the interrelationships of two pituitary hormones, the follicle-stimulating hormone (F.S.H.) mentioned earlier and *luteinizing* hormone (L.H.), and two hormones produced in the ovaries, *estrogen* and *progesterone*. Before discussing the parts which these various hormones play in the four phases of the cycle, however, it may be useful to give a brief description of the four major organs of the female reproductive system.

Organs of the Female Reproductive System

Ovaries. Within the abdomen on either side of the uterus and attached loosely to it by connective tissue lie two walnut-sized bodies, the *ovaries.* They get their name from their chief function, which is to produce eggs (*ova* is the Latin word for eggs, and *ovary* thus means "place of eggs"). In addition to being the place where eggs are kept, the ovary, as has already been mentioned, is the primary producer of the two female hormones, estrogen and progesterone. The ovary is much simpler in design than the testes. At puberty, each ovary consists of several hundred thousand eggs, each egg packaged in a little casing called a *follicle.* The space between the follicles is loosely packed with masses of otherwise useless filler cells.

Fallopian Tubes. Close to the ovaries are the open, many-fingered ends of the two Fallopian tubes. These tubes are four or five inches long—roughly the length and thickness of a mechanical pencil, only quite flexible. The inside tube running through the center of each is about as wide as thin pencil lead and, like the vas deferens in the male, is lined with tiny hair-like structures. It is attached at its other end to the uterus (Fig. 12–6) and serves as the passageway for the egg traveling toward the uterus and for the sperm traveling up from the uterus to meet it.

Uterus. The womb or uterus is a pear-shaped muscular organ located in about the center of the lower abdomen. It is the place where the baby develops before its birth. Ordinarily it can contain only a few teaspoonsful of fluid, but at full term, just before a baby is born, it may have expanded to a volume of as much as seven quarts in order to accommodate the baby and the sac of fluid in which it floats. At its upper end it has openings (Fig. 12–6) leading to the Fallopian tubes. At its lower end there is a narrow exit that projects into the vagina called the *cervix.* During pregnancy the tissue of the cervix keeps the baby from being dropped into the birth canal prematurely. At birth, the cervix dilates to permit birth to occur.

The lining of the uterus (called the *endometrium*) is a unique tissue. On top of the muscle that forms the main wall of the uterus there is a layer of tissue out of which grows a forest of glands and special blood vessels. The glands and vessels are surrounded by masses of filler cells which seem to have no other function than to support the forest. This lining is the soil in which the fertilized egg plants itself, and it is the tissue whose erosion, if no egg is planted,

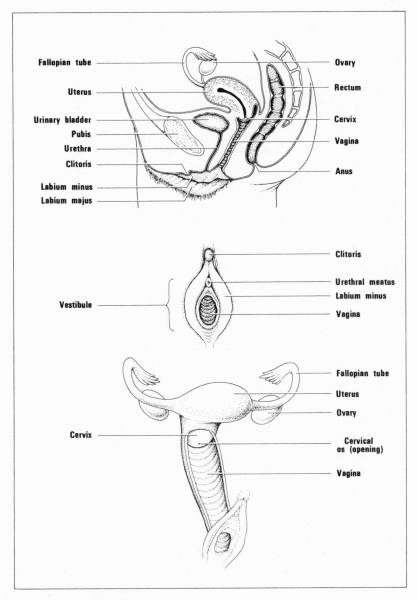

Figure 12–6. Female reproductive system.

brings about menstruation. The way that this occurs will be explained more fully in a following section.

Vagina. The neck of the uterus (cervix) opens out into the upper end of an elastic tube, roughly four inches long, called the *vagina*. The vagina itself opens at its lower end into the *vestibule* of the female external genitalia. It is so elastic that it can contract on the penis during sexual intercourse and yet, during childbirth, functioning as the birth canal, it can stretch to accommodate a baby's head. With this as background, let us return to the explanation of the four phases of the ovulation-menstruation cycle.

Phase 1: Building toward Ovulation

Ordinarily, *Phase 1* (Fig. 12–7) begins at about the time that the previous cycle has completed its last phase, menstruation. But whether it starts a little later or a little earlier than this, the thing that triggers it is an increase in the production of F.S.H. by the pituitary. This has a double effect. First of all, the follicles around the eggs in the ovaries begin to produce large quantities of estrogen, which in turn makes some of the follicles grow and also stimulates the lining of the uterus to re-establish itself. Second, in a way that is less clearly understood, it somehow reactivates certain eggs which have been waiting in an arrested state since before the individual female was born.

Events in the Ovaries. In the female fetus, by the twentieth week after conception all of the cells that will become eggs are already formed. At this stage these cells have the full number of chromosomes, forty-six. Then, in striking contrast to comparable cells in the male, these primitive female cells, while still in the fetus, begin the process of lining up the chromosomes for the special division into two cells with only twenty-three chromosomes each. The division begins, but before the process is complete it is arrested, and these cells, about 500,000 of them, remain in this state until at puberty the process is reignited in one or more cells each month. Fewer than 500 egg cells will ever complete this division begun before birth. The rest will gradually die. It is estimated that by the time a woman is thirty only about 10,000 of these cells are still able to respond to hormone stimulation.[9] Of course, 10,000 is more than enough, as only one per month is needed, but it is apparent that the rate of attrition is very high and that there is some reason for the apparently excessive supply of cells in the female just as there is in the male, namely, to offset the high mortality rate of the original cells.

Under the stimulation of estrogen some of the follicles (about ten in each ovary) begin to enlarge. No one knows what keeps the others from responding, but it is just as well because there is a very limited amount of room in the ovary for such development. As each follicle grows, the egg inside of it has more and more room, but at first it does not use it; it remains attached to the side of the follicle.

[9] N. J. Eastman and L. M. Hellman, *Williams' Obstetrics,* 13th ed. (New York: Appleton-Century-Crofts, 1966), p. 115.

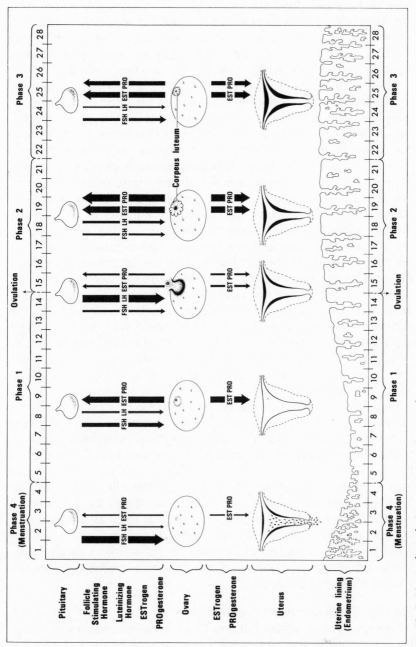

Figure 12–7. Normal ovulation-menstruation cycle.

Important things are happening to it however. At last it awakens from its long sleep and completes the cell division it began in fetal life. Two cells, each with twenty-two regular chromosomes and an X chromosome, are formed. One cell goes on to become the egg itself. The other eventually dies (although sometimes not until after reproducing itself, in which case both of the new cells die).

After about eight days of steady growth, a new hormonal message is sent to the developing follicle from the pituitary. It is luteinizing hormone, and in a way not yet understood it causes one of the twenty growing follicles to proceed in its development while all of the others recede and eventually disintegrate. In the next twenty-four hours the chosen follicle is bombarded with increased amounts of estrogen and with small amounts of a new hormone produced by the follicle in response to L.H., *progesterone*. Under these influences, the follicle grows rapidly: within a matter of hours it has formed a blister on the surface of the ovary as big as the end of one's little finger. Inside the blister the egg has broken loose from the follicle and is floating in the fluid. A special chemical weakens the wall of the ovary at the point where the blister has risen the highest. Finally, the egg pops out into the abdominal cavity, where it floats free for a moment. This release is called *ovulation*. It is the event that initiates Phase 2 in the cycle. There does not seem to be any predictable order in which the ovaries alternate from month to month in this process.[10] Before going on to the second phase, however, it is necessary to note briefly what has been happening in the uterus during Phase 1.

Events in the Uterus. At the beginning of the new cycle, the forest of vessels and glands that grow from the wall of the uterus is a field of raw stumps, which is all that is left after the previous menstruation. Under the influence of the upsurge of estrogen being produced in the ovaries, the blood vessels and glands begin to grow and come to look very much like trees. As they grow, the filler cells grow up between them to support them and cover them. By the time of ovulation the lining of the uterus is nearly as thick as it was before the last menstruation, but it is not yet ready to function as it must if a fertilized egg is implanted. For that the influence of another hormone, progesterone, is required, which is only available during the second phase of the cycle.

Phase 2: Building toward Implantation

The egg, whose release initiates Phase 2, experiences a very short-lived freedom in the abdominal cavity. It is entrapped almost im-

[10] L. B. Arey, *Developmental Anatomy*, 7th ed. (Philadelphia: Saunders, 1965), p. 49.

mediately by the finger-like flared end of the nearest Fallopian tube. Through a series of contractions the tube seems to be able to set up enough current to maneuver the egg into the opening. For the next twenty-four hours, the egg is slowly moved along the tube in a kind of swallowing motion, with the help of the tiny hair-like structures similar to those that move the sperm up the vas deferens. If it does not meet a sperm within the first day, it will die, having progressed less than halfway down the tubes in its journey toward the uterus.

The fact that an egg lives only one day after ovulation and that ovulation occurs only once a month makes the question of when that day is an important one. Ovulation takes place about fourteen days *before the next menstrual period begins.* In other words, Phases 2 and 3 of the cycle take about fourteen days and Phase 4, menstruation, can normally be expected to begin two weeks after ovulation. Unfortunately, people are more interested in knowing about ovulation before it occurs than after, and there is no such precise time interval from the start of Phase 4 (menstruation), to the end of the first phase of the next cycle (ovulation). The time may range from eight to twenty days and in exceptional cases may vary over an even wider range. The various techniques by which the time of ovulation may be determined more precisely are described in the chapter on family planning. Whenever it occurs, ovulation instigates a whole series of important reactions other than the release of the egg itself.

Events in the Ovaries. We have noted that several hours before ovulation the follicle begins producing a new hormone, progesterone. After ovulation occurs, the amount of this new hormone produced by the now empty follicle is greatly increased; in fact, this hormone more than any other is responsible for the occurrences of this second stage of the cycle. As the demand for progesterone increases, the retired follicle continues to grow and thicken until it may occupy one-third of the volume of the ovary. It turns yellow in this process and is known as the *yellow body,* or in its Latin form, the *corpus luteum.* The main function of the progesterone this yellow body produces (together with the estrogen which it continues to produce) is to prepare the wall of the uterus for implantation of the fertilized egg.

Events in the Uterus. Under the influence of progesterone the glands in the walls of the uterus begin to secrete fluid rich in a form of sugar. The blood vessels, which already look like trees, continue to grow and branch until they have to coil back upon themselves because there is no more room for them to grow normally within the uterine lining. Six or seven days after ovulation the wall of the uterus is at its maximum receptiveness for implantation. If it does occur, the newly implanted organism begins to produce its own progesterone and estrogen. In addition, it sends a special message hormone of its own, H.C.G. (human chorionic gonadotropin), to the pituitary, which then supplies it with luteinizing hormone to sustain the yellow body. If this does not occur by the ninth day of Phase 2, the pituitary stops the supply of L.H., which in turn causes the yellow body to cease producing progesterone and estrogen. The withdrawal of hormone support leads to Phase 3 of the cycle, the deterioration of the uterine lining.

Phase 3: Deterioration of the Uterine Lining

As the yellow body shrivels on the surface of the ovary, the blood vessels of the uterine lining gradually begin to deteriorate, and the blood in them becomes sludgy. Finally, on the last day before menstruation actually begins, the vessels suddenly contract, and the blood supply to the lining is cut off altogether. The tissue dies quickly. On the following day the vessels suddenly relax and hemorrhage. Just enough blood is released to seep underneath the layer of dead tissue and help slough it off.

Phase 4: Menstruation

Few women will believe it, but the average total menstrual flow amounts to about six teaspoons of blood. The old tree vessels break off down to the stumps, but constrictions in the vessels that supply them and in the muscles of the uterine wall itself keep the loss of blood to a minimum.

Menstruation is, of course, a healthy and normal part of the rhythm of life for all fertile women. When difficulties occur, a doctor should be consulted. One of the common difficulties of teenage girls is a particularly heavy flow, usually caused by failure to ovulate. Without ovulation and the resultant production of progesterone, the uterine lining continues to grow throughout the whole cycle as it did in Stage 1, and when menstruation does occur, there is likely to be a great deal more blood and tissue to dispose of.

Another common complaint of teenage girls is abdominal cramping just before and during menstruation. The reason for this is not fully understood, but it appears to be a result of the congestion of blood in the pelvic region due to progesterone withdrawal. Also it may be that uterine contractions somewhat like those of early labor may occur in some girls.

Menopause

Sometime between the age of forty and fifty-five most women observe that the ovulation-menstruation cycle begins to run down.

Generally it is the ovaries that cease to function first. They simply become unable to respond to the doses of F.S.H. sent out by the pituitary. When the estrogen level drops off, the F.S.H. level rises as the pituitary attempts to remedy the deficiency. These high levels of F.S.H. cause a periodic dilation of the blood vessels and cause the "hot flashes" which women sometimes experience during this period. It generally takes from one to five years for the body fully to adjust to the change. During this period it is not uncommon for an occasional egg to be released into the Fallopian tubes, and many a child has come into the world at least partly because his mother assumed she was infertile before that was actually the case.

IV. CONCEPTION AND IMPLANTATION

From Ejaculation to Conception

At the point of ejaculation somewhere between 200 and 500 million sperm are released into the vagina of the female,[11] a number so large that it is impossible to comprehend. Sperm are the smallest cells produced in the human body: It would take 600 of them laid head to tail to equal one inch, yet the sperm in an average ejaculation (about 300 million) laid out in this fashion would reach nearly eight miles.

The sperm itself is made up of three main units: the head, the mid-section, and the tail (Fig. 12–8). The head, which is only about one-tenth of the length of the sperm, contains little but twenty-three tightly packed chromosomes. Behind the head is the mid-section, which produces the chemicals which convert the nutrients in the surrounding fluid into energy for the sperm. The tail has as its major function the propelling of the entire cell by means of a whip-like motion. Under favorable circumstances a sperm can propel itself along at a rate of about seven inches per hour.[12] In contrast to the sperm, the egg is the largest cell of the human body and is clearly visible to the naked eye, about the size of the period at the end of this sentence. It would take three sperm, head to tail, to span the diameter of the egg, but by volume it is 85,000 times as big as the sperm that will fertilize it (Fig. 12–8).

Contrary to popular belief, there is evidence that the sperm never get beyond the vagina unless they are deposited near the time of ovulation. The mucus which plugs the entrance to the uterus is

[11] In fertility studies the sperm count is usually given per cubic centimeter rather than per ejaculation. The normal range is from 50 to 130 million sperm per cc. Less than 20 million is considered virtually infertile. The normal range of abnormal sperm produced is 10 to 50 per cent. A rate above 50 per cent may also be a factor in infertility.

[12] Arey, *Developmental Anatomy*, p. 53.

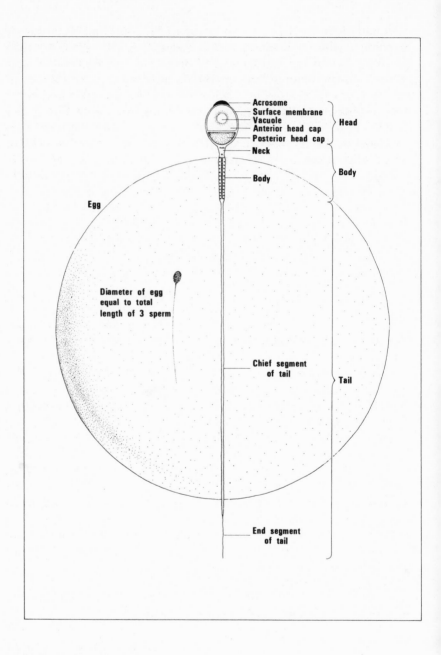

Figure 12–8. Sperm and egg.

ordinarily too thick for any sperm to get through. The hormones that trigger the second stage of the female cycle also have the effect of thinning out this mucus so that sperm may penetrate it.[13] Even under these ideal conditions, however, only about 1 per cent of the sperm do enter this passage. The rest die within a few hours in the mildly acidic and therefore hostile conditions within the vagina.

Once in the neck of the uterus, the sperm find a more hospitable environment. The uterus and tubes are mildly alkaline rather than acid and much better suited to sperm survival. It also appears that the muscular movements of the uterus help them to move along, so that their motion is no longer fully dependent on their own energy. Nevertheless, the majority die while traversing the uterus, and probably only a few thousand actually enter the tubes. Half of them, of course, will eventually find themselves in the wrong tube because, so far as can be determined, there is no special chemical attraction exerted upon the sperm by the egg, as is the case among some other animals.[14] But if all goes well, between one hour and one day after ejaculation some sperm will finally collide with the egg.[15]

The Moment of Conception

Usually the egg is reached by several sperm more or less simultaneously. At the point of contact a sperm releases a special chemical from the foremost part of its head which weakens the wall of the egg. Some studies seem to indicate that the job goes much faster if the egg is attacked by several sperm at once because this chemical is additive in its effect, and the amount of effort required to penetrate the outer membrane of the egg is much reduced when several sperm are working on it at once.[16] The relative infertility of men with low sperm counts may thus be accounted for. Not only is the likelihood of a single sperm finding its mark reduced by a low count, but the likelihood of several sperm arriving together is smaller. After some effort one or more of the sperm break through the outer membrane, and the first one in unites with the nucleus of the egg. In such a manner each of us began his life.

From Conception to Implantation

We have noted that if it is not fertilized an egg will die within twenty-four hours of ovulation, never reaching the uterus alive. The

[13] E. T. Tyler, *Sterility* (New York: McGraw-Hill, 1961), pp. 9–10.

[14] M. C. Chang, *Recent Progress in the Endocrinology of Reproduction*, ed. C. W. Lloyd (New York: Academic Press, 1959), pp. 132–36.

[15] E. S. Taylor, *Beck's Obstetrical Practice* (Baltimore: Williams & Wilkins, 1966), p. 23.

[16] Eastman and Hellman, *Williams' Obstetrics*, p. 118.

fertilized egg, however, with its full complement of forty-six chromosomes, is very much prepared for the journey. The muscular motions and the waving of the hair-like projections from the walls of the tube slowly move it along until after three days it reaches the uterine cavity (Fig. 12–9). Meanwhile, the original single cell has begun to divide. By the time it reaches the uterus the egg can boast not one but many cells. As the cells multiply they begin to specialize. Only a few represent the embryo itself. The remainder form the special mechanism which will make it possible for the embryo to implant itself in the uterus. After three or four days of further development, the implantation mechanism is ready to operate. During this period the growing fertilized egg is free to float about in the uterus, in principle. Actually it probably rests on the inside surface of the uterus near the place where it left the tube.

Roughly one week after conception, when it has become a hollow ball of over a hundred cells, the growing egg produces enough of a special chemical substance from its outer layer to attach itself to the wall of the uterus. Once attached, it literally digests its way through the outer lining, drawing nourishment from these richly supplied tissues while burying itself within them. The tissue gradually closes behind the egg and within a week of the first adhesion to the wall (second week of life) it has planted itself beneath the surface and is sending out roots.

Formation of the Placenta

The newly implanted egg sends out roots, or long columns of tissue, and, necessarily, almost the first thing that they encounter are the blood vessels within the walls of the uterus. The roots rupture the walls of the blood vessels in their path, one after another, until each root is bathed in a small lake of maternal blood (Fig. 12–10). The tissue which has invaded the uterine wall is called the *placenta*.

By the seventeenth day after fertilization a primitive mechanism of exchange has been established between mother and embryo. The mother's blood brings oxygen and nutriment to the little lakes. These vital substances are passed through the walls of the cells of the embryonic root system and passed on to the embryo itself. At the same time the embryo passes waste products back through its roots into the mother's blood where it is passed off along with the wastes from her own tissues. At no time in this process is blood exchanged between the mother and the embryo. For this reason, the root system is sometimes called the *placental barrier*: the roots permit only certain materials from the mother's blood to pass to the embryo and only certain other materials to pass from embryo to mother.

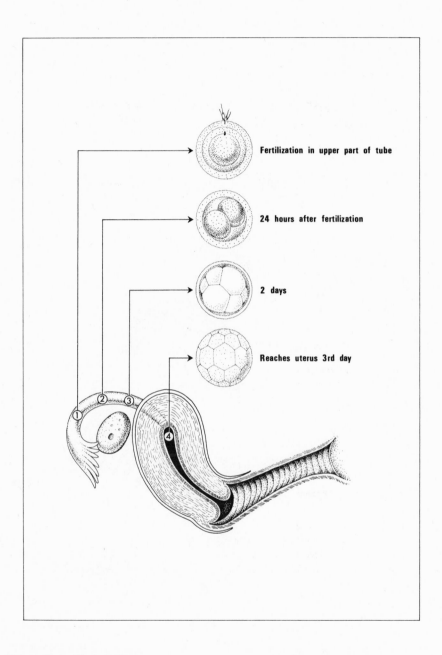

Fertilization in upper part of tube

24 hours after fertilization

2 days

Reaches uterus 3rd day

Figure 12–9. Conception.

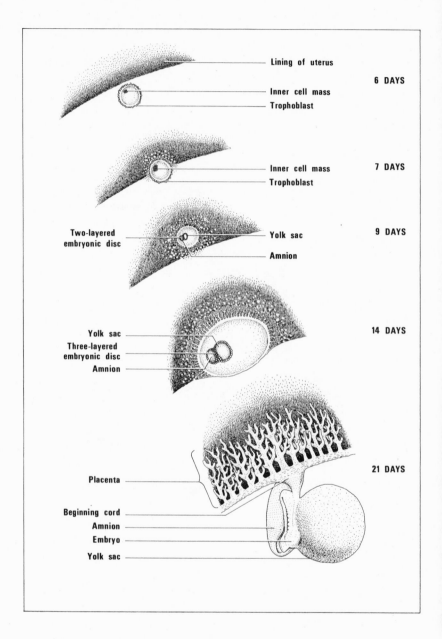

Figure 12–10. Implantation and development of placenta.

In addition to providing the mechanism of exchange, the roots perform another vital function. In their outer layer of cells they produce the hormones necessary to support the pregnancy. First they send out a hormonal signal to the corpus luteum to keep up its production of estrogen and progesterone instead of dying off, as it will if no pregnancy occurs. Then these cells begin to produce their own supply of estrogen and progesterone. Without a reliable supply of these two hormones, the pregnancy could not be maintained. The wall of the uterus would break down as at menstruation, and the embryo would abort. By the seventh week the placenta is supplying half of the estrogen in the system and more progesterone than the ovaries ever did produce. The placenta provides one other important hormone, which stimulates growth in the embryo much as the pituitary growth hormone stimulates growth in the newborn child a few months later. But at this stage there is no pituitary in the embryo, and so the placenta must do it all.

To return to the embryo itself, with its source of hormones and nourishment assured, it begins to develop and grow very rapidly. At the end of the second week it is only detectable as a small lump in the uterine lining. By the third week it has grown out on a stem into the uterine cavity, and by the end of the fourth week it is as big as the end of one's little finger, growing at the end of a quarter-inch cord.

Throughout the remainder of the pregnancy, the embryo, the placenta, and the cord that connects them grow in step with each other. A larger embryo demands a larger root system and, if it is to float freely in the fluid-filled sac, it needs also an even longer cord.

The process of embryonic development will be outlined in Section V, but first it may be useful to explain what happens when not one but two or more embryos are implanted in the mother's uterus.

Twinning

Sometimes more than one fetus is carried in the uterus at one time. This situation can occur in one of two ways. There can be two separate eggs fertilized in the tubes at one time, in which case we speak of *fraternal twinning,* or there can be only one egg, which, at some time soon after it is fertilized divides into two separate identical organisms. This is called *identical twinning* (Fig. 12–11).

Fraternal Twinning. No one knows exactly why two eggs are sometimes produced instead of the usual one. The tendency is apparently inherited in the female line, and thus may be said to run in families. Aside from inherited tendencies, double ovulation is more likely to occur in older women and in women who have already had several children, but we can only guess at the reason.

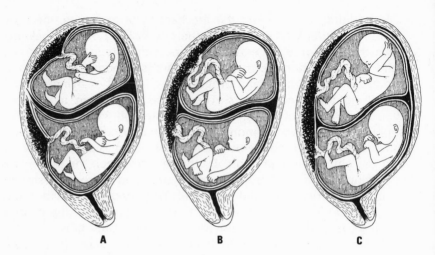

A   B   C

Figure 12–11. Twinning.

A, *fraternal twins: two placentas; each fetus has its own double sac; sexes may differ. B, fraternal twins: two placentas have merged; sexes may differ. C, identical twins: one placenta; each fetus has its own inner sac (amnion), with a single outer membrane enveloping both; sexes the same.*

Since the two fetuses develop from two different eggs and two different sperm, they are really no more closely related than any other brother or sister. One may turn out to be a boy and the other a girl, one might have dark hair and the other light hair, and so on. Each of the two fertilized eggs implants itself separately. If the implantations happen to be widely separated in the uterus, there will be two distinct placentas and two bags of waters. If, as sometimes happens, they end up close to each other, the two placentas may run together, although each embryo will have its own bag of waters. A woman with fraternal twins really has two separate pregnancies that happen to occur at the same time.

In the course of nature, it is quite rare for multiple ovulation (that is, ovulation involving three or more eggs at once) to occur. Recently, however, a number of artificially induced multiple births have been noted in the newspapers. These were connected with a new drug therapy which has been developed to help women who cannot ovulate because of insufficient F.S.H. production in the pituitary. A synthetic hormone similar to F.S.H. is given these women to induce ovulation. The problem is that the finely balanced interplay of the hormones that in nature almost always limits the ovaries to releasing one egg at a time is upset, and several eggs may be released at once. Contrary to some newspaper reports, this

F.S.H. "fertility" pill has no relationship to the contraceptive pills which are in such wide use today. It is difficult to imagine how the latter could be a factor in multiple ovulation.

Identical Twinning. The other type of twinning, in which a single fertilized egg splits into two separate organisms, is entirely different from multiple ovulation. Studies with animal eggs show that this type of splitting only occurs when the fertilized egg is under some sort of stress. For example, in the laboratory identical twinning can be induced by subjecting the growing organism to alcohol, changes in temperature, or intense irradiation. This type of twinning, then, has little to do with heredity and results from environmental factors such as poor nutrition in the mother, as reflected in the fact that there are more identical twins among Negroes than among whites and among poor whites than among middle-class whites.

In humans identical twinning has been observed to occur at any point in development between the second and the fourteenth day. Only about one-fourth of the products of these divisions survive until birth. It is believed that the most common stimulus to this type of twinning in humans is delayed implantation, which deprives the fertilized egg of nourishment at a critical point in its development. Identical twins share the same placenta and may share both membranes of the bag of waters, the outer membrane alone, or neither membrane.

Sometimes it is difficult to tell at birth whether twins are identical if they share the same placenta but have separate bags of waters, especially if the two infants have a strong physical resemblance, and it is sometimes important to know whether twins are identical because if they are they have a capacity for exchanging organs which fraternal twins do not. In some cases, organ transplants have meant the difference between life and death to an identical twin. In such cases blood types and also hand- and footprints may be relied upon. Only identical twins have the same prints.

V. PRENATAL DEVELOPMENT AND PREGNANCY

The process by which a single cell becomes a human being is probably the most fascinating mystery in the whole field of biology. Enormous strides have been made toward understanding how the genes send out chemical messengers, which in turn produce chemical keys which act upon various cells in various ways. At this writing, however, no one knows what makes one cell develop as a nerve cell, another as a liver cell, and a third as a bone cell. But if we do not know how to explain the various steps that the organism takes on its way to independent life, at least we can describe some of them.

Prenatal Development

First Month. It has already been stated that at the time of implanta-tion the seven-day-old developing organism consists of a hollow ball of cells, almost all of which are designed to facilitate the im-plantation itself. Only a handful on one edge (the edge where the ball always sets down on the surface of the uterus) are destined to develop into the embryo. At this early stage the entire compass of that potential being is a tiny disc of cells only two layers thick. Within four or five days a third layer develops between the other two. From this point onward the destinies of these three layers are separate. The top layer (*ectoderm*) is destined to provide the raw material for the skin, sense organs, and nervous system. The middle layer (*mesoderm*) develops into the skeleton and muscles and some organs, such as the heart and kidneys. The bottom layer (*endoderm*) serves as the mother tissue for the digestive system and the lungs.

The first major step in all of this differentiation occurs during the third and fourth weeks of life, when each of these three layers de-velops into a tube. The ectoderm grows in such a way that the edges curl up like a Mexican tortilla to form the *neural tube* along what will eventually be the back of the embryo. The front end of this tube in weeks to come will develop into the brain, while the rest will become the spinal cord.

The mesoderm forms its tube in a different manner. In the third week, little islands of blood cells and tiny blood vessels appear in the mesoderm. By the middle of the following week these smaller vessels have united to form a single large tube, the *heart tube*. On about the twenty-fifth day this tube begins to twitch irregularly, and then to pump. From that day until death, perhaps seventy or eighty years later, the heart never stops.

The third layer, the endoderm, forms its tube by humping in the middle to form a long ridge that eventually becomes hollow. This tube is called the *primitive gut*, and it runs from a gaping hole at the front end, which will become the mouth, to a blind alley without an opening at the back end, where the rectum or anus will eventu-ally be.

By the end of the first thirty days of life the embryo is already quite a complete organism, even though it is only about a quarter of an inch long (Fig. 12–12). About half of its total length is devoted to the head, which seems to be flopped forward on the chest. There is no face, as such. Where the mouth will be there is a gaping, ragged hole across the whole front end. On either side of the head, facing in opposite directions, are eye stalks, looking a little like wine glasses, sticking out of a primitive brain. Behind them, almost halfway back to the tail, are little spots on each side that will de-

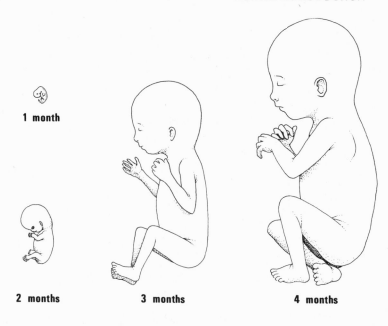

1 month

2 months   3 months   4 months

Figure 12–12. Size of embryo at one, two, three, and four months. Approximately three-fifths actual size.

velop into the ear drums. There is no sign of an outer ear, or, for that matter, of nose or chin or lips or cheeks. Arms and legs are not yet developed, but the four buds from which they will grow are already clearly discernible, and down the back of the embryo are twenty-one pairs of buds called *somites* which will form the vertebrae and ribs and muscles (Fig. 12–13).

Inside, the chambers of the heart have begun to form, and below the heart the liver has taken shape. The primitive gut has already begun to differentiate into the fore-gut which will become the esophagus, the mid-gut which will become the stomach, and the hind-gut which will become the intestine. The lung already exists as a tiny sac on the end of a tube opening off the fore-gut. The primitive kidney is clearly identifiable. Together with these familiar features, however, there are some which are less familiar. For one thing, about one third of the front of the embryo is umbilical cord, the passage through which the blood of the embryo is pumped through the placental root system. Just above the cord is a strange sac-like structure called the "yolk sac" because in some animals, although not in humans, it is full of yolk. Now the mid-gut opens into the yolk sac, but before another month has passed the sac will wither and drop off. In the region of what will be the neck there are slits that become gills in fish but develop in an entirely different

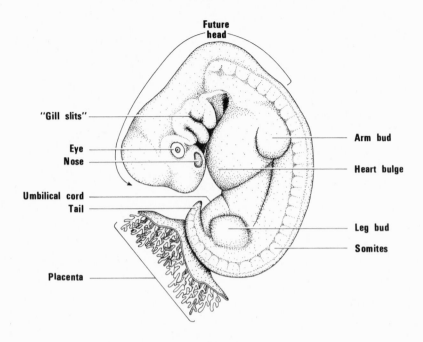

Figure 12–13. Month-old embryo in detail.

fashion in humans. And there is a very noticeable tail. All in all, this embryo could scarcely be distinguished from the embryo of a pig or cat on casual inspection. Its uniquely human characteristics have not yet developed very far, but it has come a long way down the road from the single cell it was thirty days before.

Second Month. It is in the second month that this strange-looking embryo takes on a shape and form that is easily discernible as human. The gaping orifice at the front end of the organism evolves into a face. As the head grows, the sides fill out, and the eyes, which had been facing in opposite directions like those of fish, come to focus forward in the human style. Moreover, they develop more fully until by the end of the second month they are complete down to the eyelids which cover them.

The mouth is formed by tissue growing from either side of the head and neck. One pair of buds joins to form the lower jaw and chin. (The place where they join is clearly evident in the cleft chin for which some people are admired.) Another pair of buds grows from the side of the neck to form the upper jaw, and still another forms the soft palate. One evidence of these is the bow shape of the upper lip. When fusion is incomplete, there may be a cleft palate or a "harelip." As they form the upper and lower jaws and palates, these buds also begin to fuse until they meet and form the cheeks. (It may be some consolation to those who envy the dimples of others to know that they are simply a minor flaw in this fusing process.) While the mouth is thus being formed, the tongue thrusts up from the floor of the throat. The tissue between the incipient nostrils humps to form a broad nose. The external ears begin to fuse together on the sides of the head-neck. All these developments are shown in Figure 12–14.

The rest of the body is also taking on a more human shape. The arm and later the leg buds grow and develop into arms and legs. At the end of these limbs, fan-like ridges grow and before the end of the month separate into fingers and toes. The constrictions which come to be elbows and knees, wrists and ankles, develop also. The whole trunk elongates and rounds out as muscles begin to grow between the outer skin and the inner organs, starting with the so-mites in back and growing around toward the chest. In a similar fashion the twelve ribs grow around from the back to fuse together in the sternum or breastbone in front. The thirty-three vertebrae, shoulder blades, collar bones, arm bones, wrist bones, hip and pelvic bones, leg bones, ankle bones, and foot bones all are formed during this month, although they are not made of the familiar, white, hard material we think of as bone, but rather of soft, cartilaginous ma-terial such as the "bones" of salmon. This permits growth in a way that would be impossible if the hard substance we think of as bone were deposited in the beginning.

Inside the embryo the liver is growing faster than other organs until it occupies about one-tenth of the total volume of the embryo. The other internal organs are also undergoing important differentia-

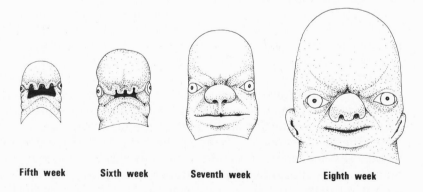

Fifth week   Sixth week   Seventh week   Eighth week

Figure 12–14. Formation of face during second month. Approximately eight times actual size.

tion and development. One other development deserves notice. Between the newly developed legs, the primitive and as yet undifferentiated external sex organ appears as a genital hump with a cleft on its underside (see Section I of this chapter for a more detailed description of this aspect of fetal development).

In this second month the length of the embryo is quintupled and its weight increases seventy-four times. However, despite the disproportionately large head, undersized limbs, and the large cord attached to its abdomen, there is no trouble identifying this inch-long being as a member of the human race. By convention, from this point onward, it is no longer called an embryo but a *fetus*. All the physical development that occurs for the rest of its life is, for the most part, merely a refinement on what has been achieved so far.

Third Month. Although, as was said, the major structural features are formed by the beginning of the third month, some interesting developments occur in this period. For example, as we noted (see Section I), this is the month in which male-female differentiation becomes evident in the internal sex organs. This is the month in which teeth buds are first noted in the gum ridges of the jaws. The vocal cords first appear during this period, although they are thick and lax and incapable of operation at this point.

Ossification (the laying down of the hard part of the bones) makes its first appearance near the centers of some of the large bones of the body. This process of gradual ossification of the bones is not completed until late in adolescence, and when it is, no further growth of the skeleton is possible. (It might be mentioned that the bones of the skull are hard from the beginning, but they do not fit together tightly and continue to grow at the edges, thus the "soft spots" in the newborn baby's skull.)

The digestive system begins to operate to the limited extent, at least, that the inner tract becomes lubricated with mucus. The pancreas begins to secrete insulin, and the liver has already begun to secrete bile. The kidney even begins to secrete urine in small amounts and voids it into the amniotic sac or bag of waters. It should be pointed out, however, that the real business of providing nourishment and excreting wastes is still performed by the placenta. The fetus's own activities in these areas are only "dry runs," as it were. The liver temporarily takes on the task of supplying the red blood cells until the bone marrow can develop to take over this function. Nails appear on fingers and toes, and although the mother cannot yet detect it, spontaneous fetal muscular movement begins to occur. By the end of this third month, the fetus is a little over three inches long and weighs about half an ounce (Fig. 12–15).

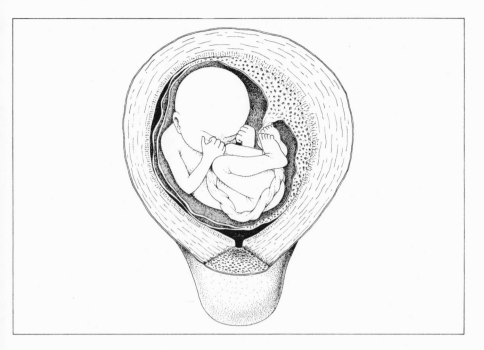

Figure 12–15. Three-month-old fetus in uterus.

Fourth through Sixth Month. One of the most striking features of the second three months of development is that approximately in the middle of this period the fetal movements become strong enough for the mother to feel the "quickening" which at one time was believed to be the moment that life entered the body.

The external genitals of the male and female become clearly differentiated during this period. Hair follicles and the oil glands that go with them begin to form in the skin, and a fine downy hair begins to grow on the body. Finger and toe prints also develop in the skin. The eyes are open, completely formed, and sensitive to light. The inner ears develop more fully and become sensitive to sound (as was first discovered by a researcher banging on the side of a metal tub with a hammer while his pregnant wife was bathing). The taste buds become operative.

The lungs form, although they would still be ineffectual in their operation if the fetus were born at this point. The centers in the brain which control breathing are not yet fully developed and babies born in the sixth month (or even the seventh) may die simply because they "forget" to breathe. Some babies delivered during the sixth month have lived, however, despite the 100:1 odds against it. The smallest to survive weighed only about one pound. Unfortunately, even if a fetus in the one- to three-pound range should survive, the probability of brain damage due to ineffective breathing is so great (50 to 60 per cent) that many parents' joy at saving the baby is marred by finding that it will be severely handicapped for life.

At the end of the sixth month, the fetus is about eleven inches long and weighs about one and a half pounds. It may be confidently asserted that "sixth-month" babies born weighing substantially more than this are inaccurately labeled; that is, they were conceived more than six months prior to their birth.

Seventh through Ninth Month. The final three months of life are devoted to several types of refinement which are important to the baby's ability to survive. In addition to growing in size, the body develops a layer of protective fat under the skin that helps to insulate the baby when it is exposed to air. The absence of this layer in premature babies is what gives them the red and wrinkled look that they have. In addition to the fatty layer of insulation, the baby's brain also develops its temperature control mechanism. The lack of this mechanism is what necessitates the use of incubators for premature babies.

This is the period when the testes descend into the scrotum in the male. As was pointed out earlier, if this descent fails to occur, and the defect is not corrected after birth, the result is permanent sterility.

Perhaps the most important developments are those that occur in the brain and lungs to prepare the infant for breathing in the outside world. The longer the baby continues in its protected environment in the womb, the more certain it is of being able to cope with the challenges of extra-uterine life when it is born.

Having looked at the process of prenatal development in the fetus, let us now look at this period as it is experienced by the mother.

Pregnancy

First Trimester. Typically, the first tentative sign that a woman might be pregnant is missing her menstrual period. Of course, this alone need not mean anything, as many physical and psychological factors can influence the regularity of the menstrual cycle. If this symptom is accompanied by 1) enlargement of the breasts (frequently resulting in a tingling of the nipple); 2) darkening of the ring around the nipple; 3) greater irritation of the bladder, as evidenced by a greater frequency of urination; and 4) possibly nausea (morning sickness),[17] then she may think it probable that she is pregnant.

All of these are only "presumptive" signs of pregnancy, however. The earliest conclusive test for pregnancy is made about the forty-first day after the beginning of the last period. At this point the embryo, if one exists, is nearing the end of its first month of life, and the placenta has begun to produce a unique placental hormone (H.C.G.) in quantities large enough to be evident in an analysis of the urine. In most urban areas laboratories equipped to do this analysis are readily available, and the question of pregnancy can be quite accurately determined in a matter of minutes.

Aside from this type of test, the doctor's examination can often detect a softening of the cervix. By the twelfth week after the last menstrual period the fetal heartbeat can be detected by special instruments, and of course this is a certain sign of pregnancy.

Spontaneous abortion, the loss of a fetus due to natural causes, is most likely to occur during the tenth to twelfth week. In the large majority of cases the abortion is caused by improper development of the fetus, the result of some defect in the original egg or sperm or some difficulty at the time of implantation.

Contrary to popular belief, the mother's activity cannot dislodge a healthy fetus. Records kept on pregnant servicemen's wives during World II and the Korean War showed them to have half as many miscarriages as the national average despite the fact that they had to carry their own luggage and do the "man's work" involved in moving and setting up new quarters. Even such experiences as falling or being struck or kicked in the abdomen can seldom be shown to cause abortion. In the early stages of pregnancy the developing embryo is securely sheltered by the pelvic bones and is effectively cushioned by the bag of waters in which the new life is suspended. Despite the fact that spontaneous abortion after a fall or blow is a vital element in several well-known novels and dramas (such as Margaret Mitchell's *Gone With the Wind*), the evidence is that any abortions which followed such incidents would probably have occurred anyway.

Second Trimester. The pregnant woman is generally most comfortable during this period. Morning sickness is usually gone by this time, but the fetus is not yet big enough to cause the discomfort experienced later in the pregnancy. By sixteen to eighteen weeks (measured always from the last menstrual period rather than from the estimated date of actual conception), the fetal bones can be

[17] About 75 per cent of pregnant women experience some degree of morning sickness during the first trimester of pregnancy.

seen upon X-ray. The baby's movements begin to be felt by about the eighteenth week. A woman who has had more than one baby can sometimes recognize the baby's movement even sooner than this, partly because the uterus itself is thinner after several births and partly because her experience makes her more sensitive to it.

By the nineteenth or twentieth week the fetal heartbeat is discernible without any special equipment. Beyond all of these technical evidences of pregnancy this is the general period when the baby begins to "show," that is, the mother's abdomen begins to bulge noticeably. This is because by the end of the second trimester the fetus has grown too large for the pelvis and, together with the uterus, now projects up into the abdomen just above the level of the mother's navel (Fig. 12–16).

Third Trimester. If any complications are going to occur in pregnancy, it is likely that they will occur in the last three months. For this reason, women generally step up the frequency of their visits to their doctors during this period. The most common serious complications of pregnancy today are hemorrhage (heavy bleeding), infection, and toxemia of pregnancy. The first two are self-explanatory. The symptoms of toxemia are swollen ankles, high blood pressure, and protein in the urine. If caught early, toxemia can generally be dealt with quite easily, but if allowed to go unchecked it can lead to convulsions (*eclampsia*) which are dangerous to the mother, or premature separation of the placenta, which of course is dan-

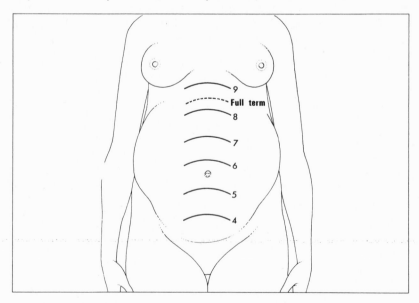

Figure 12–16. Height of uterus, by month of pregnancy.

gerous to the unborn child. In the vast majority of cases no major problems occur at all.

In the typical pregnancy the mother gains about twenty-five pounds. About fourteen pounds is lost at the time of delivery. The remainder is fluid in her own tissue which will gradually be eliminated. If she should gain substantially more weight than this, it is likely to be the result of changed eating habits rather than the pregnancy itself.

In order to accommodate the growing child, the uterus grows till it compresses the organs of the abdomen up under the lower rib cage (Fig. 12–16). This pressure against the diaphragm may cause shortness of breath, which may be partially alleviated when the baby drops into the pelvis the week or two prior to delivery, or earlier from women carrying their first child.

One aspect of married life, sexual relations, generally tapers off during this last three months. Although there is no clear evidence that sexual intercourse may harm the fetus, there is no question but that it becomes more and more uncomfortable for the wife during this period. For this reason and because of the fear (however unfounded) that they might cause a premature birth, most couples voluntarily abstain from sexual intercourse for the last few weeks of the pregnancy.[18]

The average period of gestation is about forty weeks (280 days) from the last menstrual period. However, women should not be misled by the preciseness of this number. Only about one in twenty-five actually deliver on the predicted day; about 50 per cent deliver within one week of that day. But whatever the exact timing, if all has gone well the process of reproduction ultimately reaches its fruition in the birth of a baby.

VI. LABOR, CHILDBIRTH, AND RECOVERY

Labor

The question of what starts labor is of general interest, but at present no one can give a positive answer. One factor, as in so many other phases of the reproductive process, is a hormonal message from the pituitary. The hormone involved is *oxytocin*. When it becomes necessary to induce labor, doctors do so by giving the mother a synthetic version of this hormone.

The uterus is constructed of many bands of circular, elastic mus-

---

[18] J. T. Landis, T. Poffenberger, and S. Poffenberger, "The Effects of First Pregnancy upon the Sexual Adjustment of 212 Couples," *American Sociological Review*, 15 (1950):767–72; W. E. Pugh and F. L. Fernandez, "Coitus in Late Pregnancy," *Obstetrics and Gynecology*, No. 2 (1953), p. 636.

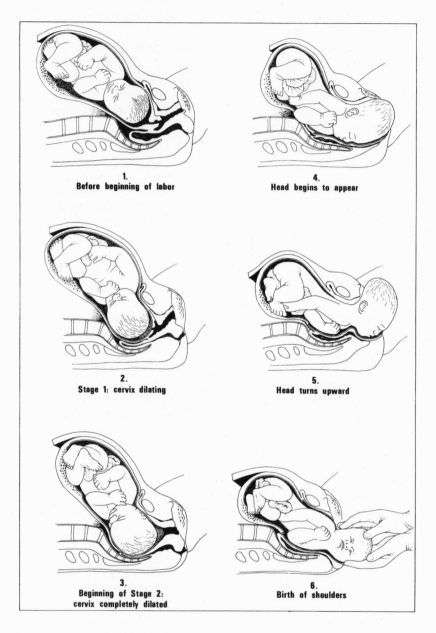

1.
Before beginning of labor

2.
Stage 1: cervix dilating

3.
Beginning of Stage 2:
cervix completely dilated

4.
Head begins to appear

5.
Head turns upward

6.
Birth of shoulders

Figure 12–17. Birth of baby.

cles. They are arranged in a complex pattern, and, like a ball of string, they do not all run in the same direction but rather in almost every possible direction. Under the influence of oxytocin these muscles begin to contract. At the same time the connective tissue of the cervix begins to soften. The contractions become more intense, and the woman feels them as though they begin in her back and work around to the front. The way her nerves report the discomfort is misleading and represents the phenomenon of "referred pain." In fact, the muscles at the top of the uterus begin the contraction and remain firm as it proceeds down through the muscles toward the cervix. This has the effect of pushing the baby's head up against the cervix, which forces it to open a tiny bit at each contraction (Fig. 12–17). Even if the baby is breech (that is, presents its feet or buttocks toward the cervix instead of its head), the fluid in the bag of waters itself puts pressure upon the cervix. As a result of this repetitive pressure, in combination with local hormonal action, the tiny network of capillaries in the cervix is ruptured, and the small show of blood that results is one sign that real labor has begun. Another event that generally occurs as the cervix begins to dilate is the bursting of the membranes of the bag of waters.

This process of gradual dilation of the cervix is called the *first stage of labor*. It is the stage that ordinarily takes the longest time, especially in women who have never had a baby before. Doctors advise women to wait until the contractions are regular, about five minutes apart, and of thirty to forty-five seconds duration before calling them. For those who have learned how to do it, the discomfort can be reduced by breathing deeply and relaxing during the contractions so as not to fight the work the body is trying to do. This stage of labor generally averages about twelve hours for first babies and eight hours after that. Gradually as the hours pass, the cervix opens to the full four-inch diameter that is necessary. The head passes through the cervix into the vagina or birth canal, which has also softened and become elastic in preparation for this event.

Childbirth

The passing of the baby through the birth canal and out into the world is the *second stage of labor* (Fig. 12–17). At this stage, assuming that she is fully conscious, the woman is generally advised to bear down and push with her abdominal muscles as she would if she were having a difficult bowel movement to help the baby along, at least until the head is out. Many doctors believe that this help from the mother is important and therefore use only local anesthetic rather than general or spinal or caudal anesthetics. In addition to permitting the mother to be a fully conscious participant in one of the most significant events of her life, it is even becoming common in some hospitals to include fathers as interested observers to increase their sense of participation.

In the case of spinal and caudal anesthesias, which leave the mother fully conscious but cut off all sensation and control in the pelvic region, the mother cannot help by pushing, and the doctor generally uses instruments to help the baby along. These techniques (local, spinal, or caudal anesthesia) all have the advantage over general anesthesia that they do not drug the baby.

If there is any chance at all that the exterior opening of the birth canal might tear under the pressure, doctors generally make a slit in it to ease the baby out and then sew it up afterward. This cut (the *episiotomy*) is the cause of the stitches that are associated in people's minds with childbirth.

After the baby is born and the cord has been carefully tied and cut (it has no nerves in it so that neither mother nor child feels the cut), the doctor helps get the afterbirth out. The afterbirth is the placenta. When it is delivered it is a flat, one-inch-thick, seven- or eight-inch-broad, pancake-shaped affair ("placenta" is the Latin word for "pancake"). The delivery of the placenta is the *third stage of labor* (Fig. 12–18).

The practice of obstetrics in a modern hospital has become so safe that the mother is in nearly as great danger of her life traveling on the highway on the way to the hospital as on the delivery table.

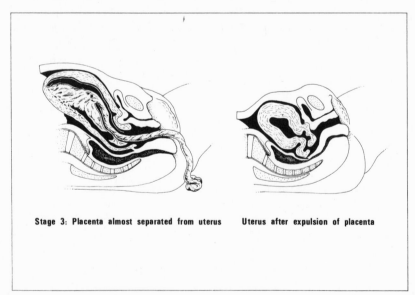

Stage 3: Placenta almost separated from uterus   Uterus after expulsion of placenta

Figure 12–18. Uterus immediately following birth.

The general rate of maternal mortality in this country is 3 per 10,000 births, and the rate is much lower than this in some states; the automobile accident mortality rate is more than half that figure for the general population in any given year.

Sometimes when a normal delivery would be difficult or dangerous for the mother or child, a cesarean delivery is called for. In this operation the doctor cuts through the abdomen and the uterine wall and takes the baby directly from the uterus without its passing through the birth canal. He also peels off the placenta before closing the incision. The whole process from the first cut to the final stitch often takes no more than one hour. Nevertheless, this is a major operation and should be avoided if normal delivery is a practical alternative. Traditionally, a woman who has had a cesarean operation is advised to have all of her subsequent deliveries in this fashion. However, the necessity for this is being challenged. When performing a second or third cesarean, a careful doctor will follow the first incision and cut away old scar tissue so that a woman who has had several cesarean deliveries need have no more scar tissue than a woman who has had only one. Of course, the recovery of the mother is slower after a cesarean than after a normal birth.

Recovery

The amount of time that it takes for the female reproductive organs to return to their normal, pre-pregnancy size, position, and condition varies from woman to woman. For about one week the uterus continues to contract as it rids itself of the surplus cellular fluid and blood-rich lining which are no longer needed. This flushing-off process produces a flow of bloody fluid (called *lochia*) much like menstruation but on a larger scale.

By the end of the first postnatal week the uterus has usually reduced in size enough to settle back down into the pelvis where it began. By the end of the sixth week, it should be back to its normal size (Fig. 12–19). The timing of the return of the vagina to normal depends on whether or not the doctor made a cut and took stitches. One of the purposes of the six-week postnatal medical checkup is to see whether the vagina is ready for the resumption of normal sex relations.

About three days after the baby's birth the mother's breasts begin to secrete milk. Prior to this they produced *colostrum*, a watery fluid which apparently has some immunizing effects on the baby. If the mother chooses to nurse the child, her breasts will produce milk for many months. About 80 per cent of all nursing mothers do not ovulate or menstruate for the first few months. This is believed to be caused by the preoccupation of the pituitary with production

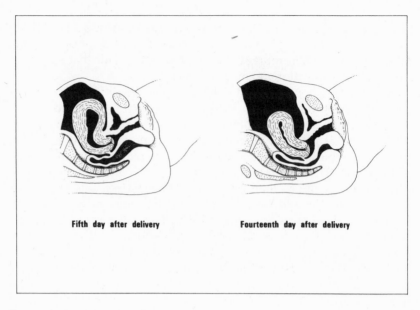

Fifth day after delivery   Fourteenth day after delivery

Figure 12–19. Recovery of uterus.

of the hormone *prolactin* (which stimulates milk secretion) at the expense of adequate levels of F.S.H. For the many centuries before birth control methods were in wide use, this period was a major factor in the natural spacing of babies at about two-year intervals. No one today should depend upon this natural protection, however, because the 20 per cent who do ovulate have at least as great a probability of conception as women who have not recently had a baby.

The cycle of life has been followed from the conception of the mother and father through their maturation as male and female adults and, ultimately, through the conception, prenatal development, and birth of their child. One full human generation has been encompassed. At many points along the way it was necessary to admit that the explanation for many stages of the cycle can only be guessed at. The knowledge of human reproduction, however, is quite possibly on the verge of a great breakthrough as the tools and techniques of biological research have been dramatically improved in recent years. As in many other fields, the answers to problems that puzzle the wisest men today may well be the common property of school children before another generation has completed its full cycle.

13   Human Sexual Response

Alfred W. Melton, Jr.

The topics discussed in this chapter are not likely to be routinely included in any sex education program in high schools, but the teacher must be familiar with them. Most students, especially girls, are likely to marry soon after high school graduation, and occasion may arise for the teacher to discuss sexual intercourse in marriage with them in personal conference and to make this material available to them. The negative uses of intercourse may come as an illumination to some of the more aggressive male and the more exploitive female students who have, in fact, used it in such ways. Knowledge of these uses may also help protect their potential victims.

SEXUAL INTERACTION

Marital Adjustment

In our contemporary marriages sexual satisfaction has been found to be closely correlated with over-all marital adjustment and satisfaction.[1] The cause-and-effect relationship between the two is not clear, but a recent evaluation suggests that the level of sexual adjustment determines the marital adjustment of the male, while the marital adjustment of the female determines her sexual adjustment.[2] Whatever the relationship, it has yet to be demonstrated that sexual adjustment is not a significant factor in the happy marriage. It is, therefore, relevant to discuss the general and specific implications of the concept of sexual adjustment.

Definition. Sexual satisfaction has often been narrowly defined in terms of an individual physical response. More accurately, the sexual experience is a total relationship between the participating persons. The level of desire and the pattern of response between the male and female may be different, but if both feel healthily gratified and made happy by their sexual expression, then they can be said to be "adjusted." Intensity of desire, frequency of intercourse, and orgasmic release may all be significant, but no one of these is the sole indicator of sexual adjustment. Positive sexual adjustment is a combination of psychological and physiological components, and the comparative importance of these components will vary from couple to couple and even from one occasion to the next for the same couple.

[1] E. W. Burgess and P. Wallin, *Engagement and Marriage* (Philadelphia: Lippincott, 1953).

[2] A. L. Clark and P. Wallin, "Women's Sexual Responsiveness and the Duration and Quality of Their Marriages," unpublished manuscript.

It would appear that among the several significant areas of marital adjustment sexual adjustment is the most difficult and requires the longest time to achieve.[3] This is possible because of the direct and continuing demands involved. A couple may find that their religious differences can be subordinated or observed individually, but they cannot readily make the same provision for their sexual relationship. For most couples, however, sexual adjustment is achieved early in their relationship.[4] Only about one out of ten couples reports being unable to adjust sexually, about two of three couples report sexual problems at some time in their marriages,[5] and to some, it is surprising that there is an "adjustment problem" at all.

Instinct vs. Learning. Some persons contend that, among all of the games that people play, the sport of love-making should be the most successful of them all. It would seem that, given the natural impetus of sexual desire plus some suitable object upon which to focus these feelings, all should simply go on from there. In fact, there are strong supporters of exactly this view. These are the people who suggest that there is no need for instruction in the process of sexual intercourse. They suggest that this is an instinctual act—witness the population explosion—and requires nothing more than opportunity. In contrast, there are those who adopt the position of the "sports-master," reducing sexual intercourse to a set of mechanical skills and the "art" of making love. Probably the reality lies somewhere in between these two positions. It is the appropriate expression of basic sexual desire that is of interest to both males and females. The erotic content of their lives is rightly their mutual concern.

Mere survival as a people depends upon some degree of eroticism. The female can conceive without becoming sexually excited. She needs only to remain reasonably passive in order for copulation to occur. However, if there is to be a successful sexual connection, the male must become sufficiently excited to achieve an erection and then to ejaculate. The interest of a couple in their sexuality will depend to some extent upon their concern with achieving or avoiding pregnancy at a particular stage of their relationship. It should be acknowledged, however, that few couples restrict sexual intercourse to the conception of children. Virtually all couples are interested in human sexual responsiveness as it affects their personal expressions to each other. Every sexual act is an expressive experience.

[3] J. T. Landis and M. G. Landis, *Building a Successful Marriage*, 4th ed. (Englewood Cliffs, N.J.: Prentice-Hall, 1963).

[4] *Ibid.*

[5] A. C. Kinsey et al., *Sexual Behavior in the Human Female* (Philadelphia: Saunders, 1953).

Sexual Expression

Positive. Sexual expression is as varied as the possible patterns of interaction between two people. There are times when the act of sexual intercourse will be deeply significant in its support and confirmation of a relationship. Here, it will be an act of love and devotion for the couple, approaching the most deeply spiritual expression of sharing. There may be few words spoken, but for both its meaning is clear beyond any verbal exchange. In the same context, they may be responding to their individual or mutual need for solace and comfort. There may be occasions when the sexual act is a shared expression of pure sensuality. In such an experience the couple may be aware of little else than the fulfillment of bodily needs. There will be still other occasions when the sexual experience will be less intense and more casual. The act will be a simple one of acceptance, performed almost with indifference. There will be other times when the sexual relationship will be an act of tension release, bringing a sense of quietness and relaxation. The sex act may even be a manner of passing the time, something a couple does instead of playing bridge or going to a show. On still other occasions, intercourse will be strictly for fun, a time spent experimenting with each other's bodies and seeking new and interesting variations and devices of seduction. In all of these situations the effect is essentially positive.

Negative. Sexual expression is not always affirmative. There are times when the sex act is a negative expression between the participants. There may be times when it reflects the struggle for dominance between the male and female. One of the partners seeks to force the other to meet demands, and the act becomes a test of power and the ability to force compliance. There may be deliberate refusal to participate, studied and dramatized in order to give emphasis to the rejection and disdain. Passivity and indifference are often expressions of rejection and hostility. Excuses of physical illness and the use of the various techniques of avoidance are common expressions of the negative tone in a sexual relationship.

It is of basic importance to be aware of the continuing interplay, either positive or negative or both, between the sexual relationship and the dynamics of the marriage as a whole. Attention must be given to those personal characteristics and characteristics of the marriage that seem to be of significance.

Significant Personal Characteristics

Factual Knowledge. There are certain personal characteristics that may be considered important. For instance, a certain amount of factual knowledge of areas directly and indirectly related to the

223

sexual experience is helpful. An understanding of the male and female genital structures, including the reproductive systems, is useful in the understanding of sexual functioning. There should also be some understanding of the basic patterns of male and female physiological and psychological sexual response.

Such factual knowledge in and of itself does not guarantee a good sexual relationship, but it is of importance to the person seeking to establish one. For example, with adequate stimulation vaginal lubrication will occur for the female regardless of whether or not she understands the process by which it takes place. However, knowing its sequence and source should heighten her awareness of her own general pattern of responsiveness. More specifically, she and the male both should know that this is only the beginning in her series of movements toward total readiness for sexual intercourse.

Capacity To Give. If sexual intercourse is defined as love-making or the simple act of giving and receiving love, then persons with these abilities are presupposed. The tone of the successful sexual relationship implies a kind of "generosity of body and soul," as described by Simone de Beauvoir.[6] This suggests not simply the sharing of oneself with another, but the ability to accept what is shared by another with oneself. This ability comes in a variety of personality types, from introvert to extrovert and every gradation in between, but it is sometimes absent even in what appears to be the most attractive personality. Somehow, in the process of development, this ability to participate in the sharing experience remains inhibited. Under some circumstances, it is possible for such persons to participate mechanically in sexual intercourse, but they never really "give" or "accept" the experience. For whatever reasons, they can never be "close" to another person, even when their bodies are interlocked. This ability to share with another and to be able to accept sharing from another would seem to be related to the total personal attitude toward sex.

Attitude toward Sex. Personal sexual attitudes are primarily a composite of sexual knowledge and sexual experience accumulated from childhood onward, which has been integrated into the total personality. Surprisingly, our current sexually sophisticated culture presents us with a contradiction here. It is now considered "right" to voice a "healthy" personal attitude toward sex. Questioned as to their attitudes, a group of young people will give an almost standard response: "I think that sex is good, right and healthy when expressed between two people who love each other," etc. Indeed,

---

[6] *The Second Sex*, ed. and trans. H. M. Parshley (New York: Knopf, 1953).

such an attitude is healthy if, in fact, it is truly felt. Unfortunately, there is sometimes a difference between the attitude that is stated and that which is actually possessed. The difference is sometimes that of the intellect versus the emotions. It is possible to know how one should feel, yet not be able to feel what one knows he should. A person can know that prejudice is illogical but still experience the emotion of prejudice. Sexual attitudes reflect one's experience and knowledge gained from a number of significant associations: parents, peers, dating, discussion and interaction with one's own sex, reading, etc. It is possible to have all the "facts of life" correct and in proper order but to have been negatively conditioned by some disturbing or inappropriate experience. There is a tendency to rationalize where negative learning is concerned. Because of the possible inconsistency between professed and actual attitudes, the personal sexual attitude of the individual must be carefully explored and evaluated. These attitudes may help the individual to participate in a shared relationship or may impede such participation.

Significant Characteristics of the Marital Relationship
Mutual Acceptance and Respect. There are characteristics of the relationship itself that affect human sexual response. The respect that persons have for each other sets the tone and the quality of the relationship and serves as the context within which sexual response occurs. This kind of emphatic sensitivity allows each person to know the other's moods and feelings, and to respond to the other as a person, not simply as an object to be manipulated. Couples will often find that some sexual experiences can be accommodated immediately, while others require slow experimentation and patience. Differences in background and previous experience may create demands that one of the partners cannot, at the moment, accept. When there is a loving relationship of mutual respect and understanding, most problems can be resolved. It is of basic importance that each person feel that the other is giving due consideration to his or her needs, for it is a rare relationship in which the needs of the male and the female are exactly the same.
Accommodation of Differences. Couples will sometimes find that there are differences in their need and response patterns. The several research studies of sexual response note a number of possible differences. Males often report more frequent desire for sexual intercourse and respond to a wider variety of sexual stimuli.[7] Male orgasmic response is almost an explosive certainty, while orgasm in

[7] Kinsey et al., *Sexual Behavior in the Human Female.*

the female is less sure and possibly more subtle.[8] The male is more likely to experiment in sex play and in variations in sexual position than the female.[9] The female is less likely to be frustrated by sexual inactivity than the male.[10] The female is more likely to relate her sexual participation to the general mood of the relationship than the male. These differences do not apply to all relationships, but every relationship should acknowledge possible differences between the male and female and be structured accordingly. Confusion and conflict result when one or both simply impute to the other their own needs and responses.

Communication. It would be difficult to overstate the importance of communication as an integral part of the sexual relationship. It is essential that there be openness and freedom of expression. The verbal expression of love for another is one manner of communication. A person will also express himself through his gesture and posture, through his dress or through music. The act of moving closer when touched communicates acceptance and response. To touch a sensitive erogenous area provides direct stimulation. All of these basic sexual expressions are important. The female probably responds to verbal expressions of affection with greater appreciation than the male. The male reacts more strongly to the female's physical response. Each couple will discover its own most meaningful communication cues.

Building Responsiveness. The expectation of instant and complete success is possibly one of the most unnecessary injustices couples impose upon their relationship. While it is true that some couples find themselves in sexual harmony from the very beginning, others will find that their initial experiences include elements of awkwardness and even disappointment. Building sexual responsiveness should be seen as a period of learning for each couple—both about oneself and about one's partner. If the couple is patient, allowing the time to profit from each bit of new information and insight gained, they will probably discover that their problems are fewer and their satisfactions greater.

Attitudes To Be Avoided

Inappropriate Comparisons. We continually measure ourselves against any number of outside variables, and this process is often helpful. But there are times when it creates problems that should not exist. For example, both males and females tend to equate pre-

[8] W. H. Masters and V. E. Johnson, *Human Sexual Response* (Boston: Little, Brown, 1966).

[9] Kinsey et al., *Sexual Behavior in the Human Female.*

[10] Burgess and Wallin, *Engagement and Marriage.*

marital experience, especially for the male, with successful sexual performance in marriage. A woman will sometimes express the hope that her fiancé has had previous sexual experience, anticipating that this will be of positive value to their marital sexual adjustment. This may or may not be the case. If his sexual experience reflects the *Playboy* philosophy with its attendant antifeminine and antisexual values, it might well work against their sexual adjustment. The attitude toward this casual experience may be carried over into the marital relationship.

There is also a tendency to stereotype experiences. If either the male or the female has had previous experiences that were negative, it is possible that they may be conditioned toward responses inappropriate to the present relationship. Every couple should recognize the uniqueness of their own sexual relationship. The frequency of sexual intercourse, types of sex play enjoyed, positions used, time and place of sex experiences, and criteria by which satisfactions are judged will be different for every couple. It is easy to fall into the trap of comparison with others. It is not unusual for a couple to say that they feel sexually inadequate because they are not having sexual intercourse as frequently as another couple of their acquaintance. Upon inquiry, it often turns out that the other couple was experiencing one of those high points in their sex life that would be humanly impossible to maintain over any sustained period of time. Women often consult their mothers or older sisters as to what is normal, forgetting the age difference involved, with some startling results. One young woman consulted her mother about her husband's desire for mouth-genital contact in sex play. Her mother's reaction was to demand that she return home immediately. Yet although certainly not essential to successful sexual experience, this form of sex play is not unusual. Some couples like to roll and tumble together as a prelude to an aggressive and violent sexual experience, while others prefer to lie quietly together, gently fondling and embracing each other. Still others will seek the unusual place and the unusual time for their sexual experience. One couple will prefer to use the sitting position in coitus, while another feels more comfortable in the traditional male-above position. All of these variations indicate the individualized nature of the sexual relationship.

Inappropriate Expectations. There are expectations that can be destructive. The differences in male and female patterns of sexual response and variations in male and female orgasmic responses have been noted. Inappropriate expectations regarding female orgasm can be a source of problems for the couple. The expectation of orgasm for the female is widespread, and indeed, for almost all women it is a reasonable expectation. However, even it can become a liability when female orgasm becomes the single criterion for successful intercourse. Some women feel that they must experience orgasm on all occasions. Males are often trapped by this expectation. There are males who feel that if their partner does not experience orgasm they are failures as lovers. Women are usually more realistic. They frequently report that although they appreciate and enjoy the experience of orgasm, such a climactic experience is not always necessary. They say that there are times when they just do not feel that excited. Some women report pretending orgasm simply to protect the ego of the male. On the other hand, almost all women want the male to furnish them the opportunity for orgasm if this is a real potential for them in the particular sexual experience. What expectations are realistic must be determined by the individual couple in terms of the different stages of the relationship.

Rigidity of Pattern. There is always danger in making rules, whether rules of conformity or non-conformity. Each couple should retain for themselves the flexibility and freedom either to accept or reject whatever sexual experiences they choose. A couple may find that they want to use only one position or even all possible positions in intercourse. The actual choice is theirs, but they should be flexible enough to choose or change as they like. When they become rigidly caught in the pattern of their relationship, whatever it may be, they have lost their freedom of choice. Perhaps it is flexibility that marks the couple which is truly sexually responsive.

THE SEX ACT

For purposes of description the total sexual experience is divided into three phases: (1) the pre-coitus period, including the initial approach and continuing through the sexual stimulation that develops into readiness for coition; (2) the act of coitus and orgasm, the actual act of connection between the partners, continuing through the experience of orgasm or climax; and (3) the post-coitus period, the portion of the sexual experience that follows orgasm and continues until both partners have returned to their previous unexcited state.

The Pre-Coitus Period

Male vs. Female Responses. Ideally, either partner should have the freedom to initiate a sexual experience, just as either partner should have the freedom to reject a sexual experience. There are fluctuations in both the male and female response, based upon a number of factors. In the past, women have often complained of too frequent male demands. There are indications that this attitude is changing as women's sexual anticipations become greater.[11]

It is not now unusual for women in the middle years of marriage to complain of the infrequent sexual attentions of their husbands. The matter of right or regularity or refusal by either male or female is of some importance. There should be a sense of obligation to one's partner unless there are reasons that strongly prohibit participation. Occasional refusal is tolerable, while frequent refusal places a relationship in some jeopardy.

Erogenous Zones and Stimulation. The importance of the pre-coitus phase is that it prepares the participants for the intercourse which will follow. This is not to imply that satisfaction is present only in the next stage: On the contrary, not a few couples report that in this, as in many other areas of life, the deepest and most meaningful pleasures are in the preparation. In this period of foreplay or sex play, the entire body becomes the conveyance and the target of sexual excitement. The act of undressing or of undressing each other can be of great erotic value. The senses of sight, sound, taste, and smell all assist touch in creating sexual response. When one is in a receptive mood, all bodily areas can become erotically responsive. The orifices or openings of the head and body are most frequently cited as the erogenous zones: the mouth, nose, eyes, ears, genitals, and rectum. These will differ in sensitivity. Other areas of the body are quite important in sexual stimulation. The male is usually more rapidly aroused, but there may be times when the female is as quickly or even more quickly aroused than the male.

A variety of kisses, from those of gentle restraint to those of harsh aggression, are effective stimulants. The light touching together of nude bodies may add to the general excitement at times, while at other times the pleasure is in the crush of a passionate embrace. Both male and female respond to being touched and stroked over the body surfaces: the neck, arms, shoulders, sides, hips, stomach, thighs, buttocks, and back. Being kissed over these same areas affords pleasure to both partners.

Breast and genital fondling of the female by the male is an important part of the period of sex play. The female is usually excited by fondling of the breast and nipples. The breasts can be gently stroked or squeezed and, in times of great excitement, firmly squeezed and pulled. The nipples can be brushed lightly with the fingertips or gently squeezed or rolled between the fingers. The female usually is excited by the kissing and sucking of her nipples, but the male should bear in mind that the breasts and nipples can

[11] Kinsey et al., *Sexual Behavior in the Human Female.*

229

become very sensitive during prolonged periods of stimulation, especially during certain parts of the menstrual cycle and during pregnancy.

The external genitals of the female can also be stimulated by the male. The mons area, the area immediately above the vaginal lips and covered by the pubic hair, can be touched and stroked. The clitoris, the small organ which lies just inside the upper apex of the inner vaginal lips, is possibly the female's most erotically responsive area. It is similar to the male penis in shape but much smaller in size. Usually the glans, or head, of the clitoris is about the size of a pea and can be touched through and inside the vaginal lips. When the female becomes sexually excited, this glans and the rest of the clitoral body, the shaft, become somewhat enlarged. Sex manuals have often mistakenly recommended direct and continued stimulation of the clitoris. Women frequently report that under such prolonged caress, the glans of the clitoris becomes extremely sensitive and causes them to lose the level of excitement they have attained. Further, as the female becomes highly excited, the clitoris retracts beneath its protective hood and is very difficult to contact directly (Fig. 13–1). In the "plateau" or fully excited stage, it can be observed that the clitoris has fully retracted from its normal pendulous position. If there is to be extended stimulation to this organ, the stroking probably should be to the area of the surface over the clitoris, thus giving the same erotic effect but avoiding over-sensitization. When the male applies mouth-genital contact, this is the organ to which he directs "genital kiss." Both the inner and outer vaginal lips are also responsive to the male's touch. When the female is

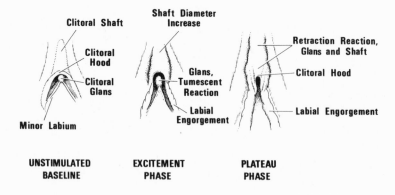

Figure 13–1. Clitoral response to sexual excitement. (From William H. Masters and Virginia E. Johnson, Human Sexual Response [Boston: Little, Brown, 1966].)

fully excited, these lips greatly enlarge and pull themselves apart, as though anticipating the entrance of the penis. In general, the skin surfaces surrounding the female genitalia, such as the inner thighs and the surfaces of the lower abdomen, are especially responsive to touching and stroking.

The entire male genitalia are responsive to the female's touch. Although completely flaccid or limp when the male is not sexually excited, the penis becomes quickly erect when arousal begins. Erection occurs when blood rushes into the otherwise empty spongy tissue that makes up a significant portion of the internal penile structure. Almost full erection can occur in from three to ten seconds after the first sexual stimulation begins.[12] The penis can be touched or stroked or kissed with much erotic effect. The scrotum, or sac surrounding the testicles, is also responsive to touch, although less sensitive than the penis. Some caution should be observed in fondling the male penis and scrotum. The glans or head of the penis is very sensitive, particularly the ring of tissue that surrounds the base of the glans where it joins the shaft. Prolonged stroking of either the glans or the shaft hastens climax and ejaculation for the male. Although it is sometimes possible for the male to maintain his erection after ejaculation, more often it will subside. As in the case of clitoral stimulation, prolonged and abrasive contact with the glans itself can be painful to the male. The scrotum containing the testicles can be touched and stroked and even gently squeezed, but aggressive squeezing of the scrotum and testicles can be painful.

The varieties and kinds of sexual stimulation enjoyed in lovemaking are extensive. Whatever seems to be meaningful and exciting to the couple's sexual relationship and does not violate either of their personalities is acceptable. Strategic passiveness, in which one of the partners lies quietly while the other takes the pleasure of his or her body, is sometimes enjoyable. But in this period of sex play and stimulation, both partners will give and receive excitement by their own participation.

Psychophysiological Response. As the male responds to sexual stimulation, several significant changes occur. He experiences general neuromuscular tension. His rates of heartbeat and breathing increase. He may experience a type of "sex flush," a red rash that spreads from the lower abdomen to the shoulders and face. His penis becomes erect and the scrotum draws upward (Fig. 13–2). When he is fully excited, a few drops of mucoid-like material may escape the opening in the glans of the penis. Psychologically, the

---

[12] Masters and Johnson, *Human Sexual Response.*

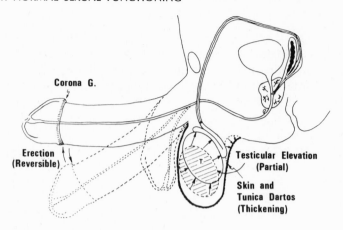

*Figure 13–2. Initial male genital response to sexual
exictement. (From Masters and Johnson,
Human Sexual Response.)*

male responds to virtually all of the stimuli presented to him and is
not easily distracted when fully excited.

The female also experiences a number of significant changes.
There is general neuromuscular tension, accompanied by rapid
heartbeat, a rise in blood pressure, and faster breathing. She is even
more likely than the male to experience the sex flush that spreads
over her body from the lower abdomen to the breasts to the shoulders and head. The response of the vaginal lips and clitoris to sexual
stimulation has been described. As she becomes fully excited, her
breasts tend to increase somewhat in size, the nipples become erect,
and the areola, or base of the nipple, swells (Fig. 13–3).

One of the early signs of female excitement is the lubrication of
the vaginal barrel. As excitement builds, the walls of the vagina
begin to secrete droplets of a mucous fluid, which coalesce to form
a film over the surface of the vaginal walls. This is the material that
prepares the vagina for the movement of the penis when inserted.
When the female is not sexually excited, the walls of the vagina are
almost touching. The vaginal opening is a narrow cylindrical form
that extends approximately from behind the vaginal lips to a point
back of the cervix or lower end of the uterus. As the female becomes excited, the vaginal cylinder or barrel opens and lengthens
somewhat. The inner two-thirds of the barrel opens even more to
form a vault-like area at the back of the vagina and surrounding the
cervix. The outer third of the vaginal barrel, already slightly opened,
undergoes tumescence or swelling. The surfaces of the walls become congested with blood, partially closing the opening by as
much as one-third. This becomes what has been labeled the "orgas-

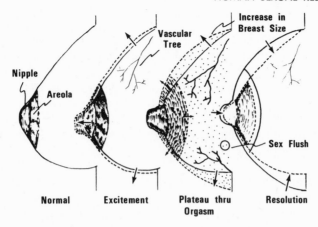

Figure 13–3. Female breast response to sexual excitement. (From Masters and Johnson, Human Sexual Response.)

mic platform" for the female.[13] The inner vaginal lips deepen in color as they engorge with blood, and the cervix and the uterus pull upward toward the lower abdomen. It is almost as though the vagina is preparing itself to receive the penis of the male (Fig. 13–4).

Insertion of the penis into the vagina should always be made with some care. The vaginal barrel is remarkably elastic and flexible, and the internal vaginal walls move readily to accommodate the angle of entry and the size of the penis. The male is often concerned lest

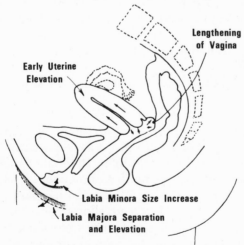

Figure 13–4. Initial female genital response to sexual excitement. (From Masters and Johnson, Human Sexual Response.)

[13] *Ibid.*

his penis be either too small or too large—more often the former. The female is often concerned lest her vagina be either too small or too large—more often the latter. Actually, there is nothing much to worry about. The vaginal barrel, in its state of repose, is capable of giving full caress to an object the circumference of an ordinary pencil. At childbirth, it is capable of expanding to approximately four inches in circumference. Very few couples have any real difficulties in "goodness of fit."

Coitus and Orgasm

The choice of position for intercourse will sometimes be made on the basis of maximum performance possibilities for either the male or the female, sometimes for the sake of experiment and variety. If the female is at an advanced stage of pregnancy, the couple will want to choose a position accordingly. Probably most choices are made on the most common basis of all, habit and comfort. Exotic literature notwithstanding, there are just a few basic positions which the human male and female can assume for purposes of sexual intercourse. The angles of possible entry into the vagina are limited. The male penis will pivot, but only within some comfortable tolerances. Actually, the male can approach the female only from either front or rear: everything else is a variation on these two positions.

Male-Above Position. Here the female lies on her back with the male positioned above her. The thighs of the male can be either inside or outside those of the female. The male-above position is the traditional position for sexual intercourse in our society. It is supposed to be related to the expression of male dominance, and may well be. However, as a specific choice, this position has both advantages and disadvantages. The male usually sets the pace of the coital movements, and the female adjusts her responses to his. When timing is properly mastered, this can be a thoroughly satisfying position. The depth of penetration can be reasonably well controlled for the couple who must give this factor consideration. The female is free to caress the male fully. There are variations on this position. The female may roll her hips up either by use of a pillow or by placing her legs over the shoulders of her partner. This variation minimizes clitoral contact and allows for deep penetration. When the female often achieves climax faster than the male, this position helps to avoid clitoral pressure. In contrast, when maximum clitoral pressure is desired in the male-above position, the male may place his thighs outside hers and move slightly up toward her hips. With the thighs of the female thus pressed more tightly together, the vagina grasps the penis with the pressure of the vaginal lips pulling against the clitoris, increasing the erotic response for both male and female.

This position has its disadvantages. The male must suspend his weight above the female because usually she cannot long bear his weight. This means that the male must support much of his total body weight upon his outstretched hands and arms, which can soon become very uncomfortable. With his hands thus occupied, the male is not free to caress the female and continue her stimulation. This position does not allow much freedom for periodic pauses for the purpose of slowing the male response, when this is desired. During the later states of pregnancy, too much weight would be placed upon the abdomen of the female and is thus to be avoided.

Female-Above Position. In this position the male lies upon his back, with the female above him. The thighs of the female may be inside or outside those of the male. The female can also move her knees alongside the hips of the male and assume a sitting position. The female now has the freedom of movement. She can adjust herself to bring maximum or minimum pressure on her clitoris. Sitting upright, she can lean back, putting maximum pressure on the penis, or forward, bringing maximum pressure to bear on the clitoris. She can press her body close to that of the male and thus minimize the movements of the penis, which has the effect of slowing the male response. At the same time, she can move her own hips so as to provide stimulation to the clitoris and hasten her own response. As she approaches orgasm, she can then lift her hips, allowing him to move in and out of the vagina according to his own needs. In this position, the male has full opportunity to caress the female's breasts, clitoris, hips, and buttocks, aiding her responses and those of his own. For the reluctant and timid female, taking this position of initiative often distracts her from herself and allows her to develop a greater sense of participation and relaxation.

The disadvantages of this position are in the muscular demands that it makes upon the female. When sexual activity is prolonged, it may be necessary for her to rest periodically. In contrast to the male-above position, here it is the female who is limited in caressing. In the terminal stages of pregnancy this position is to be avoided because penetration can be very deep in this position and therefore uncomfortable and disturbing. If the pregnant woman is leaning forward, the suspended abdominal weight is uncomfortable.

Side-By-Side Position. In this position the partners lie on their sides facing each other. The male slides his hips down and forward so as to move between the thighs of the female. The female may put one or both her thighs outside those of the male. This is often the recommended position for couples just beginning their relationship

235

together or for those who are experiencing problems. The reasons for this are simple: this is the position of least strain and of greatest control. From this position the couple can move into either the male- or the female-above position and back again. Both male and female are free to stroke and caress each other as they choose. If intercourse is to be a prolonged experience, neither partner will be under excessive physical strain, as the weight is supported on the sides. Within the recommended limits for sexual intercourse during pregnancy, this is the best position. It allows for control of depth of penetration as well as accommodation of the female abdomen. The basic disadvantage is that it limits movement for both partners. In this position it is difficult for either the male or female to gain maximum penetration or clitoral contact.

Rear-Entry Position. In this position the male approaches the female from behind and enters the vagina from between and below her buttocks. There are three variations on this position. *Side-by-side:* both partners lie on their sides, facing in the same direction; the male lies with his chest out and away from the back of the female, curving his pubis beneath her buttocks. *Kneeling:* the female kneels on her hands and knees, with the male kneeling erect behind her; the male lowers his hips beneath the buttocks of the female. *Knee-chest:* the female kneels but rests her head and shoulders against the bed, her chest resting against her knees and thighs, while the male kneels erect behind her.

The rear-entry position is probably most often used for experimentation and variation. Clitoral contact is not achieved by this position, and therefore it provides only minimal stimulation for the female. The male, however, is free to stroke and caress the entire body of the female. He can fully stroke her clitoris or mons and thus provide excitement other than through direct contact of the penis. His own depth of penetration is somewhat limited by the female buttocks and the angle of approach. This is the position that has been traditionally recommended for achieving pregnancy.

In the knee-chest position, the seminal fluid can be trapped in the basin-like area at the cervix. The female then remains in this position for a period of time, allowing the sperm to move into the uterus. More recent research has provided a re-evaluation of acceptable positions for achieving pregnancy.[14] Because the female abdomen is placed in a suspended position, neither the kneeling or the knee-chest position should be used in the later stages of pregnancy.

Sitting Position. Here the male sits in a low straight chair, while the

[14] *Ibid.*

female sits astride him with the balls of her feet resting on the floor. She sits high up on his flanks, lowering herself on his penis. This position is probably most often used for variation, but it has some functional features. It brings maximum pressure on the clitoral area and allows the female to control and adjust the degree of stimulation, while the male penis is also given full caress. This is the only position that gives both partners complete freedom of movement to caress, fondle, and embrace each other, unrestricted by the necessity of supporting the weight of their bodies. Again, because of the depth of penetration and the problem of accommodating the abdomen of the female, this position is not recommended for the later stages of pregnancy.

Each couple should begin with a position that is both comfortable and exciting to them. After they have evaluated their respective needs and patterns of response, they can experiment with other positions and variations. After a period of time they will probably find themselves relying mostly upon one position that best facilitates their particular orgasmic responses but occasionally using some or all of the others.

Possible Variations. Possibly the most common variation is the diagonal position. This is really a variation of the male-above position. All other variations are accomplished by maneuvering the bodies of the male and female into whatever positions are physically possible without injury to the bodily structure itself. The difficulties and strains encountered in such maneuvers hardly seem to justify their use.

Orgasm. Orgasm is the climax of the sexual experience for most males and females. The exact psychological or physiological mechanisms that trigger the experience are not known. An elementary description of the experience would be a building of neuromuscular tension in the body, including a more rapid heartbeat and breathing rate and a rise in blood pressure, to a point of pause and then release. The release takes the form of a series of genital contractions. Orgasm will vary in intensity in both males and females. For some persons it will often be subtle, while for others it will often be intense. Orgasm is the result of either sexual intercourse or some other form of sexual stimulation.

In the female the primary physiological response is in the "orgasmic platform" in the outer one-third of the vagina, although the entire abdominal structure is involved. The outer portion of the vaginal barrel experiences a series of muscular contractions. These contractions usually begin about four-fifths of a second apart and may be as few as from three to five and as many as from eight to twelve in number. As the contractions continue, they tend to be

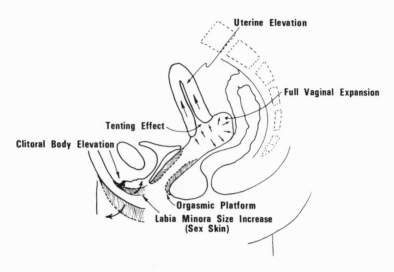

Figure 13–5. Full female genital response to sexual excitement. (From Masters and Johnson, Human Sexual Response.)

farther apart and less intense. These vaginal contractions are accompanied by wave-like contractions of the uterus and pelvic region (Fig. 13–5).

Popular fiction has often painted a false picture in its dramatic presentations of the female climax. In fiction orgasm is almost inevitably a violent and explosive experience, sometimes accompanied by fainting. While it is true that women occasionally have such an experience, it hardly represents the norm. Women often feel inadequate when they do not themselves have such an explosive experience, but for most women orgasm is more subtle.

The male experience of orgasm is accompanied by ejaculation of the seminal fluid, as a rule. These are two separate experiences, although ejaculation must be preceded by orgasm. The seminal emission is a thick, milky fluid containing millions of sperm. As much as a teaspoonful of seminal fluid might be emitted at one ejaculation. The male also experiences contractions of the penis as his orgasm and ejaculations occur. Like those of the female, the male's contractions occur at intervals beginning about four-fifths of a second apart. There are usually fewer intense contractions for the male, perhaps three or four, with some less intense contractions following at wider intervals. The intensity of response for the male appears to be closely related to the amount of seminal fluid ejaculated. The sensory experience of the male at the point of climax is associated with, first, the internal expulsion process of the prostatic region at the base of the penis, and then with the movement of the

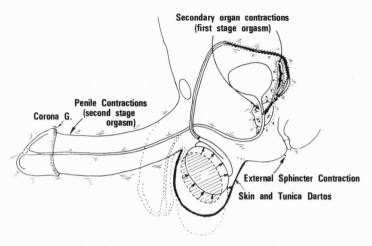

Figure 13–6. Full male genital response to sexual excitement. (From Masters and Johnson, Human Sexual Response.)

seminal fluid out through the urethra of the penis (Fig. 13–6). The seminal fluid is ejaculated under considerable pressure.

With some exceptions the male will experience orgasm rather easily. Some few males, after a brief pause, may experience a second climax. Orgasm in the female is less certain. Approximately one-half of the women studied by researchers did experience orgasm on at least some occasion within the first month after marriage. By the end of the first year, about three-fourths of these women had experienced orgasm at least occasionally.[15] Perhaps 10 to 15 per cent of married women never experience orgasm,[16] while approximately 40 per cent of married women experience orgasm in every act of intercourse.[17] This figure is higher for educated older women. Orgasm is most frequent among well-educated women twenty to forty years of age. Some women experience multiple orgasms within a single act of sexual intercourse,[18] and their number may be on the increase. Orgasm marks the termination of the most intense phase of sexual intercourse for the male and female, thus the use of the more common term "climax."

[15] See Landis and Landis, *Building a Successful Marriage*; L. M. Terman, *Psychological Factors in Marital Happiness* (New York: McGraw-Hill, 1938); and B. Thomason, "The Influences of Marital Sexual Behavior on Total Marital Adjustment" (Paper read at National Council on Family Relationships, New Brunswick, N.J., 1952).

[16] Kinsey et al., *Sexual Behavior in the Human Female*; Landis and Landis, *Building a Successful Marriage*.

[17] Kinsey et al., *Sexual Behavior in the Human Female*.

[18] *Ibid.*, p. 375.

The Post-Coitus Period

With the experience of orgasm completed, the female begins to lose the evidences of her excitement. The nipples, areolae, and breasts begin to return to their normal size and state. The clitoris loses its tumescence and returns to its former position. Both sets of vaginal lips decrease in size and move back to their unexcited position. The inner vaginal lips lose their brilliant pre-orgasmic coloring. The vaginal barrel distension begins to resolve itself, and the body loses any flush that might have occurred. The cervix and the uterus move back into their relaxed positions.

Following orgasm and ejaculation the male penis begins to return to its flaccid state quite rapidly. If the excitement state was prolonged, the erection will subside more slowly. Normally, after withdrawal the penis shrinks to approximately one-half its erect size. The scrotum and testicles return to their normal position, and the body of the male loses its flush.

This period is sometimes where the next sexual experience succeeds or fails. Some males tend to move through the post-ejaculation phase rather rapidly. It is possible for the male to experience orgasm and then to be fast asleep within thirty seconds. The female tends to move through this post-orgasmic period more slowly. Women say that they sometimes like to be reassured at this moment. They enjoy being held for a few moments and hearing words of endearment spoken by the male. Both men and women, but especially women, seem to retain memories of the tenderness of this moment, when it does occur, and these act as a source of psychological readiness for the next experience. When the male is too abrupt, the female sometimes feels that she has been only the object of gratification, that she has been used for his purposes.

AREAS OF SPECIAL CONCERN

Impotence and Frigidity

The term impotence indicates inability to participate in sexual intercourse. It is more often applied to the male than to the female, and usually indicates difficulty either in achieving or in maintaining an erection. It may mean involuntary premature or prolonged ejaculation. The term frigidity is more often applied to the female, and implies her dislike of sexual intercourse, constant discomfort or pain during intercourse, or basic inability to experience sexual excitement and orgasm. Physiological or biological problems can be the cause of such disturbances, but more often these problems are psychological in origin. There are two prevailing theories concerning impotence and frigidity. The psychoanalytic view suggests early sexual trauma or unresolved sexual-parental feelings as the principal source of disturbance.[19] The sociopsychological view suggests that the disturbed sexual response is only symptomatic of relationship problems, i.e., feelings of hostility, feelings of personal inadequacy, etc.[20] Occasional experiences such as these may not be cause for alarm. Continuous complications of this nature require the services of a therapist.

When Problems Occur

Sexual problems, like any others, tend to become serious when they are not attended to. Males somehow find it especially difficult to acknowledge sexual problems, even to their wives. Many wives also find them difficult to discuss with their husbands. There is sometimes an unwillingness to accept personal responsibility for the difficulty. However, open discussion is the necessary first step toward the solution of a problem. If both partners begin with an openness in which there is acceptance of one's own responsibility for possible error or inadequacy, they will immediately become less defensive. They can begin to search for the source of the problem and seek some adjustment and accommodation. They may find that they are not sure of the solution and need to test various hypotheses by the trial-and-error method, which is sensible if they honestly allow for the possibility of error and the need to try again. They may be unable to find the solution themselves, and at this point they should seek a competent source of assistance. If possible, they should consult a marriage counselor or a physician or therapist trained to advise on sexual problems. The real key to solving any sexual problem lies in the willingness of both persons to do something constructive about it. It is difficult for any such problem to defeat the couple who are determined that they will overcome it.

[19] A. Ellis and A. Abarbanel, *The Encyclopedia of Sexual Behavior* (New York: Hawthorn Books, 1961).

[20] E. W. Burgess and L. S. Cottrell, *Predicting Success or Failure in Marriage* (Englewood Cliffs, N.J.: Prentice-Hall, 1939).

14   Family Planning

Arthur E. Gravatt

The inclusion of a chapter on family planning in a book for teachers would have been unthinkable even a decade ago. But world-wide population problems, recent developments in the technology of contraception, widespread concern about out-of-wedlock births, and increasing permissiveness regarding sexual relations make such inclusion imperative. The teacher will not himself recommend the use of contraceptives to high school students, but he must know how the various methods work, in order to answer the questions put to him both in the classroom and in personal conferences. The teacher need not and, in fact, should not engage in a discussion of the morality of the several types; he should be able to discuss their effectiveness.

       Why do some people want small families, and others want large families?

Husband: Because of the way they were raised. . . . People from large families want large families and only children want only one child; if they have more it's a slip, somebody goofed. It also depends on their ideas about children. Some people don't want to have large families because to have more would deprive them of the luxuries of life.[1]

Wife: Not counting income it would depend on the kind of people they are. Some are just crazier about kids than others are. Also, there are men that are very demanding. . . . And, of course, there are people who are just plain careless or so over-sexed they don't think of the consequences.[2]

       Do you want more children?

Wife: Heavens, no! I'm 34 and my husband is getting close to 40. I like to be young with my children and enjoy them, and since we got married so darned young I want time alone later. My husband is in complete agreement with me. With the high cost of education and the necessity of having a child go to college, we would be foolish to have more.[3]

       What do you think is the ideal number of children for the average American Family?

Husband: I think two is ideal for the average American Family based on an average income. . . . I don't see how they could properly

---

[1] L. Rainwater, *Family Design* (Chicago: Aldine, 1965), pp. 163–64.
[2] *Ibid.*, p. 165.
[3] *Ibid.*, p. 17.

provide for more children. Personally, I'd take a dozen if I could afford them.[4]

Wife: I think four is ideal, I was an only child; that's not right. With four there is more of a family feeling, two is still not enough. I spent some rather lonely hours.[5]

These comments on family size reflect the range of motivational factors involved in family planning. This chapter explores the rationale for family planning, methods of contraception, and issues related to education for family planning.

ARGUMENTS FOR FAMILY PLANNING

The chief argument for family planning is a concern for world population growth.[6] The concept of optimum population assumes that somewhere between the extremes of the maximum number of people the earth's resources will sustain and the minimum number necessary to ensure the survival of the species there is an ideal ratio of people to resources. The ideal is certainly not absolute; it is defined by the values of society.

Another reason advanced for family planning is that of improvement in family quality. On an individual basis the determinants of family size involve the physiology, psychology, and sociology of a specific couple. The decision to practice birth control emerges from a network of personal feelings, attitudes, cultural beliefs, and family structure. As W. J. Goode has suggested,[7] lower birth rates require an important shift in the attitudes, habits, and values of individuals in their family roles. He uses the notion of *machismo* ("maleness") among Puerto Ricans to illustrate the interrelationship of sex role and fertility. *Machismo*, he argues, must be proved continually, and producing children is one way of proving one's masculinity. However, a simple correlation of personality traits and fertility may be misleading. Hill, Stycos, and Back's study of family size in Puerto Rico[8] found no support for the *machismo* hypothesis. Indeed, the men in their study were more oriented toward small families than were their wives.

A third argument for "family" planning is the prevention of pregnancy among the unmarried. An engaged couple approximates the psychosocial unit implied in discussion of family quality above.

[4] *Ibid.*, pp. 167–68.

[5] *Ibid.*, p. 168.

[6] See T. R. Malthus, *Essay on Population* (New York: Macmillan, 1909).

[7] *The Family* (Englewood Cliffs, N.J.: Prentice-Hall, 1964).

[8] R. Hill, J. M. Stycos, and K. W. Back, *The Family and Population Control* (Chapel Hill: University of North Carolina Press, 1959).

Other couples, however, are not likely to have such a total relationship, yet may be very much concerned with preventing pregnancy. The same variables (physiological, psychological, sociological) are relevant, but the referents may differ. For example, the wish to maintain her position as daughter of the family rather than as potential mother may be the referent for an unmarried girl's decision about conception control. Furthermore, her expectations or aspirations for establishing or maintaining a relationship with a man may involve sexual intercourse as a bargaining device. In other cases, pregnancy itself may be desired by either the male or the female as a basis for bargaining in a relationship.

Following C. B. Broderick's escalation theory of courtship, according to which males seek sexual involvement but not commitment, one would hypothesize greater interest in contraceptive knowledge and practice on the part of males than females. The research findings can be interpreted in this way, but they also indicate the complexity of the phenomena involved. Michael Schofield's study of 295 British youths aged fifteen to nineteen who had had sexual intercourse showed that although far more girls than boys feared pregnancy (70 per cent and 51 per cent, respectively), far fewer girls than boys (20 per cent and 43 per cent, respectively) reported that they always used some method of birth control; in fact, only two-fifths of the girls, as opposed to three-fourths of the boys, used any method of contraception.[9]

Vincent's studies show that illegitimacy rates have increased far more among females in the age group twenty-five to twenty-nine and in the group thirty to thirty-four (453 and 444 per cent, respectively) than among teenagers, for whom the figure was 108 per cent.[10] The incidence of premarital intercourse, of abortions, and of pregnant brides thus extends the potential interest in contraception to a very heterogeneous group among the unmarried, and "family planning" among the unmarried must encompass a much wider range of social networks and motivations than is usually considered in the literature.

A final argument for family planning is a medical one. Women are often advised to avoid pregnancy in order to protect their health, and A. F. Guttmacher goes so far as to maintain that almost every serious illness calls for the temporary or permanent avoidance of pregnancy.[11] Consideration for the welfare of the child that may be conceived may also suggest avoidance of pregnancy. In extremely

[9] *The Sexual Behavior of Young People* (Boston: Little, Brown, 1965).

[10] C. Vincent, "The Pregnant Single College Girl," *Journal of the American College Health Association*, 195 (1967):42–54.

[11] *Babies by Choice or Chance* (Garden City, N.Y.: Doubleday, 1959).

young mothers there is an increased risk of prematurity and even of mental retardation in the child. Persons whose children may have severe handicaps, such as progressively deteriorating diseases, as a result of hereditary traits, will have another medical reason for family planning.

FERTILITY PATTERNS

After all these arguments for family planning have been considered, however, the question remains: why do families vary so much in size? Social scientists since Malthus have been trying to explain fluctuations in birth rates. Empirical studies of American fertility patterns have been of two types, demographic and sociopsychological. Demographers have tried to explain differences in family fertility using such variables as age at marriage, length of marriage, income, education, social class, place of residence, preferred and expected family size, and others. In addition to certain demographic characteristics, sociopsychological researchers have measured sexual attitudes, conjugal role relationships, attitudes toward self, and similar characteristics. Findings from both types of studies are useful.

Demographic Analyses

Demographic studies are useful in describing general characteristics of families with different fertility patterns.[12] The growth of American families study reported by Whelpton, Campbell, and Patterson[13] is representative of the demographic approach. Most of the study was based on a nation-wide sample of 2,414 white couples, the wives aged eighteen to thirty-nine years, taken in 1960. There was also a similar sample of 270 non-whites. Of significance here are the findings concerning impaired fecundity, fertility planning status, and associated characteristics.

Nearly one-third of these couples had impaired fecundity, that is, a less than normal ability to have children in the future. Of the total group of whites and non-whites 10 per cent were reported as definitely sterile, 4 per cent as probably sterile, and 9 per cent as possibly sterile. Findings were unclear for another 8 per cent, although there was some evidence of impaired fecundity. The couples were about equally divided among three categories of impaired fecundity: those who had had operations that prevent pregnancy,

[12] See R. Freedman, P. K. Whelpton, and A. A. Campbell, *Family Planning, Sterility, and Population Growth* (New York: McGraw-Hill, 1959).

[13] R. K. Whelpton, A. A. Campbell, and J. E. Patterson, *Fertility and Family Planning in the U.S.* (Princeton, N.J.: Princeton University Press, 1966).

those who had reproductive pathologies, and those without pathologies but with long exposure and no conceptions.

Family planning status refers to the degree to which families had controlled the number of their children. Four categories of planning were identified and defined.[14] (1) Completely planned: users of contraceptives with no pregnancies and other users who deliberately discontinued them in order to have a child. (2) Partially planned: couples who had one or more conceptions before starting to use contraception because they wanted these conceptions as soon as possible, or any conception after use of contraception began other than when it was stopped in order to conceive. (3) Partially unplanned: couples who had one or more "unplanned" pregnancies but had not had more pregnancies than were wanted. (4) Excess fertility: either the husband or the wife or both did not want another child at the time of the last conception. The distribution of families in each category ranged from a high of 37 per cent in the partially unplanned group to a low of 17 per cent in the excess fertility group. A fourth of the families were partially planned. Only a fifth were completely planned. Case descriptions were used to show the characteristics of families in each category. Two examples are cited here.

Couples in the first category, completely planned fertility, had, wanted, and expected fewer children than the other groups. They took contraceptive precautions regularly except when they wanted to conceive. They generally waited longer to have their first child and spaced their children further apart than the average for the entire study.

Case 1326. The interviewer describes this 30-year-old mother of three children as "cooperative, honest, and intelligent." She lives in a well-furnished one-family house in a development near a New England city. Her husband earned $6,500 in 1959 as a lineman for an electric light company. She made $300 as a part-time saleslady in a department store. Both wife and husband are high school graduates. Both belong to the Congregational Church and attend services once a week.

They were married in 1950, when the wife was 20 and the husband 23. They used rhythm before the first pregnancy, stopped use in order to have a child, and had a girl in 1952. They resumed using rhythm, stopped again to have another child, and had a boy in 1956. After their second child they used rhythm, condom, and withdrawal (sometimes one method, sometimes another), stopped again to have a child, and had another boy in 1959.

Both husband and wife were well satisfied with three children. As the wife said, "I wanted three in the beginning. I never felt it was fair to raise an only child, and two would not be enough for me." But they did not want any more because, in the wife's words, "We have all we can take care of financially. I will feel satisfied if I can give them all they want and

14 *Ibid.*, p. 361.

need." So, they again resumed using rhythm, condom, and withdrawal to keep from having any more children.[15]

At the other extreme are the couples in the excess fertility category. These couples had not wanted another child at the time of the wife's last pregnancy. On the average, they had the highest number of births, the highest number of births expected, but not the highest number wanted.

Case 886. This couple and their five children live in a single-family house in a small town within 50 miles of New York City. The wife said that they were Lutheran, but never went to church. She had an eighth-grade education and her husband had three years of high school. He made $6,000 in 1959 as an automobile mechanic.

Both husband and wife were 17 years old when they were married in 1950. They didn't want children right away, and tried to prevent conception by using condom. However, they used this method only part-time and had a boy in 15 months. After their first child, they used condom and douche, but again only part-time and had a second boy 19 months after the first. They used the same methods part-time before the fourth (a boy, born 24 months after the third). According to the wife, they omitted use only on the days they thought she couldn't get pregnant, but apparently they miscalculated her "safe" days. After the fourth child, the wife began using diaphragm and jelly all the time. In spite of regular use, she had a fifth child 18 months after the fourth. Since the fifth child, they have gone back to using condom, and are trying conscientiously to use this method always.

Neither the wife nor the husband wanted as many children as they had. The wife wanted two, and she said that her husband wanted two or three. They definitely don't want any more: "I've got too many to take care of now. Physically and financially this is too big a job. It's always a financial struggle. I did want a smaller family. Now that I have five I love them, but it wasn't the way I thought it would be."[16]

These cases highlight the dilemma of family planning: given a certain level of fecundity, why do families fashion different patterns of family fertility? Demographers have sought to identify social factors associated with fertility. Some factors traditionally believed to be associated with fertility showed less influence in this study then previously. Among these were educational attainment, rural vs. urban residence, husband's occupation, and income. Differences in fertility appear to be most clearly related to differences in number of children wanted and ability to control fertility. Also, wives who worked after marriage had fewer births and expected smaller completed families.[17]

[15] Ibid., p. 228.

[16] Ibid., p. 235.

[17] See also L. W. Hoffman and F. Wyatt, "Social Change and Motivations for Having Larger Families: Some Theoretical Considerations," Merrill Palmer Quarterly,

Findings concerning religion as a factor are contradictory. Although this study found religious factors more significant than formerly, other studies point to the increasing similarity of practices among different religious groups.[18] Although the proportion of couples using contraception in 1960 was greater than that in 1955, most couples delay the use of contraceptives or do not use them effectively until they have reached the desired family size. Fewer Catholic children are "unwanted" (excess fertility) even though Catholic couples are less likely to plan their families systematically. Excess fertility is the highest among the least educated. Jews have the highest proportion of completely planned families and Catholics the lowest.

This is a general picture of family planning in the United States as of 1960. The advent of oral contraceptives and intrauterine devices has probably made for changes in contraceptive knowledge and methods actually used today. The simultaneous trend toward more and less effective planning observed from 1955 to 1960 merits continued study. Fertility differences between whites and nonwhites are declining as the influence of Southern farm residence diminishes, and today non-whites and whites of similar backgrounds have and expect the same number of births.

Sociopsychological Analyses

This brief presentation of a demographic study leaves unanswered the question of differences within categories (among Catholics, for example) or between categories (Catholics, Protestants, and Jews). A sociopsychological approach to family planning can suggest some answers to these questions. A paradigm for viewing the interrelationships of these variables is provided by Hill, Stycos, and Back's study of Puerto Rican families. Figure 14–1 shows their preliminary analytical model, including independent, intervening, and dependent variables. Demographic variables similar to those discussed above were related to effective planning by the intervening variables: general orientation to change, attitudes toward family size, availability of technical means for family limitation, and action potential present in the family.

Analysis of data gathered from more than 800 families showed

---

6 (1960):235–44; L. Rainwater and K. K. Weinstein, *And the Poor Get Children* (Chicago: Quadrangle Books, 1960); and Rainwater, *Family Design.*

18 See J. Blake, "The Americanization of Catholic Reproductive Ideals," *Population Studies,* 20 (1966):27–43; Alice Rossi, "NORC Poll on Abortion," cited in A. C. Wehrwein, "Abortion Reform Supported in Poll," *The New York Times,* April 24, 1966; and H. M. Schmeck, Jr., "Doctors Critical of Abortion Laws," *The New York Times,* April 30, 1967.

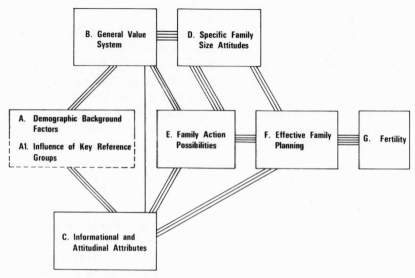

*Figure 14–1. Hypothetical interrelationships of
selected variables in fertility planning.
(From R. Hill, J. M. Stycos, and K. W. Back,
The Family and Population Control [Chapel Hill:
University of North Carolina Press, 1959], p. 220.)*

that institutional patterns and cultural norms neither hindered nor
supported family planning. Religious beliefs, *machismo*, female
modesty, lack of knowledge of contraceptive methods, and the labor
value of large families in an agricultural economy were not significantly influential in determining contraceptive use and fertility.
Many contradictory practices were present in this ambiguous situation: birth control information was acquired late in marriage, use of
contraceptives began after the family had more than its preferred
number of children, and sterilization occurred too late to affect
family size. A factor analysis showed that family organization and
individual acceptance were most closely related to fertility control.

After refining their theory in the survey study reported above,
Hill, Stycos, and Back tested it in a field experiment involving over
600 subjects. They found two sets of variables associated with
family planning, dynamic and instrumental. The dynamic variables
included adequate motivation to take action and the goal of a small
family. The instrumental variables were knowledge and acceptability of contraceptives and the family organization to implement
such planning.

Another look at the social psychology of family planning is presented by Lee Rainwater (see Chapter 9 above and his *Family
Design*). A total of 409 individuals from 257 families living in Chicago, Cincinnati, and Oklahoma City were studied. The major vari-

ables examined were social class, race, religion, and conjugal role relationship. Rainwater found only one central norm accepted as a guide to family size: "One should not have more children than one can support, but one should have as many children as one can afford.[19]

Conjugal role relationship proved the best indicator of family size preference. Nearly every couple studied knew of at least one or two contraceptive methods. However, intellectual knowledge was of little significance when compared with emotional and interpersonal factors and social class differences. Among the lower class there was a tendency to expect failure with the more effective methods and a belief in an element of "luck" in using the others, and couples with joint or intermediate conjugal role relationships were more likely to use effective methods than those with segregated role relationships, who tended to use "folk methods." Among the middle class effectiveness of contraceptive methods was not related to conjugal role relationship but to positive or negative feelings of husband or wife toward sexual relations.

We have seen that data from three quite different studies all indicate points of convergence in identifying the dynamics of family planning. Traditional institutional factors were reported as less significant by Hill, Stycos, and Back and by Whelpton, Campbell and Patterson. All three studies found that attitudes and beliefs about family planning and contraceptive methods were discriminating factors in fertility control. Even religious differences tended to disappear when degree of devoutness was included as a variable. Knowledge of contraceptive methods was reported to be widespread in each study. Hill, Stycos, and Back's conclusion that dynamic factors such as motivation and instrumental variables such as knowledge, acceptability of method, and family organization account for variations in fertility control is generally supported by the other studies. The case descriptions of family planning histories become more understandable when interpreted in motivational and instrumental terms. Rainwater's study makes somewhat more explicit the nature of the interdependence of family role organization, sexual gratification, and the meaning of parenthood. Further exploration of the theoretical and applied uses of the schema proposed by Hill, Stycos, and Back[20] is clearly warranted.

ETHICAL, MORAL, AND LEGAL ISSUES

Family planning and contraceptive practices are personal in nature yet they are not completely private affairs. Explicitly and

[19] *Family Design*, p. 150.
[20] *The Family and Population Control*, p. 220.

implicitly every society specifies its values concerning parenthood and family size. Some methods of limitation of family size are illegal: infanticide, gericide, and abortion. Therapeutic abortion is legal in some states under very stringent medical conditions, but never is the decision to abort legally made by the patient or her family. Violation of the first two of these taboos would undoubtedly lead to severe sanctions, probably imprisonment or commitment to a psychiatric institution. Other methods for limiting family size are not illegal but would be questioned by community authorities and relatives. For example, giving up a child for adoption may be accepted or recommended for a "hard-core problem family" but not for one without overwhelming problems. Other variables associated with fertility, such as postponement of marriage and limiting of intercourse within marriage, are not illegal, but there are commonly accepted limits to their use.[21]

Three issues confront couples considering family planning: the ethics and morality of the decision, the scientific basis for choosing a method, and (for low-income groups) public policy concerning dissemination of birth control information and devices by tax-supported services. The major religious groups in the United States have approved family planning in principle by their general acceptance of the concept of "responsible parenthood." In 1961 American Protestant groups in the National Council of Churches of Christ adopted a statement which held "contraception and periodic continence to be morally right when the motives are right."

The concept of "responsible parenthood" has been traced by John Rock, a well-known Catholic physician. According to Rock, responsible parenthood means "weighing the claims of procreation in relation to the total purposes of the marriage and the situation of the family in society."[22] A Catholic priest, Father Bernard Haring, has further amplified the concept:

The first consideration must be given to responsible parenthood. . . . the great majority of people, Catholics as well as non-Catholics, are convinced that procreation is essentially a question of responsibility. [A married couple] must make the decision as to whether another child is desirable *now*. They do not make a judgment once and forever. They make it only for the present time and remain open to the challenge of a new situation. Responsible parenthood can be expressed in the basic principle of Christian morality, "What can I return to God for all that he has given me?"

[21] Cf. K. Davis and J. Blake, "Social Structure and Fertility: An Analytic Framework," *Economic Development and Cultural Change*, 4 (1956):211–35.

[22] *The Time Has Come: A Catholic Doctor's Proposals To End the Battle over Birth Control* (New York: Knopf, 1963).

In the light of this principle, responsible parenthood can mean for one family not to desire more than one child. It can mean for another to desire, even after the tenth child, one more.[23]

The gradual Americanization of Catholic ideals of family size is documented by J. Blake in a comparison of official statements by the clergy with the attitudes expressed by Catholic laymen.[24] According to Blake's analysis, the clergy criticize small families and eulogize large ones, while responses to public opinion polls between 1943 and 1961 indicate that Catholic laymen prefer four or fewer children. In comparing the clerical statements cited by Blake and Rock with those of Haring, Haring appears to represent a liberal position within the Church.

Excerpts from an official text of the majority report of the Papal Study Commission on Birth Control continue the theme of responsible parenthood: "Responsible parenthood—through which married persons intend to observe and cultivate the essential values of matrimony with a view to the good of persons (the good of the child to be educated, of the couples themselves, and of the whole of human society)—is one of the conditions and expressions of a true conjugal chastity. . . . the regulation of conception appears necessary to many couples who wish to achieve a responsible, open and reasonable parenthood in today's circumstances." The report goes on to recommend other methods of birth control not now approved by the church: "If they are to observe and cultivate all the essential values of marriage, married people need decent and human means for the regulation of conception. They should be able to expect the collaboration of all, especially from men of learning and science, in order that they can have at their disposal means agreeable and worthy of man in fulfilling his responsible parenthood."[25] Criteria for choosing "a method of reconciling the needs of marital life with the right ordering of this life to fruitfulness in the procreation and education of offspring" are also discussed. The minority report, relying on historical teachings of the Church, rejected the majority argument. At present, however, the encyclical letter of Pope Paul VI, "On the Development of Peoples" (*Populorum progressio*), issued March 28, 1967, represents the official position on family planning: "Finally, it is for the parents to decide with full knowledge of the matter, on the number of their

---

[23] "Christian Marriage and Family Planning," in *The Problem of Population*, ed. D. N. Barrett (South Bend, Ind.: University of Notre Dame Press, 1964), pp. 2–3.

[24] "The Americanization of Catholic Reproductive Ideals."

[25] *The National Catholic Reporter*, quoted in *The New York Times*, April 17, 1967, p. 30. © 1967 by The New York Times Company; reprinted by permission.

children, taking into account their responsibilities toward God, themselves, the children they have already brought into the world, and the community to which they belong. In all this they must follow the demands of their own conscience enlightened by God's law authentically interpreted, and sustained by confidence in Him."[26] Church spokesmen interpreted the encyclical to support responsible parenthood and the rhythm method of conception control. The Catholic Periodical Index[27] provides a summary of current Catholic thought on family planning and related topics.

For both the dominant Christian groups, the ethical issue hinges on the role of conscience and motivation in fulfilling reponsibilities, but Catholic thought makes more explicit and binding the role of religious values in the decision to regulate family size. Resolution of the second issue, the scientific basis for choosing a contraceptive, is dependent upon resolution of the ethical and moral issue. Some effective methods of family planning are rejected on the basis of the generalized taboo against them, and for the Catholic all other methods save one are officially forbidden. The one method approved by the Church is periodic abstinence or rhythm. Hence the concern of the devout Catholic would be the scientific perfection of the prediction of ovulation. R. L. Dickinson has described the general criteria for selecting a contraceptive: "Wherever pregnancy spells serious hazard to health, to success in marriage, to essential well-being of family or community, there contraceptives must be *dependable, acceptable, harmless, simple,* and *cheap*—easy to get, easy to keep, easy to use."[28] All of the methods of contraception discussed below meet one or more of these criteria to some degree.

The third issue, public policy, has been resolved for all except the unmarried. Court decisions have now removed the legal obstacles to dissemination of contraceptive knowledge and methods in the two states that retained them. A major change in public policy on family planning was announced in January, 1966, when John Gardner, Secretary of the Department of Health, Education, and Welfare, stated H.E.W.'s support for studies and programs on population dynamics, fertility, sterility, and family planning.[29] States, local agencies, and individuals served by them are guaranteed "freedom from

[26] The New York Times, March 29, 1967, p. 24. © 1967 by The New York Times Company; reprinted by permission.

[27] Catholic Library Association, The Catholic Periodical Index (Haverford, Pa.: By the Association, 1967).

[28] R. L. Dickinson, Techniques of Conception Control, 3d ed. (Baltimore: Williams & Wilkins, 1950), p. 5.

[29] U.S., Department of Health, Education, and Welfare, Report on Family Planning (Washington, D.C.: Government Printing Office, 1966).

coercion or pressure of mind or conscience" in deciding whether to participate in family planning programs. In August, 1967, the post of Deputy Assistant Secretary for family planning and population was created. Mrs. Katherine B. Oettinger, head of the Children's Bureau, was appointed to fill the new post.

An indication of the ambivalent attitude toward birth control is the ready availability to the unmarried of some contraceptives (condoms, jels) and the inaccessibility of others. The most effective methods of contraception are the least easily available. Unmarried persons who seek to use methods requiring a physician's examination and prescription often cannot do so. Probably no other medical care is denied a patient solely on the basis of marital status. Mary Calderone opposes giving contraceptives to unmarried teenagers on the grounds that such action would not teach sexual responsibility.[30] Ira L. Reiss, discussing the same issue, concludes that there is no research evidence that availability of contraceptive information influences teenagers' morality.[31] Under certain circumstances, the present author believes it is immoral to deny youth access to contraceptive information and devices.

With these observations on issues in family planning, let us look at various methods of conception control.

CONTRACEPTIVE METHODS

Family planning is a term describing the decision-making process of determining the size of family, spacing of births, and means of regulating fertilization, including sterilization. It may also involve the decision to terminate a pregnancy by abortion. Furthermore, family planning includes studies of fertility to determine the possibility and probability of fertilization and means to enhance reproduction. In this sense, medical treatment ranging from sperm counts to post-coital cervical mucus tests and artificial insemination are part of family planning.

Assuming adequate quantity and quality of sperm, normality of the gynecological system, and correct coital technique, family planning today is primarily concerned with the prevention of ovulation, of fertilization, and of nidation. To understand the physiology of contraception, the reader should review the physiology of ovulation and menstruation presented in Chapter 12. Methods of preventing conception include suppressing ovulation ("the pill"), preventing implantation (intrauterine devices), mechanical and chemical barriers (diaphragm, foams, and jels), limiting intercourse to the in-

[30] "Contraception, Teenagers, and Sexual Responsibility," *Journal of Sex Research*, 2 (1966):37–40.
[31] "Contraceptive Information and Sexual Morality," *ibid.*, pp. 51–57.

fertile periods of the menstrual cycle (rhythm), and preventing the depositing of sperm in the vagina (abstinence, coitus interruptus, condom). Sterilization of the male (vasectomy) or of the female (tubal ligation) also prevents conception by blocking the normal route of sperm or ovum. Because the male continuously produces sperm and a female releases an ovum only once in each ovulatory cycle, the various methods of contraception must take one or both factors into account.

Historical studies of contraceptive practice indicate an almost universal interest in birth control.[32] Both primitive and civilized societies have a rich repertoire of contraceptive folklore. Indeed, some contemporary scientific preparations can be traced back to antiquity. Both the Old Testament and the Talmud offer contraceptive information and advice. J. T. Noonan's review of contraception in the Roman Empire[33] documents the attention paid in that day to developing effective birth control methods.

Methods Requiring Medical Consultation

With the exception of sterilization, contraceptive methods requiring medical consultation apply only to females. These methods in order of relative effectiveness are "the pill," intrauterine devices (IUD's), diaphragm, foam, and jel, and the rhythm method. All of these methods have been rated as highly effective if instructions are followed carefully and consistently.

Oral Contraceptives. Oral contraceptives prevent pregnancy by suppressing the pituitary hormones necessary for ovulation. The ovulation-menstruation cycle discussed in Chapter 12 is based upon the reciprocal functioning of the hypothalamus, pituitary, and ovary. The hypothalamus rhythmically paces the pituitary's release of gonadotropins. They, in turn, awaken some ovarian follicles whose hormones, among other things, operate as a control on the pituitary's further release of follicle-stimulating hormones (F.S.H.). Within the mystery of this delicate interplay in the ovarian-menstrual cycle lies the key to oral contraception.

When pregnancy occurs, the normal cycle of ovulation ceases until it is terminated. Scientists reasoned that pregnancy could be prevented by suppressing ovulation, for then fertilization could not

[32] See G. Hardin, "The History and Future of Birth Control," *Perspectives in Biology and Medicine,* 10 (1966):1–18; N. E. Himes, *Medical History of Contraception* (New York: Gamut, 1963); and A. L. Southam, "Historical Review of Intrauterine Devices," in *Intrauterine Conception: Proceedings of the Second International Conference, New York, October 2–3, 1964,* ed. S. J. Segal and K. D. Shafer, International Congress Series No. 86, abstracted in *Excerpta Medica.*

[33] *Contraception* (Cambridge, Mass.: Harvard University Press, 1965); reprinted 1967 by New American Library.

take place. Ovulation could be suppressed by simulating the ovarian-pituitary balance present during pregnancy. As Garcia and Pincus put it, "the most logicial physiological candidates" to accomplish this would be the naturally occurring hormones, estrogen and progesterone, which might suppress ovulation.[34] Subsequent research and testing have supported this hypothesis, and now we have "the pill" as an oral contraceptive. The pill reduces the likelihood of pregnancy in other ways as well. Just prior to ovulation, when it is thin and watery, the cervical mucus is very favorable to sperm penetration and progression. The pill makes it thick and sticky, forming a natural barrier to entry of sperm into the uterus and Fallopian tubes where fertilization takes place. The uterine lining also becomes hostile to implantation. Although the endometrial phases of the menstrual cycle still occur, they occur more rapidly and are less fully developed.

All oral contraceptives rely on the administration of the same synthetic hormones, estrogen and progesterone, to inhibit the pituitary gonadotropins required for ovulation. However, the method of administration differs. They may be given simultaneously or sequentially. In simultaneous administration the two hormones are combined into one pill. In the sequential method ovulation is prevented by the administration of estrogen additional to that secreted by the body, and progesterone to balance the additional estrogen. Estrogen is given alone for the first phase of the cycle and with progesterone during the second phase. As described in Chapter 12, estrogen is normally secreted during the entire menstrual cycle but not in amounts sufficient to prevent ovulation. Progesterone is normally secreted only during the second phase of the cycle. Thus the sequential method more nearly approximates the natural hormonal sequence.

Theoretically, an oral contraceptive can be taken continuously to provide protection against pregnancy. On such a schedule, however, the decline of the uterine lining and menstruation, phases three and four of the ovulation-menstruation cycle, does not occur. Instead, some unpredictable breakthrough bleeding occurs. In the natural menstrual cycle menstruation occurs following a drop in the bodily production levels of estrogen and progesterone. Hence in the oral contraceptive cycle the pills are administered for about twenty days, then withdrawn, on a schedule simulating the natural cycle. Menstruation-like bleeding follows about three days later.

Figure 14–2 illustrates the administration of the pills. In the com-

[34] C. Garcia and G. Pincus, "Hormonal Inhibition of Ovulation," in *Manual of Contraceptive Practice*, ed. M. S. Calderone (Baltimore: Williams & Wilkins, 1964), pp. 206–21.

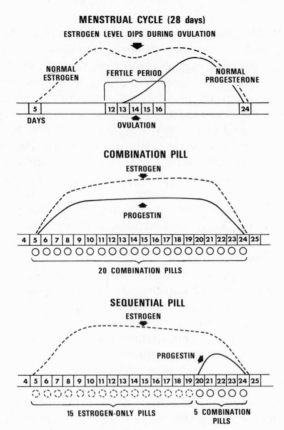

*Figure 14–2. The menstrual cycle and the oral
contraceptive pill. (Diagram by R. M. Chapin from
Time, April 7, 1967. Courtesy Time; copyright
Time Inc., 1967.)*

bination method both hormones, combined in one pill, are taken
for twenty days. In the sequential method estrogen alone is taken
for about fourteen days, and both estrogen and progesterone are
taken for about six days. The exact schedule varies for different
brands of pills. The physician's instructions for the specific pills
prescribed should be followed. They are available in different
dosages.

In general, the regimen for oral contraception is that shown in
Figure 14–3. Counting the first day of menstruation as Day 1, on
Day 5 the woman begins taking her pills and takes one each day for
a total of twenty days. Thus, from Days 5 through 24 she takes one
pill. About three days after she stops taking them, bleeding begins.
In the cycle illustrated in Figure 14–3 menstruation begins on Days
3, 30, and 26. In the second month of the diagram the patient be-

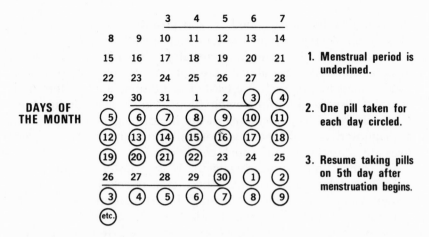

Figure 14–3. Schedule of administration of an oral contraceptive. (From D. P. Swartz and R. L. Vande Wiele, Methods of Conception Control [Raritan, N.J.: Ortho Pharmaceutical Corporation, 1965]. Courtesy Ortho Pharmaceutical Corporation.)

gins taking her pills on the fifth day following the onset of menstruation. Bleeding began on Day 30; she began taking pills on the third day following and continued for twenty days, taking her last pill on the twenty-second day of the month. Bleeding began on the twenty-sixth day of the second month. Sometimes bleeding does not follow the twenty-day regimen. When this happens the patient should nevertheless start taking the pills again seven days after taking the last one. If she misses a second period, however, she should see her physician.

If a patient forgets to take a pill, the general recommendation is to take the missed pill as soon as possible, then continue the usual pattern, taking the pill for that day and those which follow. If more than one pill is missed, she should continue the regimen but also use a local method of contraception (condom or foam) until the end of that cycle. Almost all pregnancies in women taking oral contraceptives can be attributed to lack of regularity in pill taking.

Both types of pills—combination and sequential—offer virtually 100 per cent protection against pregnancy *if taken as directed.* There have been some "failures" with the sequential pills, but many doctors believe these to be due to patient error.

Doubt about the safety of the pills has led to their being studied more extensively and thoroughly than any other product in the history of medicine. At the present time their safety factor is far higher than that of pregnancy itself. They remain under continuing study and evaluation by medical and government agencies which provide physicians with their latest conclusions.[35]

There are two reasons for fears about the pill. When certain medical conditions are already present, the use of oral contraceptives is inadvisable. Such pre-existing conditions include thromboembolic disease (life-threatening blood clots), liver dysfunctions (cirrhosis, hepatitis), carcinoma of the breast or genital organs, and undiagnosed vaginal bleeding. Generally speaking, oral contraceptives are contraindicated in such conditions.

The other doubt-producing factor is the cluster of side effects experienced by some patients. These side effects include nausea, weight gain, breakthrough bleeding, breast tenderness, dizziness, nervousness, irritability, and headaches. These side effects are transient, and reversible on stopping the drug. It is essential, of course, that oral contraceptives be taken only under medical supervision. Every user must have an initial gynecological examination and periodic medical check-ups. Young people need to be warned that taking bootleg pills can be dangerous.

Intrauterine Devices. For centuries it has been known that a foreign body in the uterus will prevent pregnancy.[36] Camel drivers in the Middle East prevented pregnancy in their camels by placing a small stone in the uterine cavity. Western medical literature of the late 1800's refers to intrauterine contraception, but it was not until 1929, when Ernst Grafenberg, a German physician, invented an intrauterine ring, that modern medicine would consider the IUD as a contraceptive device. It was initially rejected because of some complications associated with its shape and with the metal of which it was made. There were other complications erroneously attributed to it as well.

In a recent review of current experience with the IUD, C. Tietze states that "no other contraceptive method has undergone so rapid and thorough a change of medical reputation. . . . A decade ago, the IUD's were outside the field of respectable medical practice or even research. . . . Today, intrauterine contraception has received the explicit approval of numerous leaders of the medical profession, and is no longer regarded as experimental."[37]

Present-day IUD's include spirals, bows, butterflies, loops, bands, and rings. Grafenberg's ring was composed of silk threads bound by silver and had to be removed periodically. Today's spirals, loops, and butterflies are made of plastic or rings of stainless steel and

---

[35] American Medical Association, Council on Drugs, "Evaluation of Oral Contraceptives," *Journal of the American Medical Association*, 199 (1967):650–53.

[36] See Southam, "Historical Review of Intrauterine Devices."

[37] "Contraception with Intrauterine Devices 1959–1966," *American Journal of Obstetrics and Gynecology*, 96 (1966):1043.

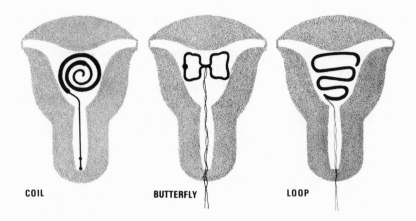

Figure 14–4. Intrauterine devices in place. Left, *coil;*
center, *butterfly;* right, *loop.*
(From Swartz and Vande Wiele,
Methods of Conception Control.)

may be left in indefinitely. Figure 14–4 shows the most common
IUD's. With a special device the physician inserts them in the uterus,
where they resume their original shape. The spiral has a beaded tail
that protrudes from the cervix so that it can be checked or removed.
The Lippes loop has two nylon threads for the same purpose.

Tietze summarized the results of studies of 22,403 women who
had used either one of the four types (spiral, loop, bow, and ring)
and nine sizes of IUD's or an experimental model for a total of
307,441 months. Pregnancy rates per hundred women ranged from
1.6 for the large spiral to 11.3 for the small bow. In every type of
IUD the large size provided greater protection against pregnancy
than the small size. Spontaneous expulsion of IUD's had been reported. Tietze found expulsion rates ranging from 30.1 per hundred
for the small spiral to 1.8 for the large bow. Expulsion rates decreased as the size of the IUD increased. The expulsion rates of
IUD's of similar size were highest for spirals, lowest for bows, and
intermediate for loops and rings. True expulsion rates for the bow
and the ring, Tietze believes, should be one and one-half times
greater than those he reported. The incidence of removal because
of bleeding and/or pain were highest for the largest spiral and
lowest for the steel ring. Perforations of the uterus were reported in
only 43 cases. The stem of the spiral was reported to have become
buried in or to have perforated the cervix of the vaginal mucosa in
1 per cent of the cases. Some husbands complained that the spiral
caused discomfort. No increase in abnormal Papanicolaou smears
was observed among the women studied.

The IUD is generally advisable only for women who have had at least one child. The size prescribed depends on the size of the uterine cavity. In order to avoid possible damage to a developing embryo before a woman knows that she is pregnant, an IUD should be inserted during or following menstruation. The mechanism by which the IUD prevents pregnancy is not known. After studying the incidence of pregnancies with IUD's in place, on the basis of statistical probability Tietze concluded that the IUD's disturb events in the Fallopian tubes, which would support Mastroianni's conclusion, studies of monkeys, that the IUD acts by speeding up the journey of the ovum through the tubes.

The disadvantages of the IUD, then, are possible pregnancy, expulsion, excessive menstrual bleeding (menorrhagia), intermenstrual bleeding (metrorrhagia), and pelvic pain.[38] Its advantages include its economy, simplicity of use, high level of protection, stability in all climates, ease of insertion and withdrawal, the fact that only limited medical supervision is needed, and, most important, the fact that it requires little or no responsibility on the part of the woman. If one considers the expulsion rate, the removal rate, and the pregnancy rate reported, its effectiveness is less than the pill's but higher than that of the diaphragm. Its popularity in the United States will probably be with those not motivated to use methods requiring daily planning or those unable to use oral contraceptives.[39]

Diaphragm and Jel. The diaphragm is a dome-shaped latex rubber cup used as a mechanical barrier to keep sperm from entering the uterus. Diaphragms, shown in Figure 14–5, are made in various

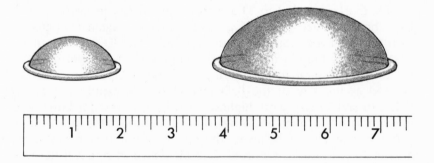

Figure 14–5. Diaphragms.

[38] G. W. Perkins, "Intrauterine Contraception," *The Canadian Medical Association Journal*, 94 (1966):431–36.

[39] See American Medical Association, Committee on Human Reproduction, "Evaluation of Intrauterine Contraceptive Devices," *Journal of the American Medical Association*, 199 (1967):647–49.

sizes to fit the patient's vaginal size and contour. In order to cover the cervix a spring is enclosed in the rubber rim to maintain a snug fit against the tissues behind the pubic bone and the posterior of the vagina. Fitting is done by a physician using a set of fitting rings. Different types of springs (flat, coiled, or flat and coiled combined) are used depending upon vaginal size, contours, and displacements of the uterus. If there is severe displacement of the uterus or adjacent organs, another method would be recommended.

A woman quickly learns how to insert and remove a diaphragm manually or with a plastic inserter. She can check with her fingers to see if it is properly placed by feeling the rim behind the pubic bone and feeling for the cervix behind the dome of the diaphragm. A spermicidal foam, cream, or jel, must be smeared inside and outside the dome. This chemical contraceptive gives added protection. Figure 14–6 shows the diaphragm in place.

The diaphragm is inserted prior to intercourse and must be left in place for at least six hours. If intercourse occurs again within this time, the diaphragm is left in place, and an applicator full of contraceptive jel or cream is used as well. Douching less than six hours after the last ejaculation is prohibited because it destroys the effectiveness of the spermicide. Even then it is unnecessary, as the normal vagina is self-cleansing. Occasionally the diaphragm may be dis-

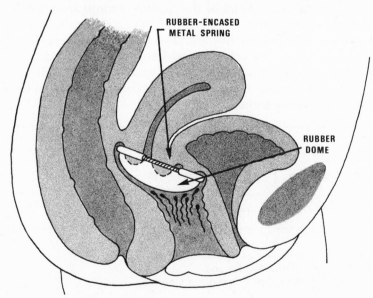

RUBBER-ENCASED
METAL SPRING

RUBBER
DOME

Figure 14–6. Diaphragm in place.
(From Swartz and Vande Wiele,
Methods of Conception Control.)

263

lodged during coitus because of frequent insertions of the penis or enlargement of the vaginal canal during coitus. The woman should check it for correct placement.

As a method of protection, the diaphragm is widely recommended. Because it can be inserted well before foreplay is begun, its use does not interfere with the sequence of coital activity. Some women object to the diaphragm on esthetic grounds; they may dislike putting a foreign object into the vagina or the task of removing, washing, powdering, and storing the diaphragm. But it is ideal when there is not frequent exposure to pregnancy, or when other methods for some reason are inadvisable.

Rhythm. As the name suggests, the rhythm method of birth control is based on the sequential and repetitive timing which is a biological fact of life for women. The discussion here will focus on the application of the rhythm method, its clinical effectiveness, and related medical issues.[40] The rhythm method is based upon the fact that fertilization can occur only when a viable ovum comes in contact with viable sperm. Abstinence is practiced during that period of the cycle when an ovum is likely to be present, and the method requires determining the time of ovulation. In the average menstrual cycle of twenty-eight days ovulation usually occurs about the fourteenth day, although it ranges from the twelfth to the sixteenth day. Variable factors in the using of the rhythm method are uncertainty about time of ovulation, the length of time a sperm may fertilize, and the life of an ovum (see Fig. 14–7). If the ovum survives for twenty-four hours, the fertile period lasts an additional day. However, since sperm live up to seventy-two hours, the fertile period begins up to three days earlier. With this magnitude of variation, the rhythm method requires careful calculation.

SPERM SURVIVAL			TIME DURING WHICH OVULATION CAN OCCUR					OVUM SURVIVAL	
9	10	11	12	13	14	15	16	17	18

DAYS OF A 28-DAY MENSTRUAL CYCLE

Figure 14–7. Variable factors in determining the "unsafe" period. (From Swartz and Vande Wiele, Methods of Conception Control.)

[40] Because rhythm is at present the only method of contraception approved by the Roman Catholic Church, any discussion of it also raises doctrinal issues and issues of public policy. For a discussion of these problems, see Noonan, *Contraception,* and Rock, *The Time Has Come.*

There are several methods of calculating the fertile period. The two most common are the calendar method and the temperature method.[41] The calendar method assumes that to compute the day of ovulation it is necessary to take into account the longest and shortest cycle experienced over the preceding year. A record kept for a year or longer should provide the range of cycle variation. Using the more cautious formula of Ogino, the beginning of the fertile or "unsafe" period is determined by subtracting 18 days from the shortest cycle: if the shortest cycle was 26 days long, the beginning of the "unsafe" period would be 26—18, or Day 8 of the cycle. The end of the "unsafe" period is determined by subtracting 11 days from the longest cycle: if the longest cycle was 30 days long, the end of the "unsafe" period would be 30—11, or Day 19. In this case the total unsafe period would be from Day 8 through Day 19, inclusive, or 12 days long. For this woman it would be relatively safe to have intercourse from the first day of her cycle through the seventh day and from the twentieth day through the beginning of the next cycle.[42]

The second method of computing the fertile period is the most effective: it uses basal body temperature to announce ovulation. During an ovulatory menstrual cycle the basal body temperature drops a few tenths of a degree immediately before ovulation, begins to rise after ovulation, and remains high for the rest of the cycle. Fertilization is believed possible for three days after the rise in temperature. When a temperature rise above the preceding six days' temperatures has been observed for three days in a row, the fertile period is over. Figure 14–8 shows a basal body temperature chart for both ovulatory and anovulatory cycles. In an anovulatory

---

[41] See M. S. Calderone, ed., *Manual of Contraceptive Practice* (Baltimore: Williams & Wilkins, 1964); R. G. Potter, Jr., "Parameters of the Menstrual Cycle," *Population Studies*, 20 (1966):223–32; J. Rock, "The Rhythm or Periodic Continence Method of Birth Control," in Calderone, ed., *Manual of Contraceptive Practice*, pp. 222–29; and C. Tietze and R. G. Potter, Jr., "Statistical Evaluation of the Rhythm Method," *American Journal of Obstetrics and Gynecology*, 84 (1962): 692–98.

[42] Other examples might be:

	Case A	Case B	Case C
Shortest cycle	26 days	27 days	28 days
minus 18 days	−18	−18	−18
Beginning of unsafe days	day 8	day 9	day 10
Longest cycle	26 days	32 days	35 days
minus 11 days	−11	−11	−11
End of unsafe period	day 15	day 21	day 24
Fertile or unsafe period	8 days	13 days	15 days

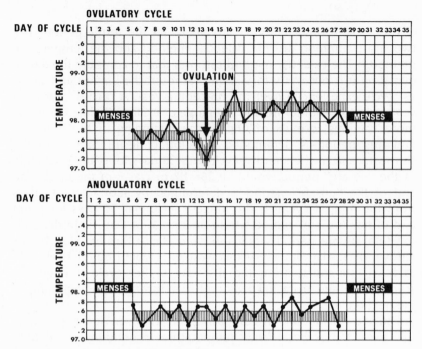

Figure 14–8. Basal body temperature during the menstrual cycle. (From Swartz and Vande Wiele, Methods of Conception Control.)

cycle ovulation does not occur. Some women show no drop in basal temperature before ovulation. In such case, the safe period following ovulation is indicated by the temperature rise. Use of this method shortens the period of abstention following ovulation.

Other methods of determining ovulation include the glucose test tape[43] and chloride spot tests.[44] In the glucose test a chemically treated paper tape is exposed to the cervical mucus. The tape turns from pink to blue in the presence of glucose. The presence of glucose is evident two or three days before ovulation and up to four days afterward. It usually precedes the lowest temperature day and may persist during or after the shift from low to higher temperatures. Rock is skeptical about these tests.[45]

The chloride spot test involves taking a sample of cervical mucus

[43] For a description of the glucose test, see C. H. Birnberg, D. J. Wexler, and M. Gross, "Estimation of Ovulation Phase by Serial Test of Cervical and Vaginal Glucose," *Obstetrics and Gynecology,* 21 (1963):194–200; J. B. Doyle and F. J. Ewers, Jr., "The New Fertility Testing Tape: A Predictive Test of the Fertile Period," *Journal of the American Medical Association,* 192 (1960):1744–50.

[44] D. J. McSweeney and A. J. Sbarra, "A Rapid Ovarian Hormone and Ovulation Test," *Obstetrics and Gynecology,* 26 (1965):201–6.

[45] See *The Time Has Come.*

with a chemically prepared swab and rubbing it on a piece of test paper. As the estrogen level rises and the time of ovulation approaches, the spot on the test paper gets lighter. After ovulation the spot gets darker again. The chloride content of the mucus is controlled by the amount of estrogen being released. Boutselis states that these two methods "may challenge the superiority of the basal body temperature method in detecting ovulation."[46]

Regulation of the ovulatory mechanism and, indirectly, the menstrual cycle is another means of implementing the rhythm method. While the oral contraceptives regulate the menstrual cycle by suppressing ovulation, other products produce ovulation on demand. Boutselis' studies indicate that ovulation can in this way be timed within two or three days. He suggests that the greatest advantage of controlling the time of ovulation would be in eliminating unexpected early or late ovulation. These same tests also tell when to have intercourse if pregnancy is desired. Conception is more likely to occur if intercourse takes place at the time of ovulation.

The advantages of the rhythm method are its ecclesiastical approval, simplicity, and economy. Its disadvantages include difficulty in determining the time of ovulation, the period of abstinence required, and the frequency of failure. A recently released World Health Organization report on fertility control by periodic abstinence concluded that lack of an accurate indicator of ovulation is the major objection to the rhythm method.[47] Variations in ovulation, lack of understanding of the method, and unwillingness to abstain are other obstacles. A statistical probability study of the theoretical effectiveness of the rhythm method showed that the chance of complete protection ranged from 90 to 95 per cent, but only when practiced under careful medical guidance.[48] The authors pointed out that these odds may be acceptable to a couple wanting to postpone pregnancy rather than prevent it completely. They concluded that the risk of conception declined sharply as the period of abstinence increased, increased with the greater variability of the cycle, and varied with the relative length of the phases of the cycle. Rock reports that the diaphragm and jel and condom are about twice as dependable as the rhythm method, but that rhythm is about six times more effective than no method.[49]

[46] J. G. Boutselis, N. Vorys, and J. C. Ullery, "Control of Ovulation Time and Cycle Length with Clomiphene Citrate," *American Journal of Obstetrics and Gynecology*, 97 (1967):955.

[47] Reported as "Better Test Needed for Rhythm," *Journal of the American Medical Association*, 201 (1967):40.

[48] Tietze and Potter, "Statistical Evaluation of the Rhythm Method."

[49] *The Time Has Come.*

Methods Not Requiring Medical Consultation

Probably the most common contraceptive method throughout the world, coitus interruptus, needs no specialized knowledge or medication. Contraceptive methods discussed in this section vary widely in their effectiveness.

Withdrawal. In Genesis 38 Onan is described as having used coitus interruptus or withdrawal, the practice of withdrawing the penis from the vagina or vulval area before ejaculation, with his brother's wife. He "spilled" his semen "on the ground," and thus "displeased the Lord: wherefore he slew him." Many Christians have interpreted this story as divine rejection of artificial means of birth control, but J. T. Noonan reviews the theological debate on the issue and points out that scholars believe rather that Onan was slain for violating the Mosaic law that a man must marry his brother's widow (the levirate).

Withdrawal is economical, always available, and simple. Because some males cannot regulate or control ejaculation and because some sperm may escape before ejaculation, the risks of pregnancy are high. Psychological disadvantages are sometimes created by interruption of the normal sequence of intercourse, particularly the orgasm patterns of both the husband and the wife. If withdrawal occurs before the wife's orgasm, she may be denied it altogether. Also, the satisfaction that some wives report of feeling the husband's ejaculatory thrust is absent, and some men feel their sense of masculinity frustrated by withdrawal. The imaginative couple can, of course, work out mutually rewarding orgasm patterns, and the universality of coitus interruptus suggests that some couples find it more rewarding than unrewarding. Its greatest disadvantage is probably its relatively high rate of failure to prevent conception. Psychiatric opinion holds that as long as it is mutually acceptable no psychological harm results from it. There is no question that much of western Europe's population stability has been achieved by the use of this method and of the condom.

Condom. Another method of birth control is the condom shown in Figure 14–9. The condom ("rubber," "sheath," "safe," "cundrum") is worn over the erect penis during coitus to prevent sperm from being deposited in the vagina. It is made of latex rubber or skin from sheep's intestine, packaged as rolled, unrolled, lubricated or unlubricated, with plain or reservoir tip, or some combination of these. Skin condoms are plain-tipped and sold dry or moistened. Some condoms are lubricated with a spermicidal jel, thus offering dual contraceptive protection. The condom covers the erect penis much as a glove covers a finger. It should be applied prior to any entry into the vagina to avoid the risk of sperm escaping prior to ejaculation. Some space should be left at the tip of a condom to

Figure 14–9. Condom.

collect semen. In condoms with a reservoir tip the space is provided automatically. With a plain-tipped rubber or skin condom the air is pressed out of the enclosed end and the condom is unrolled to cover the entire penis. A spermicidal jel is applied to the shaft of the condom and the vaginal entrance as a lubricant if the vaginal entrance and vagina do not have sufficient natural lubrication. Since the penis becomes flaccid after ejaculation, care should be taken to see that the condom is held on as the penis is withdrawn from the vagina so it will not slip off and spill its contents in the vagina.

Simplicity of use, cheapness, and effectiveness seem to be the chief advantages of the condom. Some users object to it because its use interrupts the natural sequence of sexual intercourse, it reduces the sensitivity of sexual response, and it is unaesthetic after use. Women sometimes find it irritating and report reduced responsiveness. Men who experience premature ejaculation may find their reduced sensitivity to stimulation an aid in extending their cycle of sexual response.

The Consumers Union Report on Family Planning, The Complete Book of the Birth Control, and *Planning Your Family*[50] offer detailed consumer information concerning quality and brand names of products. Along with Calderone's *Manual of Contraceptive Practice,* they provide information on the variety, efficiency, and use of contraceptives.

Foam, Cream, Jel, etc. Spermicidal preparations are widely used means of contraception which do not require a physician's services. They are available in several forms: foams, creams, jels, foam tablets, and vaginal suppositories. The foams and creams are the most effective. They block the cervical opening mechanically, thus pre-

[50] Consumers Union of the United States, *The Consumers Union Report on Family Planning* (Mount Vernon, N.Y.: By the Union, 1966); A. F. Guttmacher, W. Best, and F. S. Jaffe, *The Complete Book of Birth Control* (New York: Ballantine Books, 1961); and *Planning Your Family* (New York: Macmillan, 1964).

venting sperm from entering the uterus, and immobilize and kill sperm chemically. Foams, creams, and jels are applied by special applicator. The plastic applicator is filled and then inserted so that its contents cover the opening to the cervix. Application must be made prior to each act of intercourse. Application is shown in Figure 14–10. Effectiveness of the preparation is diminished by improper application, dilution by vaginal secretions and leakage, and incomplete distribution in intercourse. A douche is not necessary, but if desired it should be postponed until six hours after intercourse. Reapplication of the preparation is necessary before each act of coitus.

Advantages of foams, creams, and jels are ease of use and ready availability, aesthetics of application, and absence of interference with the sensitivity of response. They may be applied up to one hour before intercourse. The dripping of jels especially may make them aesthetically disagreeable to some users. Since all these preparations are water-soluble, they do not stain linen or clothing. Foam tablets and vaginal suppositories rely on their chemical and mechanical properties to prevent conception much like the preparations discussed above, but they are far less effective and not to be recommended.

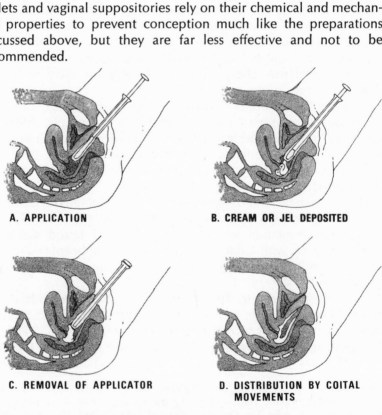

A. APPLICATION

B. CREAM OR JEL DEPOSITED

C. REMOVAL OF APPLICATOR

D. DISTRIBUTION BY COITAL MOVEMENTS

Figure 14–10. Application and use of jel.

Another popular method of supposed contraception widely used by women is the douche, which is mentioned only to be dismissed as a contraceptive. It is hardly better than no contraceptive at all, for sperm have been found in the cervix 90 seconds after ejaculation. The table below provides an evaluation of the various methods. Effectiveness is only partly due to the method of contraception. Failure of the various methods may be user failures; that is, couples' failure to follow the prescribed procedures.[51]

Effectiveness of Contraceptive Methods

Method	Effectiveness
Oral ("the pill")	Maximum
Diaphragm with cream or jel	Very high
Cervical cap with cream or jel	Very high
Condom	Very high
Intrauterine device*	Very high
Rhythm (with thermometer)†	Very high
Foam, cream	High to medium
Cream or jel alone	Medium to fair
Foaming tablets	Medium to fair
Suppositories	Medium to fair
Sponge with liquid or powder	Medium to fair
Rhythm (calendar alone)†	Medium to fair
Withdrawal†	Medium to fair
Douche	Lowest, but better than none

Adapted from *The Consumers Union Report on Family Planning.* Copyright 1966 by the Consumers Union of the United States, Inc., Mount Vernon, N.Y. 10550, a non-profit organization.

* The IUD, which was not included in this *Report,* can be ranked as maximum.

† The reliability of all methods varies with care in use; this is particularly true of the rhythm method and of withdrawal. If extreme care is assumed, both methods can be ranked as very effective.

Teachers, social workers, clergy, and others wishing help in preparing talks and lesson plans, or who wish additional information for themselves will find the following references very valuable: *The Consumers Union Report on Family Planning;* Guttmacher, Best, and Jaffe, *The Complete Book of Birth Control;* Himes, *Medical History of Contraception;* Noonan, *Contraception;* and Rock, *The Time Has*

[51] See G. Devereux, "A Psychoanalytic Study of Contraception," *Journal of Sex Research,* 1 (1965):105–34; B. Seaman, "Why Did Birth Control Fail for Me?" *Ladies' Home Journal,* 82 (1965):166–67.

Come. The G. D. Searle Company[52] and Ortho Pharmaceutical Corporation[53] have the most complete services for educators.

Sterilization

Birth control by voluntary surgery, unlike other methods of contraception, has had almost no legal opposition. It is legal in all states. However, two states, Connecticut and Utah, restrict sterilization to cases of "medical necessity," and in other states there is some concern over the legal uncertainties. Religious opposition to sterilization is expressed by both Protestants and Catholics. The theological basis for the Catholic view is discussed by Noonan. The other major religious groups do not have official prohibitions against sterilization.

Permanent sterilization may be considered under several conditions. It may be preferred when other methods of contraception fail or are unsatisfactory because of the limitations of the method or the users. When a normal, healthy couple have attained their desired number of children, permanent contraception may be indicated. Sterilization is also indicated if further births will endanger the mother's physical or mental health. In some cases involving hereditary diseases, sterilization may be recommended by a genetic counselor. Certain medical conditions such as chronic hypertensive vascular disease and cardiac disease may be aggravated by repeated pregnancies. Mental or physical illness or mental retardation which impair adequate functioning as a parent are additional bases for considering sterilization. Indeed, some states have enacted compulsory sterilization laws in such cases.

Surgical sterilization may be the result of a specific sterilizing procedure or of remedial operations performed for other reasons. The sperm or the ova are prevented from traveling the natural route leading to fertilization. In the female, sterilization is the result of cutting and tying the Fallopian tubes in an operation called tubal ligation. A tubal ligation is a major operation comparable to an appendectomy in seriousness; it is performed most easily in a hospital and preferably a few days after delivery. Males are sterilized by cutting the vasa deferentia in a procedure called a vasectomy. Male sterilization is a minor operation and may be performed under a local anesthetic in a surgeon's office.

Other operations which result in sterilization involve removal of diseased organs: the uterus (hysterectomy), ovaries (oophorectomy),

[52] Reference and Resource Program, 1841 Broadway, New York, N.Y. 10023.

[53] Professional Affairs, Raritan, N.J. See also D. P. Swartz and R. L. Vande Wiele, *Methods of Conception Control* (Raritan, N.J.: Ortho Pharmaceutical Corporation, 1965).

and Fallopian tubes (salpingectomy). Suppression of ovarian functioning by irradiation, although undertaken for other medical reasons, may also result in sterilization.

There are moral and ethical questions concerning voluntary and compulsory sterilization. In a democracy compulsory sterilization poses the problem of freedom of choice. When is the individual free or not free to exercise domain over his own body? Compulsory sterilization of institutionalized persons (the retarded, the mentally ill, and criminals) raises grave moral questions. These issues are discussed succinctly by Noonan.

Sterilization is generally considered an irreversible procedure; but what if a family's circumstances change? Suppose a sterilized widow decides to remarry and have a child by her second husband, or a child dies from an illness or accident and the parents wish to have another child? Reversal of sterilization is possible, but the ratio of success is so low that the procedure should be considered permanent.

An overwhelming percentage of both men and women report satisfaction with sterilization as a means of contraception. Laidlaw and Bass, in reviewing studies of sterilized couples, found that a majority of them reported increased sexual satisfaction and improved family adjustment as a result.[54]

Abortion

Although abortion is illegal in the United States and most other countries, it is popular.[55] It is estimated that there are one to one and one-half million illegal abortions per year in the United States. Since amateur and professional abortionists do not publicize their statistics, these figures are only estimates. Recently, some states have liberalized their abortion laws, thus focusing attention on abortion as a means of family planning.

Three kinds of abortion are identified by physicians and law enforcement officers. A miscarriage or *spontaneous* abortion is termination of pregnancy by natural causes. Interrupting pregnancy by artificial means is termed either a *therapeutic* or *criminal* abortion. A therapeutic abortion is one induced for medical reasons and is performed by physicians in a hospital. A criminal abortion is one induced for illegal reasons and is considered criminal regardless of who performs it or where it is performed. Criminal abortions may

[54] R. W. Laidlaw and M. S. Bass, "Voluntary Sterilization as It Relates to Mental Health," *American Journal of Psychiatry*, 120 (1964):1176–80.

[55] See M. S. Calderone, ed., *Abortion in the United States* (New York: Hoeber-Harper, 1958.)

be self-induced or performed by untrained persons or by health personnel such as midwives, nurses, or physicians.

Public opinion polls in the United States indicate that a more liberal attitude toward abortion as a means of birth control is emerging. A recent National Opinion Research Center study[56] showed public opinion heavily in favor of legalized abortion if the woman's health is endangered, the pregnancy resulted from rape, or there is a strong chance that the baby will be defective. There was very little difference in the views held by Protestants and Catholics. Men were more liberal than women and the more educated more liberal than the less educated. The people polled were overwhelmingly against abortion for economic reasons among the poor (79 per cent against), for the unmarried (82 per cent against), and as a birth control measure (85 per cent against). Although illegal abortions are done as a means of birth control, the public is not willing to accept this as a legal reason. Dr. Rossi considers the model abortion law discussed below as "extremely conservative."

A review of therapeutic abortions in two American hospitals from 1943 to 1964[57] concluded that social pressures were replacing medical reasons for therapeutic abortions. A survey of 40,089 physicians by the magazine *Modern Medicine*[58] reports that 86.9 per cent favor more liberal abortion laws. Of those physicians who were Catholic, 49.1 per cent were in favor of expanding the legal grounds for abortion. According to the report, no physician has ever been convicted for performing a therapeutic abortion in a licensed hospital. In June, 1967, a report prepared by the American Medical Association's Committee on Human Reproduction recommended that its House of Delegates adopt a policy statement based on the American Law Institute's model code. The statement was amended and approved by the House of Delegates.

In 1967 almost half of the state legislatures considered new abortion laws. First Colorado and then North Carolina and California adopted new abortion laws based on the model penal code of the American Law Institute. The Colorado law permits an abortion to save the life of the mother, to preserve the mother's health, when continuing the pregnancy would cause serious mental harm to the mother, when the child is likely to have a grave physical or mental defect, or when the pregnancy occurred through incest or statutory or forcible rape. Medicolegal and social problems of therapeutic

[56] Rossi, "NORC Poll on Abortion."

[57] K. R. Niswander, M. Klein, and C. L. Randall, "Changing Attitudes toward Therapeutic Abortion," *Journal of the American Medical Association*, 196 (1966): 1140–43.

[58] Schmeck, "Doctors Critical of Abortion Laws."

abortion are discussed by Calderone,[59] Guttmacher,[60] and Smith.[61] Noonan traces the ethological threads of the controversy. To avoid the conclusion that abortion is a problem only in an urbanized industrial society, read G. Devereux's analysis of abortion in four hundred pre-industrial societies.[62]

PSYCHOLOGICAL ASPECTS OF CONTRACEPTIVE USE

Contraceptive Failure

The results of failure to use contraceptives or their inadequacy when used are often alleged to be disastrous, leading to too many children and to unwanted children. The growth of American families study mentioned earlier[63] found 17 per cent of the families to be in the excess fertility category because either or both spouses did not want the last conception. The general conclusion of psychologists, psychiatrists, and other advocates of planned parenthood is that unwanted pregnancies have undesirable results for both parents and children. This hypothesis has been investigated by E. Pohlman.[64] He found that direct evidence to support the hypothesis is "almost completely lacking,"[65] not because of findings rejecting the hypothesis, but because of the lack of research. One difficulty is to define and identify an "unwanted conception."[66] Another problem is that "wanting a child" may be a neurotic want and hence not desirable for the child.

Clinicians stress unconscious motives in contraceptive failures. Patients "forget" to use the method or use it incorrectly. A husband may want to show relatives that he is virile and can produce offspring as well as his brother or brother-in-law. Wives may want to show themselves or others that they are maternal. Pregnancy may also be a way of resolving a problem. The unmarried girl may use pregnancy to force a marriage. Pregnancy may be an acceptable escape from an unhappy work or school situation. Some couples think that their problems will disappear "if they only have a baby."

---

[59] *Abortion in the United States.*

[60] *Babies by Choice or Chance;* Guttmacher, Best, and Jaffe, *Planning Your Family.*

[61] D. T. Smith, ed., *Abortion and the Law* (Cleveland, O.: Western Reserve University Press, 1967).

[62] *A Study of Abortion in Primitive Societies* (New York: Julian Press, 1955).

[63] Whelpton, Campbell, and Patterson, *Fertility and Family Planning in the U.S.*

[64] "Wanted and Unwanted: Toward Less Ambiguous Definition," *Eugenics Quarterly,* 12 (1965):19–27; "Unwanted Conceptions: Research on Undesirable Consequences," *ibid.,* 14 (1967):143–54.

[65] "Unwanted Conceptions," p. 151.

[66] See Perkins, "Intrauterine Conception."

Others may feel guilt over using birth control measures and develop medical reasons to drop the method.

Contraceptive Success

Improved emotional adjustment to marriage has been reported as a result of using contraceptives. Komarovsky's and Rainwater's studies[67] document the fears couples have over unwanted pregnancies. A more recent study reported greater emotional adjustment to marriage as a result of using oral contraceptives. Twenty-four couples in San Diego, California, were studied for four years by J. Ziegler, a psychiatrist, and his associates.[68] He found that wives who continued to use the pills were more sexually responsive and that their husbands showed an enhanced sense of well-being. Of the twenty-four families, nine discontinued the pills within a few months. These wives used the pills as a "scapegoat" for shedding responsibility for birth control. They were unwilling to continue the pills and endure the "side effects," Ziegler said, because they felt that sexuality was primarily for the husband's benefit. Wives who enjoyed sexuality, did not perceive their husbands' sexual demands as excessive, and felt responsible for managing family affairs continued the pills.

NEW DEVELOPMENTS

"Men and women have always longed for both fertility and sterility, each at its appointed time and in its chosen circumstances," according to the noted psychiatrist Karl Menninger.[69] This wish is evident in the continued search for means to regulate or control the reproductive system. Long-term anti-fertility drugs may be available in the near future.[70] Experiments are now under way on a subcutaneous capsule implant which releases mini-doses of synthetic estrogen and progesterone, providing protection for a year. Sustained release of contraceptive preparations can also be accomplished through injections. In clinical trials these have given protection for up to two years. Oral contraceptives for men, a "morning after" pill which prevents pregnancy when taken after intercourse, and a pill which prevents pregnancy by creating a "hostile climate" to sperm in the cervix are all being developed. A pill reported by Swedish physicians interrupts the normal hormonal cycle of early

[67] M. Komarovsky, Blue Collar Marriage (New York: Random House, 1962); Rainwater and Weinstein, And the Poor Get Children; Rainwater, Family Design.

[68] Cited in R. D. Lyons, "Birth Pill Found an Aid to Adjustments in Marriage," The New York Times, June 20, 1967.

[69] "Psychiatric Aspects of Contraception," Bulletin of the Menninger Clinic, 7 (1943):36.

[70] "Implantables and Injectables—Long-Term Contraception Near?" Journal of the American Medical Association, 200 (1967):33–34.

pregnancy, inducing abortion up to seven or eight weeks after conception.

The current trends in family planning may lead to dramatically different patterns of dating, courtship, and family structure. The "sexual renaissance"[71] has not yet reached its height. We can anticipate that increased control over the reproductive system will free man to integrate sex into his everyday life in new and different ways. Margaret Mead suggests that someday there will be families whose main function is child-bearing, leaving others to function as individuals.[72] The availability of abortifacients will remove many of the obstacles to premarital and extramarital sexual intercourse, but the concern for integrating man's behavior into his definition of the moral and ethical life will remain.

[71] See I. L. Reiss, "The Sexual Renaissance in America," *Journal of Social Issues*, 22 (1966):140.

[72] "The Life Cycle and Its Variations: The Division of Roles," *Daedalus*, 96 (1967):871–75.

Suggested Readings: Part III

CONCEPTION AND CONTRACEPTION

American Medical Association, Committee on Human Reproduction. "Control of Fertility." *Journal of the American Medical Association* 194 (1965):462–70.
Useful for teachers as well as physicians; discusses methods accepted at present as the best. Includes listings of commercial contraceptive products available in the United States.

Calderone, M. S., ed. *Manual of Contraceptive Practice.* Baltimore: Williams & Wilkins, 1964 (new ed. in press for 1969).
The contributors discuss the basic principles of family planning, contraceptive techniques and methods, and the psychosexual attitudes involved in contraceptive practice.

Consumers Union of the United States. *The Consumers Union Report on Family Planning.* Mount Vernon, N.Y.: By the Union, 1966.
A popular and authoritative paperback guide.

Neubardt, Selig. *A Concept of Contraception.* New York: Trident, 1967.
A clear, readable, and accurate book which presents the techniques of contraception not as a mechanical way of avoiding undesired pregnancy, but as an integral part of the sexual life of the couple.

Planned Parenthood Federation of America. *The Safe Period.* New York: By the Federation, 1962.
Has been called the best single reference on the rhythm method.

Sources of Educational Materials

American Medical Association, Department of Health Education, 535 Dearborn Street, Chicago, Illinois 60610.
Offers publications and resources for educators as well as physicians and scientists.

Planned Parenthood-World Population, 514 Madison Avenue, New York, New York 10022.
A resource for professional educators; also prepares bulletins for general distribution.

U.S. Department of Health, Education, and Welfare, Washington, D.C.
The Assistant Secretary for Family Planning and Population, the U.S. Public Health Service, and the Bureau of Family Services are all within this department. There are nine regional offices as well.

PART IV: PROBLEMS

Introduction

It seems to be human nature to be more intrigued with the problematic than with the ordinary aspects of any subject. For this reason, even though the emphasis in sex education should surely be on the positive side, it is still necessary to consider the unusual as well as the usual problems. Along with questions about "normal" problems, such as masturbation or early or late development, students do ask questions about hermaphroditism, operations to change one's sex, homosexuality, and the whole range of sexual perversions. While it would be beyond the range of this volume to cover this material in detail, it is our intention to be comprehensive enough to give the teacher a good general background based on more reliable sources than "common knowledge" or random readings. In addition, these chapters should make the professional educator much more sensitive to the small but important number of his students for whom one or another of these problems is real.

15   Sex Errors of the Body

John Money

In Chapter 12 the normal course of sexual development was described from the point of fertilization through puberty. At each point in that process development may be arrested or redirected through some accident of heredity or environment. In this chapter John Money describes the results of these "sex errors of the body" and discusses their implications for sex educators and counselors.

Most discussion and writings on sex education are formulated as though every American were named John Doe or Mary Smith. The same message is then assumed to be sufficient in the sex education of all of the John Does and Mary Smiths. Yet everyone knows that this assumption is not allowable, for each person is a special individual, unique in personality and life situation—and unique also, perhaps, in his own problems and needs in sex education. The withdrawn, shy adolescent boy born with a deformed penis that needed multiple surgical operations for repair during childhood will require encouragement even to rehearse in imagination the possibility of exposing himself to sexual intercourse. There will be far less attention to moral prohibition in his sex education than in that of the promiscuous delinquent who will try anything once, or more often for money, and ruthlessly exploits his sexual resources.

This chapter is concerned chiefly with problems of body form and function which create special problems of sex education. By and large, each one of these problems is rare, but cumulatively they occur frequently enough for the sex educator to be informed about them. Traditionally, no one else, not even the physician, has been trained to meet these exigencies, so that the professional sex educator can here perform a very important service. Moreover, the study of sexual deformities and handicaps serves as a healthy corrective to that insidious influence of old-time puritanism which tends to equate modern sex education with moral restraint. Rather, one should be reminded that healthy sexual functioning is a delicately perfected and positive achievement to be joyously celebrated.

DEVELOPMENTAL SEQUENCE

The ultimate aim of sex education is the development of a child capable of healthy sexual functioning in adulthood. Sex education thus fits into a sequence of developmental steps, the orderly progression of which is a prerequisite for normal sexual functioning. In the normal development each step follows the other in such a logical progression that one does not think of them as possibly being independent of one another. Through the study of such sexual anomalies as I have seen for the past fifteen years, in which the sequence of development is not as expected, it has been possible to differentiate one step from another and identify the developmental variables of sex which may be independent of one another. One may list these variables as follows:

1. Genetic or chromosomal sex
2. Gonadal sex
3. Fetal hormonal sex
4. Internal morphologic sex
5. External morphologic sex
6. Hypothalamic sex
7. Sex of assignment and rearing
8. Pubertal hormonal sex
9. Gender identity and role
10. Procreative sex

Each one of these developmental variables has its own probabilities of error or malfunction, each of which will bring its own subsequent problems of sex education. The major anomalies associated with each variable are presented below. Some of the syndromes overlap, and many present common problems to the sex educator, such as the issue of predicted sterility, incongruity between gender identity and other variables, transmissible genetic defect, and so on.

SEX CHROMOSOMAL ANOMALIES

As set forth in greater detail in Chapter 12, the sex of a baby is normally determined by fertilization of the X chromosome from the mother by either an X- or a Y-bearing chromosome from the father. A girl results when two Xs meet, and a boy results when the combination is XY. It is possible for a fertilized egg to carry the wrong combination of sex chromosomes, the error having taken place either before fertilization or immediately after, in the earliest phases of cell division. A few of these errors will not have any adverse effects, direct or indirect, and so will be discovered, if at all, only by chance.

Triple X Syndrome

The triple X syndrome in a female is an example of such an error. In this condition there are three X chromosomes (or even more), so that the total chromosome count is forty-seven (forty-four plus XXX) instead of forty-six (forty-four plus XX). Some women with this condition are mentally retarded, and the condition is discovered in chromosome surveys of institutions for the mentally retarded.

Others are mentally normal, married, have children, and are peacefully unaware of the chromosomal peculiarity of every cell of their bodies.

XYY Syndrome

In men there is a newly discovered anomaly, an extra Y chromosome (forty-four plus XYY). The first men discovered to have this condition were all in custody for undisciplined behavior, so there is a chance that the extra Y chromosome has an adverse influence on behavior. In any case, at least some of these males will, as youths, present a special problem to the sex educator because of their delinquent acting-out.

Klinefelter's (XXY) Syndrome

In this sex chromosome abnormality, the adverse effects are more extensive. Klinefelter's syndrome is characterized by an extra X chromosome (forty-four plus XXY), or by more than one extra X, in a person who is male in sexual morphology. XXY males have a small penis and small testes and are sterile. Typically, they are tall and skinny, with gangling legs and arms, though a few become obese. Some of them have breast growth at puberty, so that their chests look feminine, like those of a girl in early puberty. The masculine secondary sexual characteristics are usually poorly developed, and they do not respond to treatment with male sex hormones. Mentally, males with Klinefelter's syndrome are a peculiar lot. They seem to have a special proneness to one or another mental impairment, ranging all the way from gross mental deficiency to schizophrenia. A large number of them, who are not more severely afflicted, if not all, have what may best be characterized as an inadequate personality. Paradoxically, though they are typically very low-powered in sexual drive, many of them have psychosexual behavior disorders.

The sex education problem with Klinefelter's syndrome may not become evident until adulthood, when a workup for infertility reveals the diagnosis. The condition may be discovered much earlier in life, usually on the basis of physical findings at puberty. Then the task is not simply counseling for sterility (see below) but the much greater one of counseling or psychotherapy related to the over-all problems of psychopathology and life adjustment with which the individual is affected.

Turner's (XO) Syndrome

Another chromosomal anomaly with many side effects is Turner's syndrome. The basic genetic defect is that one chromosome is missing, the remaining one being always an X, so that the total is only forty-five (forty-four plus XO). There are several variants of the syndrome. In one the second X chromosome may be present but with one of its arms broken (a deletion chromosome). In another variant, the so-called mosaic, some cells of the body are XX and some XO; and there are other modifications as well.

The two symptoms of Turner's syndrome are absence of the ovaries and short stature in a person with the body structure of a girl. Should an exploratory operation be performed, the ovaries will look like streaks instead of being round and plump. They make neither eggs nor female sex hormones. The affected person will, therefore, be sterile and will remain sexually infantile in appearance until treated with female sex hormones.

The genetic defect in Turner's syndrome is associated with many other impairments which may or may not occur in a given individual. These deformities include webbed neck, webbed fingers and toes, small receding chin, pigmented moles, epicanthal folds (resembling oriental eyes), blue-baby and other heart defects, kidney and ureter defects, hearing loss, and, in cognitional functioning, space-form perceptual deficits, directional sense deficits, and motor clumsiness.

Psychologically, girls with Turner's syndrome have an unusual capacity to deal with stress and adversity. They usually cope well with the problems associated with their condition. Psychosexually, they are the epitome of femininity and very maternal in their play and child care interests from infancy onward. This femininity and maternalism may conceivably be related to their lack of gonadal hormones during fetal life (see below).

A special aspect of sex education arises in connection with Turner's syndrome—or any other condition in which sterility can be predicted before marriage and adulthood—namely, when and what to say regarding pregnancy and the future. It is generally not wise to avoid the issue on the pretense of sparing the child or teenager, for in fact the only person being spared is oneself. Children overhear much more than is believed, especially in medical history-taking and examination room conferences. They infer sex-related problems from the amount of medical interest in their genitalia. Above all, they see and hear their parents, whose anxiety has them metaphorically prancing like cats on a hot tin roof every time the subject of child-bearing, marriage, or adoption comes up.

It is not necessary to be brutally frank in order to be honest. Any revelation can be made either diplomatically or harshly. I have found that the ideal way to communicate many unpleasant medical predictions is to place them in the context of probability and the laws of chance. Most people appreciate this degree of scientific humility because they all know stories of medical predictions that proved wrong. I disclose the probability of sterility by linking it with the routine story of pregnancy and saying that, "on the basis of experience with cases like yours, doctors expect that you will achieve motherhood by adoption. When the time comes, do not, therefore, wait too long for a pregnancy." For boys there is also the alternative of donor insemination of the wife from the "sperm bank." Told in this way, the disclosure has a positive sound. It leaves the ideal of parenthood intact. Only the means is changed. Moreover, it also leaves at least a ray of hope that the prediction will prove wrong—and hope is what we all live by, to a certain extent.

In very young children it will often be sufficient to present the idea of adoption without personalizing it. It is in later childhood and certainly in teenage that the personalized reference is desirable, for then the child may build parenthood by adoption or the sperm bank into the normal rehearsals, fantasies, and expectations of marriage and family life. So prepared, the child has an increased chance of success in meeting his special role of fatherhood or motherhood—and also in making his future spouse aware of the possibilities (see below).

GONADAL ANOMALIES

Turner's and Klinefelter's syndromes nicely demonstrate the relationship that may exist between an abnormal number of chromosomes and abnormal gonads, with resultant sterility. In other cases of gonadal defects, however, an abnormal chromosome count cannot be implicated, even though there may be a hereditary factor carried in the genes.

When a primitive, undifferentiated gonad develops embryonically into an ovary, it is the rind or cortical part that proliferates. When the core develops, the gonad becomes a testis. With the exception of Turner's syndrome, it is more common to find defective gonadal development in a morphologic male than in a morphologic female, that is, in the testes rather than in the ovaries, which probably has something to do with the fact that nature's plan in differentiating a male embryonically is always to add something to the basic formula which differentiates a female. The male's development is the more complex of the two.

Undescended Testes (Cryptorchidism)

The commonest defect in testicular development is failure of one or both of the testes to descend. In the majority of instances they will probably descend of their own accord either before or at puberty. It is something of a medical dilemma to decide whether to adopt a hands-off policy or to try to induce descent by means of hormonal treatment or, as a last resort, by surgery. Any method may fail because some testes remain undescended due to being imperfect to begin with.

In rare instances an empty scrotum may be a sign of other internal anomalies, such as hermaphroditism (see below). It is even possible for a genetic female with two ovaries to be so masculinized externally that the clitoris becomes a normal penis, the labia minora becomes the skin covering the penis, and the labia majora becomes the empty scrotum. Therefore, it is wise for any child with undescended testicles to be given a diagnostic work-up, the younger the better, preferably at a major medical center where the full range of modern diagnostic evaluation is available. Once is enough, however! The first time should be the last. It is too easy for a boy to have so much anxiety and attention focused on his lack of testes that he becomes emotionally as well as physically crippled.

There will be a few boys with testes not in the scrotum who are found to have none at all, or, if they have them, they are small and may even atrophy and disappear (perhaps because of a little-understood condition in which the body becomes immunized against one of its own organs). These boys can be given hormonal replacement therapy, beginning in early teenage, so that they are developmentally indistinguishable from normal. When the testes are missing, they can be replaced with prosthetic substitutes made of silicone rubber.

There are two precautions to take in sex education of boys with this problem. One is to be medically frank with them and keep them abreast of the diagnostic implications, proposed treatment, and prognosis. The other is to make provision for them to be excused from exposing themselves naked in showers and locker rooms if they are embarrassed by their condition. Only a few will eventually need special counseling on sterility.

FETAL HORMONAL ANOMALIES

Contrary to popular belief, the testes are not dormant until adolescence. They go through a critical period of activity in fetal life, with profound and lasting effects. If this critical period of activity is absent, then the internal male (Wolffian) organs will fail to differentiate, and the external genitals will subsequently differentiate as female instead of male. The resultant simulated female will not necessarily have internal female organs (uterus and Fallopian tubes) because the primitive beginnings of these structures (the

Muellerian ducts) wither away in the male under the influence of a special inhibitor substance. This inhibitor substance works somewhat independently from the masculinizing androgen that encourages growth of the Wolffian ducts and the penis and scrotum.

It is possible to produce these feminizing effects in males experimentally by injecting the pregnant mother animal with a hormone, cyproterone. Cyproterone is an anti-androgen which cancels out the normal effect of androgen, the male hormone, on the testes of the fetus. The same effect can be obtained by castrating the fetus at the critical developmental period. It is an incredibly delicate task, if the fetus is to survive and be born looking like a female. The opposite effect—masculinizing of a genetically female fetus (with ovaries)—can be achieved experimentally by injecting the pregnant mother animal with male sex hormones. Then the daughter is born with a penis and scrotum. In this experiment the internal organs are always female. Only the external parts are affected.

Testicular Feminizing Syndrome

The human counterpart of the cyproterone experiment is the syndrome of testicular feminization. Girls or women with this syndrome appear no different externally from normal females except for a swelling or lump in each groin. The cells of the body are totally unable to respond to the male sex hormone, which is made in the testes in normal male amounts. They respond instead to the small amount of female sex hormone, estrogen, which is normally made in the testes. The effect of this unusual state of affairs before birth is that masculine internal development commences but is not completed. It goes far enough, however, to prevent internal female development. Externally the genitalia differentiate as female, except for a blind vagina which is usually not deep enough and has to be lengthened surgically in teenage. There is no menstruation and no fertility.

The special needs of these patients when their condition is diagnosed—usually in teenage because of menstrual failure—are counseling with respect to sterility and discussion of the cause of their condition and any proposed treatment. The source of greatest embarrassment and anxiety is mention of the word "testes." They should always and without exception be called "sex glands." Their paradoxical functioning and lack of germ cells should be explained; the degree of detail will differ with each patient. A nurse with such a condition, for example, will learn a great many details. In all cases, the secret of effective counseling is to tell the patient neither too little nor too much for her own needs, while maintaining her complete confidence that the channels of communication remain always open and that she can at any time return for further explanation or more information.

Sterility and, in some cases, hospitalization for vaginal surgery are two problems which a girl with testicular feminizing syndrome may have to explain to her boy friend. What to tell the boy friend, or girl friend, is always a matter of great concern to any girl or boy with a history of a sexual deformity or disability. My recommendation to them is always to say nothing until wedding plans are under very serious consideration. Giving away one's secret is giving away a part of oneself. It is not to be entrusted casually to a person who may spread it around. When wedding plans are being made, a couple are surely in love unless their relationship is and always will be perfunctory. Being in love is, like grief, an extraordinary episode of human emotion. It deserves far more scientific attention than it has ever been given. The bond that it creates between one person and another is so powerful while it lasts that the lover cannot think of separation from the beloved. Thus very few weddings are canceled even as the result of so serious a disclosure as that of reproductive inadequacy. If the marriage should break later, then the partner with the disability has gained enough in the way of experience and self-confidence to be able to try again under more auspicious circumstances.

No special issue regarding promiscuity arises among those who are told of their sterility. A person's standards of sexual conduct have much broader basis than that of fear of possibility of pregnancy. A sterile girl does not begin sexual intercourse because she knows of her sterility.

INTERNAL ORGAN ANOMALIES

Early in embryonic development the Wolffian ducts (Fig. 15–1), from which the internal accessory male organs will develop, lie alongside the Muellerian ducts, from which the female internal accessory organs will develop. At this early state both sets of ducts are present in male and female. Very occasionally, in an otherwise normal male, the Muellerian ducts do not become suppressed, as one would expect in a normal male. Consequently, a boy is born with a uterus and Fallopian tubes. They are usually found by a surgeon performing an operation for a hernia into one side of the scrotum, caused by a testicle trying to descend and tugging down these organs. Since the condition can be corrected surgically, sex educators need anticipate no untoward problems.

There does not appear to be a corresponding condition of persistence of Wolffian structures in an otherwise normal female. There are, however, problems of imperfect development of the

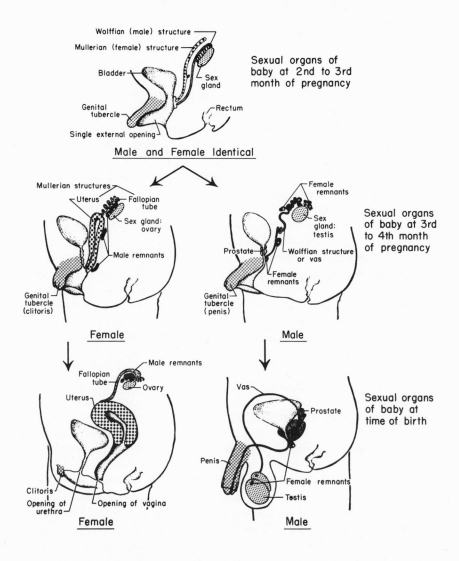

Figure 15–1. Internal sexual differentiation in the human fetus. (From John Money, Sex Errors of the Body: Dilemmas, Education, Counseling *[Baltimore: Johns Hopkins, 1968].)*

uterus in a female. It may be missing or misshapen. One such deformity is the bicornate uterus, in which the arms of the Fallopian tubes branch off too soon, like the arms of a Y instead of a T. Fertility may or may not be affected. Otherwise, there are no special problems for sex education.

EXTERNAL ORGAN ANOMALIES

Embryologically, the external organs are the last of the sexual structure to be completed. Here nature's plan is to take the same initial structures and make them components of either the male or female genitalia. The genital tubercle grows out to become the penis or retracts to become the clitoris. The skin which wraps around the penis and fuses along the seam of the underside to form the urethral canal has its homologue in the hood of the clitoris extending lengthways as the labia minora. The skin of the scrotum, which also fuses on the midline, is the homologue of the labia majora, which remain unfused to reveal the genital openings.

It is relatively simple, in such a plan of biological engineering, for the external genitals to be left unfinished (Fig. 15–2), neither fully masculinized nor feminized. The unfinished state of either sex looks remarkably like that of the other. There is a genital tubercle which could be either a large clitoris or a small penis. This organ has an open gutter underneath it instead of a covered urethral tube. The urinary orifice is at its root or base, more or less in the female position. The opening at the base may be small and may lead directly to the bladder; it may be a rather large urogenital sinus, from the interior of which the urethral passage and also a vaginal passage can be traced. The latter may either connect with the cervix of the uterus or end blindly. Outside and below the opening it will be hard to tell whether there is a scrotum with incomplete fusion or labia majora more fused than they should be.

Unfinished external sexual differentiation leaves one thoroughly confused as to the sex of a baby. From external appearances alone such a baby could be a male hermaphrodite, a female hermaphrodite, or a so-called true hermaphrodite. By definition, a male hermaphrodite has two testicles and a female hermaphrodite two ovaries. Both types are also sometimes called pseudohermaphrodites. A true hermaphrodite, by definition, has some ovarian and some testicular tissue, either separate or mixed together in the same gonad. All three forms of hermaphroditism are equally genuine. To be classified as a hermaphrodite, one need not have ambiguous-looking sex organs. The ambiguity may exist internally, as in those with testicular feminizing syndrome or the male with a normal penis and a uterus. However, the classical dilemma in hermaphroditism is that of ambiguity of external appearance.

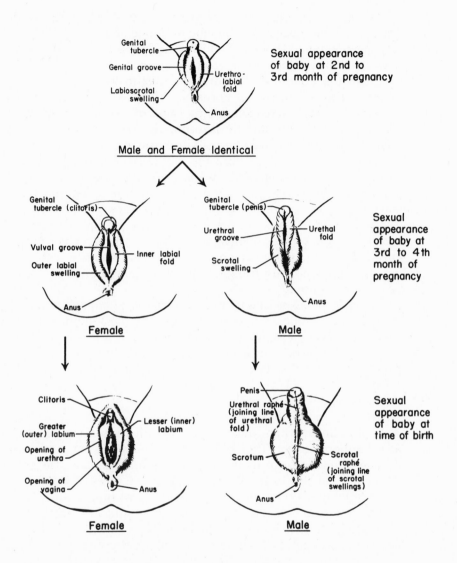

Figure 15–2. External sexual differentiation in the
human fetus. (From Money, Sex Errors of the Body.)

Female Hermaphroditism

This type of ambiguity is produced in genetic females by the presence of too much masculinizing hormone at a critical period of fetal development. This masculinizing hormone is produced in the adrenogenital syndrome by overactive, erroneously working adrenal glands. In this condition the adrenal cortex makes the wrong hormone—androgen instead of cortisone. The basic cause is a recessive genetic trait. It is the commonest cause of female hermaphroditism and can be controlled by cortisone replacement treatment.

The other type of female hermaphroditism is produced by abnormal amounts of androgen from the mother. The mother may have an androgen-producing tumor while pregnant. The greatest likelihood, however, is that she had a prescription for progestin (pregnancy hormone) to prevent a threatened miscarriage. In a very few instances of this treatment, the body utilizes the progestin as if it were androgen, so that a female fetus occasionally becomes masculinized. The metabolism of one hormone into another within the human body is not surprising, for biochemically the sex hormones are all "first cousins."

In today's medicine, the treatment for female hermaphroditism—surgical and hormonal—is very effective. The most important thing is early diagnosis, ideally at the time of birth. If this is done, a girl can grow up oblivious of ever having had a problem. Her need for special sex education is correspondingly minimized.

Male Hermaphroditism

The same ambiguities of the external organs occur in male hermaphroditism when, developmentally, there is a failure of the male hormonal effect. The failure may be either in the production of male hormone or in its utilization. The primary cause for either failure still remains to be discovered. In some cases of familial occurrence there is no doubt that a genetic factor is involved.

Complete failure of fetal masculinization results in a baby who is a morphologic female, as in the testicular feminizing syndrome. There are all degrees of failure of masculinization between this extreme and the normal male. The closer the resemblance of the external organs to those of the normal female, the less likelihood there is that anything can ever be done to permit a normal male sexual life. Therefore, there are many male hermaphrodites who, at birth, should be assigned as females, with a program then, and again in teenage, of appropriate surgical correction and hormonal treatment. If they are so treated, and the parents properly counseled, such individuals grow up and function very well as girls and develop a feminine psychosexual identity. There are no special difficulties subsequently in their sex education over and above those of all individuals with chromosomal anomalies, sterility, and contradictory sexual structures. All of these issues can be diplomatically handled, with a good outcome, as described in the discussion of Turner's syndrome and the testicular feminizing syndrome above.

A particularly tragic stituation arises when a male hermaphrodite with a phallus large enough to justify assignment and surgical correction as a boy reaches teenage and proves to have the syndrome of feminizing testes. He develops breasts and totally lacks masculine body traits. Since his body is resistant to the male sex hormone, treatment with it is useless. His voice will remain high-pitched, his face unbearded, and his body feminine rather than masculine in contour. The erectile mechanism of his penis may fail. The prostate gland may not be stimulated to produce ejaculatory fluid. Erotic feelings will not be missing, but they will not reach the true climactic peak of orgasm. Perhaps such an individual's greatest mortification is that he does not achieve a proper adult male aging appearance and is constantly thought to be much younger than his chronological age. The disparity may be so great that at age thirty-two a man is always responded to by strangers as though he were sixteen or seventeen—which was particularly galling to one man who had established a companionate marriage and was mistaken everywhere for his wife's son. In his case he did not have even a female aging appearance, as his feminizing testes had been removed earlier. His body was totally unresponsive to male hormone injections.

It is possible to forestall such an unhappy ending by using a trial test of androgen ointment on the penis in early infancy. If the penis enlarges and pubic hair growth begins, one has evidence of the body's ability to respond to the male sex hormone. Without this evidence, it is preferable to plan a program of surgical feminization and raise the baby as a girl.

In teenage and adulthood any help that can be given by sex educators and counselors is at best supportive, since the basic dilemmas cannot be resolved. Nonetheless, it is amazing how well some of these patients do develop self-confidence and rise above the adversity of their lives.

True Hermaphroditism

From the point of view of sex education, nothing is encountered in true hermaphroditism that may not also be encountered in either male or female hermaphroditism. There may be some explaining to do regarding the chromosomal contradiction if the individual has need of such an explanation. True hermaphrodites typically have forty-four plus XX chromosomes, irrespective of the presence of testes and the amount of masculine anatomy. For a true hermaphrodite raised and living as a boy and feeling like one, there is a chromosomal contradiction analogous to that in the girl with testicular feminization. A rather delicate counseling situation arises if a true hermaphrodite living as a boy develops breasts and begins to menstruate at puberty as a result of the estrogenic activity of hitherto unsuspected ovaries. Difficulties have also has been known to occur with female hermaphrodites incompletely diagnosed at birth and raised as boys and with true or male hermaphrodites, assigned and living as girls, who develop hormonal masculinization at puberty.

In such cases, and in any others where contradictions and incongruities occur, the best procedure of sex educators and counselors is to avoid creating emotional indigestion by saying too much too soon, while avoiding provoking emotional malnutrition by not saying enough at the right time. The explanation can be built around the premise that the person has been born "sexually unfinished"—an extraordinarily useful term that has saved many hundreds of patients and their parents the mortification of terms like freak, morphodite, half-boy and half-girl, neuter sex, and so on.

The concept of being sexually unfinished lends itself nicely to use of the diagrams of embryonic differentiation (see Fig. 15–1 above). From these diagrams it is possible to give a rational explanation of how elements of the reproductive system of one sex can be found contradictorily developed in the presence of organs of the other sex. In this way nature's error can be accounted for. The patient and/or parent is able to comprehend the rationale of treatment and to feel the reassurance and conviction that comes from participating in and understanding the meaning of a decision.

In most such cases of adolescent incongruity, the patient's feeling and conviction of sexual identity will be in accord with the sex of rearing, and the surgical and hormonal corrections will be made accordingly. But one dare not take it for granted that this will be the case. A chief reason for medical frankness is that it does allow the patient to state his or her own case and weigh the possibility of a sex reassignment.

Incompletely Fused Penis (Hypospadias)

The penis with an unfused open gutter instead of a closed urethal tube on its underside and the urinary orifice at its base instead of its tip represents the most extreme degree of hypospadias. At the other end of the scale is the mild degree of hypospadias in which the urinary orifice is only one or two millimeters displaced from its proper position. Mild hypospadias does not hinder effective urination or copulation and so does not need surgical intervention. Other things being equal, it is desirable for a boy to begin school with the severe abnormality corrected. For the best surgical results, however, it may not be advisable to complete the surgical repair so early. In this circumstance, sexual counseling is imperative so that the boy has a sense of the predictability of things to come. He needs special provisions for privacy in urination; for example, he should be shown the location of school latrines before the first day of school and be given permission to use them unaccompanied by a crowd of other boys. Later, he may want to be exempted from undressing in the school showers or locker room. At all ages, children need to know what is planned surgically when they go to the operating room. Mystified by the unknown, a child can easily conjecture that he will emerge from the operation minus the penis that he treasures and hopes will one day be a good one.

Absence of a Penis (Penile Agenesis)

Not far removed from hermaphroditism, in terms of its practical management, is the boy being born with agenesis of the penis, also known as microphallus. In such cases the penis is a tiny organ, no more than 2 centimeters long, usually a skinny tube with no body to it except for a small glans at the tip. Usually, the testes are small and defective. The cause of the condition is not known.

It is true that penises come in all sizes, as do hands and feet, and size may bear very little relationship to the size of the rest of the body. Though size may be a matter of vanity, a great deal of variance is allowable before a penis is too big to permit satisfactory coitus or too small to do so. Generalized obesity is more likely to be a coital handicap, because the penis is hidden under a roll of fat, than is the smallness of the penis. In the case of the microphallus, however, the organ is definitely too small to permit satisfactory copulation.

It is fairly common to recommend to the parents of such a baby that they raise it as a girl. It is, of course, a very difficult decision for them to make, and they must be given all the information needed to understand the rationale of the decision. First and foremost, they need to know that gender identity and role are not preordained by genetic and intrauterine events alone, but that psychosexual differentiation is largely a postnatal process and highly responsive to social stimulation and experience. Thus they can expect their baby to grow up normally as a girl. Surgical correction in the newborn will give the child the visible appearance of a girl, and a second-stage correction to teenage or young adulthood will produce an artificial vagina adequate for intercourse. Hormonal replacement treatment in early teenage will produce the physique and appearance of a female. Fertility is not seriously an issue, since the possibility that the testes would have been fertile had they been left in place is open to doubt. In some cases they may even have been feminizing testes.

In cases of the reversal of sex by assignment, it is of crucial importance that the parents be convinced that what they do is right. Then they will be able to rear the child consistently as a girl. If they are in doubt, their ambivalence will almost certainly communicate itself to the child. To some degree, their conviction will be shown in their equanimity in answering whatever questions the child may ask and in giving whatever information is needed to break the ice. Their simplest security device is to refer emotion-laden issues to the doctor or the professional medical sex educator, while themselves relying heavily on the formula, already mentioned, of the child's having been born sexually unfinished.

Of course there will be cases of penile agenesis in which, for some reason, the recommended treatment is not given and the sex educator is confronted with the problem of a boy without a penis. He will be particularly in need of an outsider to whom he can reveal in confidence even such secret thoughts as that perhaps he should change and be a girl. The conjectures and ruminations of childhood go much deeper than many of us surface-reading adults care to admit.

It has proved possible in some cases to lessen the childhood trials of such a boy by giving him a prescription of testosterone ointment to apply locally to the penis. The male sex hormone in the ointment produces what is actually a localized puberty. The penis grows and pubic hair appears. The boost in morale is great and overshadows the unfortunate fact that the treatment has done nothing more than accelerate the growth of the penis to its adult size, and that it will not become much larger when the rest of the body goes into puberty, at which point testosterone will have to be given again, orally or by injection. However, the increase in morale may enable the boy to join in sports and gym, appearing naked before his classmates.

As he approaches teenage, he can explore in more detail his prospects for sexual intercourse in adulthood—learn about non-genital techniques of erotic stimulation and the use of an artificial or prosthetic penis for the greater stimulation of his partner in simulated coitus. By knowing in advance that the future is not entirely black, he will be better prepared to go through the normal phases of adolescent social and romantic development. Eventually he will be able to find someone to marry—someone whose love and need for him is as great as his for her. Somewhere there is a lover for everyone who has the confidence to find her, handicap and all.

Absence or Closure of the Vagina (Vaginal Atresia)

As a life dilemma, the female deformity corresponding to agenesis of the penis is absence or closure of the vagina. The condition is often not discovered until puberty. Then there may be menstrual pain caused by the retention of menstrual blood unable to escape from the sealed-off uterus. Alternatively, there may be no menstruation at all if the uterus itself, as well as its exit passageway, the vagina, is missing or incompletely formed. In either case, it is surgically possible to construct a vaginal passage that will permit a normal coital life. The special issues in the sex education of a girl so affected are sterility, when it is present, and how and what to tell one's fiancé, both of which have been discussed above.

Tightened Foreskin (Phimosis)

Phimosis is a foreskin so tight that it cannot be drawn back over the glans of the penis. If it is forced back, it is painful and constricts the neck of the penis as if it were a tight rubber band. If in coitus the glans penis stays covered by the foreskin, which does not retract, there is no pain. The major inconvenience of phimosis for most individuals is hygienic. Circumcision may or may not be recommended. Prior to an admission for circumcision, a boy or man needs some explanatory counseling about the procedure itself and what to expect regarding sexual function.

Circumcision does not seriously alter the sensitivity of the penis and its arousal to orgasm, though there have been no pre- and postoperative studies of men circumcised in adulthood to determine whether there are any changes at all. From study of patients who have suffered severe mutilating injury or loss of the penis, or who have undergone surgical penectomy for cancer, for the correction of hermaphroditism, or for feminine reassignment, in the case of transexualism, it is evident that astonishingly large amounts of genital tissue may be removed without destruction of the capacity to reach orgasm.

The practice of circumcising male babies born with perfectly normal penises is usually a safe procedure, but cases do occur in which some of the body of the penis is removed along with the foreskin. With considerable frequency, far too much of the skin covering of the penis is removed, so that what remains is stretched too tight during erection. Many circumcisions would be cosmetically much neater had they been done by a plastic surgeon. In anatomically normal boys it would be better still if they were not performed at all.

Other External Anomalies

The various counseling issues that arise as a consequence of anomalies of the external organs have all been presented. The same principles can be applied to the other deformities that may occur, like epispadias, which involve not only the reproductive organs but also the urinary and/or defecatory systems. Epispadias is a severe condition in which the bladder empties directly through a gaping orifice in the lower abdominal wall, the penis itself appearing to be split on its dorsal (upward-facing) side. Surgical repair is possible, but urinary continence may be a problem. The repaired penis may be too small for adequate coitus and may also be not quite correctly situated. In the most severe cases it may be advisable to make surgical repair very early in life and to raise the child as a female, as is done in penile agenesis.

ANOMALIES OF HYPOTHALAMIC SEX

The pituitary gland sits in the middle of the cranium at a point approximately behind the bridge of the nose. It is, among other things, a regulator gland. One of its functions is to regulate the hormone production of the gonads or sex glands—ovaries or testes. The pituitary is situated anatomically and functionally in very close proximity to the hypothalamus, a small part of the brain amazingly diverse in its influence upon the essential vital processes of survival and reproduction.

One of the most recent advances in sex research is the discovery that in males, at the time in fetal development when the fetal testis is responsible for organizing the differentiation of male instead of female anatomy, it is also responsible for organizing the masculinity of certain nuclei in the hypothalamus. In the lower mammals these nuclei prevent in males the cyclic function of the pituitary which produces periodic estrus in females; they also regulate, in the female, mating behavior in synchrony with the estrus cycle, and, in the male, the response to the stimulus of estrus in the female.

It is still too early to say what are, or what might be, the anomalies of hypothalamic sexual differentiation in man. It is possible that a relationship may be uncovered between some of the psychosexual disorders in man and anomalies of hypothalamic function. It is possible, for example, that in certain individuals the fetal masculinizing effect on the hypothalamus did not take place at the critical time in development or that, when it did, the neural cells of the hypothalamus were unable to respond on schedule.

The hypothalamus also has another sexual role not specifically related to sex differences. It is quite likely that the hypothalamus is the part of the brain that carries the biological clock of puberty. A tumor or other lesion of the hypothalamus may set the clock of puberty going too soon and is one cause of precocious puberty, especially in males.

ANOMALIES OF ASSIGNMENT AND REARING

The sex of assignment is an official act in the signing of the birth certificate and a reiterative routine in all the daily acts of rearing that decree and confirm masculine or feminine expectations. Wrong assignment of an anatomically normal child is almost never heard of. When it does occur, one or both parents can be considered psychotic. Perfectly normal parents, by contrast, can become the unsuspecting characters in a drama of anomalous assignment when a child is born with abnormal sex organs.

Some of these wrong assignments will be, in effect, simply wrong announcements, for the initial error will be discovered within a few days of birth or, at most, a few weeks. Then the problem to be faced is simply a reannouncement of sex. It is one that does not involve the baby, as it will once he is old enough to have developed a self-awareness as boy or girl. The people for whom a sex reannouncement is a problem are the parents, older siblings, other close relatives, friends, and the community. It is not so difficult a problem as one might think.

In some older medical writings it used to be said in passing that when a new announcement of a child's sex was necessary, the parents should move to a new town and a new job, sever all connections with the past, and start life anew. I have found that this formula is completely untenable. People who have followed it live haunted lives, pursued and constantly intimidated by the ghosts of their past. There is always the nagging, realistic fear that somehow the secret will out, for it is impossible to guarantee total obliteration of one's past.

The alternative is to deal with the reannouncement openly. The first step is to make sure that the parents have the necessary medical knowledge (albeit somewhat simplified) so that they are able to explain their dilemma to themselves before explaining it to other people. This knowledge will help them to feel convinced that what is being done is correct and is their own decision as well as that of the doctor. Otherwise, they may easily feel that they are acquiescing in a trial-and-error program that could prove all error. Once again the concept of being sexually unfinished is invaluable, as are the diagrams that illustrate it (see Figs. 15–1 and 15–2). Many parents

303

find it very helpful to take with them a copy of these diagrams to use when they talk with their relatives and others. They also are helped by being given a brief medical vocabulary with which to identify their child's anomalous condition—terms like "hypospadias," "enlarged clitoris," "overactive adrenal glands," "incomplete labial fusion," "hormonal insufficiency," and so on. I usually write these terms as an aid to memory. There is a magic about words and a power in technical terms that silence idle curiosity, for the idly curious hate to have their ignorance exposed. Medical terminology also enables a parent (or an older patient) to have the last word in any silly conversation by recommending that the curious one satisfy his curiosity directly by consulting a doctor.

The first people with whom the parents have to deal are their closest relatives, usually their parents. Then they will usually explain their predicament to a few very close friends. I recommend that they deliberately choose a more or less public figure who is connected with the family, like the pastor, the family doctor, a nurse, a school teacher or lawyer, and give this person the facts of the situation. They can ask him to tell the story to other curious members of the community and at the same time request them to stop further gossip for the sake of the child's future. Some mothers have found that it is immensely helpful to show their baby, once the surgical correction has been accomplished, to a few key people, such as the babysitter mothers who take turns at caring for infants during church gatherings.

Those who are most likely to be overlooked when it comes to a sex reannouncement are the child's older brothers and sisters. They, of all people, deserve an accurate explanation in terms of the baby's having been born unfinished. Otherwise, they are logically entitled to reach the conclusion that the same thing could have happened to them, with or without their consent. Parents are often too embarrassed or squeamish to talk straightforwardly with their older children, offering instead such platitudes as God's intentions. Therefore, the professional outsider has a duty to arrange, if possible, to talk to these older siblings himself.

It will doubtless also be necessary for the counselor, as the years pass by, to talk directly to the patient. He will be able to bring an outsider's impartiality to the problem, where as the parents will be emotionally disconcerted. As in analogous embarrassing sex educational situations, they can refer their child's difficult inquiries to the professional, who, in turn, can open the channels of communication between them by conducting a final joint session in which knowledge is shared. Direct talk with the child is an absolute imperative when the possibility of changing the sex of rearing is raised not in the neonatal period but many years later, after postnatal psycho-sexual differentiation is already so far advanced as to be irrevers-ible. In this case the issue is not the simple one of sex reannounce-ment, but the far more complex one of sex reassignment.

PUBERTAL HORMONAL ANOMALIES

In girls the onset of puberty is expected from age eleven and a half through fourteen and a half and in boys from twelve and a half through fifteen and a half, more or less. Nature does not always play the game as expected, however. It is possible for puberty to begin as early as in the first year of life or to be delayed until the late teens or beyond.

Precocious Puberty

When a girl shows the first signs of sexual development at age ten, or even nine, the onset of her puberty, though early, is gen-erally considered to be within normal limits. The same is true of a boy whose puberty has its onset at age eleven. Below these ages, puberty is considered precocious. Early puberty can be explained in many cases as the result of a premature signal from the hypothala-mic-pituitary alarm clock, without any other pathology. In other cases the early sounding of the pubertal alarm clock is the result of a tumor or other pathology in the hypothalamic-pituitary structures. Such tumors or other lesions are not necessarily dangerous or fatal. Boys are less likely than girls to develop precocious puberty, and brain involvement is more likely to be its cause among boys. Girls are more likely than boys to develop early, especially at age nine, without any brain complications. For either sex, however, the first requirement when puberty begins early is a complete diagnostic evaluation to rule out the possibility of dangerous complications, especially a brain tumor. In boys, it will be necessary to rule out the diagnosis of male adrenogenital syndrome, in which early develop-ment is not accompanied by testicular maturation but is caused by excess androgens from the adrenal gland.

At the present time there is no completely effective way of hold-ing back early puberty except that of the adrenogenital variety in males, and then only provided they are treated with cortisone con-tinuously from infancy onward. A variety of new drug treatments hold some promise, however. Even with the help of drugs to slow down premature development, the management of precocious puberty relies heavily on psychologic counseling and sex education. The principle on which counseling is founded is that of reducing the disparities between chronological age, statural or physique age, and social age. Social age, including intellectual and academic age, tends to parallel chronological age, if left to its own devices, and to be divorced from physique age. Because physical size and energy permit mixing with older and bigger children, social age may become advanced over chronological age. In fact, acceleration of social age can and should be deliberately arranged by planning for academic acceleration, when intelligence permits, and for social and recreational mixing with children a year or two older. In this way the number of years that the child spends in a no-man's-land of disparity between physique and social development is reduced.

Sex education is a must for all children, as far as I am concerned, and is certainly a must for those with early puberty. Left to themselves to play, infants and children tend to rehearse in play, as do macaque monkeys and other primates, the component acts of the total mating response. In monkeys total deprivation of play, including sexual play, results in severe aberration of mating behavior in adolescence and adulthood, usually with total failure to breed successfully. Should pregnancy be achieved, mothering is grossly defective, so much so that the infant monkey perishes. One can scarcely envisage, in the near future, the social acceptance of copulation games in the kindergarten. Therefore, adults must teach in words the sex education lessons which children would spontaneously learn for themselves, were they not subject to the restraints and taboos of convention. Deeds must be replaced with words if children are to have the necessary information about the role of their bodies in reproduction and the necessary sense of gender identity to be able, in adulthood, to put this information into practice.

The sex education story which I formulated some years ago I tell with illustrative diagrams. It goes as follows: there is a baby egg, without a shell and no bigger than the dot made by the point of a pencil, and a baby nest. The egg grows, the limbs bud, and the organs form until the baby is to be born. It gets out head first, so that the shoulders can be tucked closely to the body, down the baby tunnel or canal. The egg is able to start growing into a baby only when it is joined by a sperm. Sperms are made by the father. There are three hundred million of them, and they have a swimming race, wiggling their long swimming tails, to see which one can reach the egg first. There is only one winner. The prize is to make the egg grow into a baby. The winner burrows its head into the soft wall of the egg. Then the egg fixes itself on the wall of the baby nest, where it can share the mother's blood to get food and air, and grows from a blob into a real person.

Sperms are made in the father's testicles, which are really sperm factories. They have to swim away from the testicles through a long tube inside the body and out through the penis. The penis stands up stiff and straight so that it can fit into the baby tunnel before the sperms and their swimming juice are pumped out. That gives the sperms a good start on their swimming race and makes sure that they have a fair chance of finding the egg far away inside the baby nest. Sperms are so small that a pencil point is too big to draw one. The drawing becomes a super-giant-sized sperm, instead of a real, life-sized one. You can see a real sperm only if you have a micro-scope to magnify it.

I tell this story to parents so that they can tell it to their children, in installments for the very young, and repeatedly for those who have heard and forgotten it. It solves the problem of terminology (the medical terms are added later), which for many parents has proved the biggest single stumbling block to effective communica-tion with young children on matters of reproduction. With this stumbling block removed early in life, a child and parent have mutual confidence about matters of sexual behavior and what may be called the psychology and sociology of sex, as contrasted with the physiology of sex.

During early childhood education in the sociology of sex means, among other things, advice on where and when to talk about the physiology of sex. The recommendation that it be kept a family and medical secret reserved for "your mommy, your daddy, and your doctor" is a simple expedient that prevents social embarrassment for the parents at the dinner table, in the neighborhood, and else-where. Adolescence is the age at which the sociology and psychol-ogy of sex and of falling in love are pre-eminent in sex education. It is therefore, in the sex education of adolescents that parents reap the greatest reward for having kept open the channels of mutual confidence by early frankness.

In cases where communication breaks down, the responsibility of breaking the ice lies with adults. It is not enough to follow the maxim "Answer your children's questions truthfully when they ask them" because the child who has frozen up will avoid asking any questions at all. One way to break the deadlock is to use the tech-nique of the parable, telling a story of a child in a similar predica-ment and of how he finally got enough confidence to tell and ask about thus and so. The parable technique shows a child that he is not unique, and, above all, it guarantees that the adult can listen to sex talk without exploding.

I am very frank when I talk with pubertally precocious children because I want them to know at least one person to whom they can bring any topic within the range of their sexual experience or curiosity when they need to or feel ready to do so. Normal adolescents have their own age mates from whom they learn and find reassurance about teenage sex, but the precocious child has no pubertal contemporaries to guide—or misguide—him regarding romantic feelings, dating, involvement with older teenagers, parental discipline, masturbation, and so on. Such children respond very well to counseling and guidance. They display the same range of balance and common sense as do most adolescents with normal puberty. Finally, their contemporaries catch up with them, and they become lost to view except that they, especially boys, are short in stature in adulthood. In early life their bones grew and matured so rapidly that there was not time for them to grow long.

Pubertal Delay or Failure

At the opposite end of the spectrum from too early puberty is pubertal delay. The child in whom puberty does not appear at the normal age may be showing the first signs of failure to commence puberty spontaneously, as occurs in several of the syndromes already mentioned. Alternatively, the delay may simply be a sign of "late blooming." Although it is a good general principle not to interfere when nature will do the work unaided, there are limits to the length of time one should wait for nature. In the case of pubertal delay prolonged far beyond early teenage, the deleterious effect of physical infantilism on social and psychologic maturation is too great to justify postponement of hormonal "starter" treatment. To trigger the gonads into action the treatment used may be sex hormones or gonadotropin to imitate the action of the pituitary on the gonads. In either case the treatment should be conservative, for fear of affecting fertility. It is impossible to know how extensive the risk to fertility is, especially in males, because many children who may simply seem to be late bloomers will actually have more complex problems and be destined to infertility even without any treatment.

Chronic pubertal failure is more common in males than females. It is sometimes attributable primarily to a deficit in the sex glands themselves and sometimes to a deficit in the pituitary gland's gonadotropic stimulation of the sex glands, with or without various other complications. In either case, the long-term treatment is the same, replacement in the body of the sex hormone that is missing. In boys, the result of the treatment is a perfect imitation of nature when the fault lies in the sex glands, but it is frequently much less than perfect when the fault lies with the pituitary. It is particularly difficult to get good growth of facial and body hair in the hypopituitary cases, so that the complexion often looks juvenile and is an embarrassment.

The pituitary makes many hormones. It may fail to make only one of them, or many. When only the gonad-stimulating hormone is missing, the individual's physical sexual maturation is affected, but not his statural growth. When the growth hormone is also missing, the individual is not only sexually immature but also a hypopituitary dwarf. If other pituitary hormones are also missing or deficient, then various other symptoms may be added to that of sexual infantilism. The resultant syndromes are of infrequent occurrence and do not present any really new issues in sex education and counseling.

The psychologic problem of pubertal failure with its attendant immaturity of appearance is best handled by avoiding as much as possible a discrepancy between chronological and social age, despite the retardation in physique age. The problem is particularly difficult when dwarfism is also present, for then the individual has the additional handicap of a height to which people react unthinkingly, as though a person so short must still be socially a child.

The entire problem of psychologic development in pubertal failure, even under treatment, is made more complex by personality traits and individual psychodynamics. It is possible that some forms of pubertal failure carry a predisposition to psychopathology. It is certain that some individuals with severe personality disturbances do not improve even after an excellent somatic response to hormonal replacement therapy. It is not too uncommon to find people who so resent the indignity of their condition that they try to restore themselves to normality magically by repudiating the medical help offered them or by discarding their medication.

By contrast, there are other people who have the capacity to rise psychologically above their adversity, who keep up a dating and social life despite their sexual infantilism, and who may even get married and perform coitally. Such people are examples of what the lucky personality trait of self-confidence can do. Some also exemplify the little-known fact that sexual thoughts, images and dreams, as well as sexually arousing visual and narrative sensory materials, can function in a somatically infantile male who has attained the age when the biological clock of hormonal puberty normally comes into action. The presence of androgen itself is not in all cases an absolute prerequisite for this aspect of eroticism. Androgen greatly increases the frequency of erotic arousal and the intensity of the genitopelvic component, which in some cases is non-existent without the hormone. Androgen is a libido hormone for females as well.

Sex education for sterility (see above) is one of the special issues to be dealt with in the counseling of virtually all people with pubertal failure attributable to pituitary gonadotropic insufficiency.

Breast Development in the Male (Gynecomastia)

This anomaly of sexual differentiation has already been mentioned in connection with hermaphroditism. It occurs also in otherwise normal males, with its onset at puberty. It may be small and transient or large, as in a pubertal girl, and irreversible. It is a source of mortification to the boy concerned. Its deleterious psychologic effect may be widespread and difficult to displace, even after successful plastic surgery to make the chest flat again. Sex education should include reassurance that breast enlargement is not a sign of other feminine traits or tendencies to come. Its cause is not fully known.

Hirsutism in Girls

Though the full and detailed story of the control of hair growth and baldness has not yet been scientifically ascertained, it is known that androgen plays a major role. Androgen permits the masculine pattern of body hair to develop within the limits set by hereditary type. The female body, if exposed to excessive amounts of androgen, will grow excessive body hair, distributed in the masculine fashion. An extreme example is found in the untreated congenital adrenogenital syndrome of female hermaphroditism. In the era before cortisone treatment individuals affected with this hyperadrenocortical condition grew up to look like exaggerated Mr. Atlases on a muscle-man magazine cover. There are lesser degrees of this same hyperadrenocortical condition which have their onset in adolescence or adulthood instead of childhood. These conditions can also be relieved by cortisone therapy.

The cortices of the adrenal glands are not always the abnormal source, as in the adrenogenital syndrome, of excess androgens. An abnormality of the ovary itself may be responsible. In one type of abnormal ovarian function, the Stein-Leventhal syndrome, the ovaries are enlarged with cysts. Girls with this condition develop amenorrhea, failing in their periods at the time that they become hirsute. Both symptoms can be relieved by surgical reduction of the size of the enlarged ovaries. Menstrual failure is also a usual accompaniment of androgen excess severe enough to produce considerable hirsutism. There are, however, many other sources of menstrual failure, including primary and functional or psychogenic amenorrhea. Hirsutism itself is not invariably of androgenic origin. In some instances it may be a hereditary trait.

It is much more difficult to get rid of hair growth than it is to induce it. The afflicted girl is best advised to undergo electrolysis, regardless of what help she may expect from corrective medication or other treatment. In addition, she will usually need special counseling to help prevent a serious disturbance of her social and personality development.

ANOMALIES OF GENDER IDENTITY

For the majority of the human race there is no discrepancy between any of the variables of sex. Gender identity differentiates in agreement with assigned sex and with the somatic variables, all of which agree with one another. In the case of hermaphrodites, where discrepancies may exist between the several variables of sex, there is usually concordance between the assigned sex and gender identity. This concordance is nowhere better illustrated than when two individuals with the same diagnosis are differently assigned, the gender identity in each case differentiating in accordance with the assignment and rearing.

Concordance between sex of assignment and gender identity is not, however, a universal rule. Psychosexual identity may become established in repudiation, or in partial repudiation, of an assignment which the person interprets as an error. Ambiguity of identity is especially likely to result, in the case of a hermaphrodite, when the parental attitude toward the child's sex is ambivalent and when the physique and uncorrected genital appearance evoke teasing or remarks of doubt or astonishment, especially from age mates. An ambiguous gender identity does not necessarily correlate with the chromosomal, gonadal, morphologic, or hormonal sex. Sometimes the correlation will be there, sometimes not. It is just as likely that a genetic female hermaphrodite with ovaries will have been raised as female and want to change to male as for a genetic male hermaphrodite raised as male to want to change to female.

There are some lucky instances when a definite gender identity does not become established. In such cases it will be possible to rehabilitate the individual in the other sex so as to be coitally adequate and reproductively fertile. Thus it is intellectually and emotionally more satisfactory to most medical specialists if a female hermaphrodite assigned and partly reared as a boy wants to change to live as a girl than if the same individual raised as a girl wants to be reassigned as a boy. Nonetheless, there is no point in insisting on the continuance of an unwanted female assignment—or in imposing a female reassignment—on a patient who will, irrespective of anatomy and reproductive function, retain a masculine psychosexual identity and fall in love with another girl. The same principle holds true in the case of a male hermaphrodite.

In male hermaphroditism there are some lucky cases in which the individual rejects a masculine assignment and does not develop a fully masculine psychosexual identity. These are cases in which the penis will remain forever unfunctional in coitus because of its underdeveloped, clitoral size, whereas, after surgical and hormonal feminization, the individual will function adequately as a female. The soundest rule to follow is that no child above the toddler age should have a sex reassignment imposed on the basis of an a *priori* principle. Every case should be individually evaluated and decided upon its own merits.

The most controversial type of case for sex reassignment today is that of the transvestite transexual. The transexual is a person who is typically, though not invariably, morphologically and physiologically normal by all present methods of biological testing and measurement. He (or she) is, however, a quite extraordinary person psychologically. No amount of reading can substitute for a direct personal contact with one of these patients in appreciating what manner of persons they are and fully comprehending how totally different they are from normal members of their sex. They are driven by a fanatical desire to impersonate and also by a fanatical dislike and neglect of the sexual appurtenances of their bodies given by nature. They want their bodies to look like, as well as be dressed like, the other sex, and they want to live the life of the other sex occupationally as well as erotically.

The etiology of the condition is to all intents and purposes unknown. The life history and psychodynamic history are quite variable, except that transvestitic and impersonating desires usually begin in early childhood. The response to psychotherapy or any form of psychologic therapy is poor. Surgical and hormonal sex reassignment is an ameliorative treatment, still at the investigative stage, which, in the majority of a hundred-odd cases known to have been so treated, has made life a little easier for the patients and, indirectly, for society also.

Transexuals want, and have usually ascertained, from reading and hearsay, a vast amount of information pertaining to their condition. Counseling is best directed toward rehabilitation and the day-to-day realities of living in the sex of new assignment. The parents or closest kin need counseling because they usually have been bewildered for a long time by their relative's condition. Brothers and sisters or other juvenile kin who will need to meet the patient under a new name and sex will also need counseling along lines similar to that appropriate for hermaphroditic sex reannouncement or reassignment.

In addition to problems of masculinity and femininity, there are many other psychosexual anomalies of development which in themselves rightfully constitute the subject matter of another chapter. Some of these anomalies relate to parenthood as well as to romance and copulation.

PROCREATIVE SEX IMPAIRMENTS

The assumption implicit in much of the philosophy of sex education is that all teenagers are highly fertile and must be protected from their own capacity to breed. Yet the sad fact of the matter is that many of the students in a sex education course, although quite normally developed for their age, will sooner or later have to come to terms with an injury or disease that impairs or destroys their reproductive capacity. The catalogue of such pathology is far too extensive to be dealt with here. Moreover, nothing would be gained by an attempt at complete coverage, since a few examples will illustrate the main problems.

Impotence

A weak sexual drive with slow sexual arousal and little sexual interest of any type is the natural disposition of some individuals, just as its opposite, satyriasis in the male and nymphomania in the female. Impotence is not a failure of sexual drive or of sexual arousal, but of sexual performance. In the male, it means failure either to obtain or hold an erection. The loss of erection may occur before or after ejaculation. When ejaculation occurs, it is sudden and premature, before either the male or his partner is ready for it. In many cases of impotence there is no organic lesion or deficit identifiable by current diagnostic techniques. The loss of erection, particularly in premature ejaculation, is therefore considered to be functional, and the recommended treatment is usually psychologic.

Not all forms of impotence, however, are psychodynamically functional. There are certain diseases, like sickle cell anemia, leukemia, the Leriche syndrome of occlusive vascular disease, and diabetes mellitus, in which impotence is a common symptom. Diabetic impotence may be relieved by treatment with androgen or gonadotropin. Irreversible impotence without loss of ejaculation and the feeling of orgasm may be a residual of an attack of priapism. Priapism is the inability to lose an erection. It is very painful, usually of unknown cause, and almost always results in destruction of the spongy tissues of the penis as a result of coagulation of blood in them. Thus the mechanism of erection by inflation of the spongy tissues with blood is permanently destroyed. Chronic impotence is also one of the sexual aftereffects of a spinal injury which has completely severed the nerve fibers of the spinal cord. Sexual life is terminated by such an injury, which also produces paraplegia, that is, paralysis of the lower limbs, loss of sensation in them, and loss of control over elimination. The paraplegic patient does not suffer the same pangs of mortification at being unable to satisfy the sexual partner as does the man with post-priapism impotence. The paraplegic loses most of the feelings and sensations of genitopelvic

313

sexual drive as a result of his injury, but the man impotent after priapism does not. The latter, therefore, has his ego wounded time and again by having to quit sexual play, after achieving his own orgasm, without being able to penetrate the vagina so that the partner may reach an orgasm also, in the manner she likes best.

Frigidity

The female counterpart of impotence is frigidity. The term is applied to women who are cold in the sense of having very little sexual interest or responsivity of any type. It is also applied to women who manifest a capacity to enjoy seductive flirtatiousness and the preliminaries of love play, but who "turn off" and become coldly unresponsive in the coital act itself. The frigidity may be so extreme as to cause a temporary scissor-locking of the legs, making intercourse impossible. More usually it is simply an inability to abandon oneself to the movements and enjoyment of sex and to work up to the climax of orgasm. As in the case of impotence in the male, frigidity may be psychodynamically functional and is probably so in the majority of instances. It may also be attributed to an organic lesion, as in some cases of hormonal failure and, as with the male, in paraplegia.

Loss of Organs

The sex organs may be lost through traumatic accident or through therapeutic surgical removal, especially for cancer. In the male, removal of the prostate gland—usually not necessary until old age—does not, except for untoward side effects, destroy the capacity to feel the sensations of orgasm, even though no fluid is ejaculated (dry-run orgasm). Loss of the penis also does not destroy the capacity for orgasm, provided normal androgen levels are maintained. It does, however, destroy morale as a result of incapacity to satisfy the partner. Loss of the testes, by removing the source of male sex hormones (except for the adrenal androgens) sooner or later diminishes libido, though it does not inevitably abolish it completely. Sterility is an invariable result.

By reason of their morphology, the external organs of the male are more prone to injury than those of the female. The vulnerability of the female is to disease of the uterus, with resultant hysterectomy. Some surgeons are far more conservative than others in undertaking this operation, and some are more attentive than others to the psychologic preparation of their patients for the loss of an organ by which their genealogical purpose in the world is defined. Hysterectomy, provided the ovaries are left intact, does not destroy the internal hormonal rhythm of the body, even though menstruation can no longer occur, nor does it impair sexual desire and response, including orgasm, except indirectly as a result of an adverse emotional reaction to the loss of the uterus.

Loss of Fertility

Fertility may be lost not only through the loss of the organs of fertility, but also through their functional impairment. It is well known that the mumps in adulthood may, in some men, so inflame the testicles and elevate their temperature as to kill all the sperm cells and produce permanent sterility. Male fertility may be impaired indirectly as a consequence of impotence. In a few very rare cases fertility may also be lost because of an inability to ejaculate, with no impairment of erection.

In females infertility may be the result of the failure of the ovary to ripen an egg in the monthly cycle of hormonal function, without any disorder of menstruation itself. In other instances the hormonal rhythm may itself break down with failure of menstruation (amenorrhea). The cause and treatment of such conditions can be very complex, with treatment involving hormonal and/or psychologic therapy. There may be difficulties in the implantation of the fertilized egg on the uterine wall or in its ability to stay there. Spontaneous abortion or miscarriage, like menstrual disorder, may involve hormonal and psychologic factors in its cause and treatment.

Both starvation and overeating of extreme degrees, either alone or associated with other symptoms in special syndromes, have a direct influence on hormonal cycling and fertility. In severe starvation, among prisoners of war, for example, the gonads fail to secrete sex hormones and the body undergoes various degenerative changes characteristic of starvation. Sexual function and desire disappear, and are supplanted by desire, fantasy, and talk of food. Starvation may be imposed by famine or it may be the consequence of willful fasting. An example of the latter is anorexia nervosa, a disease particularly common in adolescent girls and women. It may lead to death from an addiction to not eating. In its advanced stages sexual functioning may fail to develop or, having developed, disappear.

The converse of starvation is addictive eating and obesity. The cause of addictive eating is obscure and complex. It may involve a metabolic abnormality, a neurological defect in the brain, especially the hypothalamus, or disturbed psychodynamics, singly or all three in combination. Obesity may be associated with other syndromes, or it may constitute a syndrome of its own. There is, therefore, no simple relationship between obesity and diminution or loss of sexual function. In general, however, gross obesity is accompanied by sexual failure. In some cases of childhood obesity the onset of puberty is delayed. In such boys the immature penis looks even smaller than it is, being retracted beneath a heavy layer of fat padding. Usually there is no identifiable "glandular condition," as is often believed to be the case in medical folklore.

Painful Copulation

Sexual intercourse resulting in successful pregnancy may be made difficult or even impossible by pain. In the male, for example, there is a rare and little-understood condition, Peyronie's disease, in which the penis becomes deformed by the internal formation of scar tissue. It causes chronic pain which becomes intense when the penis erects. In females pain attendant on sexual intercourse goes by the name of dyspareunia. In some instances surgical relief is possible; in others medical or psychologic treatment may help. Dyspareunia may or may not be associated with painful menstrual periods.

Transmissible Genetic Defects

Some of the young people in any sex education class will be among those who have been called upon by fate to discover that they are the carriers of genetic defects which will show up in the next generation. They will not necessarily know of their fate, for many genetic defects, those known as genetically recessive, are transmitted by parents who are hidden carriers. A parent who is a hidden carrier of a defect will not produce a child who is an open carrier of the defect unless the other parent is also a hidden carrier. When two hidden carriers are mated, for each pregnancy that occurse there is a 25 per cent chance that the child will be an open carrier, a 50 per cent chance that he will be a hidden carrier like the parents, and a 25 per cent chance that he will not carry the defective gene at all. Parents who are afflicted with defects or weaknesses that are genetically dominant can, regardless of the genetic status of the mate, pass them on to the offspring. There are various other statistical probabilities of genetic transmission, which are dependent upon the exact nature of the genes and chromosomes involved.

Once the probability of transmitting a genetic defect is known, whether prior to or after the birth of an affected child, genetic counseling is needed. It should begin didactically, with information about the laws of chance as they affect the individual or the couple concerned. This kind of counseling is an appeal to the intellect. The emotions come next, for human beings do not make exclusively rational decisions on the basis of intellect alone. The final decision will be the product of the combined reason and emotion of both partners. The pedantic and cautious conservative will make one decision, the reckless gambler with fate another. The genetic counselor cannot dictate the actual decision about breeding, and he should not try to do so. If he does, the unlucky couple, if they disobey him, or if they have an unplanned pregnancy, will feel too guilty or ashamed to see him again for whatever further help they will need.

CONCLUSION

It is probably a good idea for all young people to have a brief acquaintance, in the course of their sex education, with the fact that genetic defects could cross their own path, with the fact that some of them will be fated to experience impairment of procreative function, and with the possibility that anomalies of sex may occur in the newborn and growing child. To be forewarned is forearmed. Knowledge is prophylactic, whether it applies to oneself or to one's community of relatives and friends. With this knowledge comes a fresh challenge to their understanding of life and of their own part in it.

16   Masturbation

Warren R. Johnson

*Many will criticize the placement of this chapter in the section on prob-
lems, in view of the fact that science has shown many traditionally held
bugaboos about masturbation to be ill founded. To be realistic, however,
it is still considered a problem by many young people, parents, and
teachers. Part of the problem, as this chapter suggests, is simply the result
of poor information. Part represents a clash of value systems that is quite
independent of the scientific question of the causes and effects of masturbation. Whether it should be discouraged or encouraged is, after all, a
matter of values. We hope that the review of the facts in this chapter will
be of use to the reader, whatever his system of values.*

INTRODUCTION

Clinicians are involved daily in the conflicted attitudes concerning
sex of the young and older men and women with whom they work.
Confusion, fomented by moral and ethical teachings of earlier
decades, is still superimposed on the findings of contemporary
physiology and psychology. What was considered wicked and dangerous to health is now seen as part of the growing up and life
processes, which needs to be understood rather than judged.
Though certain religious groups would qualify this, it is part of a
process that, to many experts, seems normal and necessary. It is
encouraging to have such a point of departure emphasized together
with the supporting facts.

Professional persons with responsibility for education and counseling of the public need authoritative help and encouragement in
connection with all aspects of sexual behavior, feelings, and attitudes. In particular they need to examine their own biases, prejudices, and underlying anxieties to be at peace with themselves before they can be basically helpful to those whom they teach and
counsel. A person who believes that sexual expression can be a
means of spiritual as well as physical communication with another
human being has the facility of helping others to relate the various
types of sexual expression into a unifying whole, within the framework of their religious or ethical convictions. This study guide
should serve as a useful step in this needed direction. Masturbation
is sexual self-stimulation. Most writers use the term *masturbation* to

This chapter is reprinted with permission from *Masturbation*, SIECUS Study
Guide No. 3, by Warren R. Johnson. Rev. ed. Copyright © 1968 by the Sex Information and Education Council of the U.S.

mean the sexual self-stimulation that leads to climax or orgasm, as distinguished from the common fondling of the genitals observed especially among infants, young children, and the retarded that is not directed specifically toward orgasm.

Various terms are commonly used to mean masturbation. These include *autoerotism, self-abuse, playing with oneself, bad habit,* and *onanism.* The last derives from Onan's "spilling his seed upon the ground" (Genesis XXXVIII:9), but this episode is thought by many Biblical scholars to refer to withdrawal from intercourse before orgasm (*coitus interruptus*) rather than to masturbation. However, traditionally onanism has been equated with masturbation. Young people among themselves ordinarily use such terms as *jerking off* or *jacking off,* or, for females, *rubbing off.*

HOW IS MASTURBATION PRACTICED?

The presumed derivation of the term from the Latin *manus*—hand and *stuprare*—to defile or rape stems from the observed fact that masturbation is commonly practiced by stimulation of the genitals by the individual's own hand. In point of fact, however, there are many other means of masturbation that do not involve the hand, i.e., rubbing the thighs together, pressure or friction against or by an object, often accompanied by erotic reading, pictures, or daydreaming. Masturbation is most often practiced in solitary fashion, but may also occur in the company of another person or persons of the same or mixed sexes.

HOW PREVALENT IS MASTURBATION?

It is not possible, for obvious reasons, to state with complete accuracy the prevalence with which solitary masturbation is practiced. Data derived from the questioning of thousands of people by means of surveys in clinical settings indicate that masturbation is extremely common among both males and females of all ages. Some authorities estimate the prevalence as high as 100 per cent (at least once to have masturbated to orgasm) among males and 90 per cent among females. Above 90 per cent for males, and above 60 per cent for females, over a period of time, however, is perhaps a more realistic figure. Be that as it may, masturbation is common rather than unusual behavior. It is more often accepted as "normal" behavior by people of the middle and upper socio-economic levels than of the lower.

Although masturbation is usually considered to be a phenomenon of adolescence, many boys and girls discover orgasm long before puberty. Prior to puberty (*and not uncommonly in the pre-school years*) the male, like the female, is capable of orgasm even though it is not accompanied by ejaculation. *Masturbation is also common in the adult years, out of as well as in marriage, and it is not uncommon in advanced years.* Indeed, for many individuals, masturbation constitutes virtually the only *overt outlet* or *release* of sexual tension. It is therefore rather universally practiced, at least occasionally, in spite of its common association with a sense of guilt. The undoubted fact that masturbation can be highly gratifying makes its wide practice inevitable.

WHAT ROLE DOES MASTURBATION PLAY IN PSYCHOSEXUAL DEVELOPMENT?

The self-discovery through self-stimulation of masturbation is one of the ways by which a young child learns to perceive his body as a possible source of pleasure. These early experiences help to lay the basis for future acceptance of sex as desirable and pleasurable—unless, of course, the child is led by his parents' negative reactions to view them as shameful and degrading.

During adolescence, masturbation and its attendant fantasies may not only be a means of releasing sex tension, but also it may serve as part of the adolescent struggle to achieve a sense of identity and a sexual self-image. Masturbation may also be used by a young person who is undergoing rapid physiological changes, to become acquainted with his sex organs and the sensations they are capable of producing.

Masturbation in adolescence can, on the other hand, be a symptom of many non-sexual conflicts. Boredom, frustration, loneliness, a poor self-image, inadequate boy-girl relationships, conflict with parents, too many pressures in school, etc., can all create tensions that the adolescent tries to relieve through masturbation. In such cases it is not the masturbation that should be treated by suitable counseling but the conflict of which it is a symptom.

WHAT ATTITUDES ARE HELD TOWARD MASTURBATION?

Not all societies condemn masturbation; some accept it. Our own condemning attitudes reflect the influence of two major sources: (1) the Judaeo-Christian tradition and (2) presently discarded medical opinion developed more or less in line with this tradition. Among the ancient Jews, whose laws strongly affected early Christian thinking in this regard, the intentional *wasting* of seed was considered sinful, a violation of the divine command imperative on all males to increase and multiply. Only the Orthodox among contemporary Jews maintain this position.

Early Christian thinking was also influenced by Augustine's belief that *concupiscence*, particularly the concupiscence associated with sex, was the result of and means of transmission of original sin; and therefore, that the use of sex could be justified only for the purpose of procreation. Later theologians rejected Augustine's view of concupiscence but taught that the deliberate sexual release outside of marital intercourse was wrong. This teaching still furnishes the starting-point for present Catholic thinking on the morality of masturbation. Among Catholic leaders, at least, there has recently been a marked moderating of view on masturbation.

Moreover, current theological refinement by contemporary religious groups continues to stress interpersonal relationships as the essence of mature and appropriate sexual expression. To the extent, then, that masturbation may turn the individual away from the use of sex as a means of "showing love and giving self to another," many Christian spokesmen would see deliberate autoeroticism as falling short of the ideal, and, for this reason, not "morally indifferent." However, many religionists today, while not ready to accept masturbation as objectively amoral in every case, are much more ready to excuse and even to tolerate masturbatory practices by individuals who, for reasons of age or specific psychological dynamics, are not always able to live successfully with the ideal.

There are no laws in the United States against masturbating alone in private, but the traditional feeling against it has been so strong that the existence of such laws is generally presumed. In Indiana and Wyoming the Supreme Courts have ruled that inducing another person to masturbate is sodomy.

Medical opinion of a century and more ago and in some instances of today was certainly influenced by the more primitive of the religious and moral traditions. In addition it had been observed that mentally disturbed people, especially those confined in institutions, masturbated where they could be seen. Masturbation was thought to be the cause of their difficulties whereas in reality it was only a symptom of lack of solitude or indifference to social restraints. Much was written on diseases, especially mental, thought to have been caused by masturbation.

The net effect of older religious and moral traditions and of medical teachings was to make masturbation a highly censored and punishable behavior—one that could have such dire results as insanity, death, and possible damnation. Thus, parents felt justified in going to extremes to "save their children from themselves." Beatings and warnings about "going to hell" were commonplace. Much of our own controversial antipornography legislation (especially that initiated by Anthony Comstock, creator of the present postal obscenity laws) was based on the fear of masturbatory activity that was likely to follow upon exposure to stimulating pictures or literature. "Masturbation Clinics" were conducted under august medical auspices, and aluminum mitts were sold to parents for incarceration of their children's hands at bedtime. Chastity belts for boys have been patented in this country.

Today, most religious groups are re-examining some of their attitudes on masturbation, and medical and psychiatric opinion no longer take seriously the alleged masturbation-disease tie-in. Traditional attitudes remain strong, however, and one finds them persisting in the continuing practice among many parents of punishing their children—verbally, if not physically—for masturbation, in the still common belief that masturbation causes various diseases, including pimples and other skin disorders, and in the fact that many professionals—even physicians, nurses, and teachers—still believe that masturbation leads to neurological and mental disorders. At best it is considered "immature" in the adult.

At the present time, therefore, it would appear that four positions regarding masturbation can be identified: (1) the traditional view, which regards masturbation as always gravely sinful and as harmful to health—with perhaps some modification of its severity and rigidity in the light of new scientific knowledge; (2) the view of many religionists, which sees masturbation often as an imperfect egocentric eroticism that deflects the individual from the Christian concept of sexuality as being ideally reproductive in intent and an essential relation with *another*; (3) an attitude of neutrality, which accepts masturbation, recognizes that further study of its various patterns is required, but is not prepared to encourage it as something positively good; (4) and the increasingly held position that views masturbation not only as completely harmless, but actually as having useful functions to perform: among younger people as a likely part of their psychosexual growth, in older people as release from sexual tension during periods of loneliness and sexual deprivation, or when a sexual partner is absent due to illness, death or divorce. The differences in level of sexual drive between two partners that so often become accentuated as both get older can also often be helped by masturbation, either solitary or mutual.

In view of this diversity of opinion, it is clear that there is need today to deal openly with the subject of masturbation in the training of professional people, especially those who will be responsible in any way for the education and counseling of the public.

WHAT ARE THE PHYSICAL AND MENTAL EFFECTS OF MASTURBATION?

Medical opinion is generally agreed today that masturbation, no matter how frequently it is practiced, produces none of the harmful physical effects about which physicians warned in the past. The physical effects of masturbation are not significantly different from the physical effects of any other sexual activity.

On the other hand, untold numbers of persons have suffered mental turmoil from childhood onward because of a sense of guilt about their practice of masturbation. For some, this turmoil has resulted in psychological damage. It should be clear, but frequently it is not, that the psychological damage is caused not by the act of masturbation itself, but by the feeling that they have done something wrong, that they are therefore bad, worthless and perhaps in need of punishment. These feelings may also occur when young people are overwhelmed by the experience of orgasm and are not prepared for this response.

CAN MASTURBATION BE EXCESSIVE?

Masturbation can only be considered *excessive* in the same sense that *excessive* reading or *excessive* watching of television can be symptoms. In other words, *neither of these things is in itself bad*, but it may suggest the presence of problems that the individual is unable to handle. Thus, if an individual is watching television too much because this represents relief from pressures or because there are no other satisfactions available in life, then the problem is obviously not his addiction to television, but the pressures or the absence of other satisfactions.

Similarly, the frequent masturbation of children has sometimes been found to be due to skin irritation, but more often to adjustment problems. When one mother complained that her ten-year-old son would do little else in his free time but masturbate, questioning revealed that, because the boy had failed to learn basic play or sport skills, he was constantly teased and ridiculed when he attempted to play with other children. He had thus also failed to acquire appropriate social skills, with the result that the range of the expected sources of satisfaction in his life was greatly restricted. Individual work with a physical educator soon led to the acquisition of the needed play and sport skills and paved the way for acceptable social play with his peers. Clearly, his excessive masturbation had been the symptom of a problem rather than the problem itself.

It should be pointed out that the term excessive is vague and undefined and that it may in actuality reflect the lesser sexual drive of the person using the term, in the light of the very wide individual variations that exist in the desire and capacity to engage in sexual activity.

WHAT IS THE ROLE OF FANTASY IN MASTURBATION?

Masturbation is usually accompanied by fantasies or daydreams in about three-fourths of the males who masturbate and about half of the females. There are differing hypotheses concerning these fantasies. It has been suggested that masturbation without any fantasy is unhealthy because it then becomes purely a mechanical act without any interpersonal sexual overtones. Some psychiatrists hold that fantasy of an affectionate heterosexual relationship can be a healthy accompaniment to masturbation, while types of fantasy that include sadomasochistic or homosexual behavior are harmful.

For many religious people, a fantasy of a sex act which, if performed in real life, would be against the individual's moral code is ethically unacceptable. On the other hand, there are those who consider that the fantasied act may substitute for the real act and thus serve as a harmless avenue of release for more violent and antisocial urges.

CAN MASTURBATION BE PREVENTED?

As already indicated, in the history of our society both cruel and fantastic measures have been taken in an effort to prevent masturbation. Little more than half a century ago, an electrical device was patented that would ring a bell in a father's bedroom whenever his son had an erection. The father could then rush to his son's bedside to "save him from himself." All evidence indicates that neither this nor any other technique of repression succeeded except in the sense that a child became ever more clever in hiding his masturbation, ever more guilt- and anxiety-ridden in the practice of it, or even repressive in the handling of his basic sexual attitudes.

DOES MASTURBATION IN YOUTH REDUCE
SEXUAL GRATIFICATION IN MARRIAGE?

There is no evidence that masturbation in youth reduces for either the male or female satisfaction in marriage. Kinsey's findings indicate that females who have not experienced orgasm prior to marriage take longer to become as good sex partners as those who already have some knowledge of sexual satisfaction. It is therefore unlikely that female masturbation reduces gratification in marriage. A woman who has masturbated in a particular way may not fully enjoy sexual activity with a husband if he fails to stimulate her in exactly the same way. In many cases, she need only explain her preferences to him.

There are males who, discovering that they suffer in marriage from premature ejaculation or impotence, jump to the conclusion that earlier masturbation was the cause, but clinical evidence suggests that the problem is generally found to have had its origin in some other cause.

Married individuals, incidentally, frequently use masturbation (solitary or mutual) for the release of sexual tension when, for any of a variety of reasons, sexual intercourse with the mate is not convenient or possible.

WHAT ADVICE SHOULD BE GIVEN CONCERNING MASTURBATION?

Students of human sexuality and of mental health seem increasingly to be taking the position that masturbation may be regarded as part of the normal process of sexual maturation. From a strictly medical and mental health point of view, there is no reason to try to prevent masturbation. As a general rule, parents and adults concerned with youth are best advised to disregard evidence of private masturbation in juveniles, not to look for it nor to try to prevent it directly, or even indirectly by attempting to divert the youngster's attention to other activities. As with other bodily functions, however, young children can be helped to become aware of the distinction that every individual must learn to make between what is acceptable as public and as private behavior, without implying that the private behavior must be in any way inferior or bad. In adulthood as well as in childhood, masturbation by individuals in private is coming more and more to be regarded as an acceptable means of releasing sexual tension.

Urging individuals troubled by the frequency of their masturbation to make earnest decisions to stop is not realistic and often may actually cause the frequency to increase. In fact, the acts may tend automatically to become fewer as the overlay of anxiety disappears. In the infrequent cases where compulsive masturbation is found in conjunction with severe personality disorders or juvenile psychoses, it is for these underlying conditions that psychiatric help is needed.

Teachers, physicians, and other counselors should recognize that full and accurate information about masturbation is required by both parents and youngsters and that the subject should be given due attention in any formal or informal program of sex education. In such discussions, a simple nonjudgmental, informative approach and manner will do much to dissipate the fears and anxieties about it that are so commonly found to block the road toward a mature acceptance of oneself as a sexual being.

17   Sexual Problems in Clinical Experience

Daniel N. Wiener

In this chapter an experienced psychologist describes the sexual problems which he commonly encounters in his clinical practice and makes recommendations to sex educators

When I began practicing psychotherapy twenty years ago, I seldom encountered sexual problems and thought that they had been over-rated as a subject for psychotherapy. Gradually, however, I began encountering them more and more, until it seemed that a sexual problem was to be found whenever a client had any other serious problem—but only if the subject was brought up. I had a similar experience with the question of extramarital sex. Seldom did the subject arise spontaneously in conversation, but when, occasionally and fortuitously, it did, then other mystifying troubles were explained. When these queries became part of my routine, it appeared that sexual problems occurred frequently and were crucial to an understanding and solution of many other complaints. Of my patients, ranging in age from seventeen to sixty, 75 per cent have had sexual problems serious enough to require help, although this was the reason for beginning therapy in only a small minority of cases. Anyone can see the ghost of sex under any bed at all: it is the most titillating of all topics. But in such professions as teaching, counseling, and psychotherapy, sex rightly takes up a large share of the discussion.

One can assume that among humans, like the animals in the Ark, there will be at least two people who have done anything that can be imagined in the realm of sexual practices, but this chapter will not focus on rarities which may be encountered no more than once in one's professional lifetime. Rather, my attempt is to describe some almost universal problems. To help students and clients with their sexual problems, we must be aware of the goals toward which, wittingly or unwittingly, they are striving. In addition, approaches to sexual problems are suggested which will help them to cope with other problems as well. Finally, practical vehicles for achievement of these goals are outlined.

UNIVERSAL PROBLEMS

Problems of Males

Because the nineteenth-century conceptualization of male sexuality as almost pure aggression still persists to some degree, perhaps the most pervasive problem of almost all males in our society is that of proving themselves, and sex is one arena of battle. While many men choose a different course of behavior, more succumb to the pressures of what they view as the sexual prowess expected of them. They worry excessively about their sex drive and performance, about how women view them sexually, about periods of disinterest in sex or sexual failure, about waning sexual powers. From adolescence to senility, males often feel that they must be aggressive and strong sexually. A good sex education program comes to grips with this attitude, with the problems that result from it, and with the variety of ways it can be made more realistic. The young man can be helped to accept and to learn from failure and to see that despite the importance accorded male potency it need not be the prime measure of personal adequacy.

An extreme version of this concept is expressed in Puerto Rico by the term "machismo," or "feeling of manhood."[1] Much of the male's behavior he measures in terms of machismo; much of what he does or fails to do reflects upon his machismo. Thus when the male slum-dweller improves his earnings, he is more likely to acquire another woman than a better house. A slight to his sexual prowess is the deadliest insult, and sexual behavior and talk overtly and specifically reflect this preoccupation.

Many of the sexual problems that plague almost every male at some time—impotence, disinterest, worry about pleasing the partner—can be understood not as purely physical or physiological phenomena (very few men are impotent when they masturbate, for example), but primarily in terms of the expectations they feel they must fulfill with a partner. What distinguishes the male with a serious sexual problem from the rest is often his view of his machismo. The stronger and more inflexible are his expectations, the less likely he is to meet his standards and the more likely he is to become upset and worried about unsuccessful behavior and reactions which others might consider transitory, trivial, and natural.

Physically the male is also more obviously put to the test than the female. The performance of the penis in sex cannot be faked or disguised, and failures are apparent. The female can and often does

[1] See O. Lewis, La Vida (New York: Random House, 1967), and Chapter 14 above, in which the concept is discussed in some detail.

simulate sexual responsiveness, and the male cannot easily detect that she is acting.

Problems of Females
The most pervasive problems for the female stem from the view that she should please men and that her own sexual satisfaction is of secondary importance. She may not seek out her own pleasure. She may develop hostile attitudes toward the male who, she believes, expects her to please (part of which is to be pleased by) him, and, because of resentment or ignorance, she may develop the habit of pretending to be pleased, or withholding herself.

Embittered about or hypersensitive to such attitudes, women may then blame men for any sexual problems they have, as though sexual behavior were the male prerogative and beyond woman's power to control or affect. They may view themselves as objects being used, or, what is worse, as required to respond sexually only to reassure the male that he can excite and satisfy a partner.

As the man must rid himself of the necessity of proving himself sexually in the woman's judgment, only when she stops measuring her adequacy in terms of the man's judgment can the woman place in proper perspective some almost universal sexual problems— disinterest, frigidity, withholding, pretense, or distaste. These problems can then be attacked as *her problems*, involving *her* pleasure and satisfaction, and subject to a substantial degree of control by wiser attitudes and actions on *her* part and for *her* own sake.

Developmental Problems
Preadolescence. Sexual problems before adolescence, with rare exceptions, primarily involve ignorance and lack of control. They consist of exploration of sex with oneself and others, of which behavior adults tend to disapprove. Perhaps when parents or others have a relationship with children in which sexual questions are freely asked and answered, there is less experimentation among children rather than more, as some persons seem to think. Such exploratory behavior among children as lifting skirts or feeling one another's bodies seem to be harmless. If adults attempt such behavior with children, however, the effect does seem to be adverse and, like the seduction of adolescents by homosexuals, apparently carries the weight of a kind of bad training, rather than a harmless kind of experimentation among equals.

Some preadolescent sexuality, however, seems to be bizarre and inexplicable and is unimportant to subsequent sex life except in rare instances. Children who grow up to be apparently normal adults may experiment on their genitals with strange devices, and

otherwise act out what would be esoteric perversions if they occurred in adults, yet these interests fade away in almost all cases in
the face of the strong sexual drive of adolescence.

Adolescence. The sexual problems of adolescents are not likely to
come to the attention of teachers or counselors except when they
surface in such dramatic forms as venereal disease, promiscuity,
or rape, or become a symptom of a general "nervous breakdown,"
psychotic break, or suicide attempt. Most of the problems that
adults suffer are also common and pressing among adolescents, but
because adolescents are often especially mystified, hopeful, igno-
rant, or ambitious in their sexual attitudes and practices, their youth-
ful rebelliousness and hopeful expectations of life will prevent them
from seeking help. If they do, it is usually because they are forced
to it by parents or drastic circumstances. Teachers, counselors, and
parents, therefore, need not hesitate to try to educate adolescents,
even though an appeal for such education has not been made. The
facts about conception and effective birth control, the spuriousness
of the notion of an inborn homosexual nature, the problems connected with promiscuity—such information can be conveyed even
in the face of the overt cynicism of the listeners. Although their
code sets a distance between themselves and adults, a fact is a fact
and will be absorbed and responded to, even unwillingly.

Adolescents also suffer from a wide range of problems peculiar
to their age. Boys are often intensely apprehensive about asking
girls for dates, and girls worry about accepting dates with boys
whom their friends may consider "jerks." Boys worry about not
talking well if they do get a date, not knowing what to do sexually
if they are offered the chance, not being bold when they imagine
the girl expects them to be. Girls fear that they are not attractive if
boys do not make advances, that they will be unpopular and rejected if they set limits on sex play, that they can earn love or
gratitude by cooperating in various forms of sexual gratification.

Young Adulthood. Young adults suffer from the same problems as
adolescents, but they have the added burden of having to seek
help on their own if they are to get it at all (teachers and parents
seldom offer it) and of the expectation that they should be married
and be skillful in sexual practices. If they are not married at this
time, they worry about that, and if they remain virgins, that too is a
worry. For men and women to keep themselves free of any sexual
outlet until their thirties seems less likely to represent a positive
commitment to a value than a negative fear of sex. Expectations in
dating tend to become much more specific; the amorphous adolescent longings, fears, and false attributions of sexual interest to the
partner become converted into more concrete sexual desires and

routines. If by the age of thirty a man or woman has not found satisfying ways of gaining sexual satisfaction, his or her problems are probably serious enough to require special counseling.

The sexual problems of young married adults usually center around specific difficulties in getting along with each other. If the husband is disinterested or impotent or unsatisfied, he usually blames his wife for the way she treats him outside of bed or for her unresponsiveness in bed. He often complains that out of bed she is too aggressive and domineering, while in bed she is too passive. The wife who is disinterested, frigid, or unsatisfied complains that her sexual problems occur because her husband is too insensitive and unsympathetic out of bed and impulsive and selfish in bed. She implies that somehow if he were a more sensitive, romantic figure she would want him and be able to respond to him.

Many of these conflicts become almost a way of life to couples; they may go on and on with their marriages, defeating or curtailing their sexual pleasures in many ways without ever making a systematic attempt to change their behavior. Sometimes they initiate divorce or separation actions, but more often they simply endure conditions as they are. Marriage counseling often is sought only when some crisis forces action. However, given the extreme frequency of such conflict, it might well be profitable to society, as well as to the individuals involved, if a mechanism were set up to deal with the problem "involuntarily." Extensive counseling services, perhaps connected with the juvenile courts and schools, might well be set up to serve married couples in trouble. These would be most important when children get into trouble because of their parents' problems or when a child has problems that parents cannot cope with alone.

Middle Age. Middle age is a time when single persons usually give up hope of achieving sexual satisfaction, when married persons frequently become depressed and consider that they are too old for sexual enjoyment or good sexual functioning, and when both single and married people often complain about too much business and not enough time to enjoy sex properly.

Perhaps the outstanding characteristic of middleaged persons who seek psychotherapy is waning hope for a better future combined with their irrational depression about the present. True, opportunities for change may have faded, though people can and do change considerably at any time in their lives right up to death. The sense of depression about the present, however, almost always is irrational. The potential for some pleasurable form of sexual activity usually exists for any male or female who can assess a situation realistically and is willing to take advantage of existing opportunities. The major problem for middleaged married persons seems to be a fear of declining powers, a resulting sense of depression, and then a diminution of activity which might have been the most pleasurable in their lives. For those who have always had sexual problems, this period often seems to be their "last chance," and they seek help lest they miss sexual pleasure entirely.

The male is often in for a particularly hard time psychologically because he undergoes no clear physical changes, even though many physicians refer to a "change of life" in the male as though it were as objective as it is in women. His sexual capacity declines only slowly until old age, and his glandular changes are very gradual. Without physiological referents, his concerns are more clearly psychological. The female, who does go through definite and dramatic glandular and reproductive system changes over a span of several years, has therefore more acceptable reasons to give herself for sexual problems at this age. She can blame them on physical changes, even thought in fact she can lead a vital and only slowly changing sexual life throughout menopause and into old age.

Old Age. Very few old people seek counseling or psychotherapy for anything, including sexual problems. Perhaps they should. It seems likely that a simple occasional sexual pleasure is as much within their power as a simple, non-intense pleasure of any other kind. It also seems likely that any kind of counseling would have to be brought to them because they characteristically isolate themselves and are isolated from the mainstream of community activity. Such counseling might enhance their vitality and help to arrest a too-quick drift into senility and death.

Conflicts between Generations. Of all the conflicts between the generations, none is so intense as the conflict between young people and their middleaged parents and parent surrogates—teachers, ministers, and others who have power over them—about sex. Changing sexual mores show up first in young people: they are the sexual leaders, the most vital sexually, and from them many of the new ways spread through society, whether their elders like it or not. How many are engaging in premarital relations, somewhat casually by older standards perhaps, but not often promiscuously. Women act more like the equals of men, and the double standard of morality is less acceptable. This is what is happening, and the parent, educator, or counselor cannot stop it. To inveigh against it is merely to risk cutting himself off from those he would help.

Sources of Problems

Marriage. Some marital problems typical of certain age groups have been mentioned above, but others are seen at all stages of a marriage. The two major problems appear to be coordination of sexual satisfaction and the handling of extramarital relationships. Outside of marriage casual sexual relationships—involving sexual intercourse once or occasionally—do not require a meshing of satisfactions or attitudes. In marriage, however, if both parties are not satisfied sexually, the capacity to get along in any way is severely strained.

The partner of a sexually impotent or otherwise ineffectual male will be hard put, over an extended period of time, to gain sexual satisfaction and to avoid feeling cheated and embittered. If she makes do with nothing, or with masturbation, it can only be accompanied, at best, by some sense of pity or maternal protectiveness toward a weak man (even though she may rationalize that sex is mainly for men, or that she does not need it). The husband with a frigid wife who has seldom or never experienced orgasm can probably get along somewhat better, though his pleasure is usually reduced when he knows that his partner is not satisfied. A multitude of other interpersonal problems go along with such a poor sexual adjustment, and successful marriage requires working together congenially on sexual as well as other problems of living.

Counselors and educators take an uncertain position on the second major problem, sex outside of marriage, perhaps reflecting changing community attitudes. Like masturbation and premarital sex, extramarital sex is so common that the counselor cannot ignore it; he must deal with it in specific situations. Like masturbation, premarital sex, and the sexual explorations of children, such incidents can be handled badly and have seriously disruptive effects or can be handled well and pass by harmlessly—or even, as Kinsey and his associates have suggested, have a positive effect. The counselor must, of course, take into account the fact that, while extramarital relations are common and are even acceptable to some spouses, they are grounds for divorce and on that account cannot be recommended.

Religion. Adherents of the more conservative religious sects in the United States often say that their sexual problems stem from the discrepancy between what their religion teaches and what they are doing. However, most members of such groups handle their sexual problems well enough to avoid the need for professional help. Those who blame their religious upbringing for their problems often seem themselves to be rigid and to attribute more rigidity to their religion on the subject of sex than in fact exists. The number of devout young church members who masturbate, use mechanical or chemical birth control measures, and engage in sex outside of marriage indicates that, like the tenets of kindness to all, racial equality, and honesty, there is a considerable gap between practice and dogma. Most religions have room for imperfections. Ministers vary widely in their attitudes toward parishioners who are not perfect in their practice. Many prefer not to be asked specific questions about sexual behavior, such as "How many times weekly is my husband entitled to sex?" In search of a rigid control over their lives by their religion some women do ask such questions, which would simply not occur to most of their fellow believers.

Voluntary Celibacy, Sublimation, and Low Sex Drive. Celibacy refers to the unmarried state, not to a rejection of sexual practices. Psychologists have never been able to answer satisfactorily the question of whether sexual need must be satisfied in some physical way or whether it can be successfully ignored. Beginning with Freud, psychoanalysts have strongly suggested that if the sexual urge is not satisfied directly it will eventually show itself in distorted, psychologically damaging forms such as displaced hatreds, phobias, excessive commitment to peculiar causes, and psychosomatic and hysterical symptoms. There is no good statistical evidence, however, on the relationship between a rejection of or attempt to sublimate sex and symptoms of conflict.

There are those who report low interest or even disinterest in sex. Clinically, low sexual interest (outlet utilized less than once or twice a week from adolescence through middle age) and disinterest seem to be related to such emotional states as fear, wish for revenge, anger, exhaustion, tension, and emotional disruption. No one can say what the "normal" range of human sexual activity is under optimal living conditions, but it is known that sexual response is particularly sensitive to environmental stresses. Perhaps one must restrict oneself to the simple observation that what is the supreme pleasure in life to many is an uncomfortable nuisance or distraction to others. If the counselor views sexual activity as at least a major pleasure in life, then he can try to encourage it so that his client can strike a balance suited to his own makeup based upon adequate experience. If he accepts a client's view that sexual urges should be sublimated, then he must at least help the client to face rationally any difficulties which arise, to take an empirical view of whether such a course seems feasible, and to aid him in resolving any consequent problems realistically.

GOALS OF SEXUAL BEHAVIOR

The sexual problems human beings encounter can be viewed in the perspective of the goals being pursued. Goals can be placed arbitrarily in four categories: reproduction, pleasure, achievement, and closeness. They will provide reference points for discovering the rewards the client may be seeking blindly in unsuccessful, even self-defeating, ways. Suppose a seventeen-year-old boy is referred to a counselor by his parents because he is withdrawn and is associating with boys who his parents think are homosexual. Suppose the counselor discovers, in interviewing the boy, that he is engaging in homosexual relations within this group and is feeling guilty and depressed about it. If the purpose of this behavior is investigated, the counselor and the boy may well decide that the goal is primarily that of being close both to a person and to a group, although physical pleasure and a sense of achievement, of being somebody, may also enter into the situation. Thus if the goal is closeness, the task of the counselor is to suggest alternative paths to the goal which do not involve the guilt and depression associated with the homosexuality that the boy keeps secret and is ashamed of. Let us now consider these four goals in more detail.

Reproduction

From the standpoint of the human race, reproduction is the most important goal of sexual behavior, and it is just as obvious that men have endowed such behavior with so much more importance that the genetic goal, which it serves in all animals, is greatly obscured. Yet many problems are generated by different partner attitudes toward having children, practicing birth control, and religious strictures. A couple usually will try to achieve some agreement on their contraceptive practices. Sometimes religious principles become an issue, but personal objections such as interruption of petting when a mechanical control is used, side effects of birth control pills, or having to plan intercourse at certain times of the month, curtailing spontaneity, are more common. If contraception is not used, either partner may feel inhibited by fear of conceiving.

Pleasure

Sexual relief or pleasure can be produced in an endless number of ways. If the genitals need not be directly stimulated to produce an orgasm (and some people can produce orgasm without any physical activity, through fantasies alone), then there is no physical limitation at all. The problems which are presented by the form which an individual's pleasure takes have little to do with the inherent merit of the practice, but only with what the individual *thinks* about it, perhaps even with a web of non-sexual associations with the person or things used in the sexual act.

Achievement

A goal the counselor often detects by default is a sense of achievement or adequacy. That a person must lead an active, satisfying sexual life to feel adequate is less often pointed out by counselors than its converse: because a person does not perform well sexually, he feels inadequate. Some counselors hesitate to say that sexual activity is a necessity but are willing to "explain" inadequacy feelings by its absence.

There are many ways in which man can gain a sense of achievement. Certainly if he places himself in a sexual situation—through marriage, a heterosexual affair, a homosexual relationship, even social bragging about sexual behavior—he may well feel compelled to measure his success at least somewhat by his sexual performance. If he avoids sexual situations or assumes an asexual role as a celibate, public adversary of sex, or puritan, he may be better able to ignore his own inadequate sexual behavior.

A sense of achievement may be gained in other ways as well. One may drive hard in his profession, another may manipulate money or people, a third may create products or works of art. Harry Stack Sullivan has said that "whenever the maintenance of self-esteem becomes an end instead of a consequent of life, the individual concerned is mentally sick."[2] The sense of adequacy may thus be viewed as the outcome of reaching one's chosen goals. If, however, it is the gnawing pain of inadequacy that drives one on to achieve, sexually or otherwise, the achieving may resemble the eating of a man with a duodenal ulcer—to keep away the pain rather than for enjoyment.

Not only one's own success is involved here, however, but the satisfaction of one's partner as well. Striving for a sense of adequacy through sex generates a problem when expectations are unrealistic as well as when performance is poor. Many people confuse their own performance and gratification with that of their partner. It may make sense to say that mutual gratification is the goal of sexual relations and that therefore one's sense of adequacy should depend upon mutual, not selfish, pleasure, but it is not a necessity where reasonable efforts by one partner fail to gratify the other.

Closeness

Sex seems to be most gratifying when it is a social act involving two persons. Apparently masturbation seldom provides the satisfaction that either homosexual or heterosexual relations—or, indeed, the various perversions involving two or more persons—do. Something more than physiological activity is involved, and that something is probably related to closeness between two persons. This closeness has its romantic aspect, where love is associated with

[2] *The Contributions of Harry Stack Sullivan*, ed. P. Mullahy (New York: Dutton, 1967).

sex, and its dependency aspect, where the two partners feel tied to one another in an intimacy which excludes the outside world.

Sexual behavior generates special problems, however, when it is the primary means of relating to others. Some homosexuals, for example, become confirmed in their way of life simply because they feel totally lost in the larger society, while the subsociety of homosexuals welcomes them. Within reasonable limits sex represents one of the best ways for human beings to draw close to each other, but if it is the only or prime basis of a relationship, there is an extra-heavy demand that it be continuously successful, varied, and stimulating. It seems likely that a single area of activity cannot carry a relationship for very long and that homosexual as well as heterosexual relationships dependent almost entirely upon sex cannot be long maintained. The hope of long-lasting closeness based exclusively upon sex seems likely to be frustrated again and again.

THE STANDARD PROBLEM-SOLVING APPROACH

In what ways can the teacher and counselor cope with these problems? I have described the principles of behavior change and the agents by which it can be accomplished in *Shortterm Psychotherapy and Structured Behavior Change*,[3] and they will be described here only briefly.

Principles

Goal-Setting. To solve problems concretely and practically they must be stated concretely and practically. For the teacher, counselor, or client to say that "sexual maturity," "adequacy," or "meaningful affectional relationships" are his goals is to say little that is useful. To say instead that frequent and mutually gratifying sexual relations, personally satisfying sexual performance, or sexual behavior with a desired and cooperative partner are his goals gives shape to the educational or counseling process.

The Measuring Process. If increased knowledge and more satisfying sexual behavior (within legal and socially acceptable limits) are the general objectives, then educational programs should be continually evaluated to see whether they are effective in accomplishing these objectives. If one of the purposes of a sex education course is "to impart healthy attitudes about sex," what can we measure except, perhaps, exactly what the teacher says? If, on the other hand, one purpose is "to provide information about the anatomy and physiology of sex," a standard test can be constructed and administered to students to measure teaching effectiveness. In counseling, if one's

[3] E. L. Phillips and D. N. Wiener, *Shortterm Psychotherapy and Structured Behavior Change* (New York: McGraw-Hill, 1966).

goal is expressed as "achievement of sexual maturity," neither counselor nor client has any clear way of determining progress. However, stated as "at least semi-weekly, satisfying sexual outlet," success can readily be measured.

Without measurement any counseling or educational program will depend more upon its initiator's optimism, salesmanship, or propagandistic ability than on its usefulness. Even if students or clients are asked their opinion of a program, the glow from their association with a clever teacher or a kindly counselor may well distort the results achieved. Teaching or counseling programs can be evaluated and improved only on the basis of a demonstrable increase in knowledge and a concrete change in behavior.

Follow-Up. To make any program of education or behavior change effective over time, there must be follow-up. In this way teaching or counseling methods are improved, new methods introduced, and successes recognized. To be most helpful, counseling and educational efforts should be reinforced and maintained within the student's or client's life. This reinforcement comes about when the environment rewards the new behavior. Often, however, when classes or interviews are over and there are no immediate applications of what has been learned, it may be forgotten, or obstacles may arise later to which students succumb. Like a booster shot, follow-up can ensure that an initial success is maintained.

Experimentation and Flexibility. For learning and behavior change to take place in the face of erroneous information or self-defeating habits, both teachers and counselors, students and clients, should be encouraged to experiment. A willingness to consider and test new information, new attitudes, and new behaviors is, in a sense, the proper goal of teaching and counseling, and the most effective teachers and counselors themselves probably serve as models. In trying to change sexual behavior one should break into ineffectual habits wherever possible, trying to block them and to initiate some possibly more successful behavior anywhere and in any feasible way. We should remember that small and specific steps toward change tend to be easier to institute than grand ones and may provide the slight push that is sometimes all that is necessary to get clients moving toward larger goals.

Problem-Solvers

While teachers and counselors are the two major groups involved in problem-solving, human beings will continue to depend much more heavily upon newspaper and magazine writers, parents, peers, friends, relatives, physicians, lawyers, youth leaders, and ministers for information and advice. In a sense, every student or client is both a receiver and a purveyor of teaching and counseling services. When he attends classes and lectures, reads books and articles, listens to conversations, observes how others behave, asks questions of acquaintances, and then tries to apply what he has heard, read, or observed, he is teaching and counseling himself. He is often capable of detachment and can be helped to develop his ability for impersonal self-appraisal.

Obtaining professional sex counseling is often laborious and/or costly, and simpler, cheaper alternatives can be described to clients when they are feasible. Because ministers, physicians, youth leaders, social workers, lawyers, and newspaper columnists are certain to be consulted much more frequently than specialized teachers and counselors, the latter might well try to develop some relationship to the non-specialists to make the work of both groups more effective. If teachers and counselors can conceive of a larger role as consultants to other agents, their views will have more impact on the community.

Parents, friends, spouses, other relatives, and peers, even if they are not necessarily dependable sources of reliable information and advice, can be of some service for whatever they do know. A person's interaction with others is almost certain to suggest new possibilities to him, and he should be encouraged to initiate conversations and participate in group discussions.

Solutions

Like problem-solvers, solutions can be highly varied. A hundred or perhaps a thousand devices can be suggested by the creative counselor to the client who wishes to overcome his impotence: relaxing beforehand to set the mood, having a drink or avoiding liquor, looking at stimulating material, seeking out a favorable partner, masturbating first or blocking it, allowing tension to build up over time, engaging in some physical activity or avoiding it, letting matters take their own course without forcing things, reading propaganda against guilt, talking to his partner about sex or avoiding such conversation. Solutions fall into four general categories: information, attitudinal change, behaviorial change, and manipulation of the environment.

Information. Facts about birth control are presented so that ignorance does not perpetuate problems. Presentation of such information is not tantamount to a recommendation of birth control: how that knowledge is used depends upon the individual. A decision not to use contraception on religious grounds is valid; a decision not to use contraception because contraceptive methods are ineffective, dirty, hard to come by, or difficult to use is not. If a contraceptive is to be used, it should be chosen to suit the convenience and comfort of two well-informed partners, not on the basis of a vague bit of whispered information.

To take another example, many females become seriously alarmed when menstruation begins. Later in life women may be concerned over a several weeks' delay in its onset. Secondary school programs effectively deal with the former worry, but the facts about widespread irregularity are not well known to older women, and much unnecessary anxiety about pregnancy results.

Sexual stimulation and improvised satisfaction should be understood if unwanted pregnancy is to be avoided. Girls should be aware of their power to excite boys, sometimes unwittingly. As for boys, what is the excited male to do? Does he have an emission, messing his clothes and hers? Does he desperately attempt to interrupt the natural progress of pleasure? Does he forcefully and blindly try to complete the reproductive process? What of the girl who may be sexually excited but feels she must maintain a relatively passive stance? Knowledge of those factors which inhibit and those which enhance sexual responsiveness, presented especially well by Masters and Johnson[4] and, in a broader review, by Ellis,[5] increases the probability of sexual success.

Attitudinal Change. Training in effective attitudes—that is, attitudes which move toward goals rather than defeat—can be important. Attitudes have been learned and can be changed. One's attitude toward mastery, control, and responsibility is crucial to success in overcoming one's problems in the sexual or any other area. If an individual believes that he is a pawn of forces beyond his control, that he is helpless to overcome his problems, that others are responsible for his sexual failures, then he is probably dooming himself to defeat unless the persons in his life or his circumstances happen to change. However, if he can be brought to see that a range of new behavior is open to him, if he then exercises his options regardless of how difficult persons or conditions are, he will have a much better chance. One has, after all, much greater power to change oneself than to change others.

Attitudes toward personal competence are also important. Sexual activity can be viewed as behavior which can be developed, like an athletic, artistic, or professional skill, with equal satisfaction. The sheer pleasure of recognizing oneself as competent is often overlooked in a discussion of attitudes.

A reasonable attitude toward spontaneity can help solve certain

[4] W. Masters and V. Johnson, *Human Sexual Response* (New York: Little, Brown, 1966).

[5] A. Ellis, *The Art and Science of Love* (New York: Lyle Stuart, 1960).

nagging sexual problems. Many people at first reject the idea of planning for sexual activity on the ground that it kills spontaneity and therefore pleasure, yet night after night their "spontaneity" is blind and self-defeating. Spontaneity has little merit in itself. If it is associated with sexual satisfaction, it should be valued; if it is not, it should be abandoned as a goal.

Behavioral Change. The success of any solution must eventually be measured by one's behavior. If unsatisfactory sexual practices are not replaced by more satisfying ones, education and counseling have probably failed. But apart from being a measuring device, behavior itself can solve problems. This particular activity or that may not succeed, but the teacher or counselor will not lack suggestions, and if they are sensible and practical, eventually one will work. Practical suggestions should be based on knowledge of local resources, imagination, and judgment. Men and women can be told where the best places are to find partners, how to approach them, and what to do with them. Often teachers and counselors hesitate to do so either through ignorance of the actions that are likely to work or through reluctance to be "overdirective." They want the client to find his own way. But success is likely to breed success, and if the teacher or counselor can increase the likelihood of the client's accomplishing his goals by playing an active role, why should he avoid it? Does it reduce the client's "maturity"? Does it make him dependent upon the teacher or counselor? Why not ask rather whether it helps him to get dates, or alleviates his sense of incompetence and loneliness? After all, these may be the pressing problems, and independence is a matter of learning to solve one's present and future problems.

Manipulation of the Environment. Manipulation of the environment will be merely mentioned here because it is seldom a function of teachers or counselors. It is, however, probably the most powerful vehicle for behavioral change, capable of affecting both the individual and the group. Parents, youth leaders, church, municipal, and other administrators are in a position to affect sexual behavior by the activities they control. Within broad limits they can determine the opportunities given boys and girls to be alone together, accessibility of contraceptives, and sanctions levied against various sexual practices in adolescence. These controls strongly affect the nature and quantity of sexual practices and should not be overlooked, as they often seem to be, as a far more potent influence than verbal instruction or counseling is ever likely to be.

18　　Problematic Sexual Behavior

James E. Moore

*Homosexuality, nymphomania, fetishism, voyeurism, exhibitionism, trans-
vestitism, sadism, masochism, sodomy—it would be hard to find topics
which evoke more curiosity and emotion. Myth and folklore about these
subjects permeate our society and often color the thinking even of the
well educated. In this chapter James Moore presents the sex educator
with an accurate and humane description of these practices and of the
people who engage in them. His annotated list of novels and plays provides the reader with a resource for the further enrichment of his own
understanding.*

This chapter will deal with sexual behavior that is commonly termed
deviant or aberrant. The dictionary informs us that "deviation"
means "marked departure from accepted norms of behavior" and
that "aberrant" means "departing substantially from the standard."[1]
We wish to draw attention to the fact that what is regarded as a
marked or substantial departure is a matter of arbitrary definition.
I would prefer to refer to many sexual behaviors that at first glance
seem strange, sexual behaviors toward which our responses are
doubtful, questionable, and uncertain, as "problematic." If this is
our definition of problematic, it follows that almost all sexual behavior is problematic. The very existence of such an organization as
SIECUS indicates that educators and the public alike find it to be so.

The first half of this chapter contains an account of the psychology and sociology of homosexuality. The second half contains
briefer accounts of a number of other problematic sexual behaviors:
promiscuity, fetishism, voyeurism, exhibitionism, transvestitism, sadism and masochism, and sodomy. It is our hope that the sensational-
ism surrounding these behaviors will be modified when the reader
understands that almost all of them have everyday counterparts in
the lives of what we regard to be "normal" persons. Marcus Aure-
lius is credited with saying, "Nothing that is human is foreign to
me." It is in that spirit that this chapter is written.

HOMOSEXUALITY

There is probably no problematic sexual behavior more common
and more widely misunderstood and feared than homosexuality. As

[1] *Webster's New Collegiate Dictionary*, 7th ed.

far as we know, it has existed in every culture, and nowhere in the Western world is it as severely penalized as in the United States. Because of this state of affairs it behooves enlightened persons to understand it.

Definition

The term "homosexuality" means sexual relations, either overt or fantasied, between persons of the same sex. It is derived from the Greek prefix *homo-*, meaning "the same as," not from the Latin word for man. Thus the term is appropriately used for sexual behavior between men or between women. "Lesbian" or "sapphic" are also sometimes used to refer to sexual relations between women; the Greek poetess Sappho, who lived on the island of Lesbos, immortalized female homosexual relations in verse.

There are other words that are sometimes used as synonyms for homosexuality, and they can be confusing. An example is "inversion." Inversion usually refers to inversion of object choice, that is, the choice of a love object of the same sex. This is the way Freud used the term. A discussion of the "inversion of inverts" is describing homosexual behavior. In some studies of human behavior, however, inversion designates sexual situations in which males assume sexual positions most often taken by females and in which females assume sexual positions most often taken by males. A better choice of descriptive terms here is "active" and "passive."

"Bisexual" is another term about which there may be confusion. The dictionary lists several definitions. In biology the term means "organisms having the anatomy or functions of both sexes" and may or may not mean having the reproductive organs of both sexes in the same body ("hermaphroditic"), depending on the context. The psychological definition of bisexual is a person sexually attracted by either sex.

It can be seen that definitions are arbitrary and switching from one frame of reference to another can be confusing. Legally speaking, a homosexual is a person who has committed a homosexual act; psychologically speaking, a homosexual may be a person who participates in homosexual behavior or he may only have erotic fantasies about it. For legal purposes it is necessary to determine whether a particular act has taken place. We do not prosecute people for what they think but for what they do. The law may be concerned with intent or motive in order to determine relative culpability, but in the final analysis it resorts to a dichotomy, guilty or not guilty, homosexual or heterosexual.

Male Homosexuality

Incidence. The Kinsey data tell us that about 13 per cent of the total male population had more of the homosexual than the heterosexual in their sexual lives for at least three years between the ages of sixteen and fifty-five, that about 8 per cent of all males are exclusively homosexual for at least three years of their lives, and that only about 4 per cent are exclusively homosexual throughout their lives. Psychologists are permitted the luxury of arranging homosexual phenomena along a continuum. Kinsey and his associates have done so on a seven-point scale which they call the "heterosexual-homosexual balance."[2] Persons were rated on the basis of their overt experience and/or their psychic reactions. The introduction of "psychic reactions" into the definition makes it broader than those used by most clinicians, who would prefer to restrict the term homosexual to persons who usually prefer sexual relations with a person of the same sex.

There are no accurate statistics on the incidence of actively practicing homosexuals in the United States. The two Kinsey reports give us the best approximation available, however. Kinsey estimated that at least 37 per cent of the male population has at least some kind of overt homosexual experience (ranging from physical contact to orgasm) between the onset of adolescence and old age. This estimate rises to 50 per cent of males who remain single until age thirty-five.[3] These estimates were quite a shock both to Kinsey and his associates and to the American public. Kinsey reports that his skepticism was gradually dissipated by the fact that regardless of the locale from which the data came the incidence was more or less the same. He felt that comparison of his results with previous incidence estimates was almost useless because on the basis of the information given it was impossible to determine where on the heterosexual-homosexual balance the men in the earlier samples would fall.

Contrary to the opinion of Freud and other clinicians who have written on female homosexuality, the second Kinsey report found the incidence of homosexual responses and contacts to be much less among females than among males. Between adolescence and old age homosexual responses to the point of orgasm occurred in about 13 per cent of the females, as contrasted with 37 per cent of the males. There were only about a half to a third as many females who were primarily or exclusively homosexual as there were males.

[2] A. C. Kinsey, W. B. Pomeroy, C. E. Martin, and P. H. Gebhard, *Sexual Behavior in the Human Female* (Philadelphia: W. B. Saunders, 1953), pp. 636–39.

[3] A. C. Kinsey, W. B. Pomeroy, and P. H. Gebhard, *Sexual Behavior in the Human Male* (Philadelphia: W. B. Saunders, 1948).

Etiology. There have been a number of theories advanced to explain the etiology of homosexuality, and we will examine their claims. To what extent does the nature of the organism itself play a role in the etiology of homosexuality? F. J. Kallman has advanced a genetic theory to account for homosexuality.[4] He studied eighty-five homosexual subjects who happened to be twins; of these forty-five were dizygotic, that is, they came from different eggs and were thus no more genetically similar than any brothers. When he examined the dizygotic subjects' twins, he found that only a few more of them were homosexual than one would expect to find in the general population. The remaining forty homosexual subjects were monozygotic twins, that is, they were genetically identical. When he examined the monozygotic subjects' twins, he found that all of them were overt homosexuals. Kallman did not claim that homosexuality was genetically determined on the basis of this remarkable finding, but he did claim that it was analogous to lefthandedness, to which genes give a powerful predisposition, which can, however, be overcome by training.

Kallman's genetic theory of the origin of homosexuality is not accepted by specialists, for two reasons. First, Kallman himself made the judgment as to whether or not each twin was homosexual, and he is an ardent proponent of the importance of genetic factors. Second, the hypothesis has not been replicated or verified by any other investigator; indeed, some evidence on twins[5] contradicts his findings. A genetic predisposition to homosexuality is thus very much in doubt, but the possibility exists that some chromosomal abnormality makes a contribution.

The nature of the organism may play a role in the etiology of homosexuality in yet another way. It has been speculated that some sort of hormonal imbalance may contribute to homosexual behavior. There is sufficient evidence to say that this hypothesis is not true.[6] A good summary is provided by John Money:

The sex hormones mature the body and thereby indirectly influence a person's social maturity. The level of sex drive or libido is hormonally influenced and androgen is probably the libido hormone in both men and women. The male and female sex hormones have a direct male and female

[4] "A Comparative Twin Study on the Genetic Aspects of Male Homosexuality," *Journal of Nervous and Mental Disease*, 115 (1952):283–98.

[5] See C. M. B. Pare, "Etiology of Homosexuality: Genetic and Chromosomal Aspects," in *Sexual Inversion*, ed. J. Marmor (New York: Basic Books, 1965), pp. 70–82.

[6] See *ibid.*, and J. Money, "Components of Eroticism in Man: Cognitional Rehearsals," in *Recent Advances in Biological Psychiatry*, ed. J. Wortis (New York: Grune and Stratton, 1960), pp. 210–25.

effect, respectively, on the genitalia, maintaining them erotically functional. The direction of content of erotic inclination in the human species is not controlled by the sex hormones. Hormonally speaking, the sex drive is neither male nor female but undifferentiated.[7]

If neither genetics nor hormones contribute significantly to homosexuality, then does the physiology of the organism itself have any importance at all? The answer is that it probably has little or none. Even though we have a cultural stereotype that the male homosexual is slightly built and effeminate and the female homosexual is huskily built and masculine, homosexuality is found in all body types. Although build and physical coordination may affect the way his parents, siblings, and playmates react to a child, they are less crucial than the actual gender role assigned to him by the people in his environment.

It is important to stress the matter of assignment of gender role. An extreme case in which gender role could be assigned either way is reported by Money, Hampson, and Hampson.[8] They studied one hundred hermaphrodites and found that their gender role and orientation were consistent with that which had been assigned to them. This correlation held true even when the assigned gender role was inconsistent with physiological findings: chromosomal sex, gonadal sex, hormonal sex, predominant internal accessory structures, and external genitals. Money, Hampson, and Hampson concluded that the acceptance of assigned gender role begins in the first few months of life and that an infant is cognizant of signs that point to his being a boy or a girl. These signs are neither all environmental nor all hereditary; they include nouns and pronouns used by parents, parental behavior, and, later, haircut, dress, personal adornment, and the appearance of the genital organs.

To our knowledge no one has yet specifically investigated sex assignment as a possible antecedent of homosexuality, and such an investigation would most likely produce ambiguous results. By this I mean that determination of human behavior is very complex and that it is naïve to expect that any behavior such as homosexuality is going to be perfectly associated with any single antecedent. In other words, dressing a boy as a girl and treating him as such for, say, the first year of his life is not going to make him a homosexual. It may provide gender role confusion in the infant, but we would expect that there would have to be other factors in his environment that would push him further along the way. Before discussing these

[7] "Components of Eroticism in Man: The Orgasm and Genital Somesthesia," *Journal of Nervous and Mental Disease*, 132 (1961):296.

[8] J. Money, J. Hampson, and J. L. Hampson, "Imprinting and the Establishment of Gender Role," *Archives of Neurology and Psychiatry*, 77 (1957):333–36.

factors, we must understand that all human beings have the propensity for homosexual behavior.

In their volume on the human female Kinsey and associates point out the widespread occurrence of homosexuality in animals. Sexual contacts between individuals of the same sex have been known to occur in almost every species of mammal which has been studied. These occur among both males and females. Where the sexes are segregated, homosexual behavior commences quickly. Where the sexes have free access to each other, heterosexual behavior occurs more frequently than homosexual behavior. Homosexual behavior does exist among primates even where heterosexual opportunities exist; however, exclusive homosexuality is a rarity in the animal kingdom, and its occurrence among humans must be the result of some specific feature of human life.[9] In fact, the evidence from comparative zoology suggests that sexual attraction to both sexes is the norm and that exclusive heterosexuality is culturally imposed.[10] Man is a mammal and is therefore bisexual, that is, capable of experiencing erotic feelings toward either sex. Anthropological studies show that in cultures that tolerate homosexual activity all men participate in it as well as in heterosexual activity.

There is no single, authoritative theory of the role of the environment in the etiology of homosexuality to which all students of human behavior would subscribe. The two existing theories are similar in that both attribute the principal cause to some disruption in the family unit. They are different in that one holds that the child's motives have their wellsprings in the unconscious, while the other holds that the child's motives are created by the approval and disapproval he receives. The "unconscious" point of view would be congenial to almost all psychiatrists; the "social learning" point of view would be acceptable to many sociologists and to most psychologists. This summary is, of course, an oversimplification, but it is not my purpose here to burden the reader with fine theoretical points of difference among social scientists.

The discussion of the etiology of homosexuality that follows will contain elements of both views, although it is difficult, if not impossible, to do justice to both. The description below must be taken as an effort to introduce interested readers to what is generally thought to be true. It should be regarded as tentative, not definitive. Those interested are referred to the literature on the subject, a small sample of which is cited in the notes to this chapter, and to the suggested readings.

Earlier it was said that homosexuality is caused by a disruption

[9] See J. Marmor, ed., *Sexual Inversion* (New York: Basic Books, 1965).
[10] See R. H. Denniston, "Ambisexuality in Animals," in *ibid.*, pp. 27–43.

in the family. The nature of this disruption is, of course, different for boys and for girls, although there are some similarities. Actually, there are a variety of conditions that may obtain before persistent, overt male homosexuality results. Any one or many of these conditions may exist for any particular case. What follows is a typical picture of such a disruption.

For heterosexual development to occur, the male child must have a male model or models with whom to identify. The typical father of the male homosexual is distant and detached from his son. He may show him little affection or even outright hostility. There are many motives the father may have for treating his son in this manner. He may not like him; he may be jealous of or indifferent to him. In any case, the son elects not to model himself after his father. The mother makes her contribution as well. The message, subtle and overt, that she is sending the boy is "don't be like your father," and the boy perceives this. When the parents love each other and show it, the chances for abnormal sexual development are immensely lessened.

Another condition appears to be a particularly intimate mother-son relationship. The mother may actually prefer her son to her husband as a companion. The potentially homosexual son may be the mother's favorite, he may be her confidant, and their relationship may involve a lot of affectionate caressing. This intimacy generates sexual guilt in the boy. There is no way that he can behave sexually toward his mother, given the incest taboos. Thus he learns to fear his own erotic impulses, and this fear and guilt generalize to other women. The male homosexual is marked by a fear of the opposite sex. He may loathe women or get along with them very well on a friendly basis, but these friendships must remain platonic; they must contain no hint of sexuality. In any case, he cannot really break away from his mother.

Along with this distant, detached father and intimate, overemotional mother, there are other factors outside the family that contribute to male homosexuality. There is a time just before adolescence when boys shun the company of girls in order to establish their own identity as males. This sexual separation is both self-imposed and supported by the culture. It is sought by the boy's peers and is encouraged by the families of girls. Girls are no longer allowed to play rowdily with boys during this stage; they are encouraged to give up tomboyism and take up more feminine pursuits. The intimacy of boys grows greater at this point, and they may look to some older men as heroes and idols. The boy with a sound family background will soon grow out of this, but the boy who has not modeled himself after his father is put in the position of adoring things masculine without having either the ability or the home encouragement to achieve this identification.

This is not to say that he will become effeminate. The folk belief that homosexuals can be told by their appearance is wrong. It has been estimated that only 15 per cent of homosexuals are obviously effeminate, and many of these develop their exaggerated poses in order to show defiance for society's disapproval. But for the homosexual boy things masculine will take on a great importance. He will admire masculinity in others but may not be able to develop much of it himself. His sexual focus, both in reality and in fantasy, will be male. His uncertainty about his own masculine sexual identity may take the form of a great concern about the appearance of his own body. For the most part, male homosexuals are not attracted by effeminate men. The "physical culture" magazines that display pictures of very muscular men are often favored as fantasy material.

The restriction of boys in this preadolescent period simply means that boys are more easily available than girls as sexual partners. After puberty boys are very much aware of their sexuality, and such experimentation as mutual examination or manual manipulation of genitals may take place. The heterosexually inclined boy may have such experiences and pass on, still heterosexual; they would take on much greater importance for a homosexually inclined boy. Male sexual partners must also be available through adolescence and into adult life. From the Kinsey data we might assume this availability, but we must also remember that homosexual impulses must be maintained in a hostile and punitive environment. There are very powerful social forces that push toward heterosexual conformity. Fear about one's sexual identity and sexual guilt have to be very strong to resist such pressures. This is why, as Marmor points out,[11] many behavioral scientists prefer the psychoanalytic assumption that persistent homosexual behavior is always associated with unconscious fear of heterosexual relationships.

Thus there are a number of conditions, both within the family and without, that may contribute to the development of a permanent homosexual adjustment. Generally speaking, I believe that at least one of the family disruptions mentioned will almost always be present.

Patterns of Behavior. There are some systematic relationships that exist between socioeconomic status as reflected by educational level and male homosexuality. Kinsey found that the males who have the greatest amount of homosexual experience after the onset

[11] *Sexual Inversion.*

of adolescence are those who enter high school but do not go beyond it. In this group 55 per cent of men still single by age thirty have experienced orgasm through physical contact with another man. The comparable figures for single men who have not gone beyond grade school is 45 per cent and for college-educated men 40 per cent. The incidence of homosexual activity rises as the men get older, but there are some minor differences in this trend in the different educational levels.

It also appears that there is a relationship between early adolescence and sexual activity, whether this be masturbation, heterosexual contact, or homosexual activity. Early maturers also appear to show the greatest sexual activity throughout the later periods of their lives, according to the Kinsey data. Kinsey also found that, although the incidence of homosexual activity appears to be less for rural than urban males, there is a generally lower total sexual outlet for farm-reared males, but there is evidence of considerable homosexual activity among lumbermen, cattlemen, prospectors, miners, hunters, and others engaged in outdoor, "masculine" occupations. There is a folk belief that homosexuals do not do manual work; that this is not true is also confirmed by the work of Michael Schofield, who found little difference between homosexual and control groups in proportion of manual laborers.[12] In summary, homosexual males are to be found at all educational levels, in all occupations, and in all social classes.

The fact that homosexuality is a forbidden topic is nowhere better demonstrated than when, as often happens, an otherwise educated person asks, "What on earth do homosexuals do, anyhow?" Even after consulting books on the subject, many people increase their vocabulary without knowing what the words mean. If it is difficult to be both polite and specific, it is preferable, I believe, to be specific.

Before answering the question, it is necessary to recall what homosexuality is. Homosexuality refers to sexual relations, either overt or in fantasy, between persons of the same sex. In order to show the utility of the heterosexual-homosexual balance, I referred to both thoughts and deeds, following Kinsey. Often, however, it is possible to find persons who think erotic homosexual thoughts who have seldom or never committed homosexual acts, and it is also possible to find persons who have committed what we would consider homosexual acts but who in no wise consider themselves homosexual. Let us consider both groups.

Kinsey reported that a very few men could become sexually

---

[12] *Sociological Aspects of Homosexuality* (Boston: Little, Brown, 1965).

aroused by observing their own genitals and that 16 per cent admitted to having some erotic response to the sight of the genitals of other men. Some males in their homosexual activities fondle the genitals of another man. This fondling may lead to mutual masturbation, which may or may not lead to orgasm; in the more experienced it probably would. Schofield reported a case of a man who made repeated visits to a particular public lavatory because there it was possible for a man in the next compartment to reach through a hole in the partition without being seen and masturbate him. Schofield also found that among a group of fifty homosexuals who had never been arrested or treated psychiatrically for their homosexuality, the preferred form of sexual activity was a kind of genital apposition, in which the two men would lie facing each other and would experience orgasm not by genital manipulation but by the general proximity of the partner's body. So one answer to the question of what male homosexuals do is that they caress, kiss, fondle, and cuddle up to each other just as heterosexual lovers do.

A very common male homosexual practice is *fellatio*. This consists of oral stimulation of the male partner's penis by the *fellator*. The male partner will almost always come to orgasm, and it is the sexual excitement of his partner that is exciting to the fellator. He may become sufficiently excited himself to achieve orgasm, or he may masturbate later. The point is that his sexual desire is focused on receiving the erect penis, just as the woman is the recipient in heterosexual intercouse.

Fellatio is not exclusively a homosexual practice, and the person on whom fellatio is performed may not regard himself as homosexual. Here one would have to know more about such an individual to rate him on the heterosexual-homosexual balance. He may not have homosexual fantasies while fellatio is being practiced upon him; he may not have had more homosexual than heterosexual experience. Kinsey reports that about forty-three per cent of college-educated husbands persuade their wives to perform fellatio on them. Does the sex of the performer of fellatio determine whether it is a homosexual or heterosexual act, or should the fantasies of the person offering the erect penis determine this? Now the reader can see more clearly some of the difficulties involved in the use of homosexual and heterosexual labels.

Many of the male partners of fellators do not regard themselves as homosexual. An example is provided by some male prostitutes, vividly described in a novel by John Rechy (see the suggested readings). A. J. Reiss studied a group of white, lower-class, delinquent boys who accepted money from adult males in exchange for allowing the adults to act as fellators. He found that boys regarded themselves neither as homosexuals nor as prostitutes; however, there was an elaborate set of norms governing the transactions, and the boys would not accept any deal in which they acted the female part, that is, the recipient of the penis. Reiss concluded that the boys were not involved in the activity primarily on the basis of its homosexuality, because as they got older they often did not become fellators themselves.[13] It should be pointed out that the peer group of these boys has very strong codes that help prevent their defining themselves as homosexual or taking part in any homosexual activity as a penis recipient. As far as most adult males involved in this activity are concerned, "This year's trade is next year's competition." From their perspective, male prostitution is but the first step toward a more overt homosexual adjustment.

When two overt, experienced male homosexuals have sexual relations using fellatio as the technique, they will usually take turns as recipient of the penis. They may decide on simultaneous oral stimulation of each other's genitals, a practice known as "69," so named because the reciprocal head-to-toe position of the 6 and the 9 suggest the position of the partners. Another common male homosexual practice is anal intercourse, pelvic thrusts after the erect penis has been inserted in the anus of the recipient. This is also known as pederasty, buggery, "corn-holing," and sodomy, although sodomy has other definitions as well.

The male homosexual may prefer to offer the erect penis, he may prefer to receive it, or he may prefer to alternate the two roles. To be the recipient is considered more completely homosexual behavior because sexual satisfaction is achieved by being receptive, a feminine behavior, and the recipient himself will sometimes experience erection and orgasm during such intercourse. Being the active offerer of the penis in homosexual anal intercourse is, of course, also a homosexual behavior. It might be possible to find male prostitutes playing the active role who do not consider themselves homosexual. This is the insistence of many male prison inmates, but their self-assessment is difficult to accept. Such men might well be located in the middle of the heterosexual-homosexual balance and be capable of erotic response to both sexes.

I believe that anal intercourse is less common than fellatio among male homosexuals. This belief is based on selected first-hand reports, although there is some evidence to support it.[14] In anal intercourse, of course, there is rear entrance and the recipient is turned

---

[13] A. J. Reiss, Jr., "The Social Integration of Peers and Queers," *Social Problems*, 9 (1961):102–20.

[14] See Schofield, *Sociological Aspects of Homosexuality*.

away and lying face down. These drawbacks, along with cultural and aesthetic objections, make it a less favored sexual activity.

It is possible for external circumstances to turn supposedly heterosexual individuals to homosexual behavior, and Kinsey's heterosexual-homosexual balance is again helpful in understanding circumstantial homosexuality. Persons whose homosexual impulses are latent may turn to overt behavior under circumstances of sexual segregation, such as in boarding schools, the armed forces, and prisons. After such experience the individual may return to heterosexual life, become involved in both heterosexual and homosexual activities, or become exclusively homosexual. B. Karpman reported that previously heterosexual men who resort to homosexual practices during long periods of imprisonment find it difficult to resume heterosexual relations when released.[15] Of course, their readjustment is complicated by the relative inaccessibility of heterosexual relations to men who are ex-prisoners.

Loneliness is a hallmark of overt male homosexuality. Many male homosexuals seem almost incapable of forming long-term, intimate relationships with other male homosexuals. One of the greatest advantages of heterosexuality is marriage and the knowledge that one is loved according to a stable model of affection within a socially acceptable and legitimate relationship. There are three reasons why enduring love relationships between male homosexuals are uncommon. First, such relationships tend to be competitive. Unlike husbands and wives, who have reasonably well-defined social and work roles, homosexual males have to decide who cooks the food, who drives the car, and who cleans the house, nor does the nature of the relationship itself determine who is the more successful in the outside world. The endless series of claims and counterclaims, conflicts and compromises, puts a heavy strain on the relationship. Second, most practicing homosexuals have an element of narcissism in their personalities, and competition over who is the more attractive may lead them to seek confirmation of their sexual attractiveness from other males. Third, they appear to be looking for a sexual ideal that no real human male could possibly be, and in their relationships, therefore, they tend to deal with others in terms of their fantasies. The average married person would be hard put to imagine the unhappy, lonely life that such homosexuals lead.

As a result of this situation a homosexual community is created in every city of any size.[16] The need to solicit new sexual partners leads

[15] "Sex Life in Prison," *Journal of Criminal Law and Criminology*, 38 (1948): 475–86.

[16] See M. Leznoff and W. A Westley, "The Homosexual Community," *Social Problems*, 3 (1956):257–63.

to the creation of homosexual meeting places: bars, hotel lobbies, steam baths, certain street corners, certain public lavatories. These are the places where the secret and the overt homosexual meet. Many of the practicing homosexuals in a city get to recognize, if not to know, one another. They have common interests and common norms, and their interaction is marked by an antagonistic cooperation. The claim by many members of the homosexual community that they are an especially sensitive, joyous, favored group is a rationalization of lonely men whose sexual behavior the larger society finds loathsome.

Female Homosexuality

Etiology. Female homosexuality has been less thoroughly studied than that of the male, and if there are differences of opinion about the latter, our notions about the origins of female homosexuality are even less clear. It should be remembered that Kinsey estimated that about 4 per cent of the male population is exclusively homosexual; the comparable estimate for women is between 1 and 3 per cent for unmarried females and under 3 per 1,000 for married females. Female homosexuality apparently occurs less frequently than male and in most places does not present itself as a social problem. The following description of the family that may well produce a daughter with a persistent, overt homosexual adjustment is presented tentatively.

For normal heterosexual development to occur, a girl, like a boy, must have a model or models with whom to identify. One of the conditions that contributes to a homosexual choice in a girl is that the mother does not present herself as such a model. There are at least two ways in which this can happen. The mother may be too intimate and too loving; her relationship with her daughter may border on the homosexual, that is, they may sleep together and caress each other. Here the daughter will seek the same kind of relationship in later life. In the second instance the mother may actually maltreat the girl and instill in her much guilt about her sexuality. In later life such a person will seek out an older woman who will provide the loving, kindly mother that she has not had.

As with male homosexuality, the relationship between the father and mother and the daughter is important. If the mother communicates to the daughter that to be loved by a husband, to bear children to him, and to rear these children is *one* important aim of feminine existence, then the chances for abnormal sexual development are immensely lessened. The father's appreciation of these attributes in his wife and their potential in his daughter is also important. I stress the point that the maternal role is only *one* feminine goal. If the mother is a career woman and the father's approval of his wife is obvious, there is no reason to suspect a disruption in the daughter's gender role identification. The father's crucial contribution here is in legitimizing the female identity that his wife has chosen. It is when the message that the father sends to the daughter is "don't be like your mother" that the possibility of disruption is increased. In no instance is this to be thought of as absolute. Girls who are treated as boys and encouraged to be competitive athletes, fishermen, and hunters or who take on other nominally masculine activities do not necessarily become lesbians. Other conditions must obtain.

As we have seen, there is a time in preadolescence when girls withdraw from boys in order to establish their feminine identities. It is also at this time that the girl may develop a crush on an older woman, perhaps a teacher, and pattern her dress or mannerisms or possible career choice after her. At first, the girl who has such crushes may feel that such ultimate femininity is utterly beyond her. But gradually her perception of her heroine becomes more realistic, and she begins to sense that this adored creature is not without blemish and that within her is the potential of becoming a desirable woman and an adequate mother. Such a girl will have a family that will reassure her about her own femininity, and she will thus have less need to adore it in others. She will also have a peer group that will provide her with an opportunity to practice feminine behavior; this will end her period of sexual isolation.

The homosexually inclined girl will not necessarily appear masculine, and certainly not all masculine-looking girls are potential homosexuals. Many women resent male superiority and dominance, and their ways of handling their resentment vary considerably. Some may become intensely competitive in some areas, and our culture interprets competitiveness as masculine. It is common for adolescents to rebel against authority; it is a normal means of establishing one's identity and autonomy. Many girls see the life of the male as powerful, independent, and adventurous, and they want it for themselves. About one out of four women says that if she were born again she would prefer to be a man, and so it is not surprising that many adolescent girls cling to masculine dress and ways of approaching things.

What is singular, then, about the potentially homosexual girl? She will most likely shun attempts of heterosexual contacts because she is frightened about her sexual identity and does not think that boys will find her attractive. In addition, she will remain in the preadolescent condition of adoring her own sex. This may range from an adoration of older women to a search for love and affection from a particularly intimate girl friend. She fears contact with men, yet wants to be like them; she adores the feminine, yet is uncertain of her own feminine identity.

As with the male, female sexual partners must be available through a homosexual girl's adolescence and into adult life. This appears to be less of a problem for the female than for the male. The female homosexual is seeking companionship and intimacy more than genital fondling. The need for overt sexual expression seems to be less than in the male, for whom sexual satisfaction is found in erection and orgasm. Females may obtain satisfaction merely by physical proximity or caressing. Our culture is much more accepting of these behaviors among women than among men, and the woman who participates in them may not recognize her own interests as erotic, much less deviant.

Many behavioral scientists would prefer the psychoanalytic assumption that homosexual women harbor unconscious fears of heterosexual relationships. Others would agree with Simone de Beauvoir[17] that female homosexuality is an attitude freely chosen and freely adopted in a given situation. In any case, the lesbian is a woman who fears sexual contact with men because she is uncertain of her own feminine identity.

Patterns of Behavior. There is a clear relationship between educational level and female homosexuality. Kinsey found a definite correlation between increased educational level and the incidence of female homosexuality. By age thirty, overt homosexual contacts had occurred between 9 per cent of grade-school-educated females, 10 per cent of high-school-educated females, 17 per cent of college-educated females, and 24 per cent of graduate-school-educated females. Kinsey speculated that the restraint on premarital heterosexual activity and the later marriage of the better educated groups both contribute to the development of homosexual behavior.

No relation between early maturation in adolescence and homosexual activity was found in women, as had been the case in men. Rural-urban differences were not sufficient to warrant any generalizations. Half of the women in the Kinsey sample who had experienced homosexual activity had done so only for a single year or part of a single year of their lives.

Among the few women in the Kinsey sample who had extensive homosexual experience, 77 per cent evidenced slight or no regrets. Overtly homosexual women who planned to continue this behavior represented every social and occupational group—store clerks, factory workers, nurses, secretaries, social workers, and prostitutes. As

[17] See her "The Lesbian," in *The Problem of Homosexuality in Modern Society*, ed. H. M. Ruitenbeek (New York: E. P. Dutton, 1963).

with men, homosexual behavior seems to be distributed across all social classes.

Women are much less likely to be erotically aroused by psychological stimuli than men; they seem to require and prefer tactile stimulation. Many of the homosexual women in the Kinsey study reported using petting techniques that amounted to little more than simple kissing and general bodily contact. Even some women with long and exclusively homosexual experience had not progressed beyond these techniques. It took some time, and, in a few cases, years, before homosexual petting was extended to breast and genital stimulation. The ultimate progression was to *cunnilingus*, the oral stimulation of the genitalia, which had occurred in about 78 per cent of women with extensive homosexual experience. However, among most homosexual women the emphasis seems to be more on generalized emotional stimulation than on genital contact and orgiastic release.

We might mention at this point what female homosexuals do *not* do, and that is simulate intercourse through vaginal penetration. Kinsey commented that the use of an object as a substitute for the male penis was quite rare. Ward and Kassebaum[18] mention female partners assuming an analogue of the woman-below–man-above heterosexual coital position, but the genital stimulation was said to come from the sensitive insides of the thighs and the mons area rather than from an artificial penis. Masters and Johnson report no physiological difference between female orgasms whose source is clitoral masturbation and those caused by vaginal penetration,[19] so there is no reason to assume the great importance of the penis, taken for granted by most males, to women with extensive and exclusively homosexual histories.

Again, external circumstances can turn supposedly heterosexual individuals to homosexual behavior. Like men, many women do participate in homosexual activities when segregated in boarding schools, the armed forces, and prisons. Ward and Kassebaum estimate that about 50 per cent of the inmates of a women's prison they studied in California will be homosexually involved at least once during their imprisonment. They give this factor so much importance that they see the prison social structure as being totally based on homosexual behavior. Very few of these women have had any homosexual experience before their incarceration, and there are no data to indicate what proportion return to heterosexual behavior after release.

[18] D. A. Ward and G. G. Kassebaum, *Women's Prison* (Chicago: Aldine, 1965).
[19] W. H. Masters and V. Johnson, *Human Sexual Response* (Boston: Little, Brown, 1966).

Female homosexuals are very seldom arrested and almost never convicted for their behavior, although it is against the law in all but five states. Our culture is permissive about open affection among women, and we are not too surprised to see them hold hands in public, put their arms about each other, and even embrace and kiss each other. Even when female homosexuality is obviously present, it is often perceived as inauthentic and many men and heterosexual women believe that it will disappear if the woman meets an attractive, eligible male. Female homosexuality is not a health problem: it does not spread venereal disease. For all these reasons, female homosexuals may live out their lives without ever posing a problem to the community. (We should acknowledge, of course, as did Kinsey, that a high proportion of the unmarried women who live together never have contacts which are in any sense sexual.)

Homosexual relationships between women appear to contain more affection, perhaps more satisfaction, and certainly much more stability than those between males. Over 70 per cent of the single women in the Kinsey sample had had sexual contact with only one or two partners. The great need to solicit new sexual partners typical of male homosexuals does not exist, and consequently there are many fewer female homosexual meeting places. Ethel Sawyer studied the behavior of a group of predominantly lower-class Negro lesbians in St. Louis who had such a meeting place and found that stable relationships were valued, although not often achieved.[20]

Encountering Homosexuality

It is likely that every person who reads this chapter will at some time have an instance of homosexual behavior brought to his direct attention. Estimates vary, of course, but it is conservatively suggested that there are between two and four million actively practicing homosexual men in the United States. I know of no human behavior so common that elicits more fright and less consideration of the effects of one's reaction to it than homosexuality. Much of this is caused by ignorance.

I know of no adolescent boy who has not "learned" that anyone who wears a particular, arbitrarily chosen color to school on a particular, arbitrarily chosen day is a "queer." In a suburban high school peopled by upper-middle-class children a new, young, male faculty member was recently accused by three boys of being a "queer" and having made inappropriate advances to them. One of the teachers brought this accusation to the principal's attention, and he responded by suspending the teacher and the three boys until an

[20] "A Study of a Public Lesbian Community" (unpublished manuscript, Washington University, 1965).

investigation could be made. By the time that it took place, the matter was already public knowledge and people were choosing sides, not on the basis of evidence but on the basis of whether they happened to like the teacher or not. The boys repeated the charges in a public hearing, where cross-examination of them was not allowed. Two of the three would not have made credible witnesses in a court of law because of previous records of delinquency and distortions of the truth. The teacher was shown to be creative, innovative, demanding, and different. He was exonerated and reinstated, but the damage to his reputation had been done.

We may suspect that this kind of incident occurs all too frequently. I once addressed a special meeting of high school guidance counselors and presented them with a hypothetical conversation between a couple of youths and a teacher, based on an imaginary reconstruction of the boys' report of the above incident. With the conversation in print before them, it took forty-five minutes of discussion of how to handle the situation before anyone noticed that the teacher had been asking leading questions and that the interpretation of homosexuality had come from him and not from the boys. This story is not told to impugn the adequacy of public school personnel to deal with sexual matters, although there are those who would do so; it is told to alert us to the difficulty of keeping one's wits about one when the fearsome subject of homosexuality arises.

Any advances made by a homosexual adult toward a minor or child must be deplored, like similar heterosexual advances. But when such cases arise, we must proceed with caution and be aware that repeated warnings by parents about forbidden encounters with adults without any explanation of their precise nature predisposes the child to be terrified of any adult who accosts him on the street. In the case of adolescents, we must be aware that pranks do occur and that adolescents are not known for their ability to assess the serious consequences of their acts. When children or adolescents are molested, offenders must be treated first and then punished, if the latter is necessary.

In the case of the youngster who is found to have homosexual relations, we should remember that his chances for normal heterosexual contacts are greatly reduced if public disclosure of his acts is made and that about a quarter to a third of all boys have had some homosexual contact after reaching adolescence.

In the case of homosexual relations between consenting adults, I see no reason for the community to be involved as long as the parties do not violate the rules of public decency. No threat to children is posed by homosexuality. Homosexuals are made by inadequate parents, not by the depredations of older homosexuals. As for their contribution to society, in a recent opinion Supreme Court Justice William O. Douglas wrote that it is common knowledge that in this century homosexuals have risen high in government, both in Congress and in the executive branch, and have served with distinction.

Every educated person should know of a clinic or other agency where psychiatric treatment is available. I do not mean to imply by this statement that homosexuality is necessarily a psychiatric problem, but treatment should be available to those who wish it and is surely indicated when a child or adolescent is failing to make an appropriate sex role identification. The prognosis for change from homosexual to heterosexual behavior depends upon many factors, one being the place of the individual on the heterosexual-homosexual balance. Once homosexuality has become a persistent and preferred mode of adult behavior, it is all but impossible to bring the individual to a heterosexual adjustment. This has been generally recognized as true ever since 1935, when Freud wrote his famous letter to the American mother of a male homosexual.[21] Some clinicians would take exception to this statement,[22] but we must remember that therapists see a selected sample of the total homosexual population and that the vast majority of homosexuals neither seek nor want any treatment.

The Kinsey reports contended that homosexuality is normal merely because it is widespread, but in our culture it is more usual to hear the comment that homosexuals are sick. It should be clear that the position of this writer is that homosexuality is not an illness of any kind. Many homosexuals have no demonstrable psychopathology.[23] If the ability to have satisfying relationships with the opposite sex is taken as a criterion of maturity, then homosexuals are by and large immature, but this does not mean that they may not have a reasonably satisfactory life adjustment. The gravest consequence of persistent homosexual behavior is that it is socially disapproved and carries with it many handicaps which may lead to strain and conflict. These strains and conflicts might well disappear entirely if homosexuality were treated with tolerance.

The fear and horror with which homosexuality is viewed in our culture is hard to explain, but in part it may stem from the refusal to acknowledge any such impulses within ourselves. Kinsey points out

[21] "Letter to an American Mother," in The Problem of Homosexuality in Modern Society, ed. Ruitenbeek, pp. 1–2.

[22] See, for example, Marmor, ed., Sexual Inversion.

[23] See E. Hooker, "Male Homosexuals and Their 'Worlds,' " in Sexual Inversion, ed. Marmor, pp. 83–107.

that there appears to be no other place in the world today in which public opinion and law penalize it so severely. The penalties are based on old religious codes which failed to discriminate between sexual relations as pleasurable in themselves and sexual relations as a means of procreating the human race. They do not in any way deter persons from living homosexual lives.

The fact of the matter is that we could not eradicate homosexuality in the next generation if we wished. We do not have either the skills or resources to identify, isolate, or provide treatment for homosexuals. Society, therefore, must learn to live humanely with homosexual behavior. Four socially responsible steps that could be adopted have been suggested by Seward Hiltner, the theologian.[24] First, we should discriminate between transient homosexual experimentation in childhood and adolescence and a persistent homosexual preference in adulthood. Second, we should provide treatment to all those who have homosexual tendencies they wish to change. Third, we should distinguish between adult homosexuals who are predatory and those who are socially responsible. Last, by accepting even practicing adult homosexuals as persons, we can confront the rationalizations many homosexuals make about the nature, meaning, and social significance of homosexuality. When fear and persecution of homosexuality are replaced by knowledge and socially responsible attitudes toward it, all persons will profit regardless of their place on the heterosexual-homosexual balance.

There are other sexual behaviors which are problematic for us. When we learn of them, we are concerned, puzzled, perhaps shocked, and certainly curious. It is important that the reader not feel embarrassed about his sexual curiosity. Every person has dreams; every person has fantasies; every person has experiences. Some sexual behaviors may seem bizarre, but upon closer examination it can be seen that many of them have their counterparts in the behavior and daydreams of so-called normal people. This is why I prefer to call these behaviors problematic. It is our task as educators and educated persons to help each other and the young make sense of them, and sense cannot be made when there is a conspiracy of silence.

PROMISCUITY

Promiscuity is indiscriminate sexual relations, whether in a man or woman. The promiscuous person does not know his succession of sexual partners as human beings, but only as shadowy figures with erotic significance. People cannot sustain a mature relationship

[24] Quoted in G. Simpson, *People in Families* (New York: Crowell, 1960).

unless they have an underlying conviction of being worthy of love. The promiscuous person has no such conviction and goes from one sexual partner to the next, partly out of the fear of being found unlovable and partly out of the compulsion to prove that he or she is acceptable in one sphere at least.

An intense, uncontrollable, and insatiable sexual desire in males is known as *satyriasis* and in females as *nymphomania*. These severe disorders are quite rare and require psychiatric treatment. These terms are frequently misapplied by laymen to the promiscuous person who is seeking reassurance that he is worthy of love and support for his masculinity, in the case of males, or femininity, in the case of females.

Promiscuity is not to be confused with prostitution. Typically the motive behind prostitution is not some emotional craving but money or material goods. In any culture where poverty and unemployment exist, prostitution, an occupation in which skill and training are not necessary, is certain to be found. Of course, not all penurious women become prostitutes, but it would be a mistake to think that those who do chose their occupation because of some emotional compulsion that made them lust for men. It is their emotional indifference to their customers that is the rule. For good summaries of the sociology and the psychology of prostitution, the reader is referred to Davis and Simpson, respectively.[25]

FETISHISM

Fetishism is an instance of magical thinking. The term "fetish" was originally applied to inanimate objects worshiped by primitive peoples who thought they possessed magical qualities. The definition has been broadened to apply to anything irrationally reverenced. In sexual fetishism "magic appears to reside, not in a whole person, but in a part of the person, an object connected with the person, or a symbolic substitute for the person."[26] The magic referred to, of course, is the capacity for sexual arousal.

The definition of sexual fetishism above is intentionally broad to show that it is widespread in our culture. A mild instance of fetishism can be illustrated in the fact that many men find women, including their wives, more alluring when wearing a negligee than when naked. Male college students sometimes conduct "panty raids." We would hardly call the average man's interest in lingerie fetishistic, but in some instances it begins to approach that level. In one family

[25] K. Davis, "Prostitution," in *Contemporary Social Problems*, ed. R. K. Merton and R. A. Nisbet (New York: Harcourt, Brace, 1961), pp. 262–88; Simpson, *People in Families*.

[26] A. Storr, *Sexual Deviation* (Baltimore: Penguin, 1964), p. 27.

which came to our attention through marriage counseling, when a husband strongly requested that his wife do a striptease of sorts with her black lingerie before sexual relations, his wife objected to being placed in this role. Other males are aroused when the female wears boots and spurs, or high heels, or a tight corset, or a skin-diving wet suit.

Many sexologists recommend that married couples wear or do anything they wish before sexual relations as long as it enhances their erotic responses. Fetishism becomes more problematic when the attraction to some aspect of the beloved becomes compulsive and irrational and when the male finds himself impotent without the fetish object. In extreme cases only the object itself has erotic qualities, and its wearer is entirely unnecessary. For instance, we might find a fetishist stealing women's underclothes from a laundry room or clothesline, which he will probably use as stimulants while masturbating.

Fetishism is almost an entirely male phenomenon. Women have no need of fetishes, for two reasons. First they do not need to achieve and sustain an erection to be sexually capable. The fears and inhibitions that affect their sexual satisfaction and enjoyment are important, but they are not so immediately focused as in the male. Second, men are more responsive to visual and psychological sexual stimuli; women are more responsive to tactile stimuli. Fetishes tend to be feminine symbols which signify the female's sexual availability. The padded bra, the plunging neckline, the bareback dress, the mini skirt, and the Bikini swimsuit all capitalize on this aspect of male sexual makeup without cultural disapproval. It is when the male's potency is disassociated from the whole person of his partner that his behavior is seen as problematic. Fetishism is another instance of sexual behavior divorced from love.

Fetishism, then, is an exaggeration of tendencies that exist in practically all males. The habitual fetishist feels excessive sexual guilt and inadequacy.[27] He tends to be extremely anxious in any sexual situation and fears impotence. He ensures satisfactory performance by insisting upon a stimulus that has served to arouse him in the past and in this way guarantees that he will get an erection. If his fetishism becomes increasingly severe, he finds himself depending more on the fetish than on his sexual partner. In general, men who practice fetishism exclusively are shy, withdrawn people who, with the exception of an occasional theft, do no harm to anyone else.[28]

[27] *Ibid.*

[28] *Ibid.*, and P. H. Gebhard, J. H. Gagnon, W. B. Pomeroy, and C. V. Christenson, *Sex Offenders* (New York: Harper & Row, 1965).

VOYEURISM

The voyeur derives sexual satisfaction from looking at sexual objects or situations. It is another problematic sexual behavior which divorces sex from love. Nearly all men on occasion have spent some time gazing appreciatively at passing women, and not a few women have been known to initiate or return a glance that signifies attraction, and some women will admit to be sexually stimulated by love scenes in movies, but the habitual seeking out of sexual objects or situations to view seems to be a male pastime.

There are a number of voyeuristic activities that our culture regards as acceptable in the male. Soldiers hang pin-up pictures in their lockers, young men carefully examine the foldout page in *Playboy*, college students watch coeds sunbathing through binoculars, and nearly every man walking down a street at night will slow his step to look through a window at an attractive woman undressing. Even voyeuristic activities that are slightly more overt are culturally acceptable, if not openly sanctioned. A man may frequent burlesque or strip shows without being regarded as deranged, and many of the stag nights at men's clubs offer movies that go beyond suggestion and actually portray sexual intercourse among humans, animals, or humans and animals.

In the most extreme cases voyeurism may become a substitute for conventional means of sexual gratification. It is then known as *scoptophilia*. Such a habitual voyeur may get to be known as a Peeping Tom. Peepers will almost never watch females whom they know well; they prefer to peep surreptitiously, and many will masturbate while watching. There is a popular notion that peepers will subsequently become rapists. This is not true; it is quite rare for peepers to use force. Peepers are more a nuisance than a danger. Of the rare peeper who does eventually resort to forceable entry, Gebhard and his associates speculated that he is the type who enters homes or other buildings in order to peep or attempts to attract the female's attention by tapping on the window or leaving notes.[29]

Habitual voyeurism is a sexual substitute resorted to by those whose sexual outlets are restricted by circumstance or emotional immaturity,[30] people for whom heterosexual relations of a traditional kind are for some reason inadequate or impossible. Voyeurism offers sexual gratification without the demands and difficulties of an interpersonal relationship.

[29] *Sex Offenders.*
[30] Storr, *Sexual Deviation.*

EXHIBITIONISM

Exhibitionism is the act of obtaining sexual satisfaction from exposing the genitals to another person in public. This is a problematic sexual behavior limited entirely to males. Although females may expose their genitals in striptease shows, they do so for the pleasure of males and do not thereby obtain sexual gratification. A great majority of exhibitionists are in or achieve a state of erection while exhibiting themselves, and a small but not insignificant number reach orgasm through masturbation at that time.[31] The persons to whom exhibitionists expose themselves are female passers-by of any age, but generally they might be regarded as attractive sexual partners. One British researcher[32] found that in slightly less than half the cases studied the female was under sixteen years old.

There are three motives that are thought to be typical of the exhibitionist. First, the act of exhibiting is in itself a primitive way of asserting masculinity. Exhibitionists are generally inept in heterosexual relationships. Exhibiting their genitals is one way of gaining feminine recognition of their masculine identity, recognition that may not be evident in their social relationships with women. Gebhard reported that one-third of the repeated offenders he and his associates studied suffered from erectile impotence. The second motive is related to the effect of the act on the female. Some exhibitionists are naïve enough to assume that the women to whom they exhibit will also be sexually excited. Exhibitionists who are more knowledgeable about female sexual psychology may derive satisfaction from the retaliatory nature of their act; they may actually intend to frighten and shock as a way of getting even with women in general because certain specific women in their lives have found them wanting. The third motive is a crude form of sexual solicitation. This is not to say that exhibitionists intend physical contact; they do not. The exhibiting is an end in itself, done in such a way that the chances of developing a relationship with the viewer are virtually non-existent—a way of establishing sexual contact at a safe distance (safe that is, to the exhibitor). It rarely occurs at arm's length; the exhibitionist is usually at a distance of two to twenty yards.[33]

Exhibitionists are more of a nuisance than a menace. An encounter with one is not likely to be damaging to any female who is warned of the possibility of its occurrence. They rarely commit more serious crimes, and when they do these tend to be of a non-sexual nature. However, they are afflicted with a compulsion to

[31] Gebhard et al., *Sex Offenders*.
[32] Storr, *Sexual Deviation*.
[33] Gebhard et al., *Sex Offenders*.

repeat their offenses in spite of legal penalties. Exhibitionism is the most common of the problematic sexual behaviors that our laws define as a crime. Exhibitionists are better candidates for psychiatric treatment than for prison.

It is hard to make a case for the view that the roots of exhibitionism exist in us all. Yet most adults wish to be thought of as physically attractive. Periodic changes in clothing styles determine how much flesh can be tastefully exposed, and we do not attribute sexual motives to muscle-displaying males or Bikini-wearing females on a public beach, although each is in a way exhibitionistic. These are the socially acceptable counterparts of a compulsion that provides a few socially inept males a means of engaging in a sexual encounter with a female with no necessity to establish a personal relationship. Exhibitionism is another instance of sexual behavior without love.

TRANSVESTITISM

Transvestitism is the act of obtaining sexual satisfaction from dressing in the clothes of the opposite sex. It is also limited to males. Women may dress in men's clothing for a variety of motives, from freedom of movement to protest against masculine dominance, but they do not appear to gain sexual satisfaction from the act itself. Male transvestites, on the other hand, do get sexually excited from dressing in women's clothes. The commonest practice is for the male to so attire himself and then masturbate.[34] The garb may be a complete outfit or it may be single items that were described above as appealing to fetishists.

What is not frequently realized is that a majority of transvestites have heterosexual interests.[35] Storr reported that one transvestite occasionally dressed in his wife's clothes and that this gave him a feeling of intense sexual arousal and potency. Ann Landers recently wrote that she was "shook" by the "avalanche" of letters she received from virtually every state in the union from married men who obviously enjoyed dressing up in their wives' clothes and who had somehow convinced their wives of the wisdom of this practice. As far as I have been able to determine, there has been no systematic research to determine how widespread this activity is.

The transvestite may have a variety of motives for his sexual behavior. He may be trying to create an imaginary female that will embody all the attributes that the real women in his life have lacked. He may fantasize her as kind or cruel, seductive or indifferent, and

[34] Storr, *Sexual Deviation*.
[35] See Kinsey et al., *Sexual Behavior in the Human Male*; M. Hirschfield, *Sexual Anomalies* (New York: Emerson, 1948); and Storr, *Sexual Deviation*.

may actually portray these traits by posturing before a mirror.[36] Thus transvestitism may be seen as an exaggeration of the tendency to identify oneself with the beloved. A male who has perceived in his mother the qualities of forcefulness, decisiveness, and dominance usually associated with the father may, paradoxically, feel more masculine when he is dressed like her.[37] Gebhard reported that in a selected sample of nine men who had been arrested and convicted for wearing female clothing in public, transvestitism had appeared in their behavior before puberty. It is widely agreed that the origins of transvestitism lie in very early childhood.

Homosexuality and transvestitism are totally independent phenomena. Some homosexuals occasionally dress in female clothes—"in drag"—but the clothing is worn to attract a person of his own sex or is meant to be symbolic of the wearer's attitude toward the male role. It is not a means of sexual gratification in and of itself.

Transvestitism (literally, "cross-dressing") is another behavior that has its socially accepted counterparts. Most people would staunchly deny that there are any such traits in themselves, yet cross-dressing is considered acceptable humor in our culture. Many theatrical productions take advantage of this, and we do not think it strange of the players or the audience. Amateur improvisations—the man who puts on a lampshade as a woman's hat—at private parties are not alarming. Every large city has transvestite entertainment, and the distinction between the casual and the habitual spectator of female impersonators is not often made. Apparently some wives are not overly concerned when their husbands don "comfortable" women's panties instead of cotton shorts. In many municipalities it is a misdeameanor for a man to appear in public in women's clothes. Apparently such behavior occurs sufficiently often for such laws to be enacted. Transvestitism only becomes a real problem, however, when it is associated with solitary sexual satisfaction.

SADISM AND MASOCHISM

The sadist obtains sexual satisfaction from inflicting pain; the masochist obtains sexual satisfaction from receiving pain. The two terms are commonly linked because it is generally believed that persons who are sexually stimulated by the one activity will also be stimulated by its opposite. Males are capable of being aroused by a wide range of psychological stimuli, while females are more likely to be aroused by tactile means. This behavior is, by and large, limited to males, but because sadism and masochism are both psychological and tactile, we do find a very few women participating in such activities.

[36] Storr, *Sexual Deviation.*
[37] *Ibid.*

It is difficult for people who regard sexual relations as synonymous with affection and tenderness to understand how the infliction and receiving of pain can be associated with sexual excitement. It is, therefore, instructive to examine the attitudes that go along with the giving and receiving rather than focusing on the pain itself. The sadist is concerned with establishing himself as the ascendant one in the relationship. He wishes his sexual partner to be helpless and at his mercy. His purpose is not so much to hurt the object of his desire as it is to dominate his sexual partner.[38] Until his ascendancy is established, the sadist's sexual partner remains compellingly frightening. It is Storr's opinion that the sadist cannot believe that anyone could invite or welcome his sexual advances, and it is only when his partner is fully helpless and at his mercy that he feels fully potent.

The few men who have these tastes have difficulty finding women who will submit to their demands. It is necessary for them to frequent expensive houses of prostitution, in which women will not only submit but will also feign pleasure while doing so. In such a house, in Newark, New Jersey, a card file was discovered, purported to contain the names of fifteen thousand clients. It would be a mistake to assume that all these men are sadists or masochists. Problematic sexual behaviors are not mutually exclusive, and many of the clients may have been men who are aroused by whips, chains, or ropes as fetish objects. The torture chamber trappings may be little more than ritual devices to ensure potency.

Masochists feel that they must be dominated by their sexual partners in order to achieve sexual potency. The masochist wishes to submit to the will of a powerful person. Storr believes that the masochist wants to take no responsibility for himself or his sexuality. In seeking out these situations he is relieving himself of guilt by virtue of the punishment he receives. The punishment may serve another function as well. Kinsey has pointed out that the psychological changes induced by fear and especially anger closely parallel those involved in sexual response. For the masochist, the figure of an authoritarian woman beating or making a slave of him allows him to become excited, perhaps even sexually excited, without having to feel guilty about it. According to this interpretation the masochist does not wish to be beaten; he wishes to establish his acquiescence. The sadist does not wish to beat; he wishes to establish his dominance. The former is assuaging his guilt; the latter is asserting his acceptability as a sexual partner.[39]

It is this view of sadomasochism that allows us to see its counter-

---

[38] *Ibid.*
[39] *Ibid.*

parts in what are called "normal" people. I believe that people select their dramatic entertainment on the basis that some of their emotional needs are vicariously satisfied through it and that producers and directors are sensitive to these needs. The James Bond books and movies and other sadomasochistic materials enjoy an enormous popularity with the American public. Harvey Cox in *The Secular City* has wisely commented that one of the attractions of the *Playboy* center foldout lies in the Playmates' apparent acquiescence; they are women over whom it is easy to fantasize dominance.

There is some evidence of sadomasochistic behavior among normal people as well. E. J. Kanin found an amazing number of sexual assaults on coeds by college men that had gone unreported.[40] In my experience on four college campuses I found that the vast majority of coeds who participate in premarital sexual relations more or less regularly refuse to admit to any cooperation on their part, including responsibility for contraception, and, that, what is more, a goodly number repeatedly get themselves into situations where they invite assault. It is not uncommon in marriage counseling to see wives who provoke their husbands into fighting them because they both enjoy making up afterward. While conducting sex education sessions, I have encountered a number of women who admit enjoying fighting with their men for the same reason. A little more extreme are the 3 per cent of females and 10 per cent of males who reported to Kinsey a definite or frequent erotic response to sadomasochistic stories. Over 25 per cent of both females and males reported definite or frequent erotic response to being bitten in foreplay. At the extreme of this continuum are the few sadomasochists described above, who require subjugation or dominance in order to be fully capable sexually.

SODOMY

Sodomy is sexual satisfaction through anal intercourse. It is not widely known that such activity may be gratifying to the recipient as well as to the male doing the thrusting. Anal stimulation may cause sexual arousal in both men and women.[41] The anal area is highly sensitive. Sexual excitement causes contraction of the muscles around the anus, and during orgasm the anal sphincter opens and closes convulsively. I have commented on the practice among homosexual males, but it is not limited to them. Some heterosexual men may occasionally prefer it to vaginal intercourse. God destroyed the city of Sodom because of this preference, according to the

[40] "Male Aggression in Dating-Courtship Relationships," *American Journal of Sociology*, 63 (1957):197–204.
[41] Storr, *Sexual Deviation*.

Bible, thus the name of the practice. The Puerto Rican women Oscar Lewis interviewed reported that the men they knew frequently preferred sodomy.[42] It is difficult to estimate how prevalent it is. Gebhard, in his study of urban males with less than college education, found that slightly over 3 per cent had practiced sodomy with their wives. In a college-educated group, among whom we would expect to find more sexual experimentation, the rate is probably slightly higher.

It is common to place other sexual behaviors under the label of sodomy. This grouping stems from legal usages and for our purposes is inaccurate and confusing. Most states have sodomy laws so worded that they apply to mouth-genital contacts (fellatio and cunnilingus), anal coitus (sodomy), and sexual contact with animals (bestiality). Thus one cannot know with any certainty what behavior is alleged to have taken place when one reads that a person has been indicted for sodomy.

I can only speculate as to the motives for sodomy. A search for new and different sexual experiences is one possible motive, although this explanation can be invoked to explain a number of problematic sexual behaviors. The most plausible theory I know is that offered by Storr, who suggests that sodomists childishly associate sex with excretion and become aroused at the notion of experiencing a pleasure associated with a forbidden area.

It is difficult to make a case for the view that counterparts of sodomy are found in so-called normal people. Most men and women would regard it as an aesthetic abomination, given their toilet training and subsequent feelings about excrement. However, we must point out that many males seem as intensely interested in female bottoms as breasts, that advertising takes great advantage of this interest, and that a slap or a pinch on the bottom is considered an erotic gesture.

CONCLUSION

Problematic sexual behaviors pose little threat to marriage and family life. There is no chance that they will replace heterosexual intercourse as a primary means of sexual gratification. Heterosexual intercourse remains the magical behavior that allows a full expression of love through intimate bodily contact and the sharing of a profound physical and psychic experience. It is a thrill of which humans do not tire; it is a joy heightened by loving cooperation; it is one of the great satisfactions of mankind.

The extremely small minorities who prefer some other form of

[42] *La Vida* (New York: Random House, 1966).

sexual expression need not be feared. Theirs is a less than completely human experience, an experience of sexual expression more or less divorced from love. Their behaviors may not be freely chosen; they are often visited upon them by their life experience. In many instances, their sexual behavior is an exaggeration of impulses found in almost everyone. It is our hope that greater public understanding will lead to compassion and humane treatment for these minorities. The reader is encouraged to further increase his understanding of problematic sexual behavior, and to that end a list of suggested readings, as well as the usual footnotes, is provided.

Suggested Readings: Part IV

SEXUAL ANOMALIES

Bartalos, M., and Baramki, T. A. *Medical Cytogenetics.* Baltimore: Williams & Wilkins, 1967.

Gardner, L. I., ed. *Endocrine and Genetic Diseases of Childhood.* Philadelphia: Saunders, 1969.

Jones, H. W., Jr., and Scott, W. W. *Hermaphroditism, Genital Anomalies and Related Endocrine Disorders.* Baltimore: Williams & Wilkins, 1958.

Money, J. "Influence of Hormones on Sexual Behavior." *Annual Review of Medicine* 16 (1965):67–82.

Money, J., ed. *Sex Research: New Developments.* New York: Holt, Rinehart and Winston, 1965.

Oversizer, C., ed. *Intersexuality.* New York: Academic Press, 1963.

Wilkins, L. *The Diagnosis and Treatment of Endocrine Disorders in Childhood and Adolescence.* 3d ed. Springfield, Ill.: Thomas, 1965.

MASTURBATION

Dearborn, L. W. "Autoeroticism." In *The Encyclopedia of Sexual Behavior,* edited by A. Ellis and A. Abarbanel. New York: Hawthorn Books, 1961.
Gives data not only on youths but on adults and the aged.

Ellis, A. "New Light on Masturbation." In *Sex without Guilt.* Rev. ed. New York: Lyle Stuart, 1958.
Presents an extremely permissive and positive view of masturbation.

Ford, C. S., and Beach, F. A. "Self-Stimulation." In *Patterns of Sex Behavior.* New York: Harper, 1961.
Discusses cross-cultural aspects of masturbation, as well as mammalian behavior.

Group for the Advancement of Psychiatry. *Normal Adolescence.* New York: Group for the Advancement of Psychiatry, 1968.
Authoritative guidance by a group of leading psychiatrists, clarifying psychosexual development and other aspects of physical and emotional development.

Hagmaier, G., and Gleason, R. "Masturbation" and "Morality of Masturbation." In *Counseling the Catholic.* New York: Sheed and Ward, 1959.
Important for understanding the Catholic position.

Johnson, W. R. "Masturbation." In *Teen Sex Counseling,* edited by K. E. Krantz and J. P. Semmens. New York: Macmillan, 1969.

Kinsey, A. C., Pomeroy, W. R., and Martin, C. E. *Sexual Behavior in the Human Male.* Philadelphia: Saunders, 1948.

Kinsey, A. C., Pomeroy, W. B., Martin, C. E., and Gebhard, P. H. *Sexual Behavior in the Human Female.* Philadelphia: Saunders, 1953.

These two volumes contain the most complete available data on male and female masturbatory practices.

Lorand, R. L. "Masturbation." In *Love, Sex and the Teenager.* New York: Macmillan, 1965.

Discusses masturbation from a psychoanalytic point of view.

Oliven, J. F. *Sexual Hygiene and Pathology—A Manual for the Physician and the Professions.* 2d ed. Philadelphia: Lippincott, 1965.

Presents medical and psychiatric advice on treatment when necessary.

Pomeroy, W. B. "Masturbation—Attitudes and Incidence." In *Sex Ways in Fact and Faith: Bases for Christian Family Policy,* edited by E. M. Duvall and S. M. Duvall. New York: Association Press, 1961.

One of the best single brief summaries of the subject, by one of the Kinsey investigators.

PROBLEMATIC SEXUAL BEHAVIOR

Albee, E. *The Zoo Story.* Signet paperback P2339, $0.60.

A one-act play which depicts an unhappy homosexual who goads a stranger into killing him. A powerful drama of the homosexual's situation.

Anderson, R. *Tea and Sympathy.* In *Famous American Plays of the 1950's,* edited by Lee Strasberg. Dell paperback 2491-LE, $0.75.

A well-known play, also a movie, about a young man in a boys' school who fears being a homosexual because he finds himself impotent with the town whore after being goaded into visiting her. Also contains a good illustration of latent homosexuality in the person of the compulsively masculine housefather.

Baldwin, J. *Giovanni's Room.* Dell paperback 0637, $0.60.

The story of a young man who discovers his own potential for homosexual behavior in France. A sympathetic and understanding portrayal.

Baldwin, J. *Another Country.* Dell paperback 0200, $0.75.

It is interesting to read this after reading Giovanni's Room and see how Baldwin's feelings about homosexuality influence his depiction of his family.

Ellis, A. *The Art and Science of Love.* Dell paperback 0294, $0.95.

For people with college-level reading ability this is a good manual about sexual technique in marriage. It will answer many common questions about sexual intercourse and also contains brief comments about a number of problematic sexual behaviors.

Fromme, A. *Understanding the Sexual Response in Humans.* Essandes paperback 1018, $1.00.

This is a book about the Masters and Johnson report (see below). For most readers it is a better buy and contains a good discussion of the implications of the Masters and Johnson work, which they, for the most part, do not consider.

Gebhard, P. H., Gagnon, J. H., Pomeroy, W. B., and Christenson, C. V. *Sex Offenders.* Bantam paperback D3279, $1.65.

This is an excellent scholarly report on sex offenders. It contains good discussions of the implications of various societal attitudes toward this group.

Kinsey, A. C., Pomeroy, W. B., Martin, C. E., and Gebhard, P. H. *Sexual Behavior in the Human Female.* Pocket Books paperback 99700, $1.65.

This is one of the two books in this list that every interested reader should purchase. It is a rich source of information; it is quite readable; it is wise in its discussion of the implications of the work. At the conclusion of many chapters are useful comparisons of the behavior of males and females. Chapter 16, "Psychologic Factors in Sexual Response," is a superb comparison of the sexual psychology of men and women, a topic all too often misunderstood. Most highly recommended.

Lewis, O. *La Vida.* New York: Random House, 1966.

Tape-recorded interviews with a poor Puerto Rican family. Their attitudes toward sexual matters are most interesting. Homosexuality is held in very low esteem; heterosexual anal intercourse is frequently preferred by Puerto Rican males, fellatio by New York City males. It reads better than most novels. The introductory essay by the author explains why serial monogamy is functional in the "Culture of Poverty."

Lindner, R. *Must You Conform?* Black Cat paperback, $0.60.

An interesting essay on the social organization of homosexuals, including the Homosexual World Organization.

Marmor, J., ed. *Sexual Inversion.* New York: Basic Books, 1965.

The best summary of current psychiatric thought on homosexuality.

McCarthy, M. *The Group.* Signet paperback Q2501, $0.95.

A novel about eight Vassar graduates which shows how overt and latent homosexuality affects their lives. The movie is a *reasonably good rendering. It is possible to get a good discussion going around the argument that all eight are homosexual.*

Masters, W. H., and Johnson, V. *Human Sexual Response.* Boston: Little, Brown, 1966.

Written by a physician and a psychologist, this is a book about the physiology of human orgasm. Its discussion of the implications of these findings leaves something to be desired (see Fromme above).

Rechy, J. *City of Night.* Grove paperback D1296, $0.95.

An excellent first novel about a young man who comes to the city and becomes a male prostitute. The descriptions of the homosexual worlds of New York, Los Angeles, San Francisco, and New Orleans are fascinating. Throughout the novel, the hero maintains that he is not homosexual, and his crisis comes when he recognizes such impulses within him. A good decription of the loneliness and futility of the homosexual way of life. Highly recommended.

Ruitenbeek, H. M., ed. *The Problem of Homosexuality in Modern Society.* Dutton paperback D127, $1.95.

An excellent collection of essays on the sources, sociology, and treatment of homosexuality.

Schofield, M. *Sociological Aspects of Homosexuality.* Boston: Little, Brown, 1965.

A very good sociological study of homosexuality. Highly recommended for the serious student.

Simpson, G. *People in Families.* New York: Crowell, 1960.

A very good psychoanalytic interpretation of family relationships; it is interesting and well written. One of the early chapters is a good brief introduction to Freudian thought. The section on the psychology of prostitution is recommended, and there is also a good section on incest, a topic not discussed in Moore's chapter.

Storr, A. *Sexual Deviation.* Pelican paperback A649, $0.85.

This is the other book in this list that every interested reader should purchase. It is superbly readable and sensible about the implications of dealing with deviates. Its two introductory chapters on sexual guilt and sexual inferiority contain information which we believe that every sex educator should know.

Vidal, G. *The City and the Pillar.* Signet paperback, $0.50.

The hero is a man who makes a high school homosexual experience on a camping trip into a life goal. It offers a glimpse into Hollywood and the upper strata of New York homosexual society.

Wylie, P. *Opus 21*. Pocket Books paperback 6C-85, $0.50.

One of the delightful things about this novel is that Wylie himself appears as a character in it. While morosing about New York waiting to learn whether he has cancer of the throat, Wylie meets a young bride who has left her husband because she found him in a compromising situation with the gardener. If you know Wylie, you can predict the bride's therapy. First the character talks her leg off and then he arranges her life so that she learns more about homosexuality. Part of the charm of this novel is that Wylie tackles many other world problems as well. A good discussion of bisexuality is included. Highly recommended, if you like Wylie.

Glossary

abortifacient (a bor ti fa' shent) [L. *abortus*, abortion; *faciens*, making]: drug or agent inducing expulsion of a fetus

abortion (a bor' shun): expulsion of the fetus within the first three months of pregnancy

abortion, criminal: interference with the progress of pregnancy which is not justified by the state of the mother's health; an illegal abortion

abortion, spontaneous: unexpected premature expulsion of the fetus with no abortive agent employed

abortion, therapeutic: termination of a pregnancy which is hazardous to the life of the mother

afterbirth: placenta and membranes, normally expelled from the uterus following birth of a child

amenorrhea (a men or re' a) [G. a-, without; *men*, month; *rhoia*, flow]: absence of menstruation

amnion (am' ni on) [G., membrane around the fetus]: innermost fetal membrane, which forms a fluid-filled sac for the protection of the embryo

ampulla (am pul' la) [L., bottle]: dilated extremity of the vas deferens where it joins the urethra; the final storage place of sperm prior to ejaculation

androgen (an' dro jen) [G. *genesis*, production]: hormone which controls the development and maintenance of the secondary sex characteristics of males

anorexia nervosa (an o rex' i a ner vo sa) [G. a-, without; *orexis*, appetite]: hysterical aversion to food, which may lead to serious malnutrition

areola mammae (a re' o la) [L. *areola*, diminutive of *area*; *mammae*, of the breast]: pigmented area surrounding the nipple of the breast

bag of waters: amniotic sac and fluid which serve to protect the fetus during pregnancy and to dilate the cervix during labor

birth control: prevention or regulation of conception by any means; contraception

bladder, urinary: hollow organ which serves as a reservoir for the urine

breech birth, breech presentation: presentation of the buttocks and/or the feet first at the cervix at delivery; called **double breech** or **complete breech** if both buttocks and feet appear

The glossary was prepared by Laura Hicks Kail.

first and **frank breech** if the buttocks alone are the presenting part, the legs being bent so that the feet lie against the face

capillary(ies) (kap' i lar i) [L. *capillus*, hair]: minute blood vessels connecting the smallest branches of the arteries with those of the veins

carcinoma (kar si no' ma) [G. *karkinoma*, tumor]: malignant epithelial tumor; a form of cancer

celibacy (sel' i ba si) [L. *coelibatus*, unmarried]: state of being unmarried, especially in accordance with religious vows

cervix (sir' vix) [L., neck]: cylindrical lower portion of the uterus, which protrudes into the upper portion of the vagina and through which the baby is expelled in childbirth

cesarean delivery (si zair' iun): delivery of the fetus through an abdominal incision; also called **cesarean section**

chorion (kor' i on) [G., skin]: outermost fetal membrane, helping to form the fetal part of the placenta

chromosome (kro' mo som) [G. *chroma*, color; *soma*, body]: bodies in the nucleus of the cell which carry the hereditary factors, so called because they stain more deeply than other cell constituents

circumcision (sur kum sizh' un) [L. *circumcidere*, to cut around]: surgical removal of the foreskin, the loose skin surrounding the end of the penis

circumstantial homosexuality: homosexual behavior induced in normally heterosexual individuals by external circumstances (imprisonment, army service, etc.)

clitoris (klit' o ris, kli' to ris) [G. *kleitoris*, to shut up]: female homologue of the penis, located just above the outer opening of the urethra at the juncture of the labia minora

coitus (co' i tus) [L., from **coire**, to come together]: act of sexual intercourse; copulation

coitus interruptus: sexual intercourse in which the penis is withdrawn before ejaculation and the semen discharged outside the vagina

conception [L. *concopere*, to take in]: fertilization of the ovum by the sperm

condom [perhaps from the eighteenth-century English physician Conton, said to be its inventor]: sheath worn over the penis during coitus to prevent conception or venereal infection

conjugal role relationships: the way husbands and wives organize their performance of tasks, their role expectations, and their patterns of communication

continence [L. *continere*, to hold back, refrain]: self-restraint, especially in regard to sexual intercourse

contraceptive: agent to prevent conception, such as medicated vaginal jelly, condom, diaphragm, or oral contraceptive

contraceptive, oral: chemical preparation taken internally to prevent conception; "the pill"

copulation (cop u la' shun) [L. *copulare*, to bind together]: sexual intercourse; coitus

corpus luteum (kor' pus lu' te um) [L., body; yellow]: yellow body formed in the ovary from a ruptured Graafian follicle; the chief source of progesterone

cryptorchism, cryptorchidism (kript or' kiz um) [G. *cryptos*, hidden; *orchis*, testicle]: developmental defect in which the testes fail to descend and remain within the abdomen or inguinal canal

cunnilingus (cun ni lin' gus) [L. *cunnus*, vulva; *linguere*, to lick]: oral stimulation of the female genitalia

diaphragm (di' a fram) [G. *diaphragma*, barrier]: contraceptive device worn internally during coitus over the cervical os to prevent conception or venereal infection; usually dome-shaped and made of thin rubber or plastic

douche (doosh) [F. from L. *ducere*, to conduct, as water]: irrigating the vagina with a jet of liquid, either to cleanse it or to apply heat or medication

dry-run orgasm: absence of fluid during ejaculation; usually caused by absence of the prostate gland

dyspareunia (dis puh roo' nee uh) [G. *pareunos*, lying beside]: pain attendant upon sexual intercourse in females

eclampsia (ek lamp' sia) [G. *eklampsis*, a shining forth]: disease occurring during the latter half of pregnancy and characterized by acute elevation of the blood pressure, protein in the urine, swelling and convulsions or coma

ectoderm (ek' to durm) [G. *ecto-*, outside; *derma*, skin]: outermost of the three primary germ layers of the embryo, from which develops the skin and the outermost lining of the primitive mouth cavity, anus, neural tube, and all structures that derive from these

egg: female germ cell produced in the ovaries; also called ovum [L., egg], pl. ova

ejaculation (e jak u la' shun): reflexive act of expelling the semen

embryo (em' bri o) [G. *en-*, in; *bryein*, to swell]; the organism in the early stages of development, through the second month of pregnancy

endoderm (en' do derm) [G. *endo-*, inside; *derma*, skin]: the inner-most of the three primary germ layers, which forms the lining of the gut, from throat to rectum, and its derivatives

endometrium (en do me' tri um) [G. *endo-*, within; *metra*, womb]: mucous membrane lining the uterus, which sloughs off during menstruation

epididymis (ep i did' i mis) [G. *epi-*, upon; *didymos*, testis]: collec-tion tubes coiled in the scrotum into which sperm pass from the testes, where they mature somewhat before passing on into the vas deferens

episiotomy (eh pi si ot' o mi; eh pis' i ot o mi; eh piz' i ot o mi; ep i sigh ot' o mi) [G. *episio-*, public area; *-tomy*, a cutting]: incision of the vulva during childbirth to avoid tearing

epispadias (ep i spay' di us) [G. *epi-*, on; *span*, to draw]: congenital defect of the anterior urethra in which the canal terminates on the top side of the penis and closer to the body than its normal opening or, occasionally, above the clitoris; compare hypo-spadias

erection: reflexive filling of the penis or clitoris with blood, which transforms these organs from flaccid structures to rigid, rod-like pillars

erogenous area (e roj' e nus) [G. *eros*, love; *genesthai*, to produce]: area of the body stimulation of which produces sexual arousal

erotic [G. *erotikos*, amorous]: arousing sexual desire

estrogens (es' tro jens): family of hormones which promote the maturation and cyclic functions of the female reproductive tract and the development of the secondary sex characteristics; they have a direct effect on the ovary itself

exhibitionism: public exposure of the genitals to another person to obtain sexual satisfaction

fallopian tubes (fa lo' pi an): tubes which transport the ovum from the uterus; also called oviducts

family planning: process of determining family size, spacing of births, and means of regulation of fertilization, including sterilization

fecundity [L. *fecundus*, fruitful]: ability to have children

fellatio (feh lay' she o) [L. *fellare*, to suck]: introduction of the penis into the mouth of another and stimulation by the lips or tongue, producing orgasm

fellator: one who orally stimulates the penis of another

fertilization: impregnation; union of sperm and egg

fetishism (fee' tish; fet' ish) [Pg. *feitiço*, from L. *facticius*, artificial]: sexual behavior focused not upon another person but upon a part of that person, an object connected with him, or a symbolic substitute for him

fetus (fee' tus) [L., offspring]: the organism from the end of the second month of pregnancy to birth

foams: foam-like liquids which serve to block the passage of sperm to the vagina and prevent pregnancy

follicle, Graafian: see follicle, ovarian

follicle, ovarian [L. *folliculus*, small bag]: small sac containing the eggs in the ovaries; its walls produce estrogen under the stimulus of F.S.H.

follicle-stimulating hormone (F.S.H.): pituitary hormone which promotes the growth and maturation of the ovarian follicles and the production of estrogens by them

foreskin: loose skin covering the end of the penis, also known as the prepuce; when the foreskin is retracted, the glans penis is exposed

fraternal twin [L. *frater*, brother]: twins resulting from the simultaneous fertilization of two eggs; they may be of the same sex or opposite sex, have a different genetic constitution, and have separate placentas

frigidity [L. *frigidus*, cold]: inability of the female to enjoy, or in some cases, even to participate in, sexual intercourse

gamete (gam' eet, ga meet') [G. *gamete*, wife; *gametes*, husband]: male or female reproductive cell; in the higher animals, egg and sperm

gene (jene): unit of transmission of hereditary characteristics; each gene is a center for specific chemical activity in the cell

genitals (jen' i tals) [L. *genitalis*, from *gignere*, to produce]: common word for genitalia, the organs of generation; in the male, the two testes with their accompanying tubes, the prostate, the penis, and the urethra; in the female, the vulva, the vagina, the ovaries, the fallopian tubes, and the uterus

gestation (jes ta' shun) [L. *gestation*, from *gestare*, to carry]: pregnancy; gravidity

glans penis [L., acorn; tail]: conical body which forms the end of the penis

gonad (go' nad) [G. *gone*, seed]: gland or organ producing sex cells; general term for ovary or testes

gonadotropin (gon a do tro' pin) [G. *gone*, seed; -*tropos*, turning]: a substance having affinity for or a stimulating effect on the gonads

gynecology (jin i kol' o jee; guy ni-; jy ni-) [G. *gyneco-*, female;

-*logy*, science]: science of the diseases of women, especially those affecting the sexual organs

gynecomastia (jin i ko mas' tia) [G. *gyneco-*, female; *mastos*, breast]: excessive development of the male mammary glands, even to the functional state

hermaphrodism, hermaphroditism (hur maf' ro di tiz um) [G. *Hermaphroditus*, a bisexual god]: the coexistence in an individual of ovaries and testes; true cases are rare in humans, pseudo-hermaphrodism appearing more commonly

heterogeneous (het er o ge' ne us) [G. *hetero-*, other; *genus*, kind]: differing in kind or nature; composed of different substances; not homogeneous

homosexuality [L. *homo-*, same; *sexus*, sex]: state of being in love with or attracted by members of one's own sex

hormone (hor' mone) [G. *hormaein*, to excite]: specific chemical product of an organ or of certain cells of an organ transported by the blood or other body fluids and having a specific regulatory effect upon cells remote from its origin

human chorionic gonadotropin (H.C.G.) (kor i on' ik): hormone secreted by the placenta and appearing in the blood and urine early in pregnancy, its presence or absence being the basis of tests for pregnancy

hypospadias (hy po spay' di us) G. *hypo-*, beneath; *span*, to draw]: in the male, a congenital malformation of the penis and urethra in which the urethra opens upon the underside of the penis or at the base of the penis; in the female, a congenital malformation in which the urethra opens into the vagina; compare epispadias

hypothalamus (hy po thal' a mus) [G. *hypo-*, beneath; *thalamos*, chamber]: a small part of the brain with great influence on the essential vital processes of survival and reproduction

hysterectomy (his ter ek' to me) [G. *hystera*, womb; *ektome*, excision]: total or partial removal of the uterus

identical twin: twins which have developed from a single egg, are always of the same sex, have the same genetic constitution, and have the same placenta

implantation [F. *implanter*, from L. *in-*, in; *planta*, sprout]: imbedding of the fertilized egg in the tissue lining of the uterus

impotence (im' po tence) [L. *impotens*, powerless]: inability of the male to participate in or enjoy the act of sexual intercourse

infanticide [L. *infans*, infant; *caedere*, to kill]: the murder or murderer of an infant

inguinal canal (ing' gwi nul) [L. *inguinalis,* of the groin]: canal in the groin through which the testes descend into the scrotum prior to birth

insemination (in sem i na' shun) [L. *inseminare,* to implant]: introduction of semen into the vagina; impregnation

insemination, artificial: instrumental injection of semen into the vagina or uterus to induce pregnancy

intercourse, anal: see sodomy

intercourse, sexual [L. *intercursus,* from *intercurrere,* to run between]: sexual connection; coitus

interstitial cell-stimulating hormone (I.C.S.H.): pituitary hormone in the male which stimulates the production of testosterone by the testes; identical chemically to L.H. (luteinizing hormone) in the female

intrauterine device (I.U.D.) (in tra u' ter ine) [L. *intra-; uterus,* womb]: contraceptive device placed semipermanently within the uterus for the purpose of preventing conception

jel, contraceptive: any one of a number of viscous substances introduced into the vagina to prevent conception

Klinefelter's (XXY) syndrome: a form of testicular dysfunction caused by genetic abnormality, associated with hardening of the seminiferous tubules and characterized by elevated excretion of gonadotropin

labia majora (sing. **labium majus** (la' bi a ma jo' ra) [L. *labia,* lips; *majora,* large]: large outer lips of the female genitalia

labia minora (sing. **minus**)   [L., small]: inner lips of the female genitalia

lesbianism (lez' bi un iz um) [from Lesbos, home of Sappho]: homosexuality between women

lochia (lo' ki a; lok' i a) [G., discharge after childbirth]: discharge from the uterus and vagina during the first few weeks after delivery

luteinizing hormone (L.H.) (lu' ten iz ing): pituitary hormone which functions in the female to promote the secretion of estrogens by the follicles undergoing maturation and causing ovulation, promotes the formation of the corpus luteum, and causes the corpus luteum to secrete progesterone and estrogen

masochism (maz' o kiz um) [after Leopold von Sacher-Masoch, 1835–95]: obtaining sexual gratification while receiving pain; compare sadism

masturbation (mas tur ba' shun) [L. *masturbari*, to defile oneself]: production of orgasm by self-manipulation of the genitalia

menopause (men' o pawz) [G. *men*, month; *pauein*, to stop]: the cessation of menstruation, usually between the forty-fifth and fiftieth year; also called climacteric

menstruation (men stru a' shun) [L. *menstruus*, monthly]: periodic discharge of bloody fluid from the uterus, occurring during the period of a woman's sexual maturity, from puberty to the menopause

mesoderm (mes' o durm) [G. *meso-*, middle; *derm*, skin]: the germ layer between the endoderm and the ectoderm which gives rise to the connective tissues, muscles, urogenital system, and vascular system

metrorrhagia (mee tro ray' juh) [G. *metra*, womb; *rhegnynai*, to burst forth]: uterine hemorrhage independent of the menstrual period; also called intermenstrual flow

miscarriage: spontaneous expulsion of the fetus before it is viable; see abortion

mons [L., mountain]: the area of the female body immediately above the vaginal lips, covered by the pubic hair

morphology (mor fol' o jee) [G. *morpho-*, form; *-logy*, science]: the form and structure of an organism; the study of form and structure

mucoid (mu' koid) [G. *mucus*; *eidos*, form]: resembling mucus

neural tube (new' ral) [G. *neuron*, nerve]: embryonic tube formed from the ectodermal neural plate; it differentiates into the brain and spinal cord

nidation (ni day' shun) [L. *nidus*, nest]: implantation of the fertilized egg in the lining of the uterus

nymphomania (nim fo ma' nia) [G. *nympho-*, female; *mania*, madness]: excessive sexual desire on the part of a woman

obstetrics (ob stet' riks) [L. *obsetrix*, midwife]: branch of medicine that cares for women during pregnancy, labor, and the period of recovery after birth

optimum population: an ideal ratio of people to resources, somewhere between the maximum number of people the earth's resources will sustain and the minimum number necessary to ensure the survival of the species

orgasm (or' gaz um) [G. *orgasmos,* from *organ*, to lust]: culmination or climax of sexual excitement, accompanied, in the male, by ejaculation of the seminal fluid and followed, in both sexes, by relaxation and detumescence

ossification (os si fi ka' shun) [L. *os*, bone; *facere*, to make]: formation of bone; conversion of tissue to bone

ovarian follicles: see follicle, ovarian

ovary (o' va ri) [L. *ova*, eggs]: female sex gland; one of a pair of organs producing ova

ovulation (o vu la' shun): maturation and escape of the ovum from the follicle

ovum (pl. **ova**) [L., egg]: female germ cell or egg cell; in humans, a large spheroidal cell containing a large mass of cytoplasm, a large nucleus, and a large germinal spot

oxytocin (ok si to' sin) [G. *oxys*, quick; *tokos*, childbirth]: hormone from the pituitary which increases contraction of the uterine muscles in late pregnancy and during delivery and labor

paradigm (par' a dim) [G. *para-*, by the side of; *deigma*, to show]: an example or model

pathognomonic (pa thog no mon' ik) [G. *pathos,* disease; *gnomonikos*, skilled in a thing]: characteristic of a disease distinct from other diseases

pathology (pa thol' o jee) [G. *pathos*, disease; *-logy*, science]: that branch of biology which deals with the nature of disease through the study of its causes, its process, its effects, and the alterations of structure and function associated with it

penile agenesis (a jen' e sis) [G. *a-*, without; *genesis*, production]: a genetically caused abnormality in which the penis is no more than 2 cm. long, usually a skinny tube with no body to it except for a small glans at the tip; also called microphallus

penis (pe' nis) [L., tail]: the male organ of copulation and urination

Peyronie's disease: hardening of the penis because of internal formation of scar tissue

phimosis (fi mo' sis) [G., a stopping up]: tightness of the foreskin so that it cannot be drawn back over the glans of the penis

pituitary gland (pi tu i ter' i): small endocrine gland, oval in shape, located in the skull directly beneath the brain, which secretes a variety of hormones

pituitary gonadotropins: sex hormones produced by the pituitary gland

pituitary hormones: a wide variety of hormones produced by the pituitary gland

placenta (pla sen' ta) [L., flat cake]: organ on the wall of the uterus to which the embryo is attached by means of the umbilical cord and through which it receives its nourishment; also serves an endocrine function by producing hormones; composes the larger part of the afterbirth

placental barrier: tissue intervening between the maternal and fetal blood of the placenta which prevents or hinders certain substances, including bacteria, from passing from mother to fetus

plateau phase (in sexual response cycle): the fully excited stage of sexual stimulation which immediately precedes the orgastic phase

pre-eclampsia (pre ek lamp' sia) [L. *prae*, before; G. *eklampsia*, a shining forth]: same disease as eclampsia, but without convulsions or coma

pregnancy [L. *praegnaris*, pregnant]: being with child; the state of a woman from conception to childbirth

priapism (pri' a pizm) [G. *Priapus*, god of generation]: persistent erection of the penis, usually unaccompanied by sexual desire

procreation (pro cre a' shun) [L. *procreatio*, from *procreare*, to beget]: begetting of offspring

progesterone (pro jes' tur own): hormone from the corpus luteum which cooperates with the estrogens in regulating the female cycle, prepares the uterus for implantation of the ovum, and maintains pregnancy

prolactin (pro lak' tin): hormone which stimulates milk production in the mammalian breast

prostate gland (pros' tate) [G. *prostates*, one who stands before]: organ surrounding the neck of the bladder and the beginning of the urethra in the male which supplies 15 to 20 per cent of the seminal fluid; in middle age it often becomes enlarged and may interfere with the emptying of the urinary bladder

prostatic fluid (pros tat' ik): a milky alkaline substance produced by the prostate gland, counteracting the uric acid which has previously passed through the urethra and which would be destructive to sperm; helps to activate the sperm

pseudohermaphrodite (su do hur maf' ro dite) [G. *pseudo-* false; *Hermaphroditus*, a bisexual god]: an individual with external genitalia resembling one sex and gonads of the opposite sex

puberty (pu' ber ti) [L. *puber*, adult]: period at which the generative organs become functional and bodily signs of sexual maturity first appear as a result of changes in the sex glands

rectum (rek' tum) [L. *rectus*, straight]: the lower part of the large intestine

referred pain: pain whose origin is not in the area in which it is felt

rhythm method: limitation of intercourse to the infertile periods of the menstrual cycle

sadism (sad' iz um) [after Count de Sade, 1740–1814]: obtaining sexual gratification by inflicting pain upon another; compare masochism

satyriasis (sat y ri' a sis) [G. *satyros,* lascivious demigod]: excessive sexual desire in man

scoptophilia, escopophilia (skop to fil' e ah) [G. *skopein,* to examine; *philos,* loving]: derivation of sexual pleasure from looking at the genital organs

scrotum (scro' tum) [L.]: pouch of skin in which the testes and related structures are located

semen (se' men) [L., seed]: fluid produced by the male reproductive glands containing the male sex cells and secretions from the testes, the prostate gland, and the seminal vesicles

seminal emission (sem' i nal): thick milky fluid containing several million sperm which is ejaculated by the male through the penis during orgasm

seminal vesicles [L. *vesicula,* bladder]: two small sacs at the base of the bladder which secrete a fluid constituting 40 to 80 per cent of the semen; connected to the testes by the vas deferens

seminiferous tubules (sem i nif' ur us) [L. *semen,* seed; *ferre,* to bear]: tubes in the testes in which sperm are continuously produced in the post-pubertal male

sex flush: a temporary red rash that may occur in either sex during sexual excitement, spreading from the lower abdomen to the shoulders and face

sex gland: see gonad

shaft, penile: body of the penis, composed of spongy tissues and a network of blood vessels and covered by two long muscles and by skin

sodomy (sod' um i) [from the wicked city of Sodom in the Bible]: sexual intercourse by the insertion of the penis into the anal orifice; in legal terminology sometimes used to refer to any illegal sexual practice

somite (so' mite) [G. *soma,* body]: segment of the body of an embryo, one of a series of paired segments derived from the mesoderm; they run along the back of the embryo and the muscles and bones of the torso largely develop from them

sperm, spermatozoon (pl. **sperm, spermatozoa**) [G. *sperma,* seed; *zoion,* animal]: the mature male germ cell

sterile [L. *sterilis*]: not fertile; not capable of reproducing

sterilization: any procedure which renders an individual incapable of reproduction

testes (sing. **testis**) [L.]: the pair of male reproductive glands; after maturity the source of sperm and the chief source of male hormone

testosterone (tes tos' ter own): male sex hormone produced by the testes, controlling maturation and functioning of the male reproductive tract, development of secondary sex characteristics, and direct stimulation of the testes themselves; also influences sexual behavior

toxemia of pregnancy (tox e' mi a) [G. *toxikon*, poison; *haima*, blood]: eclampsia or pre-eclampsia are collectively referred to as the toxemia of pregnancy; see eclampsia and pre-eclampsia

transexual: one whose sex has been surgically changed

transvestitism (trans ves' ti tism) [L. *trans-*, across; *vestire*, to clothe]: obtaining sexual gratification from dressing in the clothes of the opposite sex

trimester [L. *trimestris*, of three months]: a period of three months; one of the three divisions of a pregnancy

tubal ligation [L. *ligatio*, from *ligare*, to bind]: sterilization of the female by cutting and tying the fallopian tubes

Turner's (XO) syndrome: genetic abnormality associated with incomplete ovarian development, short stature, and webbing of the neck; other congenital defects may be present

urethra (u re' thra) [G. *ourethra*, from *ouron*, urine]: canal through which the urine is discharged; from 8 to 9 in. long in the male, about 1.5 in. long in the female

uterus (u' ter us) [L., womb]: the organ which receives and holds the fertilized ovum during the development of the fetus and becomes the principal agent of its expulsion during labor; a pear-shaped, muscular organ ordinarily measuring 3 in. long, 2 in. wide, and 1 in. thick, it expands greatly during pregnancy

uterus, bicornuate [L. *bi-*, two; *cornutus*, horned]: uterus divided into two compartments because of arrest of fetal development

vagina (va ji' na) [L., sheath]: the flexible canal in the female in which the penis is inserted during coitus and in which the sperm are deposited; the cervix, which constitutes the lower end of the uterus, opens into the vagina; during the birth the vagina is the birth canal

vaginal atresia (a tree' shuh; a tree' zee uh) [G. *a-*, without; *tresis*, perforation]: the absence or closure of the vagina

vas deferens (vas def' e rens) (pl. **vasa deferentia**) [L. *vas*, vessel; *deferens*, carrying down]: abdominal tube running from the testes to the urethra

vasectomy (vas ek' to mi) [L. *vas*, vessel; G. *ektome*, excision]: sterilization of the male by cutting and tying the vasa deferentia

venereal disease (ve ne' re al) [L. *venereus*, from Venus, goddess of

love]: collective name for diseases such as syphilis and gonor-
rhea which are transmitted by sexual intercourse with an in-
fected person

vestibule [L. *vestibulum*, vestibule]: that portion of the vulva
bounded by the labia minora

voyeurism (vwa yur' izm) [F. *voyeur*, one who sees]: obtaining sexual
gratification from looking at sexual objects or situations

vulva (vul' va) [L., covering, womb]: external genital organs in
women

wet dream: discharge of semen without coitus during sleep; also
called nocturnal emission

withdrawal: see coitus interruptus

womb: see uterus

X chromosome: a sex-determining factor in both ovum and sperm;
ova fertilized by sperm having the X chromosome produce
female offspring

Y chromosome: a sex-determining factor in the sperm, producing
male offspring

yellow body: see corpus luteum

Index

Names

A

Abarbanel, A., 112n, 116n, 241n
Anderson, O. W., 114
Arey, L. B., 194n

B

Back, K. W., 244, 249, 250, 251, 275
Baer, D. M., 41n
Bandura, A., 41n
Barrett, D. N., 253n
Bass, M. S., 273
Beach, F. A., 42n
Bell, Robert, 35, 110n, 116n
Berelson, B., 123
Bernard, Jessie, 110n
Best, W., 269n
Bieber, I., 25n
Bigelow, M. A., 5n, 6–12 passim, 19
Bijou, S. W., 41n
Birnberg, C. H., 266n
Blake, J., 249n
Bordua, David J., 129n
Botella-Llusia, J., 175n
Bott, E., 132n
Boutselis, J. G., 267
Broderick, Carlfred B., 15, 27n, 28n, 31n, 35n, 43, 47n, 110n, 124, 245
Burgess, E. W., 121, 122, 126, 221n, 226n, 241n

C

Calderone, Mary, 88, 255, 265n, 269, 273n, 275
Campbell, A. A., 246, 251, 275n
Carpenter, George R., 117, 158n
Cayton, H. R., 136n
Chang, M. C., 199n
Chapin, R. M., 258
Christensen, Harold T., 110n, 117, 158n
Christenson, C. V., 364n
Clark, A. L., 221n
Clark, K., 50n, 136n, 137n, 139n
Clausen, J. A., 24n
Cook, Paul, 19
Cooley, Charles Horton, 155
Cottrell, L. S., 126, 241n
Cox, Harvey, 115, 370
Cuber, J. F., 38

D

Davis, Allison, 129n
Davis, K. E., 33n, 252n, 363
De Beauvoir, Simone, 224, 357

Denniston, R. H., 348n
Devereux, G., 271n
Dickinson, R. L., 86–87, 254
Dollard, John, 129n
Douglas, William O., 361
Doyle, J. B., 266n
Drake, St. C., 136n

E

Eastman, N. J., 192n, 199n
Ehrmann, W. W., 109, 110, 114, 120
Ellis, A., 112n, 116n, 122, 241n
Erikson, E. H., 41n
Ewers, F. J., Jr., 266n

F

Farber, S. M., 32n
Farrell, C. B., 25n
Feldman, H., 38
Fernandez, F. L., 215n
Foote, Nelson N., 126
Force, Elizabeth S., 19
Ford, C. S., 42n
Fowler, S. E., 27n, 28n, 124n
Frazier, E. F., 136n
Freedman, M. B., 110
Freedman, R., 246n
Freud, Sigmund, 28n, 140, 334, 344, 345, 361

G

Gagnon, J. H., 364n
Garcia, C., 257
Gardner, John, 254
Gebhard, Paul H., 110n, 114, 131n, 345n, 364n, 365, 366, 368, 371
Glassberg, B. G., 85
Goode, W. J., 244
Grafenberg, Ernst, 260
Graham, S. R., 123
Green, A. W., 136n
Greenwald, Harold, 122
Gross, M., 266n
Gruenberg, Benjamin, 6, 7, 10, 12, 17
Guttmacher, A. F., 245, 269n, 271, 275
Guyton, A. C., 188n

H

Hammond, Boone E., 42n, 136n, 137n
Hampson, J., 347
Hampson, J. L., 347
Handel, G., 138
Hardin, G., 256n

Haring, Bernard, 252
Harroff, P. B., 38
Hellman, L. M., 192n, 199n
Heron, A., 116n
Hill, R., 244, 249, 250, 251
Hiltner, Seward, 362
Himes, N. E., 256n, 271
Hirschfield, M., 367n
Hoffman, L. W., 24n, 248n
Hoffman, M., 24n
Hooker, E., 361n
Hotchkiss, R. S., 188n
Hubble, D., 182n
Hudson, J. W., 15

J
Jaffe, F. S., 269n, 271, 275n
Johnson, V. E., 42n, 226n, 230, 231n, 233, 239, 340n, 358n
Johnson, Warren R., 6, 7

K
Kagan, J., 24n
Kallman, F. J., 346
Kanin, E. J., 370
Karpman, B., 354
Kassebaum, G. G., 358
Keefer, C. S., 175n
Kerckhoff, A. C., 33n
Kimbrough, R. A., 175n
Kinsey, A. C., 30n, 36, 37, 42, 47n, 109, 110, 129–35 passim, 222n, 225n, 226n, 229n, 239n, 345–70 passim
Kirkendall, Lester A., 6, 7, 8, 36n, 110, 120n, 125n, 126n
Kirsch, Felix, 9, 10
Kleegman, S., 177n
Klein, M., 274n
Komarovsky, Mirra, 131n, 138, 276

L
Ladner, Joyce A., 42n, 49n
Laidlaw, R. W., 273
Landis, J. T., 37n, 215n, 222n, 239n
Landis, M. G., 37n, 222n, 239n
Lewis, Oscar, 132n, 328n, 371
Leznoff, M., 354n
Libby, Roger W., 110n
Lion, E. G., 122
Loeb, M. B., 123
Lull, C. B., 175n

M
McSweeney, D. J., 266n
Malthus, T. R., 244n, 246
Manley, Helen, 55n
Marmor, J., 25n, 348n, 361n
Martin, C. E., 345n
Maslow, A., 124

Masters, W. H., 42, 226n, 230, 231n, 233, 239, 340n, 358n
Mead, Margaret, 277
Melton, Alfred W., Jr., 38
Menninger, Karl, 276
Money, John, 293, 295, 346, 347
Morley, Margaret, 9
Morrow, Prince Albert, 5, 7
Moynihan, D. P., 139n
Mullahy, P., 336n
Muuss, R. E., 166

N
Niswander, K. R., 274n
Noonan, J. T., 256, 264, 268, 271, 273, 275
Novak, E. R., 175n
Nye, F. Ivan, 156

P
Pare, C. M. B., 346n
Patterson, J. E., 246, 251, 275n
Paul VI, 253
Perkins, G. W., 262n, 275n
Phillips, E. L., 337n
Pike, James, 115
Pincus, G., 257
Pineo, P. C., 38
Poffenberger, S., 215n
Pohlman, E., 275
Pomeroy, W. B., 345n, 364n
Potter, R. G., Jr., 265n, 267n
Pugh, W. E., 215n

R
Rainwater, Lee, 42, 110n, 138, 243n, 249n, 250, 251, 276
Ramsey, G. V., 42
Randall, C. L., 274n
Reevey, W. R., 35n
Reiss, Ira L., 15, 165n, 255, 277n, 352, 353
Robinson, John A. T., 115
Rock, John, 252, 264, 265n, 266, 267, 271
Rossi, Alice, 249n, 274
Rowe, G. P., 28n
Rubin, Isadore, 39

S
Safir, B., 122
Sagarin, E., 122
Sawyer, Ethel, 359
Sbarra, A. J., 266n
Schmeck, H. M., Jr., 249n, 274n
Schneider, A. J., 33n
Schofield, Michael, 31n, 110, 120, 124, 245, 351, 352, 353n
Schorr, A. C., 45n

Schultz, W. C., 126
Seaman, B., 271n
Shafer, K. D., 256n
Sherwin, Robert, 110n
Shettles, L. B., 176n
Shope, D. G., 35n
Short, J. F., 136n, 139n
Simpson, G., 362n, 363
Slater, E., 132n
Smith, D. T., 275
Southam, A. L., 256n, 260n
Southard, H. F., 88n
Spinley, B. M., 132n
Steiner, G. A., 123
Stokes, W. R., 11n
Storr, A., 363n, 365n, 366n, 367, 368n, 369, 370n, 371
Strain, Frances Bruce, 6, 10
Strodbeck, F. L., 136n, 139n
Stycos, J. M., 132n, 244, 249, 250, 251
Sullivan, Harry Stack, 336
Swartz, D. P., 259, 261, 263, 264, 266, 272n

T
Taylor, E. S., 199n
Terman, L. M., 239n
Thomason, B., 239n
Tietze, C., 260, 261, 265n, 267n
Tyler, E. T., 199n

U
Ullery, J. C., 267n
Umbiorsky, Father, 91

V
Vande Wiele, R. L., 259, 261, 263, 264, 266, 271n
Vincent, Clark E., 110n, 114, 138, 245
Vorys, N., 267n

W
Wallin, P., 121, 122, 126, 221n, 226n
Walters, R. H., 41n
Ward, D. A., 358
Weaver, Jean, 31n
Weinstein, K. K., 249n, 276n
Westley, W. A., 354n
Wexler, D. J., 266n
Whelpton, P. K., 246, 251, 275n
Whyte, W. F., 136n
Wiener, Daniel N., 337n
Wilson, R. H. L., 32n
Woodruff, J. D., 175n
Woodside, M., 132n
Wyatt, F., 248n

Y
Yeomans, E., 13n

Z
Ziegler, J., 276
Zink, M. S., 16n

Subjects

Pages on which tables and figures appear are given in italics

A

Aberrant sexual behavior, 343–72: of adolescents and young adults, 123; defined, 343

Abortion: illegal, 114; public attitude toward, 274; in urbanized and pre-industrial societies, 275 —types: criminal, 114, 252, 273–74; spontaneous, 213, 273; therapeutic, 252, 273, 274–75

Abstinence, 109, 254

Adolescents: sexual intercourse among, 31; sexual problems of, 330; social pressures on, 32. *See also* Sex information and experience

Adults: inadequate sex education of, 79–80, 90; programs for, 83, 87, 88

Affection: effect of, on sexual behavior, 120–21; effect of sexual intercourse on, 121–22; an element in sexual relations, 111; male embarrassment concerning, 143–44; reliance on, in permissiveness, 109

Aggressiveness, male: as measure of adequacy, 328; shift in emphasis on, 142–43

Agricultural Extension Service: sex information programs, 92

American Law Institute: model code on abortion, 274

American Medical Association Committee on Human Reproduction, 274

Ampulla, 185, 189

Anal intercourse, 353–54. *See also* Sodomy

Androgen, 291, 301, 309, 310

Anomalies of body form and function, 285–317. *See also names of anomalies*

Artificial insemination, 255, 289

Asexuality: in preadolescents, 43

Assignment and rearing anomalies: child born with abnormal sex organs, 303–5; sex reassignment, 312

Attitudes toward sex: dangers in rigid, 228; knowledge as basis for, 224–25; problems created by comparisons and expectations, 226–28. *See also* Sex information and experience

B

Bachelorhood, 36, 150

Birth. *See* Childbirth

Birth control: attitudes of mothers in deprived families, 94–95; demographic and religious factors, 246–49; instructing teenagers about, 33–34, 255; public policy on, 254–55. *See also* Contraceptive methods; Family planning; Fertility planning

Births: multiple, 204–5; ratio of live male to live female, 177

Bisexuality: defined, 344, 348

C

Cana Conference of the Roman Catholic Church, 91

Catholic Church: on family planning, 253–54; on family size, 253; on masturbation, 322; periodic abstinence and rhythm approved by, 254, 264n; on "responsible parenthood," 252–54

Celibacy, 334

Cervical cap: with cream or jel, 263; effectiveness, 271

Cervix, 190, 217, 233

Chastity, 159, 110

Childbirth: anesthesias in, 218; cesarean delivery, 219; labor, 215, 217, 218; maternal mortality rate in (U.S.), 219; mother's recovery, 219–20. *See also* Uterus

Chromosomal (genetic) anomalies: Klinefelter's XXY syndrome, 287; Triple X syndrome, 286–87; Turner's syndrome, 287–89; XYY syndrome, 287

Chromosomes: defined, 176; biological inheritance determined by, 176; regular, X, and Y, 176, 177, 178–79, 182

Churches: sex education programs in, 18–19, 86, 91–92

Circumcision, 186, 301–2

Claire Elizabeth Fund (Flint, Mich.), 86, 87

Cleveland Health Museum, 86

Clinical psychology. *See* Psychology, clinical

Coitus. *See* Sexual intercourse

Colostrum, 219

Community work in sex education: appraisals of school programs, 89, 90; involvement of parents and educators in, 53–54, 79–80; sources of financial support, 96; work with deprived families, 94–95

Community work in sex education
(*continued*)
—institutional cooperation: churches,
91–92; county and state health
departments, 85, 95, 96; family
service agencies, 93; parent groups,
93; social agencies, 89
—programs: councils on venereal
disease, 89; discussion groups,
lectures, and films, 86–87, 90, 91;
local radio stations and mass media
articles, 83–86; orientation meetings
for high school and college students,
88; training in leadership, 93–94
Conception and implantation: from
ejaculation to conception, 197, 199;
moment of conception and
implantation process, 199–200; sperm
and egg illustrated, *198*; uterine
cavity reception of fertilized egg, 200,
201, *202*, 203. See *also* Determination
of sex at conception
Conception control. See Birth control;
Contraceptive methods
Condom method of conception control,
268–69: effectiveness, 271; illustrated,
269
Conjugal role relationships: indicators
of family-size preference, 251;
variables in mutual adaptation, 132
—husband-wife integration: and
emotional closeness, 138; and joint
interests, 132
—husband-wife segregation:
intermediate vs. high segregation, 132,
133, 134, *135*; and separate interests,
132, 133; and sex gratification in, 137,
138
Contraceptive methods: dissemination
of knowledge of, 254; effectiveness
of, 271; failures and success in,
275–76; methods not requiring
medical consultation, 268–72;
methods requiring medical
consultation, 256–67; new
developments in, 276–77;
psychological aspects of, 275–76. See
also names of methods
Corpus luteum (yellow body), 195, 203
Counseling and therapy, 17, 18, 72–74
Courtship: as encouragement of
premarital intercourse, 114, 115, 117;
escalation theory of, 245; functional
courses on, 33; system, in urban
society, 112–13
Cream or jel: as contraceptive method,
271
Cultural patterns: personality and

behavior molded by, 155; premarital
intimacy patterns in Scandinavia and
America, 158–64; restrictiveness in
American, 161, 164–65; sex norms in
different cultures, 159–60; variations
among students, 68–69
Cunnilingus, 358, 371
Cryptorchidism, 289

D
Dating: "functional" courses on, 33;
"going steady," 32, 116, 124, 159,
160; preadolescent, 29. See *also*
Courtship
Decision-making in sexual matters: and
adolescents, 14–16, 31; interpersonal
relationship and, 125
Denmark: sexual permissiveness in, 117,
158–64 *passim*
Determination of sex at conception:
spermatozoan male and female
population, 176, *177*, 286
Development of male and female
reproductive systems. See Fetus;
Puberty
Deviant sexual behavior, 343–72. See
also name of behavior
Diaphragm and jel: application and use
of jel. *270*; diaphragms illustrated,
262; diaphragm in place, *263*;
effectiveness of, 271; function in
conception control, 262–64
Douche: as contraceptive method, 271

E
Eclampsia, 214
Ectoderm, 206
Educators, sex: avoidance of personal
counseling and therapy, 72–74;
consideration of students as
individuals, 68–69; as guides in the
search for values, 74–75; need for
psychological maturity of, 76, 81;
as pseudo-parents, 75–78; and
teaching techniques, 78n, 79;
teamwork with community personnel,
81; tests and grades, 79. See *also*
Sex education in school curricula
Egg: production, 189; release and
movement, 194–95; size compared
with sperm, 197, *198*; sperm breaks
outer membrane of, 199
Ejaculation: mechanism of, 186–89. See
also Sexual intercourse
Embryo: at end of one month, 206–8,
208; human shape and formation
of face at second month, 208–10,

209; size in first through fourth months, *207;* third- through ninth-month development, 210–12. *See also* Fetus
Endoderm, 206
Endometrium, 190
Epididymis, 185
Episiotomy, 218
Erogenous zones: orifices of head and body, touch of entire body, 229; stimulation of female, 229–31; stimulation of male, 231. *See also* Response to sexual excitement
Estrogen, 179, 189–203 *passim,* 257–58, 291
Exhibitionism: deferred and explained, 366; socially acceptable counterparts of, 367
External organ anomalies: embryological unfinished sexual differentiation, 294; epispadias, 302; hypospadias, 298–99; penile agenesis, 299–301; phimosis, 301–2; vaginal atresia, 301. *See also* Hermaphroditism
Extramarital coitus, 164, 333

F
Fallopian tubes, 190
Family life: and sex education, 19, 90; and sexual behavior, 67, 68; situations involving sex experiences, 24
Family planning: Consumers Union report on, 269, 271; defined, 255; ethical, moral, and legal issues, 251–55; motivations in choice of family size, 248–49; reasons for, 244–46; and religious groups in U.S., 252–54; variables associated with, 250–51. *See also* Fertility planning
Fellatio, 352–53, 371
Female reproductive system: illustrated, *191;* ovulation-menstruation cycle, 192–96
—organs: fallopian tubes, 190; ovaries, 190; uterus, 190–91; vagina, 191–92
Femininity: defined, 141, 145, 152–53; fiction as aid to understanding, 150–51; girls' desire to marry and have a family, 141; job discrimination against women, 152; rights formerly denied, 145–46; women's perception of the creative quality of men, 153. *See also* Male-Female differences and similarities
Fertility: American patterns, 246; impaired, 246–47; loss of, 315–16
Fertility planning: categories and case

histories, 247–49, 275; demographic studies of, 246–49; hypothetical interrelation of variables in, 249, *250;* sociopsychological factors in, 249–51. *See also* Family planning
Fetal development of sex organs. *See* Fetus
Fetal hormonal anomalies: effect of testicular feminizing syndrome on females, 291–92; feminizing of males through lack of development of testes in fetal life, 290–91
Fetishism: defined, 363; examples of, 363–64; objects used in, 369
Fetus: development of sex organs, 178–80; external sexual differentiation, *295;* internal sexual differentiation; *293;* three-month-old, *211. See also* Embryo
Fiction: and sex education, 62, 150–51, 352, 370
Foam, cream, and jel: application and use of, 263, 269–70, *270;* effectiveness of, 271
Foam tablets, 269, 270; effectiveness of, 271
Follicle-stimulating hormone (FSH), 180, 189, 192, 197
Frigidity, 240–41, 314
FSH. *See* Follicle-stimulating hormone

G
Gender identity anomalies: ambiguity of identity, 311; transvestite transexual, 312
Genetic defects. *See* Procreative sex impairments
Gonadal anomalies: cryptorchidism, 289–90; embryonic relationship between abnormal chromosome count and abnormal gonads, 289
Group for the Advancement of Psychiatry, 113
Guilt feelings: in masturbation, 321, 324, 325; in sexual relations, 134, 164, 276, 349, 350, 355
Gynecomastia, 310

H
Health, Education, and Welfare, Department of (HEW): support for family-planning programs, 254–55
Hermaphroditism: female, 296; male, 296–97; true, 297–98
Heterosexual-homosexual balance, 345, 351, 353, 354, 361, 362
Heterosexual intercourse: primary means of sexual gratification, 371

HEW. *See* Health, Education, and Welfare, Department of

Homosexuality: adolescent encounters with, 359–60; adult, 360–61; defined, 344, 351; development of, 24–25; distribution among social classes, 357–58; psychiatric treatment of, 361, 362

—etiology: assignment of gender role, 347–48; disruption of father-mother-child relationships, 348–49, 350, 355–56; fear of contact with opposite sex, 349, 356, 357; genetic and hormone theories, 346–47; segregation of sexes in boarding schools, armed forces, and prisons, 354, 358

—female homosexuals: incidence of, 345, 355; patterns of behavior among, 357–59

—male homosexuals: communities of, 354–55; incidence of, 345, 351; patterns of behavior among, 350–55

Hormones: fetal, 179; response to stimulation of, 192; supply during puberty, 180, 182

Human chorionic gonadotropin (HCG), 196

Hypothalamic-pituitary structures and functions, 180, 302, 305, 309

Hypothalamic sex anomalies: and male-female differentiation, 302–3

Hysterectomy, 314

I

Illegitimate births, 159, 160: rates among various age groups, 245

Impotence, 39, 240–41, 313–14

Incest taboos, 85, 349

Infertility, male, 199

Institutionally centered sex education programs: example, 86; joint parent-child sex programs, 86–87

Internal organ anomalies: imperfect embryonic development of male and female organs, 292–94

Interpersonal relations. *See* Personal relations in sexual matters

Intimacy-commitment bargaining spiral, 32–33, 34

Intrauterine device (IUD): advantages and disadvantages, 262; effectiveness, 271; Grafenberg's ring, 260; in place, 261; pregnancy with use of, 261, 262; present-day types, 260–61

IUD. *See* Intrauterine device

J

Jel. *See* Diaphragm and jel

Jews: completely planned families among, 249

Judaeo-Christian position on sex, 156, 159, 321

K

Kansas: statewide sex instruction programs, 14, 21

Kansas City: televised sex instruction in, 18; workshops for teachers, 21

Kissing games, 30, 124

L

Labor. *See* Childbirth

Lesbian. *See* Homosexuality: female homosexuals

LH. *See* Luteinizing hormone

Love: absence in deviant sexual behavior, 363, 365, 372; meaning of, 112; puppy love and childhood crushes, 29; relation to sex, 14, 116

Luteinizing hormone (LH), 189, 194, 196

M

Machismo: Puerto Rican notions of, 244, 250, 328

Male-female differences and similarities: convergence and divergence of male-female pattern, 163–64; division-of-labor transformation, 144–45; old and new distinctions in, 145–46; in physical, social, and psychological development, 70–71; in sex awareness and drives, 70, 72, 163, 188. *See also* Sex characteristics

Male reproductive system: illustrated, *187*; production of sperm, 182, *184*, 185

—ejaculation mechanism: moment of discharge, 189; penis, 186; prostate gland, 188–89; seminal vesicles, 186, 188

Marital sexual relations: accommodation through communication, 225–26, 241; adjustment and satisfaction in, 37, 221–22; mutual acceptance and respect in, 225; range of, from enjoyment to rejection, 130–31; refusal of intercourse, 229

—and social class: attitudes toward the function of, *135*; interest in and enjoyment of, by class, *131*; lower-class vs. middle-class, 132, *133* See also Conjugal role relationships; Personal relations in sexual behavior

Marriage and parenthood: as universal goal, 36

Masculinity: defined, 141, 143, 145; father role as test of, 149, 151; fiction as an aid to understanding, 150–51; need for male perception of creative quality of woman, 153; physical and moral strength shown in, 147–48; satisfying the female as gauge of, 144; threats to masculine identity, 146–47. See also Male-female differences and similarities

Masochism: counterparts in "normal" people, 370; sexual satisfaction from receiving pain, 368–69

Masturbation: in childhood and adolescence, 27, 31; excessive, 324; fantasy in, 325; meaning and prevalence of, 320–21; past and present attitudes toward, 10, 319, 321–23; physical and mental effects of, 323–24; and psychosexual development, 321; relation to sexual gratification in marriage, 325–26; and social class differences, 35

Menopause: bodily adjustment to changes in, 196–97; physical and psychological stresses of, 38

Menstruation, 182, 195, 196, 340

Methodists: Chicago Conference on the Family, 91; Michigan youth groups, 92

Michigan sex education programs: Child Study Program, 86; Council on Family Relations, 96; Family Service Association, 95; Health, Mental Health, and Social Welfare departments, 95; Merrill-Palmer Institute (Detroit), 86, 95; Parent Education Associates, 93–94

Middle-aged persons: disenchantment in marriage, 38; programs for, 39; sexual problems of, 331–32

Middle-class children: parents shield from "facts of life," 44–45

Midwest: sex norms in, 158–62 passim

Minnesota: teacher conferences on sex education, 21

Montana: "Education for Parenthood" programs, 16

Morality and sexual behavior: as issue in schools, 13; modernist's view of, 156; theory of normative morality, 157, 165–66

Mormons: sex norms among, 158–64 passim

Muellerian ducts: role in embryonic development of female internal accessory organs, 291, 292

Multiple ovulation, 204–5. See also Twinning

N

Narcissism, 354

National Association of Independent Schools: and sex education for adolescents, 13

National Council of Churches of Christ: approval of family planning, 252

National Council on Family Relations: and adult sex education, 96

National Opinion Research Center: poll on abortion, 274

Negroes in slum areas: myth of "Negro sexuality," 42–43; sex and stresses of ghetto life, 47; sexual attitudes compared with those of poor whites, 131; socialization patterns and behavior norms of children, 47–48, 51; vocabulary for the sex act, 46n

—adolescents: non-use of contraceptives and pregnancy, 47, 50; sex as survival strategy and "belonging," 47, 49; venereal disease among, 50–51

—preadolescents: exposure to sex conversations and acts, 43–44, 45–46; sexual precocity of, 43–44, 46

Nocturnal emissions, 10

Nymphomania, 122, 313, 363

O

Old Testament: on contraception, 256

Older persons: sexual problems of, 39, 332

Oral contraceptives: effectiveness of, 271; menstrual cycle and "the pill," 258; ovarian-menstrual cycle as key to, 256–57; safety factor of, 259–60; schedule of administration, 258–59, 259

Oregon: sex education programs for high schools, 21

Orgasm, 131, 189. See also Sexual intercourse

Ovaries, 190, 192, 194, 195

Ovulation-menstruation cycle: hormones produced in, 189–90; menopause, 196–97; normal, 193

—phases in the reproductive process: (1) building toward ovulation in the ovaries and uterus, 192, 194; (2) building toward implantation, 195–96; (3) deterioration of uterine lining,

Ovulation-menstruation cycle
(continued)
196; (4) menstruation, 196. See also
Female reproductive system
Ovum. See Egg

P
Papal Study Commission on Birth
Control, 253
Parents: ambivalence about sex
education, 142; concern about
"sexual revolution," 12–13;
"responsible parenthood," 252–54;
and school programs, 79–90
Peeping Tom, 365
Penis, 186, 231, 233
Permissiveness. See Premarital
intercourse
Personal relations in sexual behavior:
as central issue, 119, 120, 122–24,
125–27; components of successful,
126; maturity and, 124–25;
mutual satisfaction in, 37;
prostitutes vs. fiancées, 120–21
Petting: among adolescents, 30–31;
boy-girl bargaining about, 34–35;
intimate, 110, 113, 116, 159
Phimosis, 301–2
"Pill." See Oral contraceptives
Placenta: development, 202; expulsion
in last stages of labor, 218;
formation, 200, 203; hormone-
producing function, 203
Planned Parenthood, 86, 93
Poverty culture. See Sexual behavior
by social class
Preadolescents: dating among, 29;
developmental sexual problems of,
329–30
Pregnancy: determination of, 213; first,
second, and third trimesters, 212–15;
pathological complications in, 214–15;
sexual relations during, 215. See also
Embryo; Fetus
Pregnancy among the unmarried, 47,
115, 116, 244: calculating conception
and timing of marriage, 161;
incidence among brides, 114, 245
Premarital intercourse: autonomy of
choice, 115; control of consequences
through contraception information,
114–15; liberal vs. traditional views,
107; middle-class view, 109, 117; as
moral issue in classroom, 13;
permissiveness and conflicting values,
110–14; relation to social status,
135–38; religious and cultural
prohibitions, 107, 115–16

—standards concerning: abstinence,
109, 111, 112, 117; double standard,
111, 112, 113, 135, 136; permissiveness
with affection, 109, 111, 113, 116;
permissiveness without affection, 111,
112
See also Courtship
Prenatal determination of sex, 177–78
Prenatal development: first through
ninth month, 205–12. See also
Embryo; Fetus
Preschool children, 23–24, 24–25
Procreative sex impairments: frigidity,
314; impotence, 313–14; loss of
fertility, 315–16; loss of organs,
314–15; pain in copulation, 316;
transmission of genetic defects,
316–17
Progesterone, 189, 194, 195, 203, 257–58
Progestin, 296
Prolactin, 220
Promiscuity: caused by personality
deficiencies, 122–23; disapproval of,
109; motives for, 362–63; among
Negro lower-class adolescents, 48;
among white lower-class groups, 136
Prostate gland, 186, 188–89
Prostitution: and emotional deprivation
in childhood, 122; houses of, 112;
motives for, 363; in Negro slums, 139
Protestant groups: position on
contraception, 252
Psychology, clinical, and sexual
problems, 328–34
—factors in problem-solving:
counseling on goals, 337; flexibility
of counselors, 338; follow-up
reinforcement, 338; groups involved
in, 329–32, 338–39; measurement of
increased knowledge and behavior
changes, 337–38
—goals of sexual behavior: achievement,
335–36; closeness, 336–37; pleasure,
335; reproduction, 335
—special problems: of females, 329; of
males, 328–29; marital, premarital,
and extramarital situations, 332–33;
religious tenets, 333–34; voluntary
celibacy, sublimation, and low sex
drive, 334
—solutions suggested: acquisition of
information, 339–41; attitudinal and
behavioral change, 340–41;
manipulation of the environment, 341
Psychotherapy, 123
Pubertal hormonal anomalies: breast
development in males, 310; delay or
failure in pubertal development,

308–9; hirsutism in females, 310–11; precocious puberty, 305–8
Puberty: development of sex organs during, 180, 182
Puerto Rico: sex behavior and fertility patterns in, 244, 249

Q

Quaker Committee (England): permissive position on sex, 116

R

Religion: views on sexual problems, 115–16, 333–34. See also names of denominations
Reproduction. See Female reproductive system; Male reproductive system
Response to sexual excitement: psychophysiological, 231–34
—female: breast, 233; clitoris, 230; full genital, 238; initial genital, 233
—male: erection of penis, 231; full genital, 239; initial genital, 232
Responses in sex act: "adjustment" defined, 221; building responsiveness, 226; instinct vs. learning, 222; knowledge and attitudes of each partner, 223–25; positive vs. negative expression, 223
Rhythm method of birth control: advantages and disadvantages, 267; determining unsafe period, 264; use and effectiveness, 264, 271
—computing fertile period: basal body temperature during menstrual cycle, 265–66, 266; calendar method, 265; chloride spot tests, 266–67; glucose test tape, 266
Roman Catholic Church. See Catholic Church
Roman Empire: birth control methods in, 256

S

Sadism, 368–69, 370
St. Louis, Mo.: radio programs on sex, 85
San Francisco Psychiatric Clinic, 122
Satyriasis, 313, 363
Scandinavian countries: sexual standards in, 116, 149, 159, 160, 164
Scoptophilia, 365
Scrotum, 179, 185, 231
Segregation, sexual, 144
Sex characteristics, primary and secondary: of mature female, 181; of mature male, 183

Sex education in school curricula: euphemisms for, 19–20; fears concerning, 8–13, 65; historical background, 5–8; male-female ratio of high school teachers and preference for married teachers, 149–50; methods and procedures, 11–19, 72–81; objectives and limitations, 14–16, 65–67; relevance, 151–53; segregation of classes and teachers by sex, 11–12, 62, 71; specialized courses vs. subject-matter courses, 80; teacher training and qualifications, 21, 54–56, 62, 150, 152. See also Educators, sex
Sex education school programs: audiovisual aids and other source materials, 63, 77; intermediate grades, 57–59; junior high school, 59–61; kindergarten through twelfth grade, 17–18, 20; primary grades, 56–57; senior high school, 61–62; student evaluations of, 78, 79; suggestions for administrators and teachers, 62–63
—in California: Anaheim, 18; Castro Valley, 17; Elk Grove, 16, 18; Hayward, 17, 18; San Diego, 19; San Jose, 21; San Lorenzo, 17; Santa Rosa, 21
—in various locations: Corvallis, Oreg., 17; Kelso and Longview, Wash., 88; Orono, Me., 16; Phoenix, Ariz., 21
Sex Information and Education Council of the U.S. (SIECUS), 20, 88, 96, 117, 343
Sex information and experience: social skills and sociosexual development, 25, 29–30, 33–34, 37
—attitudes toward opposite sex: of adolescents, 32–33; in middle childhood, 28–29; of preschool children, 24–25; of young adults before marriage and early in marriage, 36, 37–38
—self-directed attitudes: of adolescents, 31–32; in middle childhood, 27; of preschool children, 23–24; of young unmarried adults, 35–36
Sex offenders, 360, 367
Sexual behavior by social class: among the poor, 129–40; changes in working-class, 138
—lower-class patterns: of Negroes in slum communities, 136, 137, 138; sexuality of Negro and white girls compared, 135–36; socioeconomic factors in, 139; of white adolescents and young adults, 135, 136

Sexual behavior by social class (*continued*)
—middle-class patterns, 131, 132: double standard, 135
—upper-middle-class patterns: sexual enjoyment, 130
See also Marital sexual relations
Sexual intercourse, act of: 228–40
—positions in coitus: female-above, 235; male-above, 234–35; rear entry, 236; side-by-side, 235–36; sitting, 236–37; variations, 237
—pre-coitus period: kisses and embraces, 229; male and female excitement, 228–29; stimulation of erogenous zones, 229–31
—termination ("climax") marked by orgasm: building up of neuromuscular tension, 232, 237; male experience and ejaculation of the seminal fluid, 238–39; "orgasmic platform" in female and vaginal contractions, 232–33, 237–38; return to normal state, 240
Sexuality: concept of, 14, 144
SIECUS. *See* Sex Information and Education Council of the U.S.
Single girls: a minority by age twenty, 35
Sodomy: practice of, 370–71; and state laws, 322, 371
Sperm: described, 197, 199; entrance of, into uterus, 199; production of, 182, *184*, 185; size, *198*; X-bearing (female) and Y-bearing (male), 176
Sponge with liquid or powder: as contraceptive method, 271
Sterility, 246–47
Sterilization method of conception control: ethical questions, 273; Protestant and Catholic opposition to, 272; vasectomy and tubal ligation, 256, 272
Suppositories. *See* Vaginal suppositories

T
Talmud: on contraception, 256
Testosterone, 178–79, 180
Textbooks on sex, 15
Transexuals, 312
Transvestitism, 367–68
Twinning: fraternal twins, 203–5; identical twins, 205; organism involved in, *204*

U
United Church of Christ: youth programs, 91
Unwanted pregnancies, 115: consequences for parents and children, 275
Unwed mothers. *See* Pregnancy among the unmarried
Urethra, 179, 185
Uterus: described, 215–16; development of baby in, 190–91; events in, 194, 195–96; height by month of pregnancy, *214*; immediately after childbirth, *218*; recovery after childbirth, *220*

V
Vagina, 180, 191–92, 232–33, 237–38
Vaginal suppositories: as contraceptive method, 269, 270, 271
Values, sexual: adolescents' search for, 74–75; changing, 156–57; conflicting, 113–15; defined, 155; relevance to behavior, 157–58; sociologist's contribution to, 157, 164; in various cultures, 160–63
Vas deferens, 185
Venereal disease: information in mass media, 116; among Negro adolescents, 50–51; among teenagers, 114
Virginity: attitude of white lower-class groups toward, 136; extent of non-virginity, 110–11
Voyeurism, 365

W
White House Conference on Child Health and Protection, 6, 7, 11
Withdrawal as contraceptive method: disadvantages, 268; effectiveness, 271; practiced by Onan, 268, 320
Wolffian ducts, 290–91, 292–94

Y
Yellow body. *See* Corpus luteum
YMCA and YWCA sex education programs, 92, 93
Young married adults: sexual problems of, 37–38, 92, 331
Young unmarried adults: sexual problems of, 34–36, 330–31